Costume in the
Drama of Shakespeare
and his
Contemporaries

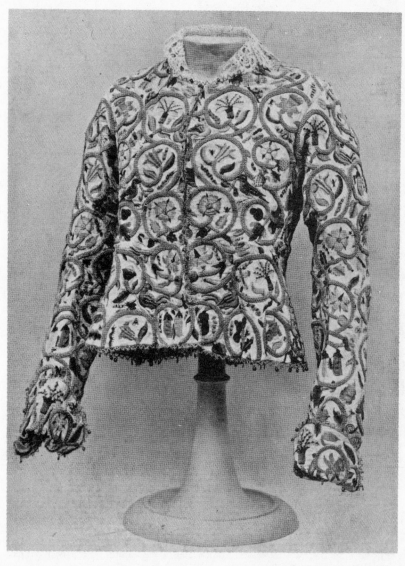

I. Lady's kirtle body embroidered in coloured silks. Insects, birds, and flowers typical of late 16th century

Metropolitan Museum of Art, New York

Costume in the Drama of Shakespeare and his Contemporaries

BY

M. CHANNING LINTHICUM

New York

RUSSELL & RUSSELL

1963

FIRST PUBLISHED IN 1936

REISSUED, 1963, BY RUSSELL & RUSSELL, INC.

L. C. CATALOG CARD NO: 63—15169

PRINTED IN THE UNITED STATES OF AMERICA

TO
G. A. L. and G. E. G. F.

PREFACE

To be valuable to a student, editor, or producer of drama, a work on costume should give dated information supported by evidence, documentary and pictorial. Such testimony is needed to clarify lines which unwarranted emendation and misinformation have confused, and to ensure the chronological placement of modes in costume. An accurate knowledge of the periods of fashion will contribute to the dating of literature.

Costume in the Drama of Shakespeare and his Contemporaries attempts (1) a *brief* survey of sixteenth- and early seventeenth-century colours, their production, symbolism, and periods of fashion; (2) a similar discussion of costume textiles and garments; (3) the earliest known date of the use in England of each colour, textile, garment, accessory, trimming, fastener, mentioned in the plays of dramatists who were writing during the age of Shakespeare; (4) a definition, with illustrative quotation from drama and contemporary accounts—such as wills, diaries, letters, tailors' bills, wardrobe expenses, merchants' and household inventories, ulnage accounts, court cases, reports of travel, costume books, literature, &c.—of each of these colours, textiles, garments.

Dramatic references to some garments, colours, &c., are very numerous; a representative selection has therefore been made, with no attempt at being exhaustive. The study aims at giving sufficient historical background for an understanding of references to costume; it does not intend to give a *complete* historical or economic discussion of any one phase, for these pages embody only a part of the results of the author's research in this complex and extensive subject. It does not enter into the question of authorship of plays, but merely accepts the attribution of the editions cited.

During the early years of its composition this work was guided by Professors T. W. Baldwin, Ernest Kuhl, and Allardyce Nicoll. Its publication has been assisted by a generous grant from the American Council of Learned Societies. The European Fellowship of the American Association of University Women gave the author access to manuscripts and sources in European libraries, galleries, and museums. She is indebted for valuable comment on the proofs to Sir Edmund Chambers, Mr. Percy Simpson, and Mr. J. L. Nevinson of the Victoria and Albert Museum.

WASHINGTON, D.C.   M. C. L.

March 1936

CONTENTS

LIST OF PLATES

*Plates I, IIb, IV, IX, XV, XVII, XVIIIa and XIX are
reproduced by the courtesy of the Metropolitan Museum of Art.*

ABBREVIATIONS EMPLOYED IN FOOTNOTES IN QUOTATIONS FROM SHAKESPEARE'S WORKS

Ant. & Cleop.	= Antony and Cleopatra
A.Y.L.	= As You Like It
Com. of E.	= Comedy of Errors
Cor.	= Coriolanus
Cymb.	= Cymbeline
Haml.	= Hamlet
1 Hen. IV	= The First Part of King Henry IV
2 Hen. IV	= The Second Part of King Henry IV
Hen. V	= King Henry V
2 Hen. VI	= The Second Part of King Henry VI
Jul. Caes.	= Julius Caesar
Lear	= King Lear
Lover's Comp.	= A Lover's Complaint
Love's L. L.	= Love's Labour 's Lost
Macb.	= Macbeth
Meas. for M.	= Measure for Measure
Merch. of V.	= The Merchant of Venice
M. Wives	= The Merry Wives of Windsor
Mid. N. D.	= A Midsummer Night's Dream
Much Ado	= Much Ado about Nothing
Oth.	= Othello
Rich. II	= King Richard II
Rich. III	= King Richard III
Rom. & Jul.	= Romeo and Juliet
Tam. Sh.	= The Taming of the Shrew
Timon	= Timon of Athens
Troilus	= Troilus and Cressida
Tw. N.	= Twelfth Night
Two Gent.	= The Two Gentlemen of Verona
Wint. Tale	= The Winter's Tale

COSTUME COLOURS

I

DYEING

PLINY states that dyeing was invented by the Lydians in Sardis. Certainly the art is an ancient one, for the staining of textile substances with permanent colours derived from plants and shell-fish was perfected in Egypt, Babylonia, and Phoenicia, a fact attested, not only by records, but by pieces of such textiles preserved in museums. Ancient Egyptian art indicates a knowledge of yellows, orange, tawny, brown, certain reds, a bluish-green, and black—colours known also to the Greeks. Latin authors noted a greater variety of colours than did Greek writers.[1]

European countries derived their knowledge of dyeing from the Orient. Italy's supremacy in this industry began in the middle of the thirteenth century, with Florence as a leader,[2] though the earliest extant book on processes of dyeing, *Mariegola dell'arte de tentori*, was published at Venice, 1429.[3] Knowledge of dyeing was carried into Germany, Flanders, and France; and by the sixteenth century Flanders was vying with Italy for the world's coloured cloth trade.

[1] F. E. Wallace, 'Color in Homer and in Ancient Art', *Smith College Classical Studies*, ix. 4 ff.; T. R. Price, 'The Color-system of Virgil', *American Journal Philology*, iv. 1 ff.; N. G. McCrea, 'Ovid's Use of Colour and of Colour Terms', *Classical Studies in Honour of Henry Drisler*, 180 ff. (Macmillan, 1894).

[2] The first experiments with white moss or *oricello* were carried on by Bernardo, called 'Rucellai', a Florentine, about 1261, and the rich scarlet derived from *oricello* became the required colour for robes of state. Staley, *Guilds of Florence*, 125–8.

[3] In 1510 a second edition was published under the editorship of Rosetti, who later studied in the Orient and published, 1540, his *Plictho del arte de tentori*. . . . In 1514 appeared at Strassburg *Mengmeistery von mancherlei Farben auf Garn, Leinwandt, Holtz, Beyn*. . . . In 1536 Alexis of Piedmont, *De secretis libri sex mira quadam rerum varietate*, appeared at Bâle, and was translated into German, Italian, French, and English. In the English language it was published six times before 1600 and was the greater part of the frequently quoted *A profitable boke . . . how to die velvets and silkes, linen and wollen fustiã and thread*, translated by L. M., 1583, 1605.

Records show that English dyers had practised their 'mystery' since late in the twelfth century, but the encouragement to foreign workers given by Edward III[1] helped to improve the industry. Organizations of dyers are mentioned throughout the fourteenth and fifteenth centuries, though they did not form a gild until 1472;[2] and not until the sixteenth did they make scientific attempts to perfect their art.

Sources of Dyes used by English Workmen

Materials used by English dyers may be classed as: (1) plants and woods, such as indigo, sumach, saffron, madder, woad, greenweed, anil, logwood, brasil; (2) mineral, as verdigris, alum; (3) insects, as kerms, cochineal, and galls. In addition to these sources, salt and lye derived from ashes and such obnoxious sources as brine of pickled fish, and animal or human excretions, were used.

Since indigo and sumach were not produced in England for dyes and were not as extensively used as were other dyestuffs, they need not be discussed. Saffron and greenweed were prolific. The true saffron was introduced by the Greeks, and the herb first brought to England in the reign of Edward III—according to Hakluyt, by a pilgrim who concealed a dried 'head' of it in his palmer's staff.[3] Saffron did not greatly flourish in England until Shakespeare's age. The dried stigmas of the flower of this plant produced orange and yellow dyes.

Madder was a climbing herb, the dye of whose roots, when combined with certain mineral products, yielded

---

[1] *Cal. Pat. Rolls*, Aug. 1337, m. 4: protection for Nicolas Appleman, dyer, and 'dyers . . . in his company who lately came to the Realm, and are exercising their mistery in the city of Winchester according to the late Proclamation inviting workers of cloth of whatever land to come to the Realm'. Dyers are mentioned in Worcester, 1173, *Pipe Roll*, 19 Henry II (p. 165); Lincoln, 1200, *Curia Regis Rolls*, 21, m. 5 d; Yorkshire, 1212, ibid. 56, m. 9; Richmond, 1280, *York. Arch.*

Soc. Rec., ser. xii. 230; Halifax, 1297, *Wakefield Court Rolls*, i. 272; London, 1298 (regulations for dyers), *Lib. Cust.* i. 129. At the end of the twelfth century, Northampton had established a penalty for 'any deyster' who 'dyze the cloth of any wikkedliche', *Lib. Cust. Northampton*, ch. li. 37.

[2] *Let. Bk. L*, 194.

[3] *Voyages*, v. 241. Harrison, *Des. Eng.*, bk. iii, ch. 8, gives discussion of saffron, 1587.

colours of the greatest permanence: yellow, orange, red-brown, and purple. Used with woad, it produced black. Madder was imported into England until the sixteenth century, but succeeding centuries saw it, with saffron and woad, established in English soil. Harrison states that the growing of madder which had formerly been an occupation in England had been long neglected, but was, in 1557, 'a little revived and offerreth itselfe to prove no small benefit unto our countrie'.[1]

The woad plant, whose pulped leaves yielded a blue dye, was native to south-east Russia but grown in Europe by the sixteenth century. The Exchequer accounts of King Richard I and subsequent rulers show how large was the importation of woad[2] before England cultivated the herb extensively. As stated in *Thomas of Reading*, woad made 'all colours sound', i.e. it was used as a ground colour. During Elizabeth's reign the cultivation of woad was encouraged, but the yearly acreage was limited and twenty shillings per acre was paid into the Exchequer to compensate for the loss of customs on foreign woad.[3] The leaves of the woad were ground in mills, the juice pressed out, and the resulting pulp, according to Heresbach,[4] rolled into balls and allowed to dry on boarded floors. When dry, the balls were fermented in water. This fermentation produced such an unpleasant odour that Queen Elizabeth, in 1580, forbade the planting of woad within

[1] *Des. Eng.*, bk. ii, ch. 20; bk. i, ch. 18. *Port Bk. Southampton* for 1428–9, pp. 2, 23, 254, shows importation of madder.

[2] Madox, *Hist. Exch.*, ch. xviii, 3. For the year 1214, duties on woad imported into Kent and Sussex amounted to £103 13s. 3d.; Yorkshire, £98 13s.; Lincolnshire, £17 3s. 4d.; Norfolk and Suffolk, £53 6s.; Southampton, £72 1s. 10d.; Essex, £4 2s.; London and other ports, £214 12s. See also *Records Norwich*, ii. 209; *Little Red Book Bristol*, ii. 16–22. The use of woad as a foundation for certain colours was mandatory by statute of

3 & 4 Edward VI, c. 2. Cf. May, *Estate of Clothing*, 30.

[3] 1587, *C.S.P.D.* xxx. 22. In 1594 licence was granted two Grooms of the Chamber to sow 100 acres in each of the counties of Berks., Wilts., Gloucester, Dorset, Warwick, Worcester, ibid. ccxlix. 23. Laud MS. cxi gives directions for planting woad. For a complete discussion of woad, see J. B. Hurry, *The Woad Plant and Its Dye*, Oxford, 1930. Also Stephen Dunn, *Alien Flora of Britain*, London, 1905.

[4] *Foure Bookes of Husbandry*, 1577, bk. i. 38.

eight miles of the royal residences.[1] In 1601 she revoked
this order, allowing woad to be sown within three miles
of London or any royal palace but 'she prayeth thus much,
that when she cometh on Progress to see you in your
Countries; she be not driven out of your Towns by suffer-
ing it to infect the Air too near them'.[2] Jonson humorously
refers in the *Poetaster* to the unpleasant odour of woad by
contrasting it with that of frankincense (II. i. 57).

In his notations for Mr. S., who was sent to Turkey,
1582, to study dyeing, &c., Hakluyt observed: 'There is
a wood called Logwood or *Palo Campechio*, it is cheape
and yeeldeth a glorious blew, but our workmen can not
make it sure. This wood you must take with you and see
whether the silke diers or wooll diers in Turkey can doe
it. It may bring downe the price of Woade and of Anile.'[3]
From the custom of putting logwood on the market in
large blocks weighing 290–400 lb., it was termed 'block-
wood', as it is called in a statute of 1581 forbidding its
use in dyeing woollen materials.[4] The use of this forbidden dye caused litigation and legislation throughout
this century,[5] none of which, however, proved wholly
effective. In March 29, 1619, a proclamation was issued
declaring that 'As the import of logwood cannot be prevented, and as it is useful in dyeing coarse stuffs, linen,
caddoes, ribband, inckle, tape, caps, gloves, hats, &c.,
licence has been granted to Sir Thomas Compton to
import 50 tons of logwood yearly and no more. It is to
be ground and sold in an appointed place in the City of
London, and the buyers' names registered.'[6]

Brasil, originally the brownish-red wood of the East
Indian genus *Cæsalpinia* (Sappen), was, after the discovery of South America, found to be obtainable from

[1] *Tudor and Stuart Proc.* i. 782. No
person might sow woad within four
miles of a market town or within eight
miles of any residence of the Queen.
Changed by proclamation 1581 to
five miles of royal residences.

[2] Ibid. 922; D'Ewes, *Jour. Parl.*
653.

[3] *Voyages*, v. 239. Logwood was the

heartwood of *Haematoxylon Campe-
chianum.*

[4] *Statutes at Large*, 23 Elizabeth, c. 9.

[5] Exch. K.R. Mem. Rolls, Mich., 33
Elizabeth, 465, 5; Mich., 34 Elizabeth,
152–4; Mich., 26 Elizabeth, 368;
Mich., 29 Elizabeth, 367, &c., *Statutes
at Large*, 40 Elizabeth, c. 11.

[6] *Tudor and Stuart Proc.* i. 1275.

several species, notably the *echinata*.[1]   The wood was ground, allowed to ferment in the air, and boiled in water, usually in copper, to extract the dye. The addition of salts of alumina produced red; salts of iron produced purple. Though its use was forbidden, 1532–3, in dyeing scarlet—when it was described as having been 'first invented by aliens to the great hurt and slander of woolen cloths dyed within the realm'[2]—it was the foundation of the shade called incarnate. Notes on trade, 1575–85, show that brasil was still used in dyeing, but was producing 'very deceitful vading collor' so that it was 'almost out of request' in England.[3]

Verdigris, the greenish-blue pigment formed by action of acetic acid on copper, was used not only in the dyeing of textiles but in artists' paints, and in cosmetics. *A Profitable Boke*, 1583, gives the recipe for preparing dye with verdigris:

'Take an ounce of verdigreace, and crush it well in a wooden dishe, then put thereto the yolke of an egg and two blades of saffron, then take leaues of spurge half a handfull, and beate them in a morter, and therto cast a good glassfull of vinegar and strayne it throw a cloth. Then take of this stuffe and put therof in a dishe with the Verdigreace, and stirre it well together and make it thin, that it may be better to dye' (fol. 19).

Of all mineral sources of dyestuffs, alum—used as a mordant—was the most important. Until 1460, alum was a Turkish product, but about that time John de Castro, who had been trained in Constantinople, began to make alum from a deposit at Tolfa; whereupon, alum became a papal monopoly. Large quantities were im-

---

[1] That part of the country producing these woods was named—according to tradition, by Emanuel, King of Portugal 1495–1521—Brazil. The origin of the name brasil is disputed. It may have been derived from the glowing colour of the wood or from the custom of placing it on the market in fragments, i.e. ground in pieces. The wood was used in dyeing in Chaucer's age, *Nun's Priest's Tale*, 4649, 'Him nedeth not his colour for to dyen With brasil ne with grain of Portingale.'

[2] *Statutes of Realm*, 24 Henry VIII, c. 2; renewed, 3 & 4 Edward VI, c. 2.

[3] *Eng. Hist. Rev.* xxix. 522. An important brasil-mill was located at Wandsworth, 1571, *Surrey Arch. Soc. Coll.* xvii. 168.

ported into England throughout the early centuries.[1]
Sixteenth-century attempts to produce alum profitably in
England failed.[2] The failure was caused partly because the
experimenters did not have sufficient knowledge, partly
because the Crown was reluctant to give up the revenue
derived from large customs on alum imported from the
Pope's dominions.[3] In 1600 Sir Thomas Chaloner, who
had visited the Pope's alum works and studied the rock
formation of surrounding areas, discovered at Guis-
borough, Yorkshire, a rich deposit of alum rock. He imported workmen and began the manufacture of alum.
With a company, he was granted, 1606, a monopoly for
thirty-one years.[4] The domestic output of alum having
increased, importation of foreign alum was forbidden in
1609. Four years later, the Crown took over the Chaloner
works and appointed overseers to direct them. By 1625
£150,000 had been spent in bringing them to perfection,
but King Charles leased them, 1627, to Sir Paul Pindar
and William Turner,[5] and they never became as profitable
to the Exchequer as King James had expected.

Kermes were the chief insect source of red dyes. These
were the larvae of the *Coccus ilicis*, which fed upon oaks,
especially the holm oak, and were supposed by naturalists
to be a product of that tree.[6] It was thought that when
the berries or 'graines' became overripe, or blood-red,

[1] *Port Bk. Southampton*, 2, 17, 29, 32, &c.; Macpherson, *Annals Commerce*, i. 667.

[2] 1565, Cornelius de Vos had tested alum ores in the Isle of Wight, and received indenture for their working. 'Alym de Wyght' had been known as early as 1346, but was not then permitted to be used in Bristol. *Little Red Book Bristol*, ii. 6. In the sixteenth century Lord Montjoy spent his patrimony in an attempt to produce alum and copperas—used in dyeing black—near Skipton. In 1576 W. Kendall of Cornwall was granted sole privilege of making alum for twenty years. The story of these attempts can be read in *C.S.P.D.*, 1565, xxxvi. 72; 1567, xlii.

24; 1572, lxxxv. 45; 1576, cx. 39; 1593, ccliv. 109; &c. Cf. Hakluyt, 1582, *Voyages*, v. 237.

[3] *C.S.P.D.* 1581, cxlix. 11.

[4] *Cowper MSS.* i. 84.

[5] For fuller information, see *Cowper MSS.* i. 84; ii. 50; *C.S.P.D.*, 1609, xlv. 134, l. 64; 1611, lxvi. 79; 1613, lxxii. 111; lxxiv. 19–21, lxxv. 67, 68; 1614, lxxviii. 21; 1619, cx. 149; cix. 73; 1621, cxx. 7; 1622, cxxxi. 43; 1627, liv. 79.

[6] Pliny, *Nat. Hist.*, bk. xvi, ch. 8. Gerard, *Herball*, 1158–9: 'The oke which beareth the scarlet graine is a small tree. . . . Besides the acornes, there is found cleauing vnto the woody branches, a certaine kinde of berrie . . .

they bred a 'sort of worm' which, if it were not killed by sprinkling the berries with vinegar, would soon escape, become a red fly, change colour and, after a brief time, die. The original method was to gather the berries, and watch them carefully; when 'theye began to move of themselves', to catch the worms as they escaped, kill them, roll them into balls, dry them in the sun, and put them away for future use.[1] The oak 'berries' were in reality the husky, globular coverings—containing 1,800 to 2,000 eggs—prepared by the female insect to protect her young. As the eggs hatched, and the larvae ate the food provided for them in the globular covering, the so-called 'berries' naturally became soft and the redness of the worms inside gave them the appearance of ripeness. The ancient belief concerning them is therefore understandable. The worms yielded a permanent dye, so that any colours produced from immersion in the concoction of which they were a part were said to be 'ingrain'. Such colours[2] could be depended upon to endure wind and rain; hence the statement in *The City Match*, 'Colours not in grain, make a fair show, but are more apt to stain'. By weakening the dye of 'grains' or kermes, many colours could be produced, varying from scarlet to ash, or to quote Binet, 1622:

'Chose estrange que d'vn seul breuuoer, voyage, ou chauderonnée . . sans rien euacuer, se font ces couleurs suiuantes, adioustant nouuelles eaux & estoffes . . .: 1. rouge cramoisi de haute couleur: 2. sort le brun de mesme breuuoer: 3. le passe-veloux: 4. le pourpre: 5. fleur de peschier: 6. l'incarnat: 7. couleur de chair: 8. le gris lauandé ou cendré argentin.'[3]

in which are engendred little magots . . . wherof is made the most perfect scarlet.'

[1] Dr. L. Eichstadio in his work *De Confectione Alchermes*, 1634, ch. v, gives an account of the insects.

[2] I. i. *Damon and Pythias*, sig. B ij; *Tw. N.*, I. v. 257. The term *ingrain* is noted in the *Wardrobe Accts. Edward II*, 1320. See also *Cal. Pat. Rolls*, Nov. 6, 1347, m. 24, customs on 'every cloth of scarlet and other cloth of whole grain, cloth of half grain, or in which the grain has been mixed'. *Cal. Close Rolls*, June 1, 1367, m. 17. *Statutes at Large*, 12 Henry IV, c. 2.

[3] *Les Merveilles de nature*, ch. 45, 387. Purple and crimson in-grain are mentioned in English wardrobe accounts, 1545-6, E. 351/3025; violet-in-grain, *Durham Wills*, xxxviii. 230; rose-in-grain: 1816, E. 101/434/14; tawny-in-grain: 1623, E. 101/435/20.

The Latin term *vermiculus* gave *vermilion* to the English
language; and from the Arabic *qermazi* (from *qermez*,
from Skr. *krmija*, produced by a worm) came the English
crimson. Crimson and vermilion did not then indicate the
particular tones of red now known by these names.
Crimson indicated an encrimsoned[1] or engrained tone;
so that such expressions as 'blood-red crimson velvet',
mentioned in *Love's Sacrifice* (ii. i. 60), or crimson-incar-
nate, crimson purple, crimson-violet, found in accounts,
need not confuse the reader.

In addition to kermes, cochineal (*Coccus cacti*)—classed
in *The Devil's Law Case* with gold and spices—was used
to produce shades of red. When the Spaniards reached
Mexico, 1518, they saw cochineal employed by the natives.
Accounts were given the Spanish ministry, 1523, and
Cortez was ordered to multiply the source, but the real
nature of the insects was not known. Robert Tomson,
a London merchant, who travelled in *Nova Hispania*,
1555–8, reported that the 'cochinilla is not a worme or
a flye, but a berrie that groweth upon certaine bushes in
the wilde fielde'; and, as late as 1666, members of the
Royal Society of London listened to a highly fictitious
account of cochineal.[2]

Galls, or excrescences on leaves of trees and plants, produced by parasitic aphids and gallflies, were also used in
dyeing. Oak galls contained much tannic acid. *A Profitable Boke*, previously mentioned, tells how to make 'a
goode blacke dye' from a pound of 'galles', a 'fourth part
Rye meal', 'half as much swarte of grindstone' (metallic
particles from grinding tools), and 'so much elder barke'
—certainly not a definite recipe. Another recipe gives
directions for dyeing 'as red as a rose' with a concoction
of galls, alum, greenweed (*Genista tinctoria*), and brasil.
For dyeing velvet or linen black, a mixture of galls or
oak bark, elder bark, copperas, swarf, and water, allowed

[1] Monet (quoted from Gay, op. cit.
i. 488): 'Le cramoisi n'est pas couleur,
mais qualité de teinture commune à
plusieurs et diverses couleurs.'

[2] Tomson's voyage, see Hakluyt,
Voyages, ix. 358. Royal Society *Transactions* for 1666 contain the account
of cochineal.

to stand three weeks in a herring barrel, is recommended.[1] Directions are usually vague: 'let it seeth therein so long till it ware a fayre black . . . so let it boyle a little . . . styrre it with a staffe six or seven Paternoster whiles.'

In order to increase the number of fast colours and to obtain cheaper dyeing materials—for England had to import much of her dyestuffs—men were sent to the Orient to learn processes of dyeing and to bring back to England skilled workmen. Morgan Hubblethorne, a dyer, was thus sent to Persia in 1579 with written instructions given him by Richard Hakluyt. He was to study the processes by which the Persians dyed their carpet thrums, 'which are so died as neither raine, wine nor vinegar can staine. . . . For if the colour hold in yarn and thrumme, it will hold much more in cloth'; he was also to learn silk dyeing, for the English merchants had a 'mind to bring much raw silk into the Realm'. He was to become acquainted with any dyer of 'China or the East parts of the world' who might be in Persia, and to learn all he could of him.[2] The use of *anil*, a fabaceous shrub which was one of the sources of indigo, had been the object of dyers' study for years. In 1577 Pedro de Vaaz had been sent by the King of Portugal to England to demonstrate its use to the dyers of London.[3] He had shown how to produce durable blue, azure, and watchet with a compound of anil and woad; and a committee of dyers had reported that the process would be profitable, provided anil could be imported for less than twenty shillings a pound. Anil, therefore, was the subject of part of Hubblethorne's instructions: 'If you can procure the herb either by seed or by plant to carry into England, you may do well to endevour to enrich your country; but withal learne you the making of the Anile and if you can get the herbe, you may send the same dye into England for possibly it groweth here already.' He was ordered to learn 'to fixe and make sure the color to be given by loggewood; so shall we not need to buy woad so dear, to the enrichment of our enemies'. He was

[1] Fol. 25, 31, 37.
[2] *Voyages*, iii. 249 seq.
[3] Lansdowne MS. 24, art. 66; also *Acts Privy Council*, July 11, 1577.

to set down in writing the nature of every herb that produced dyeing material, with a description of the place
where it grew, whether near a city, sea, or portable river.
In a little pot in his lodgings he must make daily trial
of his newly acquired knowledge of processes, and write
the results, 'lest you should forget, or lest God should
call you to his mercy; and by ech returne I wish you to
send in writing whatsoever you have learned or at least
keepe the same safe in your coffer, that come death or
life, your countrey may enjoy the thing that you goe for.'

In 1582 Hakluyt gave similar instructions to a friend
sent to Turkey. Not only was anil to be brought in by
seed or root, but 'all other herbes used in dying, all trees
whose Leaves, Seeds, or Barkes, or Wood doe serve to
that use to be brought into this Realme by seed or roote'.
He was to learn all earths and minerals used in dyeing
and their natural sources, 'for possible the like may be
found here upon sight'. In 'Remembrances for Mr. S.'
sent to Constantinople in the same year, Hakluyt asks
that skilled dyers of wool and silk be brought back to
England. If his credit be not sufficient to 'worke this by
ordinarye meane', he must 'insinuate' himself into the
acquaintance of the French Ambassador and 'worke it
with his helpe'. He also suggests that 'Mr. S.' promote
the sale of cloths in greens and yellows because 'Ode and
Greenweed wherewith they be died be natural here'.[1]

Among the notes given Pette and Jackman, sent by the
Merchants of the Muscovy Company for the discovery
of the North-east Strait, was the direction: 'Or if you can
find the berrie of the Cochenile with whiche wee colour
Stammeles, or any Roote, Berrie, Frvite, wood or earth
fitte for dying, you winne a notable thing for our clothing.'
Berries, leaves, barks used by the natives for dyeing were
always mentioned in reports of voyagers, especially by
those to Virginia and Guiana, from the latter of which in
1595 came the report of great quantities of brasil-wood
and 'diverse berries that die a most perfect crimson and
carnation: and for painting, all France, Italy, or even

[1] *Voyages*, iii. 250–1; v. 229, 235–6, 240, &c.

East Indies yeelde none such, for the more the skin is washed, the fairer the colour appeareth'.[1] What news for English women, who sought an in-grain complexion that would, like Olivia's, 'endure wind and weather'!

In spite of laudable attempts on the part of English dyers to produce fast dyes, all of their work was not dependable. They succeeded well with certain shades. Waters in parts of the country, such as at Bristol and Coventry, enabled dyers there to create famous colours. As early as 1522, Thomas Howell, a member of the London Drapers, who had business in many countries, records the purchase by his London agents of English cloths in 'violets in grayne medleys, mostyns, light Greyne, light tawney, brown-blue, Friar colour, Long fine Blue, green medley'. Between 1522 and 1527 he was indebted to Thomas Huck, dyer, for 'pukes, Redds, Light Green, Pink, Croyde, Popingay Green' in addition to the above.[2] Dyers' attempts in other shades were not, however, so successful; and 'so many false and deceivable colours' were being made 'whereby many of the King's loving subjects' were deceived, that a statute was passed in 1552 prohibiting the sale of cloth of any other colours than scarlet, red, crimson, murrey, violet, puke, brown-blue, black, green, blue, orange-tawny, russet, marble, 'sad new colour, watchet, sheeps colour, lions colour, motley, or iron grey'.[3] Much English cloth was exported undyed to Flanders, France, Holland, and Italy. It was finished in these countries and re-imported into England, or sold to other countries under the name of the dyers, so that England lost the profit and even the name of her commodities. Sir Walter Raleigh estimated that over £491,000 yearly was thus lost to England.[4]

Six years later, Alderman Cockayne, reflecting on the

---

[1] Ibid. x. 426.

[2] Johnson, *Drapers*, ii. 252. London was famous for a blue and a light green.

[3] *Statutes at Large*, 5 Edward VI, c. 6. The subject of false colours concerned dyers and Council throughout this century: *C.S.P.D.* lxxxviii. 24; 3 & 4 Edward VI, c. 2; 23 Elizabeth, c. 1; 39 Elizabeth, c. 11.

[4] Anderson, Adam, *An Historical and Chronological Deduction of the Origin of Commerce*, London, 1787–89, 4 vols., ii. 220.

profit made by Hollanders on English cloth, proposed to undertake the dyeing and dressing of all English cloths at home. He formed a company, which, after nearly a year's petitioning, royal consideration, and Council discussion of the project, obtained a patent. The old Merchant Adventurers, in February 1515, surrendered the charter which allowed them to export undyed cloths. To celebrate their first year of success in meeting their contract to ship 6,000 or more cloths, the King's Merchant Adventurers, as the Cockayne company was called, held a banquet, June 14, 1616, which the King attended. Dyers, cloth workers, and weavers with their shuttles were presented to His Majesty, 'and spake such language as Ben Jonson putt in theyre mouthes'.

The venture looked auspicious. But foreign countries wanted undyed cloth, and soon forbade the importation of English coloured cloth. The Cockayne company, deprived of its best foreign markets, found that even the home buyers did not want their work, for it was more expensive than Holland's cloth, and not as well finished. The weavers, cut off from employment, clamoured against the project; so that, in order to quiet the people, a few white cloths were allowed to be exported; and by January 1617,[1] the charter of Cockayne's company had been annulled, and that of the Merchant Adventurers restored. Dyers continued their search for perfect colours; and could Cockayne have lived a century he would have seen his premature experiment become almost a success.

[1] *Cal. Pat. Rolls*, 13 James I; 1616, *C.S.P.D.* lxxx, 38; lxxxvi. 51, 67; 1617, ibid. xc. 9. For a complete discussion, see Astrid Friis, *Alderman Cockayne's Project and the English Cloth Trade*, London: Humphrey Milford, 1927. The above discussion does not include Friis's treatment.

II
COSTUME COLOURS AND THEIR SYMBOLISM

To a suggestion that all English cloths be dyed before export, Richard Manningham, a successful London merchant, replied in 1601: 'We may as well make it into clokes and garmentes as dye it in colours before we carry it ouer; for both are variable, and as much change in colour as in fashion.' Although this statement sounds extreme, fashion in colours changed from season to season, as they do now. The list named in the Statute of 1552[1] contained those which were then fashionable, but even at that time others were worn at Court. King Edward wore 'blod', turkey, incarnate, carnation, sea-water. Ruby, crane, and 'old medley' were some of Queen Mary's favourites. In 1577 Harrison railed against 'phantastical colours' which were then in use: 'gooseturd greene, pease-porrige tawnie, popongaie blue, lustie gallant, the devil in the head (I should say Hedge)'; and a series of directions for English merchandise to be sent to various countries, 1575–8, advised taking for sale in Brittany 'all new collors: stannel Reds and lustie gallantes'; and to 'Biscaye, popingaye grenes, violets, skye collors, azars'.[2]

Fanciful names are apparent not only in the literature of the period, but in wardrobe accounts and inventories of mercers and drapers, showing them to have been actualities. Inventories between 1586–7 add: gentleman's gray, partridge, maiden-hair, pheasant, beggar's gray, milk and water, hair, straw, rat, ginger,[3] and the

---

[1] *Statutes at Large*, 5 & 6 Edward VI, c. 6 (xlvi); Manningham, *Diary*, 12.

[2] Harrison, *Des. Eng.*, bk. ii, ch. 7; *Eng. Hist. Rev.* xxix. 518. 'Lustie gallant' was a light red.

[3] *Durham Wills*, xxxviii. 163; ii. 256–7. Milk-and-water colour, and drake or mallard colour were known in Scotland in 1511 and 1541 respectively. *Accts. Lord High Treas. Scotland*, iv. 245; viii. 22.

Great Wardrobe accounts are colourful with such names as: 'brasell, celestial, clay, drake, flybert, goselinge, horse-flesh, Isabelle, marigold, meal, palme, Paul, peach, sande, pearl, soppes-in-wine, synamon, turtle, willow'—all of which were fashionable by 1559. Some of the Tudor favourites, as ash, blush, carnation, de roy, hair, peach, popingay, puke, sea-water, watchet, willow, continued during the Stuart period, but new ones were added: brick, 'greediline, gingerline, muske, pepper, grape, fawne, sage, corke, tobacco, Virginia-ffrog'. Colours reflected the interest in newly founded colonies and discoveries, though many of the names were importations from France. *D'isabel, gris de lin, couleur de roy, zinzolin, verd de mer, triste tanne, merde d'oye, de rat, de ciel, de paille, de fleur de pescher, feuille morte*, were either rendered in English by such approximated pronunciations as: Isabelle, greediline, deroy, gingerline, follimort, or translated: sea-water green, sad tawny, goose-turd, rat, sky, straw, peach colour.

An advertisement of la Maison Bovant-Caillet de Neuchâteau addressed, 1607, to drapers, lists seventy-four colours and tones of colours as 'la mode', many of which are as fanciful as d'Aubigné's *couleur de Judas, de racleurs de cheminée, de temps perdu, d'Espagnol malade, de baise-moi-ma-mignonne*. But, to the credit of the English, many of the obscene and objectionable names current in French colour fashions were omitted.[1]

If evidence of the drama may be credited—and records indicate that the stage reflected life—beards were dyed to harmonize with costumes or to reflect the mood of the wearer. Grey beards were transformed into black ones through the constant use of lead combs; happiness over

[1] Roy, *La Vie . . . et le costume au 17e siècle*, Plate X; *Les Aventures du Baron de Faeneste*, i, ch. ii. For English colours, see Wardrobe Accounts 1600–27, A.O. 1/2344–50, nos. 31–58; also E. 101/434–36; L.C. 9/90–101. Puke was a dusky brown between russet and black; grisdelin was grey-violet. This colour was mentioned in *Parson's Wedding*, iii. ii. *Feuille morte* is self-explanatory. Isabella was pure yellow. An 'Isabella colour' gown of satin was listed among the costumes provided for the entertainment of King James at Oxford, 1605. *Malone Soc. Coll*. i. iii. 259.

the return of a favourite might be expressed by dyeing
the beard carnation 'speckled with green and russet';
Catherine-pear-coloured beards indicated a wicked disposition, and cane, straw, French crown, and Abraham-
colour beards had each a language. Such language or
colour-symbolism, traceable to several sources, is the
subject of the next chapter.

SOME SOURCES OF COLOUR SYMBOLISM

'Thus taking his leave, he marched toward his chamber,
which he found hanged with white and black. Who,
knowing well the vertue of each color and the mixing
of the same, thought varily he swimmed against the
stream.'[1] This passage suggests the colour symbolism
practised by Elizabethan England. Sources of colour-
language trace to ancient man; the summary in book
form seems to have been a product of the sixteenth
century.

Certain meanings had naturally become associated with
colours even in pre-Christian times: red with blood, and
hence with power; yellow with the sun, therefore with
warmth and fruitfulness; green with spring, youth, hope-
fulness; brown with autumn and despair; grey with
winter and barrenness; white with purity; black—the
absence of colour—with darkness, constancy, gloom, woe,
death. Greek dramatists used colour-symbolism effectively
on the stage, as Pollux suggests in the *Onomasticon* (bk. iv,
ch. xviii), and as even a hasty reading of the chief plays
of Aeschylus will show.

Early in the Christian era the clergy sought to substi-
tute, for existing associations of colours, others expressing
Christianity: red with the blood of Christ, therefore with
justice and mercy; blue with truth and eternity; impure
yellow with the clay from which the body was made,
therefore with earthly passions; white with purity of soul,

---

[1] Grange, *The Golden Aphroditis*,   were symbolic of eternal virginity.
1577, sig. D, ii. 1. Black and white

&c. Colours are used symbolically in the Bible: the white robes of joy in Ecclesiastes ix. 8; the purple of royalty, Judges vii. 26; the blue of Jehovah, Numbers xv. 38, &c. Early miniatures and still earlier paintings and windows in cathedrals suggest a colour significance. The Virgin appears in blue; the Infant Christ in tawny, but in white after the Resurrection; Saint Peter in a blue tunic with a yellow mantle—indicating his two natures; Chastity in white, often with a blue cloak; and other examples too numerous to list here.

Before the eleventh century, English bishops were wearing chasubles in colour. For instance, *c.* 962, Theodred, Bishop of Elmham, bequeathed four chasubles to friends, one red, one white, two yellow;[1] but not until 1198 were rules for the use of colours in vestments made for the Christian world by Pope Innocent III in his *De Sacro Altaris Mysterio*—rules which are observed to-day.

Colour nomenclature is meagre and conventional in Anglo-Saxon poetry, and Chaucer is the earliest English writer to use symbolism of colour freely. The burden of his *Ballade Against Women Unconstant*: 'In stede of blew thus may ye were al grene,' refers to the accepted meaning of two colours, as does also Lydgate's: 'Watchet blue of fayned stedfastnesse';[2] for watchet was not a pure blue. By Malory's time, heraldry had done much to fix the association of colours with virtues—and vices. Morality plays, masques, and pageants helped to establish colour symbolism. In *The Castle of Perseverance*, Mercy is in white, Righteousness in red, Peace in black;[3] in *Three Lords and Three Ladies of London*, Dissimulation has motley hair and beard,[4] Jonson presents Veneration in ash, Gladness in green, Truth in blue, Affection in crimson and flame-colour, Safety in carnation;[5] Middleton

---

[1] Blomefield, *County of Norfolk*, ii. 324.

[2] *Falls of Princes*, i. 6445. Chaucer's physician wears perse and sanguine to indicate his knowledge, and his cruel cupidity.

[3] Directions for presenting the play, conclusion of MS.

[4] II. i, stage directions.

[5] *Works* (Gifford), vi. 408, 9, &c., vii. 75.

costumes Truth in white, Error in ash, Envy in red, Zeal
in carnation;[1] and, in various pageants, Fame appears in
watchet, Honour and Eternity in blue, Justice in red.[2]
Illustrations could be extended for pages, but the purpose
of these selections is to show that certain meanings had
become attached to colours.

As previously stated, a potent source of colour-symbolism was heraldry. Interest in this subject had demanded
treatises on blazonry, which, though early limited to
colours borne in arms, gradually extended their range, or
changed their purpose, to include all colours. The most
popular early book on colour-symbolism was written by
an author who disguised himself under the name Sicile,
Herald of Alphonso V, King of Aragon. A copy of the
first edition of his work has not been found, all extant
copies having the statement, *nouvellement imprime*. Only
two of the eight known French editions of the sixteenth
century are definitely dated, the earlier of the two bearing
the date 1528, and representing what appears to be the
sixth edition. What seems to be the earliest known edition
is entitled: *Le Blason des couleurs en Armes Liurees et
deuises. Liure tres utile et subtil pour scauoir et congnoistre
dune et chascune couleur la vertu et propriete.* Italian transla-
tions of this work were published in 1565, 1593, 1595.
Brydges notes an English translation by R(ichard)
R(obinson), 1583, called *A Rare True and Proper Blazon
of Coloures and Ensignes Military with theyre Peculiar
Signification . . . translated oute of a little French Booke
printed at Paris 1546.*

Since the influence of Sicile's work must have been
widespread, a review of its presentation of colour-
symbolism is desirable. According to Sicile, white indicated faith, humility, and chastity; black, grief and constancy; obscure grey, patience; bright grey, despair; ash,
trouble and sadness; silver, purity; yellow, hope, joy,
magnanimity; russet, prudence; yellow-red, deception;
green, love, joy; blue, amity; turquoise, jealousy; perse,
knowledge; red, prowess; vermilion, courage. Of the

---

[1] *Works*, vii. 238, 241, &c.   [2] *Prog. James*, i. 355; ii. 569, 710.

colour combinations, white and black meant grief; white
and blue, courtesy; white and green, virtuous youth;
white and grey, hope of coming to perfection; white and
purple, grace; white and red, honesty; white and tawny,
patience in adversity; blue and violet, loyalty in love; red
and purple, strength; red and tawny, unholiness; red and
violet, wanton love; red and yellow, cupidity; incarnate
and grey, hope of riches; incarnate and tawny, misfortune;
incarnate and violet, hope of great things; incarnate and
yellow, riches not tempered. The most curious part of the
book is the description of the 'habit moral de l'homme
selon les couleurs'.[1] Sicile undoubtedly set down for some
colours the symbolism which had come through ages, but
to others, he probably, as Rabelais accused him,[2] attributed meanings on his own authority.

Fulvio Pellegrino Morato, professor in the University
of Ferrara, author of the oldest known book of rhymes:
Rimario di tutte le cadenze di Dante e Petrarca, 1528,
father and teacher of the learned Olympia Morata—the
second edition of whose works was dedicated to Queen
Elizabeth, as the only woman scholar who could compare
with her—published in 1535 his *Del significato de' colori*,
which, unlike that of Sicile, had no interest in the
blazoning of arms. It was published nine times before
the end of the century: 1545, 1551, 1559, 1564, 1584,
1586, 1593, 1599, with one edition undated.[3] All later
writers on colour-symbolism were indebted to Morato's
work. He presented his ideas in a sonnet which he said
'me era cadutto delle mani non so a che modo' (sig. A iiij).
He avoided future Rabelaisian attacks by supporting his
attribution of meanings to colours by 'le auttorità di tali
ch'io posso dire me hauer molto & bouni testimoni', and
by 'el prouerbi'. His chief authorities are the Bible,
Homer, Virgil, Plautus, Ovid, Petrarch, and his Italian
contemporaries, and many of the proverbs which he

[1] This description, too long to quote, is given on pages 40 ff. The costume for woman is also given.

[2] *Gargantua*, ch. ix, x.

[3] Morato died in 1547, so that future revisions were the work of editors, but they seemed to make only negligible changes except in improvement of the index in editions between 1559–99.

quotes had their origin in works of these authors. His
sonnet is as follows:

> Il color verde esser ridutto a niente
> Dimostra. Il rosso ha poca sicurezza.
> Il nero ha'l suo uoler pien di mattezza.
> Il bianco ha'l suo appetito, e uoglie spente.
> Il Giallo ha la speranza rinascente,
> Corpre il Taneto in se saggia sciocchezza,
> Il Morel morte per Amor disprezza;
> Chi veste Beretin, gaba la gente.
> Amorosco piacer ha l'incarnato.
> Il mischio mostra bizzaria di testa,
> Il Torchino ha'l pensier molto eleuato,
> Che ha fede, e signoria d'oro si uesta.
> L'argentino dimostra esser gabbato.
> Al verde Gial poca speranza resta.

Although Morato's symbolism for green, ash, incarnate, and turquoise differs from that of Sicile, the systems
for the most part agree. The green referred to by Morato
is the obscure or willow green,[1] and he thus explains the
origin of the Italian proverbial saying 'lui giunto uerde',
indicating that one is in extreme misery or near death:

'Fv consuetudine appresso li antichi ... che offerendo le facelle sopra
le Alteri alli Dei, collocauano la parte di quelle secca in un legno
uerdo, il quale fusse in uece di sostentacolo, & candeliero alle tede
ardĕti. ... Quando dunque quelli luminari erano del tutto consumati
del fuoco, & erano già peruenuti a quel calce del tronco uerde, niĕte
piu di quelli da esser abbrucciato restaua.'

His connexion of parti-colour with an unsound mind
is especially interesting, as is also his attempt to correct
the attribution of jealousy to turquoise. He shows how,
throughout the ages, turquoise had been the symbol of con-
templation and elevated thought, but he explains its association with jealousy: 'Il Certaldese Cicerone, desiderando la
Reina hauer per sua, & conoscendo quella impresa esser
ardua & difficile, di tal habito si ornò e perche chi affetta
cosa grandi, facilmente sospetta a teme massimamente in
Amore, p tal colore può interpretar sospetto e tema' (sig.

---

[1] 'Il color uerdo ... è quello che noi uolgarmente addimandiamo uerdo
scuro' (sig. A v).

C iij). He tells how the *poco sicurezza* of *il rosso* originated in a custom of cowardly soldiers who wore that shade to appear valiant; and how yellow, as the colour of Aurora and of the marriage veils of Roman brides, symbolized hope. Jews also in some countries wore this colour in head-dress to signify their hope of the coming of the Messiah.[1] He failed to state that other countries compelled them to wear this colour as a badge by which they could be known.

The *Trattato di Colori*, of Coronato Occolti, published 1557, with a second edition in 1568, also expressed in rhyme the significance of colours.[2] Occolti's attribution follows Morato's in part. White indicated humility;[3] black, constancy;[4] gold, faithfulness;[5] silver, high desires,[6] but obscure greys such a *beretin* and *cincereo* showed undesirable qualities, lack of firmness, deceit, death of good;[7] pure red showed courage;[8] vermilion, scorn, wrath;[9] *cesio*, sanguine, fierceness, cruelty; incarnate, passionate love;[10] turquoise, elevated thoughts;[11] pure green, hope;[12] willow-green, willingness to die;[13] yellow-green, desperation;[14] orange-tawny and *zizolino*, probably the English ginger-line, a certainty of nobleness of mind or high courage—a symbolism which did not accord with later English significance;[15] straw colour, abundance;[16] murrey, passionate love;[17] violet, coldness, aloofness;[18] the pale, indeterminate colours, such as the *zallolino*,[19] *pallido*,[20] *mischio*,[21] showing respectively, fraud, fear, dubious or unstable condition. Occolti also gives the significance of combinations of colours. Clear or pure colours signified good qualities; obscure colours or hues or colours having evil symbolism destroyed the significance even of sacred colours. Thus white and friar's grey signified wanton love; white and *zallolino*,

---

[1] Sig. B viij. For discussion of colour in dress of Jews, see *P.M.L.A.* xliii. 761 ff.   [2] Edition of 1568, p. 1 seq.
[3] pp. 5, 38, 49.   [4] pp. 6, 39, 50.
[5] pp. 8, 40, 50.   [6] pp. 9, 40, 51.
[7] pp. 10, 42–3, 51–3.   [8] pp. 14, 43, 53.
[9] pp. 37, 49.   [10] pp. 19, 45, 55.
[11] pp. 16, 44, 54.   [12] pp. 17, 44, 54.
[13] pp. 45, 55.   [14] pp. 19, 45, 55.

[15] pp. 46, 55. Red signified valour; gold-yellow, faith, 25, verso.
[16] pp. 47, 56. Straw of the grain which signifies fruitfulness.
[17] pp. 25, 47, 56.   [18] pp. 30, 39.
[19] pp. 35, 48, 57. *Zallolino* is defined as 'genera di color bianco debile che tira al rosso, il quale è color uile'.   [20] pp. 33, 48, 57.
[21] pp. 24, 48, 56.

weak deceit.[1] With *cesio*, white lost its significance entirely.

A reader might expect Ludovico Dolce, historian, grammarian, philosopher, poet, editor, and translator, whose work was known and copied in England, to add much to the knowledge of colour-symbolism, but his *Dialogo nel quale si ragiona delle qualita diversita e proprieta dei colori*, 1565, quotes Morato's words on many of the colours. He gives additional quotation and information on some colours omitted by his predecessor. The *Dialogo* represents Cornelio's instruction of Mario in the definition of *argentino, bigio, pullo, ceruleo, turchino, mischio, incarnato, roseo, rubro, rosso-secca, vermilio, ostrino, oro, giallo, flameo, glauco, purpureo, perso, ferrugineo*, and *porro-verde*, and the symbolism of those named in Morato's sonnet.

The eighties and nineties saw an unusual demand, especially in Italy, for books on colour-symbolism and blazoning of arms. In 1593 Andrea Viani published a translation of Sicile's work, an edition of Morato's, and one of Giovanni Rinaldi's *Il Mostrovissimo Mostro*, which had appeared previously in Ferrara and Venice, 1584, 1592. This work was republished in 1599, 1626. Rinaldi was indebted to the preceding authors, but he neither quotes nor acknowledges their works, listing as his references twenty-nine philosophers, poets, and historians—Greek, Roman, and Italian—from Empedocles to Tasso. Rinaldi wrote a poem and a sonnet on colour-symbolism, the latter of which lists more colours than does the former and so is quoted here:

> Fà di speme, e letitia il Verde mostra,
> Di spene il Verdegial già quasi morta;
> Di mano il Rosso à ria uendetta sorta;
> Gior soaue l'Incarnato mostra.
> L'alto pensiero altrui il Tvrchin dimostra,
> E di dominio il Giallo inditio porta;
> Si fà d' alma sincera il Bianco scorta;
> Co'l duol d'un core il Ner di pari glostra.
> D'animo inuito è il Leonato essempio,
> Salda uoglia il Morello apre in amore;

[1] p. 38 seq.

Inganno il Beretin sin falso, & empio.
Mente instabile il Mischio nota. Honore
L'oro e ricchezza manifesta: Esempio
Di Gelosia l'Argento, e di dolore.

Briefly, his symbolism is: gold, sovereignty, honour, love;
silver, passion, fear, suspicion, jealousy; black, sadness,
grief; white, purity, chastity, faith, truth, sincerity of
heart and spirit; ash, fraud, poverty, vileness; yellow,
arrogance; tawny, regal grandeur, intrepid spirit; murrey,
firmness, constancy in love; reds (*rosso* to *incarnato*),
cruelty, vengeance, joy; turquoise, noble thoughts; green,
happiness; yellow-green, wan hope; parti-colour, unstable mind, discord. Rinaldi's summary was carefully
made. He selected from his sources, ancient and modern,
the accepted symbolism of each colour, and justified his
choice.

Although these were the most important works devoted
wholly to colour-symbolism, the subject had attracted
grammarians, such as de Guez, 1527,[1] poets, as Forcadel,
1550,[2] and innumerable authors interested in the blazoning of arms. England produced no book on colour-
symbolism alone, but English authors must have been
familiar with the work of Sicile, Morato, Dolce, if not
with that of Rinaldi. Gerard Legh's *Accedens of Armory*,
first published by R. Tottell, 1562, recalls to a reader
familiar with Sicile's work, the latter's manner, but contains no direct evidence of indebtedness. Legh's book,
written in the popular dialogue form, discusses the
blazoning of arms, and gives in part the symbolism of the
seven colours used in that art, treating each colour

---

[1] *Grammaire*. His symbolism is:
'Noir, duel; blanc, humilité; rouge,
orgueil; verd, amourous; bleu, constant; pers, deception; tanné, fatyga-
tion; jaulne, jouissance; gris, espérance;
pourple, majesté; sanguin, cherité;
violet, trahison; carnation, dissymulation.'
    Evidently de Guez was familiar with
Sicile's work.
    [2] *Anciens blasons*, 310:

Pour fermeté et deuil le noir est pris
Le gris travail, le verde dénote espoir;
Le blanc est foy, ainsy que j'ay apris,
Et le tanné mostre le désespoir,
Le rouge veult par luy vengeance avoir,
Et l'incarnat tousjours est douleur,
Contentement porte jaune couleur
S'il est paille; car l'orange est change;
Le violet d'amour a la chaleur,
Et puis le bleu sur le jalous se renge.

separately and in combination with others; for instance, gold indicated wisdom, riches; silver, chastity, virginity, charity; vermilion, strength, boldness; sanguine, 'not hasty in battle but victorious'; azure, good disposition; black, constancy; green, joy, gladness; purple, jurisdiction; tawny, glory. Sanguine with gold meant 'victorious in youth'; with silver, 'rather die than be captive'; with vermilion, 'hot in love, soon cold'; with azure, 'whom no man resisteth'; with black, 'disloyaltie'; with green, 'as lieve be hated as loved'; with purple, 'keepeth good hospitality'; with tawny, 'every day a new faith', &c.[1] Of Legh's successors in the sixteenth century, Sir John Ferne is next in importance. Ferne's *Blazon of Gentrie*, 1586, indebted to Legh's work, offers little originality except his attribution of colours to the seven ages of man: white to infancy, azure to puerility (7–14), yellow to young adolescence (14–20), green to 'lusty green youth' (20–30), vermilion to virility (30–40), purple to 'grey hairs' (40–70), black to decrepitude (169–71).

Not until the seventeenth century did an English author attempt to compile the meanings attached to most of the shades, tones, and tints of colours known to Tudor and Stuart England. Thomas Blount added to Peacham's *Compleat Gentleman*, in 1661, a summary on colour-symbolism drawn from the work of other authors on this subject and from literature, especially that of the period between 1580 and 1640. He attempted to reconcile conflicting meanings attributed to the same colours; often, however, reporting one meaning and retiring behind a vague 'but some would have it otherwise'. Except as a compilation, his work is of little value, and will not, therefore, be discussed.

---

[1] verso. This work was published again in 1568, 1576, 1591, 1597, 1612. Only 10 of the 142 pages are devoted to colour-symbolism.

COSTUME COLOURS IN THE DRAMA

Shakespeare and his fellow dramatists mentioned in their plays most of the colours known to their age. Shakespeare was the master colourist; Ford, Middleton, and Marston, the leaders in the multiplicity of colours used; Marston used rare and beautiful colour combinations.

The aim of the following discussion will be, not to show how many times a dramatist used certain colours, nor what colours each mentioned, but to note: (1) how early the colours mentioned by dramatists were known in England; (2) what these colours were; (3) their significance in the life of the time and in drama.

Drama followed the generally recognized attribution of certain colours to persons of certain status. Followers of the Court wore yellow in part of their costume; servants wore livery of blue, or tawny; fools wore several colours, of which yellow was usually prominent; persons in high church or civil positions wore scarlet. An interesting comparison between the status of an inherited title and an acquired one is noted by Massinger in *A New Way to Pay Old Debts*, when Lord Lovell gives as his reason for not marrying Margaret Overreach:

> I would not so adulterate my blood
> By marrying Margaret, and so leave my issue
> Made up of several pieces, one part scarlet,
> And the other London blue. (IV. ii. 224.)

The bride and bridegroom had colours, as indicated by Jonson's 'Let us know your bride's colours, and yours at least'.[1] Colours connected with lovers especially interested

[1] *Silent Woman*, III. ii. 223. The curious tract, 'Fifteen Comforts of Marriage' tells how various colours were discarded when a selection was made for the bride. Violet, signifying religion, was considered too grave; popingay, meaning wantonness; flesh colour, meaning lasciviousness; willow, meaning desertion; sea-green, meaning inconstancy, were likewise rejected. Finally, blue, peach colour, and orange-tawny were selected for the favours; flame, straw, grass-green, and milk-white were chosen for the knots, and gold for the garters.

dramatists. When Charella of *Fancies Chaste and Noble*
remarked that women in their love affairs were more
secret than are men, Romanello sneered:

> You secret, when your dresses blab your vanities?
> Carnation for your points? There's a gross blabber.
> Tawny? heigho! the pretty heart is wounded;
> A knot of willow ribbons? She's forsaken.
> Another rides a cock-horse green and azure,
> Wince and cry 'Wee-hee', like a colt unbroken;
> But desperate black puts 'em in mind of fish days.
>
> (III. iii. 100–6.)

The lover wore the colours of his mistress, and by means
of the language of colours could carry on a silent conversation or flirtation with her. Amorphus thus instructs Asotus
in the language of a lover's colours:

'Or, if you can possesse your opposite, that the *greene* your mistris
weares, is her reioycing or exultation in his seruice; the *yellow*,
suspicion of his truth, (from her height of affection:) and that he
(greenly credulous) shall withdraw thus, in priute, and from the
aboundance of his pocket (to displace her jelous conceit) steale into
his hat the colour, whose *bluenesse* doth express truenesse, (shee
being . . . nor so affected) you giue him the *dor*.'[1]

In *Captain Underwit*, Shirley admirably satirized the
use of 'such variety of Ribbands every day':

Device: 'Your colours to an understanding Lover carry the interpre-
tation of the heart as plainly as we express our meaning one to
another in characters. Shall I decipher my colours to you now?
Here is Azure and Peach. Azure is constant and Peach is love;
which signifies my constant affection.'
Sister: 'This is very pretty.'
Device: 'Oh, it saves the trouble of writing, where the Mistress and
Servant are learned in this amorous blazon. Yesterday, I wore
Folimort, Grisdelin, and Isabella. Folimort is withered, Gris-
delin is absent, and Isabella is beauty, which put together, express
I did wither and languish for your absent beautie.'

---

[1] *Cynthia's Revels*, v. ii. 28–35. Cf.
Aurillio's reproach to Lucretia: '. . . besides, I was so simple to wear your
foolish colours', *The Antiquary*, Dodsley, xiii. 441; 'Let me wear your
colours, Lady', *Bondman*, I. iii. 432;
'Nor wear his colours like a tumbler's
hoop', i.e. Cupid's colours, *Love's
L. L.*, III. i. 198; also *Every Man Out
of His Humour*, I. ii. 83; *Astrophel and
Stella*, stanza liv.

Sister: 'But is there any reason for these distinctions?'

Device: 'Yes, Lady: for example, your Folimort is a withered leafe, which doth moralize a decay; your yellow is joy, because——'

Lady: 'Why, yellow, Sir, is Jealous.'

Device: 'No, your Lemon colour, a pale kind of yellow is Jealous. Your yellow is perfect joy. Your white is Death; your milk white, innocence; your black, mourning; your orange, spiteful; your flesh colour, lascivious; your maide's blush, envied; your red is defiance; your gold is avaritious; your straw, plenty; your green, hope; your sea-greene, inconstant; your violet, religion; your willow, forsaken.'[1]

When a rejected lover behaved in approved fashion, he adopted black and tawny—sign of extreme sadness—or like Sir Abraham in *A Woman Is a Weathercock*, threw off all colour insignia:

> Well, since I am distained, off garters blue!
> Which signify Sir Abraham's love is tree;
> Off cypress black! for thou befits not me;
> Thou art not cypress of the cypress true
> Befitting lovers. Out green shoe-strings, out! (i. ii. 533.)

Symbolism will be discussed in more detail under the separate colours, but one interesting reference in *Tamburlaine* should be noted. Tamburlaine pitches white tents, as sign of amity, outside of Damascus, but remarks that, if the governor does not yield, those tents will become vermilion; and, if the city still holds out, 'fury and incensed hate' will fling 'slaughtering terror from my coal-black tents'. Stage directions note that Tamburlaine dresses successively in these colours.[2]

Allusions to colours can best be understood through consideration of their definitions and the history of their periods of fashion. Of the blues: azure and watchet are the chief mentioned in the drama; of the browns: Abraham, russet, hair; of the greys: ash and rat; of the greens: goose-turd, popingay, sea-water, willow; of the reds: blush, Catherine pear, carnation, flame, gingerline, horse-flesh, murrey, nutmeg, peach, scarlet, stammel; of the

---

[1] Bullen, *Coll. Old Plays*, iii. 345 ff. summarizes this list. This play was given previous to 1641. Peacham, *Compleat Gentleman*, 1661,   [2] *1 Tamb*. iv. ii. 111–18; iv. iv; v. ii. 8.

yellows and orange: cane, French crown, primrose, roy, saffron, straw, tawny, orange-tawny, and whey. Succeeding pages will discuss each of these colours.

Blue

Livery of a shade lighter than the midnight-sky-blue, but near the sky-blue of a clear October day, was the mark of servitude in the sixteenth century. Blue in connexion with the dress of servants is noted in *Every Man In His Humour*, *Taming of the Shrew*, *1 Henry VI*, *Roaring Girl*, *Eastward Hoe*, and *Two Angry Women of Abington*, &c.[1] Possibly the custom had been introduced by the Romans.[2] In Shakespeare's age, they were called 'blue-coats', 'blue bottles', or said to be of the 'blue order';[3] but, judging from Lucre's remark that 'since blue coats have turned into cloaks, we can scarce know the man from the master', servants of the early seventeenth century wore cloaks, and the colour was not unlike that worn by their masters.[4] During Mary's reign, apprentices wore blue cloaks in summer, and blue gowns in winter.[5] Waits or pensioners,[6] orphans of the city hospitals,[7] as well as the beadles of hospitals or prisons, according to *2 Henry IV* and *Micro-*

[1] In order of mention: II. iv. 12; IV. i. 93; I. iii. 47; III. iii. 123; III. ii. 9; *M.S.R.*, line 729. Azure was worn by servants at Cambridge, 1583, *Agriculture and Prices*, VI. 550 (Cambridge blue?).

[2] Pliny noted that blue was a mark of servitude in Roman times, *Nat. Hist.* xvi. 18.

[3] Blue-coats, *Mad World My Masters*, I. i. 79; blue bottle, *Northward Hoe*, I. iii; blue order, *Case Is Altered*, I. vii. 27; *Tu Quoque*, fol. D ij: 'Seruingman wears broadcloth . . . and for his colours, they are according to the season; in the summer he is apparelled like the heauens in blew, in the winter, like the earth in freese', i.e. in russet. 1536, *Rutland MSS.* iv. 279: 'Blewe cloth for my Lordes servaunts agaynst his goyng to Dunkaster with my Lord of Norffolk. . . .' In 1564,

Robert Wild bequeathed his eldest son his 'blve cote wch was my lord of northfolks leverye', *Durham Wills*, ii. 226. See also Machyn, *Diary* (1544), 74, 76.

[4] *A Trick to Catch the Old One*, II. i. 158; *The Fleire*, ii, line 202.

[5] Stowe (Howes, 1631), *Annales*, 1039–40.

[6] *Hist. Lord Mayors' Pageants*, 23.

[7] Children of St. Mary's, Machyn, *Diary* (1553), 53. Those of Christ's Hospital, see Stowe and Strype, *Survey of London*, 1633, i. 175: 'In 1552 the month of September they took in neer 400 orphans and clothed them in russet, but ever after they wore Blew coats, whence it is commonly called Blewcoat Hospital. Their habit being now a long coat of blew warm cloth, close to the arms and body, hanging loose to their Heels, girt about their waste, with a red leather Girdle

cosmus; and prisoners of Bridewell, indicated by scenes in *City Madam*, and *Promos and Cassandra*, also wore this colour.[1]

Although azure, brown-blue, Coventry blue,[2] indigo, perse, sky-blue, violet, and watchet besides other blues are mentioned in accounts, statutes, &c., of this period,[3] few occur in the drama. Azure and watchet only will be discussed.

AZURE

Azure, derived from the French *azur*, a form of the term lapis-lazuli, was the blue of that precious stone. The name azure does not seem to have occurred until the first quarter of the fourteenth century, but the colour was known in the period of illuminated manuscripts, for the stone was used in that beautiful art. By the late sixteenth century, the natural colour had been imitated in plant and chemical dyes. Of the symbolism of azure, Ferne says: 'Azure signifieth power, honour ... wisdome',[4] but a combination of azure and green, according to Legh, 1562, indicated excess of gladness or joy;[5] so that Ford's phrase 'ride a cock-horse green and azure'[6] evidently meant to be too merry.

WATCHET

Watchet, also a French term, indicating light or pale blue inclining towards green, occurs 1198 in the *Curia*

buckled; a loose petticoat underneath of Yellow cloth, a round thrum cap tied with a red Band, yellow stockings, and Black Low Heeled shoes.' Girls wore the same livery except that they used kerchiefs instead of caps.

[1] *2 Hen. IV*, v. iv. 22; *Microcosmus*, Nabbes, *Works*, ii. 213; Heath, *Grocers*, 407, records expense for blue coats for beadles for the four hospitals; *City Madam*, v. iii. (stage direction); *Promos and Cassandra*, III. vi. 2.

[2] Coventry was known for various colours (1581, L.C. 9/73), but was famous for its blue. W. S., in a *Discourse of the Common-Weal of England*, 1581 (?), states that the decay of Coventry, whose wealth had been 'in

making blew threde', was due to the importation of thread 'from beyond the sea'. Greene refers to this thread in *Quippe for an Upstart Courtier*, xi. 222; in *Vision*, xii. 255; *Pinner of Wakefield*, xiv. 140. Jonson mentions it in *Gipsies Metamorphosed*, vol. vii. 389; and *Masque of Owls*, line 115.

[3] Purple is, of course, frequently named. Purple-in-grain beards, *Mid. N. D.* I. ii. 97; purple velvet, *London Prodigal*, I. i. 101, but since this colour is so well known, it will not be considered.

[4] *Blazon of Gentrie*, 143.

[5] *Accedens of Armory*, 10.

[6] *Fancies Chaste and Noble*, III. iii. 108.

Regis Roll,[1] and was fashionable from the thirteenth century, as wills and accounts indicate.[2] It was worn by King Edward VI, Queen Elizabeth, and King James. Chamberlain describes, disapprovingly, a suit worn by King James on June 5, 1619, four months after the death of the Queen. It was of 'watchet satin laid with silver lace', and he looked 'more like a wooer than a mourner'. Chamberlain wonders what the Duke of Lorraine and his twenty-four attendants, dressed in black, who were soon to arrive to condole with King James, would think of such a suit.[3] Burton tells a story of Henry IV and his jealousy of his son, afterwards Henry V. This jealousy, 'the prince well perceiving', caused him 'to visit his father in his sickness in a watchet velvet gown, full of eyelet holes and with needles sticking in them (as an emblem of jealousy)'.[4] But watchet was not a colour reserved to royalty. In *Your Five Gallants*, it is worn by courtesans; in *A Trick To Catch the Old One*, by servants; and combined with sea-water green, in *Malcontent*, by farmer boys who were to attend their lord at Court.[5] As previously stated, the symbolic meaning of watchet was 'fayned stedfastnesse'.

Brown

Abraham, hair, and russet are noted in the drama, the first used in descriptions of hair and beard; the others, of costume materials.

ABRAHAM

Blount defines Abraham colour as brown, though he does not designate the shade. It was evidently a swarthy

[1] i. 63: 'et ei abstulit j. scapelarium de Waschet.' Hakluyt, *Voyages* (1589), 282, mentions 'watchet or sky-coloured cloth' (see *O.E.D.*); Florio, 1598, defines *celestro* as azure, 'skie colour or watchet'; 1620, *Household Bk. Howard*, 123: 'green watchet.'

[2] 1283, *Lincoln Wills*, i. 3; *Somerset Rec. Soc. Pub.* xvi. 31; 1545-6, E. 351/3025 (wardrobe accounts Edward VI); 1566, *Durham Wills*, ii. 256-7; 1599, L.R. 2/121 (inventory wardrobe Queen Elizabeth); 1609, *Shuttleworth*

Accts. xxxv. 183; 1613, E. 154/4/4 (inventories of drapers).

[3] Birch, *Court and Times James I*, ii. 171.

[4] *Anatomy of Melancholy*, III. iii. 1, i. The story leaves the reader to guess whether the colour of the gown, the eyelet-holes, or the needles symbolized jealousy. Turquoise was the usual colour for jealousy.

[5] *Your Five Gallants*, III. v. 160; *Trick to Catch the Old One*, IV. iv. 31; *Malcontent*, III. i. 58.

tone, since he lists auburn next as a 'blacke-brown'.[1]
Abram colour heads are mentioned in *Coriolanus*, a spelling
changed by some editors of Shakespeare to 'auburn',
which is an unwarranted emendation; especially since
Soliman and Perseda contains the phrase 'that Abraham-
coloured Trojan', and 'Abram coloured beard' occurs in
Blurt, Master Constable.[2] It is possible that an ephemeral
fashion in colours, named after Biblical characters, following the interest in 'holy embroideries', brought forth
stage satire.

MAIDEN-HAIR

Maiden-hair brown, or hair, as it is more commonly
called, was a bright tan.[3] 'Unam tunicam de maydenhare'
occurs in a will of 1359,[4] but this tone of brown is infre-
quent in accounts until the late sixteenth century, when
it was used by the nobility and by the Queen.[5]

Hair colour is named in *Westward Hoe* as the colour of
a forepart, and it seems to have been a favourite in stage
costumes. When King James visited Oxford, 1605, many
elaborate costumes were provided for the drama and
pageants presented in his honour. One of these accounts
itemizes the gowns. One was a 'lose gowne of silvr
Tabine with workes of hayre colour velvet faced wth orenge
colour and white spotted shag', another a 'longe cloake of
Hayre coloured saten lyned wth ash colour plushe'.[6]

RUSSET

Russet, a dusky, reddish-brown, or ashy-grey, was an
ancient tone of brown, called from the homespun cloth
of that name. Russet, like pure blue, symbolized stead-

---

[1] *Compleat Gentleman*, ed. 1661, 155.
[2] *Cor.* II. iii. 21; *Soliman and Perseda*, v. iii. 70; *Blurt, Master Constable*,
II. ii. 213.
[3] For directions for dyeing this
colour, see Markham, *English Housewife* (1631), 168.
[4] *Test. Ebor.* iv. 71.
[5] 1581, Egerton MS. 2806; 1599,

L.R. 2/121, inventory the Queen's
wardrobe; 1600, *Prog. Elizabeth*, III.
507; July, 1594, wardrobe of Bacon
family, Bacon MSS., Univ. Chicago.
[6] *Malone Soc. Coll.* I. iii. 258. *Westward Hoe*, I. i. 77. See also inventory
apparel Lord Admiral's men, Mar. 13,
1598, Greg, *Henslowe Papers*, 118.

fastness.[1] French russet, defined by Florio, 1598, as
violet, was, judging from Middleton's 'Scorch me 'em
soundly, burn 'em to French russet',[2] the violet-brown of
burning paper. French russet was worn by the king of
Scotland in 1512;[3] and in 1587 woollen cloth of that
colour in the inventory of a Durham draper was valued
at the high price of nine shillings a yard.[4]

Green

Green symbolized youth and joy,[5] and was therefore,
as Shakespeare said, 'the colour of lovers'.[6] Sometimes
these lovers were betrothed; sometimes bride and groom;
not infrequently, especially on the stage, courtesan and
libertine. Sea-water green and popingay were the courtesan's tones of green; but, since dramatists did not always
mention the tone to which they referred, modern readers
gain the impression that any tone of green had numerous
meanings, from pure joy to lechery.

The rough sport of rolling girls on the grass, thus
staining their dresses, probably originated the phrase 'to
give a green gown'. The phrase is as old as the fourteenth
century. In 1350 William Fox, a parson, with several
accomplices, was charged with abducting Margaret de
Everyngham, nun of the house of Brodholm, Nottingham-
shire, 'et induentes eam robam viridem secularem'.[7] The
phrase is used in *George-a-Greene*,[8] and in many ballads
and poems of the sixteenth century. Green gowns and
green sleeves, therefore, were unpleasantly associated with
whores. When Knockem had persuaded Win and Mrs.
Overdo to lead 'the life of a lady', he tells Ursula: 'Open

[1] Grange, *Golden Aphroditis*, sig.
G iij:
'Yet will I, woeful wight my corps
  with steadfast colour clad
As russet deck'd with blue, as stead-
fast colours as may be had.'

[2] *A Game at Chess*, II. i. 117.

[3] *Accts. Lord High Treas. Scotland*,
IV, 421.

[4] *Durham Wills*, xxxviii. 290.

[5] *Faerie Queen*, VII. vii. 11, 8;

Rinaldi, op. cit.; *Percy Soc. Pub.* xv.
11, a story of a gentlewoman who calls
for silks to make a sampler, but re-
quests: 'No green at all, Youth, you
and I must part.'

[6] *Love's L. L.* I. ii. 91.

[7] *Inter Brevia Regis Edwardi III*
135. They were pardoned, *Cal. Pat.
Rolls*, 26 Edward III, m. 25.

[8] Greene, *Works*, xiv. 140.

thy wardrobe and fit them to their calling. Green gowns,
crimson petticoats.'[1]

But lovers' adoption of green caused trouble if they
travelled in Mohammedan countries. The Turks rough
treatment of 'an English pirate's whore, with a green
apron' mentioned by Massinger in *Renegado*, was probably founded on an actual occurrence, similar to that
related by William Biddulph in 1600. He wrote from
Aleppo in that year:

'for greene they account Mohamets colour, and if they see any
Christian wearing a garment of that colour, they will cut it from
his backe, and beat him, and aske him how he dare presume to wear
Mohamets colour, and whether he bee Kin to God or not? This I
have knowne put in practise upon Christians (not acquainted with the
customes of the countrey)... one for having but greene Shooe-strings
had his Shooes cut away. Another wearing green breeches under his
Gowne had his Breeches cut off and he reviled and beaten.'[2]

Green shoe-strings were one of the insignia of lovers. In
Les Arrêts d'amours, a decision was rendered in favour of
three ladies accused of usurping some of the masculine
love insignia, i.e. 'de fermer leurs souliers d'esquillettes
verdes'.[3] This custom explains Sir Abraham Ninny's
exclamation when he was rejected: 'Out green shoe-
strings, out! Wither in pocket!'[4] Jonson's amusing
description of a lover receiving instruction in wooing his
mistress by means of colours was not mere satire: 'Or if
you can possesse your opposite that the greene your mistris weares is her rejoicing or exultation in his seruice. . . .'[5]

Some tone of green, never designated by authors, was
worn at weddings by rustic bridegrooms. The first
Shepherd in *The Prophetess* mentions as part of the costume
he will assume in honour of the Emperor's visit, 'my
green slops I was married in' (v. ii. 35), and Tompkins,
the bridegroom of Greene's *Vision* was dressed 'all new
from top to toe with a paire of greene garters tyed cross
above the knee'.[6]

[1] *Bartholomew Fair*, IV. iii. 395.
[2] *Purchas His Pilgrimes*, viii. 265;
Renegado, I. i. 57 ff.
[3] Martial d'Auvergne, *Les Cinquante*
et un arrêts d'amours, 408.
[4] *Woman Is Weathercock*, I. ii. 537.
[5] *Cynthia's Revels*, V. ii. 28 ff.
[6] *Works*, xii. 228. The modern

In addition to the term green, four tones of this colour are mentioned in the drama: goose-turd, popingay, sea, and willow.

GOOSE-TURD

Goose-turd, probably an importation of the French *merde d'oie*, was a yellowish-green. It does not occur, seemingly, in extant English wardrobe accounts or mercers' inventories, but it was mentioned by Harrison among the 'phantasticall colours' in use in 1577.[1] Jonson named it in *Bartholomew Fair* as a colour of starch, and again in the *Alchemist*,[2] and Marston used it to describe unclean teeth,[3] but it seems to have been avoided by other dramatists of this period.

POPINGAY

Popingay, or the green of the parrot, is a blue-green, containing some yellow. Because of its blue cast Harrison lists it among the colours used in England, 1577, as 'popingay blew'. This blue was mentioned in Arnolde's *Chronicle*, 1503 (sig. Q iii, verso). It appeared in an indenture of the goods of Edmund Dudley six years later,[4] and was apparently a fashionable colour by 1520[5] and is frequent in the wardrobe accounts of Henry VIII,[6] but, like so many other tones of colours, lost popularity during the next years and was not revived until Elizabeth's reign. In the drama, Bilioso's use of it is typical. The farmers' sons who are to attend him when he goes as ambassador, 'shall go apparelled thus: in sea-water green suits, ash-colour cloaks, watchet stockings and popingay green feathers'.[7]

SEA-GREEN

The bluish-green of the sea becomes yellow-green in sunlight, and blue in shadow. This variation accounts in

Shropshire girl will not be married in green, believing that colour will bring bad luck.

[1] *Des. Eng.* (1587), bk. ii, ch. 7.

[2] *Bartholomew Fair*, II. i (Nightingale's song); *Alchemist*, IV. ii. 67: 'And my lord's goose-turd bands.'

[3] *Dutch Courtezan*, III. i. 21.

[4] E. 154/2317.

[5] Accounts of Lestranges, *Archaeologia*, xxv. 433. 1522, cloths dyed for Thomas Howell, Johnson, *Drapers*, ii. 252.

[6] E. 101/420/13; 422/11; 423/9, &c.

[7] *Malcontent*, III. i. 58–61.

part for its symbolism. Pure yellow, or pure green, symbolized good qualities, but bluish-green signified questionable qualities, as was ever the case of hues of colours.
In *The Falls of Princes*, Lydgate describes Delilah's preference for hues, a description which characterized her better
than could any discussion of her disposition:

> She wered colours of many dyvers hewe,
> In stede of bleu, which stedfast is and clene,
> She loued chaunges of many dyuers grene. (i. 445.)

In other words, she loved changeable, or sea-water green.
So Moth in *Love's Labour's Lost*,[1] describes Delilah's
complexion as 'sea-water green', and the allusion must
have provoked a laugh, for the popularity of sea-green was
much ridiculed on the stage, even though the Queen had
a few garments of that colour. A good example of that
ridicule is Bilioso's plan to dress his attendants in hues
that indicated dissoluteness and deception: sea-green,
popingay, and watchet.

WILLOW

The connexion of willow-green with despair probably
arose from one of two sources. The sombre green of the
'weeping willow' shared the symbolism of tragedy and
grief attached to the tree itself, which from the time of
the captivity of the Jews in Babylon is said to have drooped
its branches. Allusions in literature to willow, of which
Desdemona's plaintive song[2] is sufficient reminder, are
too numerous to list. Romanello, in telling how the dress
of a woman betrays her heart, refers to the association of
grief for the loss of a loved one, when he says: 'A knot of
willow ribbons? She's forsaken.'[3] The second source of
the sombre-green-and-tragedy association is, as previously
discussed in the summary of Morato's *Del significato de'
colori*, the ancient custom of placing torches in green wood.
When the torch had burned to the green wood it was

---

[1] I. ii. 87. Sea-green was a fashionable colour in Chaucer's day. Garments and purses were of this colour.
1378, *Let. Bk. F.*, ccxxii.

[2] *Oth.* IV. iii. 51. Cf. Grange, *Golden*

Aphroditis, sig. m, v: 'Overloved, soon
lost; Betroth not your hand, lest you
gain to your cost, a willow garland.'

[3] *Fancies Chaste and Noble*, III. iij.
109.

extinguished, hence the Italian *esser giunto al verde*, meaning to be in extreme misery or death. So Petrarch expressed Laura's grave illness in 'Quando mia speme già
condotto al uerde'.[1]

Grey

ASH

Ash and rat's colour are the only greys mentioned in
drama of the sixteenth century. Ash was used as early
as 1518, and occurs in many dramatic accounts and wardrobe inventories of the period.[2] Its popularity was due
in part to its neutrality of tone, which formed an excellent
background for the rich embroideries fashionable in
Shakespeare's age. It does not seem to have any special
symbolism in English drama, though Morato said it
indicated a disposition to deceive. A gallant mentions it
as a colour of velvet in *A London Prodigal*, and Randolfo
describes the Italian in *What You Will* as wearing 'a black
beaver felt, ash-colour plain'.[3] The line is evidently in need
of emendation, since the hat could not have been both
black and ash colour. The line should read: 'In a black
beaver felt, ash-colour band.'

RAT'S COLOUR

Rat's colour is described by Adam in a *Looking Glass
For London* as half black, half white—a description that
would suggest an equal mixture of black and white hairs,
giving the appearance of dull grey (line 222). 'Rattes
colour cloth' was purchased for Francis Willoughby in
1550;[4] Machyn records that at the funeral of Raff Warren,
a mercer of London, 1553, fifty poor men were given

[1] *Sonetto* xxvi.

[2] *Letters and Papers Henry VIII*,
ii. 2, 1517; 1530, Accounts Lestranges,
Archaeologia, xxv. 507. Henslowe,
Diary, i. 61, records a loan to 'Thomas
dowtan to fetch owt of pane' (pawn)
'an embrawered cloke of ashe-colerd
velluet'. Gowns and kirtles of this
colour were used in plays at Oxford,

1605, *Malone Soc. Coll.* I. iii. 257–8.
L.C. 9/72; 1587–8, L.C. 9/79; 1599,
L.R. 2/121. Ash colour is mentioned
by Chaucer, but he does not apply it
to costume.

[3] *A London Prodigal*, I. i. 101:
What You Will, I. i. 149. Also ash-
coloured feather, *Poetaster*, III. iii. 1.

[4] *Mid. MSS.* 401; 1588, 412.

gowns of this shade;[1] in 1580 John Amyas, gentleman, requested his brother in London to send him two and three-fourths yards of ràt-colour cloth at ten shillings a yard to make him a cloak.[2] These references show that the shade was used by the very poor, as well as by families of knights, but its absence from royal wardrobe accounts leads one to the conclusion that it was not a shade fashionable at Court. Claudio tells the bandits in *The Guardian* (II. iv. 128) that cheating vintners are to be known by their 'ratcolourd stockings and shining shoes', a puzzling allusion, for rat's colour was not used in the Vintners' livery. It is possible that rat's colour and ash may have been confused and so have shared the association of deception.

Red

MAIDEN'S BLUSH

Red, one of the earliest Anglo-Saxon terms for colour, designated during Elizabethan times, over a dozen tones varying from the delicate 'maiden's blush' to the vivid 'lusty gallant'.

Maiden's blush is presumably the damask rose colour. It was well known from 1590 until the nineteenth century. Jonson and Marston mention it as a colour of suits worn by gallants,[3] and it occurs frequently in the Queen's wardrobe accounts,[4] especially those of the nineties.

CATHERINE PEAR

Pear shade, as used in *Honest Whore* and *Westward Hoe*,[5] indicated the russet-red, characteristic of the

---

[1] Machyn, *Diary*, 36. In 1565 Sir Martin Bowes made a will providing that twenty-four poor men be given a gown each of such a colour as of late has been accustomed to be given at burials, that is to say 'Rattes culer' or 'Shepes culer', *Hustings Wills*, pt. ii. 695.

[2] *C.S.P.D.* xxvii. 20 (Addenda). For other references to the colour, see *Cal. Pat. Rolls*, May 13, 1553, m. 23: 'unum pallium coloris rattys color'; *Middlesex Sessions Rolls*, Dec. 28,

1561; 1586, *Durham Wills*, ii. 163.

[3] *Every Man Out of His Humour*, III. v. 2; *What You Will*, v. i. 100.

[4] 1599–1601, L.R. 2/121; L.C. 9/92, &c.

[5] *1 Honest Whore*, I. xiii. 420; *Westward Hoe*, II. i. 361. Suckling's *Ballad on a Wedding*, 1641, thus describes this shade:

'Streaks of red were mingled there
Such as are on a Catherine Pare
The side that's next to the sun.'

See *Works* (1709), 31.

Catherine pear. This tone of red evidently shared the odium attached to all yellow-reds. It does not occur in wardrobe accounts, and was probably only a name given by Dekker to that particular shade of red beard.

CARNATION

Carnation was a shade deeper than Catherine pear. It resembled incarnate; and Shakespeare was seeking a laugh from his audience when he put the words: 'A' could never abide carnation' into Mistress Quickly's reply to the narration of Falstaff's last words. Womanlike, she had interpreted incarnate[1] as a colour and as synonymous with carnation. Since carnation was a tone resembling raw flesh, an Elizabethan audience probably enjoyed her remark as an excellent characterization of Falstaff who had played such a passive part in the Battle of Shrewsbury. From the first quarter of the century, carnation is associated with courtly and noble wardrobe accounts. The cost of 'hose of carnation' is listed in the expense accounts of Lestranges of Hunstanton, 1524,[2] and the wardrobe of Henry VIII included carnation hose, stomachers, and entire suits.[3] Princess Mary, Edward VI, and Elizabeth[4] also had garments of carnation, but it was not limited during the latter part of the century to use by nobility, as Love's Labour's Lost (III. i.1 53) shows. Some of the dramatists seem to have recognized it as a courtly shade. Marston's Balurdo, going to Court, wears 'a yellow taffeta doublet cut upon carnation valure';[5] King Amyclas of The Broken Heart shows his joy over the return of his favourite by having his beard made that shade (II. i. 51). In 1 Honest Whore, a lover appears dressed in a flame-coloured doublet, red satin hose, and carnation silk stockings.[6]

[1] Hen. V, II. iii. 35. Phillips, World of Words, 1662: 'Carnation is a kind of colour resembling raw flesh.' Blount, Glossographia, 1656: 'An incarnate colour is a carnation colour.'

[2] Archaeologia, xxv. 480.

[3] 1527, E. 101/419/20.

[4] P. P. Ex. Prin. Mary, 96; 1548–9,

E. 351/3026; 1590–1600, L.C. 2/82; L.C. 2/121; Prog. Elizabeth, iii. 454.

[5] Antonio and Mellida, v. i. 82. Sicile, op. cit., wrote that it was commonly worn by young lovers, gallants, principally by courtiers.

[6] I. viii. 32; see also Scornful Lady, I. i.: 'Carnation jersie stokins.'

In his symbolism of colours de Guez, 1527, says that carnation indicated 'dissymulation'; Forcadel, 1550, noted sadness as its meaning; Rinaldi, 1592, mentioned peaceful love. Among the devices at an entertainment for the Queen at Westminster, 1581, was 'a chariot whose horses were apparelled in white and carnation silke, being the colours of desire'.[1] This last symbolism probably explains Romanello's reply to Charilla when she remarked that women in their love affairs were more secret than were men. Romanello shows how a woman's costume reveals her heart: 'Carnation for your points? There's a gross blabber.'[2] In Jonson's masque prepared to celebrate King James's coronation, 'Safety' was dressed in carnation, 'the colour signifying cheer and life'. The disagreement as to the symbolism of carnation supports the conclusion that there was an ecclesiastical and a secular meaning which were connected but not alike, and that this shade, once meaning pure love and desire, had, through evil associations, acquired also a meaning of questionable qualities.

FLAME COLOUR

Flame-coloured cushions were provided for the chariots of the Queen and Court Ladies on November 1, 1327.[3] This is the earliest noted reference to this hue in English use, but, since Romans wore flame colour, it was probably known to England centuries before. Like carnation, flame colour was associated with lovers—*Henry IV* and *Honest Whore*[4]—usually with the dissolute; but Rowe's emendation of 'dam'd coloured' in *Twelfth Night*[5] to 'flame-coloured' has no support. The damned were as often black as flame-coloured.

GINGERLINE

Gingerline, mentioned with nutmeg hue in Middleton's *Anything for a Quiet Life*,[6] was seemingly an Anglicization

---

[1] Holinshed, *Chronicle* (1808), iv. 444.

[2] *Fancies Chaste and Noble*, III. iii. 100.

[3] *Archaeologia*, xxvi. 343; 1468, *Test. Ebor.* xlv. 162.

[4] *1 Hen. IV*, I. ii. 11; *1 Honest Whore*, I. vii. 29.

[5] I. iii. 146; *fl* could hardly have been misread for *d*.

[6] II. ii. 5. Nutmeg colour is mentioned also in *Hen. V*, III. vii. 20, but,

of the French *zinzolin*, a reddish colour containing some violet, which may have been originally derived from the jujube. It had no connexion with ginger, as is commonly thought.[1] *Zinzolin* was used in France by 1595,[2] and was fashionable there during the early seventeenth century,[3] but seems not to have been much used by the English. 'Gingilene peropus' was purchased at Cambridge in 1617.[4]

HORSE-FLESH

Horse-flesh colour is the bronze shade peculiar to the hide of bay horses. Palsgrave lists it among colours in 1530, but it does not appear in costume until Elizabeth's reign, when it became a favourite.[5] Like other fantastic reds, it was usually, on the stage at least, mentioned as a colour for the costume of gallants. It is one of the shades of silk which Bubble in *Tu Quoque* (sig. C 4) desires.

MURREY

Murrey is explained by *O.E.D.* as 'mulberry colour', the term being derived from Old French *moré*. Palsgrave, 1530, defines it as 'cramosyn'; *A Very Proper Treatise* on the art of 'limming', 1573, describes it as sanguine; Vernon, 1575, as synonymous with 'ferrugo, chestnut or sad blue'; Baret, *Alvearie*, 1580, as 'darke blue like rusty iron'; Florio, 1598, as dark red; Rider, *Dictionarie*, 1612, as a 'lively ruddy colour'; Minshew, 1617, as 'blackish, dunne'. It was evidently a dull purplish-red, but owing to the inability of dyers of this century to reproduce

since it is well recognized, it needs no exposition.

[1] *O.E.D.* defines it as a possible 'perversion of It. *giuggioline*', representing ginger colour. Florio, 1598, defines *gioggiolino* as horse-flesh or brick colour; and, in 1611, *zuzzulino* as a 'kind of reddish colour called Gingerline'. The It. for jujube is *giuggiola*, from which, according to *Vocab. della Crusca*, 1612, was derived the colour *giuggiolino*, 'che è tra giallo e rosso, come da carne scarnatino . . . quasi del color della carne'. See *Phil. Quart.* ix. 212–13, for more complete discussion.

[2] Gay, op. cit. i. 806: 'Une demie aulne de satin geisolin'; 1599, 'un capot et une devanture de satin couleur zizolin'. Occolti mentions *zizolino* in 1557.

[3] Roy, *La Vie, la mode et le costume au XVIII siècle*, Plate X; D'Aubigné's *Les Aventures du Baron de Faeneste*, livre I, ch. ii.

[4] *Agriculture and Prices*, vi. 553.

[5] It is found in accounts of both rich and poor. For examples, see *Middlesex Sessions Rolls*, June 14, 1582, i. 76; 1599, L.R. 2/121; *Prog. Elizabeth*, iii. 505.

colours exactly, it probably varied a little; hence the lack
of agreement among lexicographers. This shade was
known in England in 1249,[1] and it was a favourite for
costume through succeeding centuries, especially the sixteenth. It was used in the royal wardrobe,[2] in Court
revels,[3] in dress of common people, and even in liveries.
It is alluded to in *Every Man Out of His Humour*, and
Michaelmas Term,[4] but with no special significance.
Rinaldi gives its symbolism as 'steadfastness in love'.

PEACH-FLOWER

Peach or peach-flower colour was a deep, fresh pink.
As a textile colour it was known in France in 1315,[5] but
seemed new to England in the late sixteenth century. In
1572 it was the colour of cloth for a safeguard for the
mistress of Hengrave,[6] and it is frequently mentioned in
Queen Elizabeth's wardrobe.[7] Allusions to it in the drama
are in connexion with gallants and would-be courtiers. It
is descriptive of stockings in *Henry IV* and *Queen of
Corinth*; of suits in *Measure for Measure, London Prodigal*,
and *What You Will*, and of a shirt in *Every Man Out of
His Humour*.[8] If peach-colour had the symbolism which
Sicile attributed to it, i.e. diminished riches, lost courage,
little nobleness, its occurrence in comic scenes must have
provoked laughter; for instance, in *What You Will*:
'There's no way to redeem his peach-colour satin suit from
pawn but by the love of a citizen's wife.'

[1] *Cal. Close Rolls*, m. 11 (p. 157);
1338, *Cal. Pleas, London*, p. 148: 'A
piece of morre cloth'; 1358, *Test. Ebor.*
iv. 70: 'cotam de murre', 1362, *Test.
Karl.* 4; 1459, *Paston Letters*, i. 478:
'clokys of murry derke'.

[2] It occurs frequently in the Great
Wardrobe: 1524, E. 101/209; 1548,
E. 351/3026; 1553, L.R. 2/119; 1576,
A.O. 1/2340/6; 1580, L.C. 9/72; Harl.
MS. 1419 B, fol. 458.

[3] See Feuillerat, *Revels at Court*, 35,
39, 146.

[4] IV. iv. 85. In *Michaelmas Term*,
I. i. 256, it is applied contemptuously
to a woman.

[5] Gay, op. cit. i. 457. 'Apple blom'
was known in England in 1339, *Cal.
Pleas, London*, 109, &c.

[6] Gage, *Hist. Hengrave*, 196.

[7] *Prog. Elizabeth*, ii. 77; L.R. 2/121;
1586-7, L.C. 9/77: 'Pro . . . scarf de
taffeta peachcolour.' It was used also
by commoners: *Middlesex Sessions
Rolls*, Dec. 28, 1594 (*M.C.R.* i. 219).

[8] *2 Hen. IV*, II. ii. 19; *Queen of
Corinth*, II. ii. 24; *Meas. for M.* IV. iii.
12; *London Prodigal*, I. ii. 101; *What
You Will*, III. iii. 112; *Every Man Out*,
IV. v. 114. It was a stage favourite,
Henslowe Papers, 118-20, inventory
apparel Lord Admiral's men, 1598.

SCARLET

Scarlet was a vivid red which had in it more of yellow
than of purple. 'Pannos de Scarlatto' were purchased in
Lincoln, 1249,[1] and, though scarlet cloth was made in
many colours, this reference seems to indicate the scarlet
colour. It was an ingrain colour produced from the dye
made of *Coccus ilicis*. Because kermes had to be imported
from southern Europe, scarlet-coloured cloths were very
expensive and could not be afforded by poor persons.
The servant in *Anything for a Quiet Life* tells how his
mistress had persuaded the master that underfeeding the
servants 'would make him wear scarlet the sooner' (v. i.
75). In contrast to other tones of red (which did not need
unadulterated dye-bath of kermes, and so were cheaper),
scarlet[2] was originally worn only by royalty and those of
high position. Ferne, 1586, states that 'by command-
ment of the old law of armes, none might use this cullor
of vermillion (represented by robes scarlet) except he had
been a prince, or thereunto licenced by the Soveraigne'.[3]
In the drama, scarlet is worn by royalty, the Lord Mayor
and Aldermen of London, and by heads of gilds. Subtle's
prophecy of Drugger, *The Alchemist*,[4] indicates that he will
have a phenomenal rise in rank in the Grocers' Gild,
receiving livery 'this summer' and 'next spring called to
the scarlet', i.e. he will be sheriff. The Lord Chamberlain's accounts for 1603, recording the expenses for King
James's progress through London, gives one example of
the wearing of scarlet by persons 'licenced by the Soveraigne'. On the occasion of this progress Shakespeare, and
each of the actors of his company, was allowed four and
a half yards of scarlet, to be used in his costume.[5]

[1] *Cal. Close Rolls*, m. 11 (p. 157).

[2] Monet, 1635, quoted from Gay, op. cit. i. 488: 'Le kermes n'est autre que la couleur d'escarlate.' See discussion of sources of dyes, previous chapter.

[3] *Blazon of Gentrie*, 170. Also Pliny (1606), bk. xxii, ch. 2: '. . . to say nothing of the graine brought out of Galatia, Affricke, and Portugall, wherof is made the royal Scarlet, reserved for princes only and great captains of war.'

[4] I. i. 568. See also Atkins's speech in Grocers' Hall, 1647, Heath, *Grocers*, 417. Cf. *City Madam*, I. ii. 143: 'They will never wear scarlet.'

[5] L.C. 2/4 (5).

Scarlet cloth was credited with many virtues. A cloth of scarlet used in the application of cosmetics was thought to beautify the face.[1] Scarlet kept out summer's heat, and also, as indicated in *The Bondman*,[2] kept one warm in winter.

STAMMEL

The colour called stammel was a slight variation of scarlet[3] probably derived from cochineal,[4] and not a 'coarse red', as it is usually defined.[5] Warren's description in *Friar Bacon* of the damsel that seemed 'so stately in her stammel red' (i. i. 15) implies its association with scarlet. Stammel was revived as a new colour in 1575–80, for it was listed then among 'new colours' to be taken for sale in Brittany.[6]

SYMBOLISM OF RED

From the previous exposition of the shades and hues of red, one may conclude that the pure red symbolized good qualities, though some hue of red indicated evil. An excellent illustration of the association of red with evil is the connexion of red hair and beard with Judas. The particular shade of red attributed to Judas was never designated. Medieval and Renaissance painters represented Judas with black, brown, or blonde hair; though Giotto painted him with reddish-yellow hair in his *Judas Conspires with the High Priest*.[7] Reddish-yellow was connected with treachery, a connexion originating possibly in the association of that colour with foxes. Red beards were fashionable in England in the early seventeenth century, according to Tafata's reply to Andriana in *Ram Alley* (i. i. 200), but remarks in *Bussy d'Ambois, The Family of*

---

[1] Borde, *Dietary*, 95; *Volpone*, III. ii. 108.

[2] II. i. 52. Borde, ibid. 249, recommends it for summer wear.

[3] Florio, 1598, 'escarlatino, the colour we call stammel red'.

[4] Hakluyt, *Voyages*, v. 135: 'Or if you can find the berries of cochenile with whiche we colour Stammelles....'

[5] The Shuttleworths wore stammel: *Accounts* xli. 240. Persons of their status would hardly have worn coarse red.

[6] *Eng. Hist. Rev.* xxix. 518; 1577, *Welsh Port Book*, 285: 'stammell kerseys'; 1557, *Durham Wills*, ii. 422: 'j pettie cote clothe of stamell coller.'

[7] For more complete discussion of the question, see *P.M.L.A.* xlvii. 905-7.

Love, A Very Woman, indicate an antipathy to red hair or beard.[1]

Celia's description of Orlando's hair as 'something browner than Judas's'[2] and Hieronimo's directions to the painter to present the pattern of the notorious Spanish villains with beards 'of Judas his own colour' do not connect red with Judas; but such expressions as: 'Sure that was Judas then with the red beard', 'That hungry fellow . . . with a red beard (Corporal Judas)', and 'by his red beard, he would prove a Judas',[3] testify that Judas's red beard was familiar to early seventeenth-century writers.

YELLOW AND ORANGE

'As touching yellow', wrote Pliny, 'I find that it is a most auncient colour, and highly reputed of in old time; for the wedding vaile which the bride ware on her marrying day was all of yellow.'[4] Yellow, orange, and tawny were favourites in the sixteenth century. There were French crown and whey-coloured beards; primrose, *de roy*, Isabelle, straw, orange-tawny, and tawny cloths, silks, and leather.

CANE-COLOUR

Various identifications of cane-colour have been made since Theobald, in his edition of *Merry Wives of Windsor,* changed the Quarto spelling of 'kane' to 'Cain'. The only justification for this emendation is the fact that an Abraham colour and a Judas colour are also mentioned in drama. But since the cane used for stiffening farthingales was very familiar, and was yellow, as was also the beard in question, Theobald's change may be probable, but is hardly necessary.[5] Other dramatists do not mention cane-colour, and it does not appear in wardrobe accounts or bequests.

---

[1] *Bussy d' Ambois,* III. ii. 18; *Family of Love,* v. i. 79; *A Very Woman,* III. i. 36; *The Witch,* v. ii. 55.

[2] *A.Y.L.* III. iv. 8.

[3] In order of mention: *The Spanish Tragedy,* iii. 12 a, 130; *Chaste Maid in Cheapside,* III. ii. 44; *Bonduca,* II. iii.

81; *Insatiate Countess,* II. ii. 38. See also *Sea Voyage,* II. i. 160.

[4] Holland's trans., bk. xxi, ch. viii.

[5] *M. Wives,* I. iv. 23: '. . . he hath but a little whey face, with a little yellow beard—a cane-coloured beard.' Folio spelling is *Cain.*

WHEY

French crown colour offers no difficulties, and whey-colour is self-explanatory. It is the pale bluish colour of the watery part of milk left by the separation of the coagulated curd. It was an admirable description of the faded beard of an elderly man,[1] and is so used as early as 1553. It is descriptive of a beard in *The Hog Hath Lost His Pearl* and of a sallow face in *Merry Wives of Windsor* and *Macbeth*.[2]

PRIMROSE

Primrose, the pale yellow of the English flower of that name, was especially beautiful combined with silver. The wardrobe accounts for the family of Sir Nicholas Bacon, May 1597, itemize the expenses for a lady's nightgown of primrose minikin bays trimmed with silver 'clowde' lace.[3] Marston had probably seen on some gallant the 'silver hose and primrose satin doublet' which he gave Laverdure in *What You Will* (II. i. 88–9).

COULEUR DE ROY

In October 1531 'vij ½ quartaris collour du roy' cloth to be 'ane galcot with slevis' was one of the purchases for the King of Scotland;[4] and during the next four years many garments in this colour were made for him. By 1536 it was being used for his saddle cloths, and for the wardrobe of his officials and household attendants, thereafter seldom appearing in his wardrobe. Before 1538, the colour had been imitated by dyers of Scotland, and future references to it in the *Compota Thesaurariorum* carefully distinguished between 'Scottis' and French *couleur de roy*.[5]

---

[1] 'as soon as he waxed whey-berded'. See *O.E.D.*

[2] *Hog Hath Lost His Pearl*, Dodsley, xi. 479; *M. Wives*, I. iv. 22, which is sometimes interpreted as referring to fine down on the face; *Macb.* v. iii. 16.

[3] 'For making a nyghte gowne of mennekinne trymmede with b & silver Clowde Lace . . . viij s. For viij yeardes primrose menekinne at iij s. ii d. (a yd.). For vij oz. di b and silver cloude lace 5 s. vi yards of Ribben & Ribben for the syde seames ij.' Bacon MSS., Univ. Chicago.

[4] *Accts. Lord Treas. Scotland*, vi. 18. For more complete discussion of this colour, see *Rev. Eng. Stud.*, 1934.

[5] April, 1538, vi. 286, 'iij elnis . . . Scottis colloure de roy'. 1538, vii. 91, 'xx elnis of French colour de roy to be thame cotis', also 143, 305, &c.

English wardrobe accounts do not note it, but English dyers had attempted it before 1549, for a statute of that date required that wool to be dyed certain colours, including 'Royes' be first 'perfectly woaded, boiled, and maddered'.[1] Colour de roy seemed not to have gained English fancy in the sixteenth century. In 1602 Marston mentions it to describe the colour of a nose, and among the velvets for young Flowerdale,[2] of *London Prodigal*, 'colour de roy' is listed. Other dramatists do not note it in plays. Among the costumes for the drama and entertainment given at Oxford for King James, 1605, was a 'lose gowne of colour de roye nett worke'.[3]

Possibly, King James brought the fashion to Court. The wardrobe accounts of Prince Charles contain numerous items of cloth and silk in this colour. As its name implies, it was French. Cotgrave defines it as 'bright tawny', but research has revealed neither its origin nor its early history.[4]

STRAW

The yellow of straw was fashionable in England by 1578, as many wardrobe accounts, including Queen Elizabeth's, testify.[5] Jonson mentions straw-colour stockings, and Shakespeare and Middleton, straw-colour beards.[6] Its symbolism is given as that of abundance, presumably because it was the colour of harvested wheat.

ORANGE-TAWNY

Orange-tawny, known in England by 1523,[7] was a gay colour, usually associated in the drama with courtiers: the colour of Stephen's cloak in *Woman Never Vexed*, of Bubble's velvet in *The City Gallant*, and Balurdo's stock-

[1] *Statutes at Large*, 3 & 4 Edward VI, c. 2.
[2] *Antonio's Revenge*, I. ii. 79; *London Prodigal*, I. i. 105.
[3] *Malone Soc. Coll.* I. iii. 259.
[4] For Prince Charles's wardrobe accounts see E. 101/434/9; E. 101/436/9, &c. For other references to colour de roy, see *Rev. Eng. Stud.*, cited.
[5] Egerton MS. 2806; *Antiquary*, xxxii. 78; *Prog. Elizabeth*, iii. 510; L.R. 2/121; 1589, L.C. 9/18.
[6] *Tale of a Tub*, I. iv. 8; *Mid. N. D.* I. ii. 96; *Anything for a Quiet Life*, II. i. 56.
[7] *Rutland MSS.* iv. 262, bought for liveries of servants. For other references, see 1550, E. 154/2/36; 1556, Add. MS., 35328.

ings in *Antonio and Mellida*.[1] If orange-tawny symbolized pride, as suggested by Device of *Captain Underwit*, these allusions as well as that to Hoard's[2] plan of dressing his retinue in orange-tawny caps, and Bianca's desire[3] for an orange-tawny quilt, have a special meaning, but, since the clerk's coat of *A Tale of a Tub*[4] had nothing to do with pride, Device's list is probably only satire.

TAWNY

Tawny, a yellowish tan, or lion's colour, composed of deep red and much yellow, was ancient. In 1298 dyers of blue cloth were forbidden to dye tawny.[5] In the sixteenth and seventeenth centuries it was much used in liveries:

> The nobles of our land
> Were much delighted then
> To have at their command
> A crue of lusty men;
> Which by their coats were known
> Of tawney, red or blue
> With crests on their sleeves showne.[6]

In 1522 tawny liveries are provided for the Lestrange servants;[7] when Henry VIII entertained the French King at Calais, 1533, all the 'seruyng menne of England' wore coats of French tawny;[8] in 1581, on the occasion of the Devices at Tilt Yard, the pages were 'all apparalled in loose jerkines of tawnie taffetie . . . and Venetian hose of the same';[9] servants of bishops wore coats of tawny in *I Henry VI*,[10] as did also summoners at Court. Tucca's

---

[1] *Woman Never Vexed*, I. i. 109; *Tu Quoque, or The City Gallant*, sig. (C 4); *Antonio and Mellida*, v. i. 83.

[2] *A Trick to Catch the Old One*, IV. iv. 32.

[3] *Women Beware Women*, III. i. 28. The will of Sir William Fitzwilliam, 1597, leaves an orange-tawny quilt of 'taffata lyned with russet fustyan', *North Country Wills*, cxxi. 181.

[4] IV.ii.44. Bottom mentions orange-tawny beards, *Mid. N. D.* I. ii. 97.

[5] *Lib. Cust.* II. i. 129.

[6] 'Times Alteration', *Roxburghe Ballads*, ii, pt. 3, 583.

[7] *Archaeologia*, xxv. 452.

[8] Hall, *Chronicle*, 793.

[9] *Prog. Elizabeth*, ii. 317; also *Prog. James*, iv. 895: Prince Charles's grooms wore clothes of tawny for this occasion. E. 101/434/20 gives the expenses of his trip to Spain.

[10] I. iii. 47. See also Harington, *Nugae Antiquae*, ii. 22.

reference in *The Poetaster*[1] to Histrio's wearing a tawny coat may allude to the time when, as a player, he was seeking a master.

From the Middle Ages, tawny was considered a sign of sadness;[2] hence Romanello's: 'Tawny? ... the pretty heart is wounded.'[3] In Lodge's *Euphues Golden Legacy*, Montanus is apparelled in tawny 'to signifye that he is forsaken'.[4] Combined with black, it was worn in mourning:

> Tawney and black my courtly colours be,
> Tawney (because forsooke I am) I weare;
> Black (since my Albas love is dead to me).[5]

The Duchess of *More Dissemblers Besides Women* wore black and tawny for her 'seven years deceased lord', discarding them only when she forgot him in her love of the Cardinal's nephew (II. i. 2).

SYMBOLISM OF YELLOW

Of all colours, yellow had the most diverse symbolism: treachery—at least in France, where the doors of a felon's house were painted yellow; heresy, from its connexion with the Jews;[6] charity—according to Spenser;[7] youth, in its heraldic significance;[8] jealousy, marriage, and love, both human and divine. The confusion is somewhat lessened when one considers that gold, lemon, saffron, tawny, though all called yellow, had different associations and therefore different symbolic meanings. Although there are no allusions in Tudor drama to yellow as a colour symbolic of treachery, those which connect it with marriage, love, and jealousy are very numerous. Following

---

[1] III. iv. 134. Tawny livery was worn by servants of others besides nobles and civil officials, Machyn, *Diary*, 86.

[2] Portal, *Des Couleurs symboliques*, 277.

[3] *Fancies Chaste and Noble*, III. iii. 101.

[4] *Works*, i. 128.

[5] Tofte, *Works*, xi. 104. Also Edward de Vere, 'Complaint of a Lover', *Paradise of Dainty Devices*, 70:
'For blacke and tawnie will I weare,
Which mournyng colours be.'

[6] 'Sur les vitraux de l'église de Ceffonds, en Champagne, vitraux qui remontent au seizième siècle, Judas est vêtu de jaune', Portal, op. cit., 89. For discussion of colour in costume of Jews, see *P.M.L.A.* xliii. 757 ff. Also Morato, op. cit. 137, who explains Jews wore yellow to express hope of the coming of the Messiah.

[7] *Faerie Queene*, I. x. xxx.

[8] Ferne, *Blazon of Gentrie* (1586), 169.

classical example, Jonson costumed Hymen in a saffron
robe in his *Masque of Hymen*.[1] His robe is saffron also in
Unfortunate Traveller, *Philaster*, and *Unnatural Combat*,
but is described as yellow, without reference to shade, in
Women Beware Women.[2] A husband's first journey without his wife is indicated in *Malcontent* by saying: 'Hymen
begins to put off his saffron robe' (III. i. 182).

Allusions to yellow as indicative of jealousy are too
numerous to mention. *Eastward Hoe*, *Fancies Chaste and
Noble*, *The Fatal Dowry*, *More Dissemblers Besides Women*,
The Winter's Tale[3] are a few of the examples.

Yellow in hose or footwear had three meanings in
drama: love, marriage, and jealousy after marriage. Its
connexion with love probably grew out of its association
with Hymen. In the fifteenth-century *Les Cinquante et
un arrêts d'amours*, a lover is allowed to wear a yellow boot
for love of his lady.[4] The many lovers at Court possibly
account for the fact that Marston's, Deloney's, and Overbury's characters who go to Court assume yellow hose.[5]
Malvolio's yellow hose of course indicate love.

As previously stated, Hymen is dressed in yellow. Jonson also represents the rustic John Clay and Stub in yellow
stockings on their wedding days.[6] Perhaps this colour,
as indicative of hope of marriage, explains the ancient
English custom that an elder, unmarried sister of a bride
must dance in yellow stockings at her wedding to avert
ill luck and get a husband.[7]

After marriage, yellow hose—meaning either stockings

[1] *Works* (Gifford ed.), vii. 47; see
also Greene, *Works*, vii. 80.

[2] *Unfortunate Traveller*, Nashe,
Works, ii. 274; *Philaster*, v. i. 114;
Unnatural Combat, III. ii. 63; *Women
Beware Women*, v. i. 90.

[3] In order of mention: v. v. 185; II.
ii. 96; III. i. 151; v. i. 105; II. iii. 106.

[4] *Le XLIII arrêt*, 408.

[5] Balurdo wears orange-tawney,
Antonio and Mellida, v. i. 81. 'He may
in time grow great and a well-graced
courtier, for he wears yellow already',
The Fawn, IV. i. 44–6. 'When Robin

and his fellows went to court, on their
legs, they had yellow stockings', *The
Gentle Craft*, pt. ii, ch. iv. 'If he go to
court, it is in yellow stockings', is said
of the country gentleman in Overbury's *Characters*, 106. Malvolio's
yellow hose, *Tw. N.* III. iv. 29, are
discussed in *Mod. Phil.* xxv. 87.

[6] *Tale of a Tub*, II. ii. 126; *Love's
Welcome at Welbeck*, vol. viii. 124.

[7] Lean, *Collectanea*, ii. i. 382. Chambers, *Book of Days*, i. 723, says green
stockings were worn in the west of
England.

or breeches—signified jealousy because of unfaithfulness. Such allusions as 'What stockings have you put on this morning, Madam? If they be not yellow, change them; that paper is a letter from some wench to your husband';[1] or Dekker's more direct: 'at length he was thrust into hell; for his wife cast aside her wedding stockings and drew on a pair of yellow hose',[2] show that yellow hose worn by a wife meant jealousy. Whether the jealous one, man or woman, ever actually wore yellow hose except as a stage costume is an unanswerable question, but the statement in *2 If You Know Not Me*: 'Many of our young married men have ta'en an order to weare yellow garters, points and shoetyes, and 'tis thought yellow will grow a custom',[3] suggests that they may have assumed yellow hose also. Whether used metaphorically or actually, yellow hose was symbolic of marital discord. 'If I were the Duke,' said Stephen, voicing his suspicion of Marcelina, 'I should wear yellow breeches.'[4] Similarly, in *Northward Hoe*, *Thomas of Reading*, and *Look about You*,[5] jealousy is indicated by reference to yellow hose. An old rhyme shows that the association was a common one:

> For he that's jealous of his wife's being bad
> Must have his legs in yellow stockings clad.[6]

Other uses of yellow connected directly or indirectly with the drama should be noted. It was worn by fools in court revels[7] and on the stage;[8] but the Court fool did not dress like the stage fool; for instance, William Gower wore a purple gold tinsel branched frock at the coronation of Elizabeth,[9] and Henry VIII's fool wore green in 1536.[10] Yellow and black in *More Dissemblers Besides Women*

---

[1] *2 Honest Whore*, I. i. 123.

[2] *The Raven's Almanacke* (Grosart ed.), iv. 198.

[3] I. i. 197. Note also the statement that yellow 'has long been used' at London, ibid. 199.

[4] *Duke of Milan*, IV. ii. 24.

[5] In order of mention: I. i. 256; p. 217; Dodsley, vii. 474; also Middleton, *World Tost at Tennis*, 197; also ballad, 'Give me my Yellow Hose Again'.

[6] Lean, *Collectanea*, II. i. 275. Cf. Borghine, *Il Risposo*, 240: 'Chi porta il giallo, vagheggia il fallo'; and the French saying concerning a man whose wife has been unfaithful. He is said to be *peint en jaune*.

[7] Feuillerat, *Revels, Edward VI*, 114, 120.

[8] *Henry VIII*, prologue, line 16.

[9] L.C. 2/4 (3).

[10] *Archaeologia*, ix. 249.

(II. i. 12) suggest constancy, which is also the significance of this combination in Shakespeare's arms. In Spring's song of *Summer's Last Will and Testament* black and yellow may indicate constancy, but also sadness at departure:

Falangtado, Falangtado, to wear the black and yellow;
Falangtado, Falangtado, my mates are gone, I'll follow.[1]

Malvolio's 'not black in my mind though yellow in my legs'[2] has a double meaning. He wears yellow to indicate that he is a lover, but he is not a black-minded or melancholic lover. He refers also to a musical composition well known to Elizabethans: 'Black and Yellow'. Doctor Edward Rimbault, in his *Musical Illustrations of Bishop Percy's Reliques of Antient English Poetry*, reproduced a version of this composition which he found in a copy of a Jacobean virginal book. The tune must have been a popular one, probably serving the words of many songs. In 1567 (?) appeared 'A Doleful Ditty or Sorrowful sonet of the Lord Darnley . . . to be sung to the tune of Black and Yellow'; and sometime between this date and 1580 came the ballad 'The Cruelty of Gernutus', the story of the Jew of Venice, which was also sung to this tune.[3] Shakespeare's reason for having Malvolio allude to the tune may be widely conjectured, but proof is lacking. He may have desired only to call attention to a familiar tune; or he may, at this peak of Malvolio's elation, have made him foreshadow his own downfall.

With few exceptions, only single colours have been considered in the foregoing discussion, but a study of colour combinations is a revelation of the refinement of taste and appreciation of chromatic harmony which char-

[1] Nashe, *Works*, iii. 239. Cf. Lady Clifford's *Diary* November 1616, 42: 'All this time since my lord went away, I wore my black taffety nightgown with a yellow taffety waistcoat.' The connexion of sadness with black and yellow may be a transfer from that of black and tawny. In the ballad 'Corydon's Doleful Knell', black and yellow ribbons are used on the funeral gar-land of Phillida.

[2] *Tw. N.* III. iv. 29. For more complete discussion, see *Bulletin, Shakespeare Assoc. Am.*, October 1933.

[3] The ballad is given by Percy, the tune by Rimbault, op. cit. 53. During the German boycott of the Jews, 1933, stores of the Jews were indicated by signs painted black and yellow.

acterized the Tudor age. A sense of colour is no mean
index of the quality of a people. Dull of imagination must
a reader be who cannot respond to such descriptions as
'a cloake of crymsin sattin garded with green cloth of
golde and lyned with black sarsenett', 'a gowne of white
sattin layed with pasmane of golde lyned with strawe
collored sarceonet', 'a cloake of peache colour clothe of
silver, lyned wth aishe colour unshorn vellet', 'a saufegard
and jupe of willowe vellat fased with orange colour plushe'.[1]

Such beautiful combinations of colours existed not only
in the garments but in the fabrics themselves. To a person
who loves colour, the study of a collection of Renaissance
velvets and silks such as that in the Victoria and Albert
Museum, London, is a satisfying experience. Framed in
case after case through a great room are hundreds of
pieces: delicate azure and cream colour satin; ruby
damask on golden ground, emerald uncut velvet patterned
against silver, two pile velvet—so darkly, deeply, glow-
ingly red that neither photography nor paint can reproduce
its texture, lights, and shades. Any student soon realizes
that the originals of many of these pieces must have been
created by artists. Books of artists' designs for velvets
and silks are treasured in the Musée du Louvre, and one
cannot doubt that Lady Cressingham's rebuke of her
mercer in *Anything For a Quiet Life* was usual. 'The rich
stuffs which my husband bought of you,' she said, 'the
works of them are too common; I have got a Dutch
painter to draw patterns, which I'll have sent to your
factors, as in Italy at Florence and Ragusa, where these
stuffs are woven, to have pieces made for mine own
wearing, of a new invention' (i. i. 293). Nor can one
doubt that tapestries were 'tailors' libraries'. From these
they gained suggestions both for style and colour combinations, and some of their beautiful costumes show how
conscious they were of the play of light and shadow
achieved by combining in a single garment the sheen of
satin, the soft glow of velvet, and the dull tone of taffeta.

---

[1] In order of mention: 1525, *Antiq.* A.O. 3/110; 1599, L.R. 2/121; L.R.
Rep. iv. 357; 1553, E. 154/2/40; 1565, 2/129.

Nor were the dramatists unmindful of the appeal produced by reference to fabric and colour, with the added suggestion of colour-symbolism. A reader is constantly surprised and delighted by lines of beauty—sometimes glittering: 'Cloth of silver and tabine, That like beaten gold will shine'; sometimes soft and subtle: 'silver hose and primrose satin doublet'; sometimes thought-teasing and iridescent: 'And the tailor make thy doublet of changeable taffeta, for thy mind is a very opal.'

COSTUME TEXTILES

III

WOOLLEN CLOTH

CARLYLE's statement that 'Society is founded upon cloth' is profoundly true; for fabrics have played an important part in the exchange of commodities between nations. To the vending of cloth, England owed much of her sixteenth-century supremacy. Her trading companies were founded chiefly to sell her cloth. New trade-routes were sought for the sake of new or more accessible cloth markets. Lands were discovered by the trade-route seekers, and these lands were always examined for new plants and new dyestuffs which would contribute to the cloth industry.

Cloth in this discussion will indicate materials made wholly or partly of wool. Wool fibre differs from that of hair and plants in three ways: (1) it grows in locks or staples; (2) it is curly, tending to twist around anything with which it comes in contact; (3) its surface is covered by imbrications, all serrations pointing one way, so that, if fibres lie across one another, there is a tendency to interlock. The under surface of these serrations, however, offers some resistance to interlocking, and this resistance must be overcome in manufacture through the application of lubricants and pressure. When combed, the long staple wool tends to lie in parallel direction, but the short staple, being more curly, twists about the comb. They are therefore separated in the first process of manufacture. The short is easily felted by carding, and when spun into cloth the fibres composing warp and woof become so entangled that the resulting fabric is a thick, strong maze of inseparable fibres. Such cloth is called woollen. When long staple is spun into yarn, it forms a thread in which there is no interlocking, but only twining of fibres around each other in parallel directions, so that the surface is smooth with no protruding ends. Cloth woven from such yarn is called worsted.

The yarn was spun with the distaff, known as 'rock spinning', or with the wheel. The making of yarn was a domestic occupation of which Shakespeare presents a picture in his 'spinsters and knitters in the sun'. After the cloth had been woven, it was fulled, dried, and its nap raised by the 'rower', who drew it over the dried heads of the teasles fastened in a board. Unevenness of nap was trimmed by shearmen, and the cloth was then dyed and 'tented', i.e. stretched on a long wooden frame, and pulled to the dimensions from which it had shrunk in the fulling process.[1] After drying, it was ready for pressing and folding, and was offered for sale to mercers. With the rise of guilds, each of the aforementioned processes had become the work of a single craft, and no craft was allowed to exercise more than one 'mistery'. The cloth-making crafts always took an important part in the presentation of miracle and mystery plays.[2]

The fifteenth century had been one of expansion in the cloth industry. More persons were employed in it; greater acreage was given to sheep raising; more cloth was exported. *The Libelle of Englyshe Polycye*, 1436, gives a

[1] Cloth manufacture in England was ancient. Mercia exported cloth 796, *English Hist. Source Book*, ed. Wallis, i. 59; there were organizations of weavers at Lincoln, 1131, *Pipe Roll*, 31 Henry I; 109; Oxford, 1140; Huntingdon, 1140; London, Winchester, 1159, Madox, *Hist. Exch.* i. 467, 340, 338, 41. 1159, 1166, weavers at York and Nottingham paid fees into the Exchequer, ibid. 340; ordinances for weavers and dyers at Northampton were made during the reign of King John, *Lib. Cust.*, ch. 52, 37; scarlet cloth and saye were purchased at Lincoln 1182, *Pipe Roll*, 28 Henry II, 50; Stanford and Northampton were making dyed in-grain cloths, 1235, *Cal. Close Rolls*, m. 14 (p. 73); Lincoln was making russet and scarlet, 1236, ibid. m. 6 (p. 301); there was a fulling-mill in Cassiobury, 1255; one in Hemel Hempstead, 1290, that continued in use for three centuries,

Victoria County Histories, Herts. ii. 452, 221; one in Wakefield, 1296, *Wakefield Court Rolls*, i. 250; fullers and spinners are mentioned in Dunster, 1260, Maxwell-Lyte, *Hist. Dunster*, 297; John Pecok was appointed alnager Aug. 30, 1315, *Cal. Pat. Rolls*, m. 25. He was to have ulnage of canvas, woven linen kerseys, sayes, other serges and scarlets and cloths of Lincoln, Essex, Norfolk, Suffolk, Kent, Stanford, Beverley, Devon, and Cornwall. These references are only slight evidence of cloth manufacture in England before the supposedly epochal event of July 1331, when Edward III issued letters of protection to John Kempe, and offered similar favour to all foreign dyers, fullers, and weavers. Much more evidence is available.

[2] *Beverley Town Documents*, xiv. 33; Davies, *Municipal. Rec. York, 15th century*, 235–6.

picture of world trade showing how all nations were dependent upon England for wool and cloth (ll. 79–540); Fortescue, in his *Comodyties of England*, written before 1451, boasts that England had 'wooleyn cloth redy made at all tymes to serve the merchants of any two kyngdoms crysten or hethyn'.[1] In 1463 Edward IV had struck a blow at foreign cloth manufacture by forbidding the importation of woollen caps and woollen cloth, and his successor forbade the export of thrums and woollen yarn.[2] By 1470 the textile industry was largely concentrated in the West of England, East Anglia, and Yorkshire.

The sixteenth century saw East Anglia leap to first place, chiefly through the introduction of the 'new draperies'; but Yorkshire's industry declined. The reasons for the decline in the old cloth centres were many; but continued wars which caused decay in trade were partly responsible. Pestilence found an easy victim in the cloth-worker because of his sedentary habits. Specialization required by the guilds made the cloth-worker dependent upon a single process. Broadcloth, which was formerly made of the finest wool from Lincolnshire and southern counties, and kersey—only slightly inferior to broadcloth—were the staple products of the North of England and had been of commercial importance; but with the growth of the demand for the 'new draperies', and the superior fabrics of the West of England, the price of these cloths was comparatively low. Clothiers began to make the cloths to suit the price, so that by 1591 it was said of the northern counties: 'the clothes shipped . . . bee course clothes and most of them made of course wooll of the growthe of those countryes and ffloxe and thrummes'.[3]

Economic conditions of the sixteenth century called for

---

[1] *Works*, ed. 1869, 551 ff. From the thirteenth century, foreign manufacturers maintained merchants in England to buy wool and unfinished cloth: 1275, *Rot. Hund.* i. 353, 396, 405; ii, 4; Oct. 12, 1282, *Cal. Pat. Rolls*, m. 3; 1317, Madox, *Firma Burgi*, 273; *Cal. Close Rolls*, Apr. 22, 1395, m. 9; Feb. 20, 1393, m. 17; see also *Cal. Pat. Rolls* for numerous letters patent granted foreign merchants.

[2] *Statutes at Large*, 3 Edward IV, c. 3; 8 Henry VI, c. 23.

[3] *S.P.D.* ccxxix. 54. This statement was not wholly true, though the fabrics were of a lower grade than those of previous centuries.

an expansion which was not possible under the old guild regulations. Up to the middle of the fifteenth century, the domestic system of manufacture had been practised; but from that period native capitalists arose, who sought investment not in large cities under guild rule, but in districts and small towns where aliens could supply labour. A class of clothiers like the Springs of Lavenham, and William Rysby—though Hollinworth's Cuthbert and Hodgkins were mythical—started a kind of factory system. They bought wool and other raw materials and hired workers to produce the finished cloth. Deloney represents John Winchcombe as employing 100 carders, 200 spinners, 200 weavers, 150 children sorting wool, 50 shearmen, 80 rowers, 40 dyers, and 20 fullers.[1]

But cloth production in that machineless age was necessarily slow. A document, 1588, shows that in the making of broadcloth sixty persons were employed in producing four cloths, twelve by one and three-fourths yards, a week.[2] But since kersies were sold undyed, and were only a yard wide, thus requiring but one person to a loom, sixty persons could produce ten kersies eighteen yards long a week.[3] A weaver at this rate of manufacture could earn about five pence a day. Having capital, the clothiers could always secure wool by engaging the clip, seasons in advance.[4] Poor spinners and weavers, unable to get wool, had no alternative but to hire out to them. Their

[1] *Works*, 20, 21. There is no proof that the factory system presented in Deloney's romance of business men was founded on reality, but facts suggest that it was not wholly fictitious.

[2] *Kenyon MSS.* iv. 573; 12 were employed in sorting, dressing, and dyeing the wool; 30 in carding and spinning; 12 in weaving and shearing; 6 in carrying wool to the spinners and returning the yarn, taking cloth to the fulling-mill, &c.

[3] Six persons were occupied in sorting and dressing wool, 40 in carding and spinning, 8 in weaving, 6 in shearing, 2 in helping the other workers.

See also Rogers, *Agriculture and Prices*, vi. 597–8; and MS. Titus Cotton B, v. fol. 254, 'a survaye of the benefits wᶜʰ cometh to the state by colloringe of the woole and cloth made in Suffolk'. Robert Reyce, *Breviary of Suffolk*, 1618, 22, stated that a clothier who made twenty broadcloths a week employed 500 persons.

[4] Numerous laws were made against the buying up of wool and the accumulation of looms. *Statutes at Large*, 5 and 6 Edward VI, c. 7; 2 & 3 Philip and Mary, c. 11; 1577, *C.S.P.D.* cxv. 28, but none was wholly effective in ensuring the independence of weavers, &c.

methods increased the dependence of workers, for until law was made against the practice in 1464, and again in 1512,[1] they could force their employees to take payment in 'pins, girdles, and other unprofitable ware'. Whole towns were dependent upon a few clothiers or a venter of cloth. In 1525, for instance, when the clothiers of Laneham, Sudbury, and other towns were taxed for Henry's proposed wars in France, they declared themselves unable to bear the burden of production and dismissed

> The spinsters, carders, fullers, weavers, who
> Unfit for other life, compelled by hunger
> And lack of other means, in desperate manner
> Daring the event to the teeth, are all in uproar,

an event thus admirably described by Shakespeare in *Henry VIII*.[2] A century later, 1,400 persons of Godalming, makers of Hampshire kersies, were unemployed because Samuel Vassel who had vented these kersies had given up the trade.[3]

Cloth has been called the favourite child of legislation, as indeed it was. Statutes for lengths and widths had been made as early as 1328,[4] and frequently thereafter until 1552, when sizes for all English cloths were fixed.[5] This statute was the basis for all further legislation. Though it was slightly amended during the next fifty years,[6] it stood until 1607, when all cloths were reconsidered and their sizes fixed.[7] Since cloths over a yard wide required large looms and two persons to a loom, frequent changes in the size of cloths worked a hardship upon weavers and venters of this commodity. Also frequent legislation encouraged deceit, for when a cloth-owner found his product

[1] *Statutes at Large*, 4 Edward V, c. 1; 3 Henry VIII, c. 16.

[2] I. ii. 30 seq.; Hall, *Chronicle*, 699. In 1528, the cloth trade was disturbed by war with Emperor Charles V. England depended upon foreign markets and largely upon foreign supplies of woad, alum, oil, &c. At that time clothiers had most of their cloth on hand. Cf. Deloney, 43.

[3] 1630, *C.S.P.D.* clxxv. 105.

[4] *Statutes at Large*, 2 Edward III, c. 14; also 47 Edward III, c. 1; 13 Richard II, c. 10; 9 Henry IV, c. 10; 11 Henry VI, c. 9; 18 Henry VI, c. 16; 4 Edward IV, c. 1; 12 Henry VII, c. 4; 5 Henry VIII, c. 8; 33 Henry VIII, c. 18; &c.

[5] 5 & 6 Edward VI, c. 6.

[6] Ibid. 4 & 5 Philip and Mary, c. 5; regulations concerning cloths newly devised were added by 8 Elizabeth, c. 12; 27 Elizabeth, c. 17, 18; 35 Elizabeth, c. 9, 10. [7] 4 James, c. 2.

much shrunken, upon its return from the fullers, he naturally was unwilling to lose it. He simply had the cloths 'tented' to a legal size. This practice gave rise to over-stretching, as cloths woven short could be thus legalized; but over-stretching caused breaks in the thread and consequent thin places. He remedied these by gumming into the cloth a mixture of lamb's wool, flocks, chalk, and starch.[1] Cloth of inferior workmanship was often given a superior appearance by the use of gum which added gloss. A statute of 1514 attributed the origin of this practice to strangers.[2] It was not limited to woollens, as numerous allusions in the drama to gummed velvets, satins, and taffetas will testify. Naturally, gummed or tentered cloth lost both its beauty and size after wear, and, if wetted, shrank to its original dimensions. Leake's famous complaint in 1577, that many northern cloths 'will not hold their contentes being wette',[3] reminds one of Honeysuckle's statement in *Westward Hoe* that 'old thinges must shrinke as well as new Northern cloth' (II. i. 44). Perhaps John May referred to northern cloth in 1613, when he wrote that a gentleman may have livery made for his man, which 'after the first showre of raine may fit his Page for Bignesse'.[4]

In order to ensure the proper making and size of cloths, searchers and aulnagers[5] were appointed to examine and measure the cloth before it was offered for sale, and seal it to signify that it was according to statute. Such aulnagers had been appointed first in 1279,[6] but the custom of farming out aulnage, begun by Henry IV, gave rise to deceitful practices. Some aulnagers extorted more than

[1] The following statutes were against stretching cloth: 4 Richard III, c. 8; 4 Edward IV, c. 1; 3 Henry VIII, c. 6; 6 Henry VIII, c. 9; 3 & 4 Edward VI, c. 2; 39 Elizabeth, c. 20; 43 Elizabeth, c. 10. Laws against flocks in manufacture were: *Lib. Cust.*, ii, pt. 1, 125; 2 Edward III, c. 3; 27 Edward III, c. 5; 50 Edward III, c. 7; 13 Richard II, c. 7; 7 Richard II, c. 2. 'Flocks' were short fibres gigged, fulled, or sheared from cloth in the finishing rooms.

[2] 5 Henry VIII, c. 4. The statute states that 'a coarse worsted' of twenty-six shilling value is made to appear like one of forty. But upon being wetted these cloths become 'spotty and foul'.

[3] *C.S.P.D.* cxi. 38.

[4] *Estate of Clothing*, 38.

[5] A term derived from *aln* or ell, a measure of 45 inches.

[6] *Cal. Pat. Rolls*, 7 Edward I, m. 3.

the legal fee for measuring.[1] Dishonest aulnagers sealed cloth without measuring, if the owner paid a fee.

Since all cloths of illegal measurement could be seized and sold for the benefit of the Crown, frequency of legislation worked a hardship. The changes in size were detrimental to the trade and unfair to manufacturers, especially to those in the north who could not always learn the latest statute before sending their cloths to London. An interesting example of this fact is afforded by a case before the Privy Council, 1588, when 'Dyvers clothiars of sundry partes of the realme havinge repayred to this Barthylomewe Fayre with a great nomber of course clothes and karseys to be uttred and solde there' forebore 'to open their said clothes . . . fearing they be not made according to the Statute'. They therefore made 'humble sute' to the Council who notified officers of the fair not to 'seasin uppon their saide clothes, as forfett . . . untyll they shall have recyved order from hence'.[2] Wilful deceit and illegal manufacture reacted upon the workmen, and cloth of districts which had consistently offered defective goods for sale remained unpacked in the cloth halls.

The cloth trade, which had declined under Henry VIII but increased under Edward VI, showed a marvellous expansion in the reign of Elizabeth. English cloth was carried to nearly every nation by merchants and trading companies.[3] Guicciardini presented an excellent account of Antwerp's trade in English cloth, stating that England

[1] Exch. Dep. by Com. 38–9 Elizabeth, Mich. 23.

[2] Acts Privy Council, Aug. 23, 1558, 378–80. Each shire had a room in a hall to which the country clothiers could send cloths to be sold. Keepers were maintained who received the cloth. Sales took place usually from Thursday noon to Saturday noon each week.

[3] Wheeler, Treatise Commerce, 1601, gives an excellent history of the Merchant Adventurers. Roberts, Treasure of Traffic, 1641, reviews the histories of all the companies. 1527, Thomas Howell was exporting to Spain: broadcloths, scarlets, Kentish cloths, tawny, russets, marble, kerseys. See Johnson, Drapers, ii. 253. 1560, C.S.P.D. xv. 67, gives the sale of English cloths on the Continent. A letter from M. Arthur Edwards, Aug. 8, 1566, Shamaki Media, to his company, is typical: 'I was asked by the Shauh if you were able to bring him yearly 10,000 pieces of kersies and cloths. The Armenians and others are desirous to barter with us giving silks for kersies.' Hakluyt, Voyages, iii. 56 seq.

was making cloth in very large quantities.[1] A manuscript written probably between 1575-85, giving special directions for foreign trade in English merchandise, lists sixteen trading cities to which English cloths were taken, making the interesting allusion to Flanders wool that it was 'of so course a staple that it will not runne in threade unles they mingle our woolles withall'.[2] England was importing from these countries furs (Russia); linens (France); silks (Levant); dyestuffs (Brazil and West Indies); gold and silver (West Indies); friezes and linen yarn (Ireland); holland cloth and linens, &c. (Flanders); cotton (Tripoli), &c. In 1601, according to Wheeler,[3] the Merchant Adventurers were exporting 6,000 white cloths besides coloured cloths of all sorts: kersies, bays, cottons, northern dozens, or about £600,000 worth of white cloths and £4,000,000 worth of coloured cloth. The imported cloths offer an interesting commentary on English taste and manufacture of the period:

'Of Dutch and Germain Merchants they buy Fustians, Linnen cloth; of Italians—all kinde of silke weares, velvettes, wrought and unwrought, Satins, Damaskes, Sarsenettes, Milan fustians, clothe of gold and silver, Grograines, Chamlettes, Satin and sowing silke, orgazine; of Low Countrie Merchantes—handwork not made in Englande, Tapestrie, Buckrams, white threed, incle, Linnen clothe of all sortes, Cambrickes, Lawnes.'

The greatest influence upon English cloth of the sixteenth century was wrought, however, not by the growth of trading companies, but by the influx of aliens. Taking advantage of the Reformation in England, many Protestant weavers flocked there during the reign of Edward VI. Though some immigrated during Mary's reign, they came in larger numbers when Elizabeth's tolerance became known, settling in Norwich, Colchester, Sudbury, and other East Anglian towns; though some of the serge workers remained at Southampton.[4] These aliens introduced the 'new draperies', a name given to stuffs woven

---

[1] 1567, *Descrittione di tvtti paesi bassi*, 119–22.
[2] *Eng. Hist. Rev.* xxix. 516 ff.
[3] Op. cit., pp. 25–8.
[4] 1567, *C.S.P.D.* Add. xiii. 81; *Court Leet Rec. Southampton*, 106, 278.

of 'rock spun' worsted or worsted mixed with flax or silk. They were softer and finer in texture than the 'old draperies' of broadcloth, kersey, penistone, russet, marble, &c.,[1] and had a high gloss obtained by use of the hot press.

In order to revive worsted manufacture in Norwich, which was 'almost wholly decayed', Queen Mary, 1554, had granted twenty-one persons letters patent to make 'Russels, Sattens, Sattens Reverse, and Fustian of Naples'. These stuffs 'had been made beyond the Seas, of the Wools bred in the County of Norfolk', and the mayor and aldermen of Norwich had imported strangers to teach these 'mysteries' to the weavers of the city. Eleven years later, Elizabeth granted letters patent to thirty Dutch master cloth-workers with ten servants each 'to exercise the faculties of making bayes, arras, says, mockadoes, stamen, carsey—and other outlandish commodities as has not been made within this our realm of England'.[2] Other foreign cloth production was introduced in 1569 when John Hastings got a patent for making 'freezadoes after the manner of Haarlem'.[3] In 1578, when rates of duty on the 'Norwich stuffs' were drawn up, some idea of the quality and lengths of the materials was given. Bays were thirty-four yard materials, weighing from twenty-four to forty-four pounds; 'rass or staminett', twenty-two yards, of thirty-two pounds; sayes of the 'Flanders sort', twenty-seven pounds; grograins, fourteen yards, five pounds; moccadoes, fourteen yards, three to six pounds; 'plommette', 'carrells', and fustian of Naples fourteen yards, four to six pounds; blankets 'called Spanish Rugges', ten pounds.[4] A year later 'buffiner and mockado' are men-

---

[1] Marble, known to England by 1303, was a cloth woven of irregularly coloured wools which produced a marbled appearance. Riding coats, jackets, kirtles, and in some cases, servants' livery were made of marble cloth; see 1541, E. 154/21/20; 1545, 1549, *Knaresborough Wills*, C. iv. 42, 54, 57; 1551, *Thoresby Soc. Pub.* ix. 350; 1554, 1558, 1559, *Test. Leod.* xxvii. 27, 30, 31, 231, 283, 289; 1551,

Mid. MSS., 403. Its price ranged from 2s. 9d. to 10s. a yard, *Agriculture and Prices*, iii. 502, 508; *Durham Wills*, ii. 256, 363.

[2] Lansdowne MS. 7, art. 81. Sayes, stamels, and kerseys had been made in England before, but the new products were not wholly of wool.

[3] *C.S.P.D.* cvi. 47.

[4] Lansdowne MS. 27, art. 60; 28, art. 25.

tioned as having grown into much favour 'to the decay of the use of cloth'. These 'new draperies' had captured the fancy of cloth wearers and caused jealousy among the weavers of the 'old draperies' who, unable or unwilling to learn the new, suffered from loss of work. In Yorkshire, for instance, few of the 'new draperies' were being made in 1595,[1] and most of those were from Halifax; but when in 1619, in an endeavour to teach the new to York's poor, Edward Wally of Norwich was brought in, the project failed.[2]

A manuscript of 1592 gives further particulars concerning the 'new draperies'. Frizadoes of 'Pennystones', 'Worseters', Hastings, are mentioned, showing that they were made in both the north and south of England; 'grograines, called Buffines', which were fourteen yards long, weighed four pounds and were valued at £1. 'Carrolles' were similarly expensive. 'Rash or Stammetts of Florence' at £6 was evidently the kind of rash which England had formerly imported from that city. 'Russells' seem to have declined in popularity. None had been 'entered in custom of long time'. Serges broad and narrow, weighing six to eleven pounds, were rated at £6 to £6 10s. Sayes also were of two kinds: silk sayes and 'broad sayes', the silk rated 10s. higher than the other, but weighing ten pounds less. Valures were valued at £1 10s. 'Tukes—being a kind of Buckram', weighing six pounds, were 8s. 'Grogranes Chamblets', weighing five pounds, were listed at £1 6s. 8d. Spanish ruggs were reported 'not now used'; no English ruggs were being made, and no Irish ruggs 'shipped over'.[3] Only one kind of moccado is mentioned; though single, double, and tuft had been listed in 1578. The 'new draperies' did not come under the control of the aulnager until June 1594, when their aulnage was farmed out to Sir George Delves and William Fitzwilliam for twenty-one years. The patent does not define these draperies. They are spoken of as

[1] Peck's 'Certificate of New Draperies in the Countie of Yorke', *C.S.P.D.* cclii. 2.

[2] Heaton, op. cit. 65–6.
[3] Lansdowne MS. 81, art. 51.

'divers sortes of wollen clothes and other commodityes commonly cauled duble midle and single bayes, rashe, stammelles of Florence, serge of French sorte, sayes of Flaunders sorte, narrow worstedes, narrow grogranes, maccadoes of every sorte, Plummetes, fusades, carrells, Fustian of Naples, blankets cauled Spanishe rugges, knitt hose of worsted yearne & all sortes of nue draperies & other nue stuffs & commoditys now made of woll only or most parte of woll have ben of late yeares chiefly devised & made within England by straungers.'[1]

Probably the patent does not list all the draperies made, or possibly new kinds were invented rapidly. To use Fuller's quaint expression: 'The nimble woof, its artificial dancing in several postures about the standing warp, produceth infinite varieties in this kind.' If the patent to Delves and Fitzwilliam in 1594 had named them all, then the woof was indeed nimble during the next seven years, for the Delves case against Norwich for the payment of aulnage, August 18, 44–5 Elizabeth, named the following:

'cloth of arras, bayes, bewpers, boulters, boratoes, buffins, bustyans, bombaces, blanketts, callimancoes, carrells, felts, flannels, grograines, garterings, girdelings, knitt hose, knitt pettycots, knitt sleeves, knitt gloves, knitt capes, knitt hatts, knitt coifes, knitt sockes, linsey-woolseyes, mockadoes, minikins, mountaines, makereles, oliotts, Paris cloths, pomettes, plumettes, perpetuanas, perpicuanas, rashes, rugges, russells, russells-sattins, sattin-reverses, sattins of Cipres, Spanish sattins, serges, sayettes, sayes, saye lace, grograine lace, and laces of all sorts, stammells, stamenes, scallops, tapestry, tukes, tamettes, tabines, thrummes, valures, woadmelles, worsteds, worsted yarn, woolen yearn.'[2]

If one will note the stock of a draper of the early years of Queen Elizabeth's reign, and one of the first decade of the seventeenth century, he will see how far the 'new draperies' had replaced the old.[3] When English ships were bringing products of the world to English ports, it is small wonder that Elizabethans preferred materials with foreign names. Dramatists were quick to use the names of the 'new draperies' in their plays; buffin, calamanco,

[1] *S.P.D.* ccxlix. 80.
[2] *Exch. Bills and Answers*, 44 Elizabeth, Mich., *Norfolk*, no. 301.
[3] Cf. 1579, *Richmond Wills*, 275 ff.; 1613, *Durham Wills*, xxxviii. 289 ff.

frizado, grograin, mockado, rash, stammel not only give them effective descriptions of costumes, but enable them to suggest, without description, the status of the characters. Dramatists also noted the change of fashion, when plush succeeded rash, or mockado was out of favour.

The 'new draperies' did not advance without opposition. Every possible complaint, petty or serious, was lodged against the strangers: they dumped their 'filthy dye waters into the street', they 'cheated the Crown' by using the finest wool, which formerly went into expensive kersies, for 'sleight' materials that paid little subsidy.[1] London merchants tried to prevent dealers of Norwich and Colchester from selling in London.[2] The makers of bays were accused of injuring the spinsters and weavers of Sudbury, 1618.[3] The question as to whether these stuffs were woollen or worsted and so governed by the statute of 1465 caused continual litigation. In 1618 the worsted weavers of Norwich presented to the Privy Council a statement to prove that 'the stuffs of new invention do not vary from the materials of the worsteds, nor from the texture', but in order to make them 'more vendible' they had been given new names. 'Buffyn, catalowne, and pearl of beauty' were shown to be one cloth; 'paragon, peropus, and philiselles', one; 'saye and primides' one. The 'paragon peropus, and philiselles' were double 'chamblets', though the one was double in the warp, the other in the weft. 'Buffin', &c., were single chamlets, with difference only in the width. To make a worsted a stamin was to make it narrower and thinner 'in the stay'. A worsted was wrought with four treadles; a bustian with three; a double chamlet with the two right-foot treadles; a single chamlet, the two left-foot treadles; a 'catalowne' was a 'buffyn' made with twisted threads of colour; a 'pearl of beauty', 'a buffyn' striped by colours in the warp and tufts in the 'stricken'. From the ancient motley or checker worsted, all damasks and branched works took their beginning.[4] The 'new draperies' were therefore new names

[1] 1594, *S.P.D.* ccl. 47.
[2] Ibid. lxvii. 143.
[3] Ibid. cix. 55.
[4] Add. MS. 12504, art. 64. Para-

only. Obviously this statement cannot be wholly accepted, for improvements in manufacture had been made, and new weaves were given new names.

The seventeenth century saw the 'new draperies' firmly established, whether they owed their popularity to weaving or to name. In 1615 an appeal was filed urging the use of wool for new draperies rather than for old.[1] Three years later, a proposal was made to the Privy Council for encouragement of the new draperies, especially the 'perpetuanies', by issuing charters for their manufacture in Devonshire and other counties according to the charter granted to Hertfordshire;[2] and on February 25, 1625, a warrant was issued authorizing a corporation for Hereford, Essex, Middlesex, Berks., Devon, Dorset, to introduce the manufacture of the new draperies.[3]

Unfortunately, James had not the foresight and wisdom of his predecessor on the throne. His granting of monopolies helped to ruin, for his reign, England's cloth trade. The most disastrous of these monopolies was Cockayne's dyeing experiment,[4] 1615–1617, because it closed the best foreign markets. Considerable deceitful practice in cloth weaving and dressing added to the ruin of trade. Misselden,[5] 1622, says 'the perpetuanaes and other new draperies have little by little been made worse and worse so that now they are become quite out of use, the trade lost, the traders ruinated, the manufactures by other nations supplied'. Thousands of cloth-workers were becoming beggars and thieves because there was no work. On February 9 of that year the Privy Council sent mandates to all cloth manufacturing towns requiring that their citizens be set to work so they would cease to be 'a nuisance to the Government'.[6] The answers sent by these towns

gon and peropus were especially fashionable in the late Jacobean period. Philip Hutton paid £24 for a suit of 'water'd paragon' in 1620, and £1 2s. for a doublet of peropus, and mending breeches and gown, *Hutton Accts.* 224. See also *Shuttleworth Accts.*

[1] *C.S.P.D.* lxxx. 15.

[2] Ibid. xcvi. 40.

[3] Ibid. clxxxiv. 44.

[4] See p. 12.

[5] Op. cit. 101. Worcester was then making broadcloths, kersies, perpetuanas; Colchester, says; Canterbury, says. Ibid. 128.

[6] *C.S.P.D.* cxxvii. 76.

to the Council show a desperate situation. Two hundred
towns of Suffolk had cloth on hand worth £39,280, and
the clothiers, having lost £30,415, had not funds to re-
employ their workmen.[1] Oxfordshire manufacturers expressed a willingness to re-employ the cloth-workers at
once if unsold cloth were taken off their hands.[2] The
keepers of the 'halls' of Gloucestershire, Worcestershire,
Reading, Somerset, Suffolk reported 1,133 pieces unsold,
though some of this was defective. In Manchester 'Hall'
853 pieces of friezes, cottons, baise were unsold; Hampshire cloths were not even unpacked. 5,159 pieces were
reported in Northern 'Hall'; 323 in Wiltshire; 207 in
Oxfordshire; 3,057 in Leadenhall.[3]

A commission was appointed to find the cause of the
situation, and clothiers from all the shires were asked to
send delegates or opinions concerning conditions. Some
shires expressed the futility of sending delegates, but all
gave their opinions. Essex, for instance, thought the
makers of the new draperies responsible, because they did
not make cloth according to statute, and did not regard
the laws of apprenticeship;[4] Oxford considered the secret
export of wool to be one cause.[5] The Drapers of England
traced the ills to remissness of alnagers, to interlopers in
the trade, and to night funerals.[6]

To relieve the clothiers, the Merchant Adventurers
were ordered to buy up cloth on hand, but they replied
that they had bought all possible, for, with the foreign
markets closed, they could not sell. Besides, much of the
cloth on hand was faulty and contrary to statute.[7] Conditions seemed indeed serious. After examination of all
opinions the 'Council on the decay of the cloth trade'
reported its findings on June 23, 1622. They were:

1. Increased manufacture of cloth abroad.
2. Deceits in making and dyeing English cloth, and
   the heavy burdens on it.
3. Foreign wars.

[1] C.S.P.D. cxxviii. 67.   [5] Ibid. cxxviii. 51.
[2] Ibid. cxxviii. 51.   [6] Ibid. cxxx. 140–1.
[3] Ibid. 73–80.   [4] Ibid. cxxx. 65.   [7] Ibid. cxxix. 12.

4. Close policy of the Merchant Adventurers.
5. Scarcity of coin.
6. Want of returns for cloth exported.
7. General wearing of silk and foreign stuffs instead of cloth.[1]

The Council offered remedies for all these causes, and, acting upon this advice, James issued a proclamation, July 28, 1622, prohibiting the export of wools, woollen yarn, fuller's earth, and wood ashes; forbidding deceitful dyeing of cloth; and commanding that nothing be worn at funerals except black English-made cloth.[2] By September the situation had somewhat amended, but, to ensure a plentiful supply of wool, suggestion was made that Scotland and Ireland send their wools only to England. The proclamation of 1622 was the first which absolutely forbade the export of wool for any length of time. Previously, it had been only temporarily forbidden, subject to royal convenience, licences being granted to favourites to export during the king's pleasure.

The commission was continued for the purpose of further studying the situation; especially of investigating the price of English cloth beyond the sea, to determine whether the restrictions imposed by the Merchant Adventurers had raised it too high; and to devise measures for encouraging a greater home consumption of English woollen cloth.[3]

During the disastrous Cockayne experiment, the Dutch had begun the manufacture of the kinds of cloth which they had hitherto purchased from England, an industry which interfered seriously with the sale of English cloth in the Netherlands and elsewhere. The imposts set by the Merchant Adventurers were a grievance, since this company had thus secured the sole right to trade with Germany and the Low Countries. The House of Commons therefore resolved that all merchants might transport northern and western 'dozens', kersies, and new draperies everywhere, and all might freely trade in dyed

[1] Ibid. cxxxi. 55.
[2] Ibid. cxxxii. 61.
[3] *Foedera*, xvii. 413 ff.

and dressed cloths with Germany and the Low Countries; but, as a favour to the Eastland Company, in 1629, the export of broadcloth, dozens, kersies, &c., to the Baltic countries was forbidden to all except those who were free of that company.[1] A year later, Charles confirmed his father's proclamation against the export of wool and materials used in the manufacture of cloth.[2] In 1631–2 he appointed a commission for the counties of Somerset, Wilts., Gloucester, and Oxon. to see to the proper making of cloth.[3]

The appointment of commissions was in vain. The cloth manufacture had been given too serious a blow by the Cockayne experiment. Attracted by the bounty which the Dutch Government offered to all who set up looms, many English weavers of serges and broadcloth had emigrated to Holland.[4] Aided by protective tariff, and supplied with raw materials from England which were smuggled, in spite of laws prohibiting their export, Holland's cloth industry flourished.

England's decline and the Low Countries' rise in cloth manufacture was further accelerated by the over-zealous Laud. In 1634 Laud recommended to the king that all English-born children of foreign parentage be compelled to attend the parish churches. The Walloon, Italian, and Dutch settlers in Norwich, Suffolk, Canterbury, Colchester, and Sandwich vainly pleaded for the toleration allowed by Edward VI and subsequent Protestant rulers. Denied that religious freedom for which their ancestors had sought refuge in England, these settlers emigrated to America and to Holland, giving an impetus to Holland's cloth industry which was prejudicial to that of England, for both capital and workers were lost. Thus closed that chapter of England's supremacy in cloth-making—a supremacy admirably expressed by Deloney in his introduction of *Thomas of Reading*: 'Among all craftes, this was the onely chiefe, for that it was the greatest merchandize by the which our country became famous throwout all Nations.'

[1] *Foedera*, xix. 129.   [3] Ibid. 215.
[2] Ibid. 155.   [4] 1632, *S.P.D.* ccxxiv. 44.

WOOLLEN CLOTH IN THE DRAMA

CLOTHS mentioned in the drama might be classified as 'old' or 'new' draperies: woollen, worsted, and mixed cloths of wool-linen-silk, but since none of these classifications would be of particular advantage to a student of the drama, all cloths are described alphabetically, giving, whenever possible, four points in the history of each: (1) its origin; (2) the date of its earliest use in England; (3) a discussion of its use and price; (4) its mention in the drama.

BAYS

Two and a half yards of orange-tawny 'baise' were purchased for the personal wardrobe of King Henry VIII in 1546. Originating in Baia, baize, or 'bays' as it was commonly called in the sixteenth century, was a napped material, half worsted, with a warp of combed wool. Its manufacture was introduced into England by Dutchmen in 1563, when the Queen granted letters patent to thirty master workmen to exercise the 'faculties of making bayes, arras, sayes . . . and other outlandish commodities as has not been made in this our realm of England'.[1]

Previous to this date, bays had been made in Flanders of English wool and imported into England. By 1594, England was sending great quantities of bays into Italy.[2] Bays of Sudbury, Coggeshall, and Maidstone were called 'minikins', and were in 'waight length and bredth equal to short Suffolk clothes saving they are afted and cottoned lyke unto a Baie'.[3] They were exported, converted into frizadoes, and often re-imported into England at high prices.[4]

Because of its nap, bays was especially suited to lining garments, and during the sixteenth century was worn

---

[1] Lansdowne MS. 7, art. 81. For discussion of bays, see *Walloons and Their Church*, 80, &c.

[2] Dec. 17, 1594, *S.P.D.* ccl. 47, 76.

[3] Ibid.

[4] *Book of Rates* for 1624 gives the customs rate on 'Bayes voc. minekin or Frizados the peece containing 54 pounds upward'.

chiefly by the wealthy. Sir Nicholas Bacon paid three
shillings a yard for 'primrose mennekine' in 1597; and
the Shuttleworths nearly eight in 1619.[1] The 'minikin
breeches' mentioned in *Scornful Lady* were evidently not
expensive, or because of their old condition were contemptuously alluded to. Bays was out of favour by the six-
teen-thirties. Shirley expressed in *A Bird in a Cage* the
change in fashion when bays had been superseded by
plush, and had become middle class:[2]

> At masks and plays, is not the bays
> Thrust out to let the plush in?

BROADCLOTH

Jonson showed England as the home of broadcloth
when he compared the bringing of broadcloths to that
country with taking fresh oranges to Spain.[3] Broadcloths,
distinguished from yard-wide 'straits', were originally
fine, woollen cloths of plain weave, two yards wide, exclusive of the wide selvedge or 'list'.[4] The full length of
a broadcloth was twenty-four yards, but the 'dozen', or
broadcloth of twelve to thirteen yards was an important
commercial product. Broadcloths had come 'into great
perfection' in England at the beginning of the reign of
Edward III;[5] and until the introduction of the 'new
draperies' they were the chief export of England. William
Cholmeley wrote in 1553 that 150,000 undressed and
undyed broadcloths were yearly sent out of England. He
gives no account of the finished cloths which were exported.[6] Even in 1577, Harrison stated that the 'wares'

---

[1] Bacon MSS., Univ. Chicago
(wardrobe of Bacon family, May 7,
1597). *Shuttleworth Accts.* xli. 237 (kind
of bays is not stated). For other references to bays, see, for 1578, *Archaeologia*, xxv. 566; 1623, *Eng. Hist. Rev.*
vii. 98 (3s. 2d. a yard); *Kenyon MSS.*
36 (2s. 10d. a yard).

[2] *Scornful Lady*, I. ii. 338; *Bird in
a Cage*, v. i (Dyce ed. ii. 442).

[3] *Devil is an Ass*, II. i. 205. See also
Knack to Know a Knave, sig. (G 4);

Fair Maid of the Inn, IV. i. 488.

[4] *Statutes at Large*, 2 Henry VI,
c. ix; 1 Henry VIII, c. 2; 4 James I,
c. 2. The lists were used for caps and
garters, &c. *Fatal Dowry*, V. i. 50;
Tam. Sh. III. ii. 69—Grumio's garters were probably of broadcloth lists.

[5] Sir Edward Coke, *The Institutes of
the Laws of England*, i. 41.

[6] *Request and Suite of a Truehearted
Englishman*, Camden Soc., 1853, 1–20.

which were carried out of England were 'for the most part Brode clothes'.[1]

The demand for broadcloth declined as that for the 'new draperies' grew, and this cloth became, by the seventeenth century, the wear for servants.[2]

BUFFIN

Buffin has always been defined as a coarse cotton material. Florio's definition of *gottomato* as 'a kind of cotton, frezado, penistone, or buffin sarge', does not indicate that it was cotton, but a napped material. Buffin was a narrow grograin or single chamlet, as weavers testified in the Delves *v.* Norwich case, 1602,[3] and it was made in both wool and silk.[4] Since it cost from one to one and a half shillings a yard,[5] it could not be classed with the *very* cheap materials. The earliest noted reference to this material is 1572,[6] and it was first manufactured in England in 1589.[7]

Buffin was usually worn by tradespeople, so that Milliscent of *The City Madam* would have been shocked at Lady Frugal's wearing it; and Gertrude, *Eastward Hoe*, in her ambition to be a lady, would naturally have scorned it.[8]

CADDIS

Caddis was a woven tape; also a cloth in a coarse, thick quality, resembling *bureau*, and a fine quality resembling flannel.[9] It was made of the cadace or 'flocks' of wool,[10] so

[1] *Des. Eng.* bk. ii, ch. 5.

[2] *Tu Quoque, or The City Gallant*, sig. C 3 verso.

[3] Exch. Bills and Answers, 44 Elizabeth, Norfolk, 301. See Lansdowne MS. 81, art. 51, for definition.

[4] 1585, *Durham Wills*, xxxviii. 134, 'a remblet of black and red silk boffyn'.

[5] 1588, 'Wray Accounts', *Antiquary*, xxxii. 54, tawny; 1593, 365, striped; 1593, 280, orange-tawny changeable, 281, purple; *Durham Wills*, xxxviii. 281.

[6] *Durham Wills*, ii. 373.

[7] *Walloons and Their Church*, i. 78.

[8] *City Madam*, IV. iv. 34; *Eastward*

Hoe, I. ii. 16. One finds buffin garments in wills and inventories of bailiffs, constables, tradesmen, and merchants, but not in those of nobility. See *Durham Wills*, xxxviii (1586), 138; (1592), 210–11; (1593), 233, 236, &c.

[9] Gay, op. cit. i. 224.

[10] 1400, *Coventry Mysteries*, 241: 'Cadace woole or flokkys.' 1440, *Promp. Par.* : 'Cadas—bombacin.' 1463, 3 Edward IV, c. 5: 'Persons having income of less than forty shillings a year are not allowed stuffing of wool, caddis, nor cotton in their doublets.' 1530, 'Caddes or crule'. 1612, *Customs on Goods Imported Into Scot-*

that allusions to caddis may indicate the wool, the yarn, the tape, or the cloth. The tape, in many colours, was used for girdles,[1] or for garters by the poor folk of Shakespeare's age, who could not afford silk ribbon. The allusion in *1 Henry IV* (ii. iv. 80) is a contemptuous reference to the vintner's poor clothing. Caddis is named in the inventory of a chapman's goods, 1446;[2] and was usually among the wares of every pedlar such as Autolycus[3] pretended to be.

CALLAMANCO

The origin of callamanco is unknown. It may have been invented and named by foreign cloth-workers at Norwich. In the Delves *v.* Norwich case of 1602, Henry Fasett, aged thirty-six, testified that some of the materials mentioned by the interrogators were made before his time, but he knew that grograins and callamancoes were worsted cloths. Callamanco does not occur in the list of cloths made sixty years before this case, nor among those invented 'within these few years'.[4] One must assume, therefore, that it was not known in England before the second half of the sixteenth century, but must have been familiar when Lyly mentioned it in *Mydas* (iv. iii. 20). No contemporary definitions of it have been noted. Florio, 1598, defines *tesserino* as 'a kind of fine stuff like calamance'; and Cotgrave explains *boccasin* as a 'kind of fine buckram that hath a resemblance of taffeta, also the stuff callimanco'. Callamanco was evidently the name, not of a certain material, but of a weave of such irregular design or pattern as to explain Lyly's allusion: "'Tis the best calamance in the world, as easily deciphered as the characters in a nutmeg.' It was made in both wool, as indicated in the Delves *v.* Norwich case, and silk. In a list of merchandise imported into Scotland, 1612, it is classed

---

land, 293: 'Caddes the pound thairof in woll . . . x s. Spun in yairne the pound . . . xv s.' 1631, *Book Rates*: Caddas or cruell ribband.'

[1] 1552–3, Feuillerat, *Revels at Court*, 99: 'Item, 11 pyces of grene and yellow caddas for girdles.'

[2] *Test. Ebor.* xlv. 104: 'De cadis vj d.'

[3] *Wint. Tale*, iv. 208.

[4] Exch. Dep., 44 Elizabeth, Mich., iii, 1.

as silk;[1] it occurs under 'wrought silk' in the English *Book of Rates*, 1631; and Roberts, *Treasure of Traffic* (21), 1641, mentions 'throwne silk wherof is made all manner of silk-laces, Sattins, Plushes, Taffetas, Cally-mancoes'. The callamanco named in *London Prodigal* (i. i. 112) and *Lady's Trial* (ii. i. 47) seems to be of silk.

CHAMLET

Chamlet was originally a soft, fine fabric made in Syria, Asia Minor, India, and Tibet, of the hair of chamois. The hair from kids born dead or taken before birth from the mother afforded the most beautiful chamlet. Early in the fifteenth century, Venice produced a silk-and-hair imitation of the oriental fabric, and Norwich made a worsted chamlet;[2] but the silk chamlet, and that given a silky appearance by the 'hot press', seemed to have been the favourite of English wearers from 1423.[3] By a sumptuary law of 1532 only noblemen were allowed to wear it.[4] It was expensive material, priced from two to twelve shillings a yard.[5]

Allusions to chamlet in *Henry VIII* and *Fancies Chaste and Noble*[6] seem to be to a material of hair, in the latter of which Savelli said Octavio 'merited well to wear a robe of chamlet' for his crimes—evidently suggesting a hair-robe of repentance, though chamlet of camel's hair was

[1] Halyburton, *Ledger*, 327. Miège, 1691, de fines callamanco as 'sorte d'éttoffe de soie'; but *Diccionario de la lengua castellana*, 1737, defines its Spanish cognate *calamaco* as 'Tela de lana delgada y angosta, que tiene de Portugal y otras partes, la qual tiene un torcidillo como jerga.'

[2] Marco Polo says that the city of Kalaka manufactured beautiful chamlets from camel's hair and also of fine wool, bk. i, 237. Coles, *Dictionary*, 'Cameletto, a stuff partly silk, partly camel's hair'. 1602, Exch. Dep. Norfork, 44 Elizabeth, Mich. 1, 'Chamlettes, stryped sayes . . . have ben named worsted Clothes'.

[3] 1423, *Test. Ebor.* xlv. 73; 1473,

Rot. Parl. vi. 155: 'Camelet and every other clothe of silk.' See also 1502, P. P. Ex. Elizabeth *York*, 70; 1520, *Letters and Papers, Henry VIII*, iii, pt. 2, 1554; 1525, *Archaeologia*, xxv. (6s. a yd.), 1536, *Lancashire and Cheshire Wills*, liv. 46; 1582, *Durham Wills*, xxxviii. 65.

[4] *Statutes at Large*, 24 Henry VIII, c. 13.

[5] 1502, P. P. Ex. Elizabeth *York*, 44, 2s. 4d.; 1561, Lansdowne MS. 86, 3s. 4d.; 1631, *Agriculture and Prices*, v. 576.

[6] *Hen. VIII*, v. iv. 96, *Fancies Chaste and Noble*, I. i. 4; also *The Woman's Prize*, v. i. 107, but here the material may be either silk or hair.

soft and non-irritating. By 1525, chamlets were made to show a 'watered' or moire appearance, and thereafter they were designated 'unwatered', or 'watered', the latter called 'cold water chamblets' in *Philaster*.[1]

CREWEL

The 1467 'Ordinance of Girdlers of York' forbade members to set any 'bucle pendante uppon any girdilles that are made of threde or of cruyles'.[2] The ordinance referred to the fine, coloured, woollen yarn,[3] used in sewing[4] and embroidery, in making fringes,[5] laces,[6] and gartering tape, as in *Two Angry Women of Abington*;[7] hat-bands, as in *The Noble Gentleman*;[8] nightcaps, as in *Scornful Lady* (ii. i. 108). The word offered excellent opportunity for punning. In *King Lear* (ii. iv. 7), crewel garters and stocks afford double puns.

DURANCE

Durance referred to a class of closely woven, worsted fabrics of lasting quality named specifically, according to their patterns: 'mountains, mackerels, scallops, oillets'.[9] Durance was made in several colours, and priced two to seven shillings a yard.[10] The earliest reference which the

[1] v. i. 254. Also 1536, wardrobe accounts Henry VIII, *Archaeologia*, ix. 248: 'a long gowne of unwatered chamblett'; 1580, Baret, *Alvearie*, 'Chamblet, pannus undulatus vel sericum undulatum sive cymatile'; 1633, *Household Bk. Howard*, lxviii. 297: '2 peeces of black waterd chamlett'; 1638, *Merchant's Map Commerce*, 94.

[2] *York Mem. Bk.* cxx. 185; 1571, *Durham Wills*, ii. 362: 'Crewle beltinge.'

[3] 1585, *Durham Wills*, xxxviii. 134; 1589, E. 154/3/19: 14 lb. black 'double crewell' at /18 a lb. By 1581, the Walloons were making linen crewel, *Walloons and Their Church*, 78, but references are usually to woollen.

[4] 1592, *Durham Wills*, xxxviii. 211: 'iij lbs. sowing cruell', 10s. It was used in working the button-hole stitch in embroidery, 1503, *P. P. Ex. Elizabeth York*, 83; 1623, *Household Bk.*

Howard, 217.

[5] 1536, *Archaeologia*, ix. 249; 1582, *Durham Wills*, xxxviii. 103.

[6] *Hist. Hengrave*, 23.

[7] Line 490, *Malone Soc. R.* 1912: 'he will have His Cruel garters crosse aboute the knee.'

[8] v. i. 70; 1571, *Durham Wills*, ii. 362: 'vj peces gartoring crewle.'

[9] 1602–3, testimony of Francis Smalpeece, Delves *v*. Norwich case, Exch. Dep. 44 Elizabeth, Mich. I: 'And the stuffs that he doth usually sell are these as followeth videlicet . . . mountaines, mackerelles, skallopes, Ollyettes which foever goe under the name of durances.' The 'duretta' of *City Match*, Dodsley, xiii. 222, was also a durance.

[10] 1589, *Account Bk. Wm. Wray*, xxxii. 54, 5/8: '1 pece blacke durance xxiij s'; 1587, ¾ yd. 'birdseye durance

author of this discussion has found to durance, i.e. 'Pro un toga . . . de durance watchett',[1] 1575, illustrates its most frequent use. It served also in aprons,[2] sometimes lace-trimmed, in 'bodies', and in petticoats as mentioned in *Eastward Hoe* (I. ii. 23). The usual dramatic allusions, however, are puns on durance, the cloth, and durance, a prison commitment.[3]

FLANNEL

'I am not able to answer the Welsh flannel', said Falstaff in *Merry Wives of Windsor* (v. v. 176). The author's search has not disclosed that Wales originated flannel or led in its manufacture, even in the sixteenth century. Welsh port books between 1550 and 1603 note the export of very little flannel; 'wedmolles', 'frises', 'cottons', and kerseys lead in the cloth lists.[4]

It was a thin, fine material, both linen and woollen, the former manufactured in England before 1345,[5] the latter appearing in the wardrobe accounts of Elizabeth of York, 1502, and in those of noble families throughout the century. A flannel petticoat trimmed with billiament lace, stolen in 1596, was valued at thirty shillings.[6] Lady Anne Clifford sometimes wore flannel gowns, but in *Ram Alley* flannel is classed with buckram as material to be worn out of sight.[7]

FRIEZE

'Item ordeigne est et establi qe nulle subside ou aulnage soient paiez lavez ne demandez des draps appellez Friseware queux sount faitz en Irland, ou autrement en Engleterre de leynes Irreises

---

xvi d', 76; 1593, '1 pece cremsen branched durance xxxx s,' 370; 1595, 'd yeard & nail gren durance, xviii d,' 370; 1592, *Durham Wills*, xxxviii. 211, '1 peace crimsine durance 27/6; 1 elle orringe durance 2 s'; ibid. 281, 4s. 3d. a yd. for crimson.

[1] A.O. 3/1108.

[2] 1585, *Durham Wills*, ii. 114; Overbury, *Characters*, 160.

[3] *Comedy of Errors*, IV. iii. 26; *1 Hen. IV*, I. ii. 49; *Westward Hoe*, III. i. 147.

[4] *Welsh Port Books*, 11, 16, 30, 33,

40, 60, 67, 76, 84, 255, 280, &c.

[5] 1345, *Cal. Close Rolls*, July 13, m. 22: 'flannel of linen thread called "coverchiefs" of Salle, in co. Norfolk'; 1502, *P. P. Ex. Elizabeth York*, 94: 'iiij yerds of fflanel iiij s.'; 1520, *Letters and Papers Henry VIII*, iii. 2, 1551, cost 2s. 8d.; 1551, *Middleton MSS*. 403, 1s. 4d.; 1597, *Durham Wills*, xxxviii. 282; *Household Bk. Howard*, 161, 1s.

[6] *Middlesex Sessions Rolls*, i. 230.

[7] Clifford, *Diary*, Jan. 1617, 52; *Ram Alley*, Dodsley, x. 357.

amesnes deinz le Roialme d'Engleterre a cause qe celles draps ne contienent longeure et laieure ordeinee par estatut.'

This statute of 1376[1] which exempted friezes from the subsidy paid on cloth of ray and colour is the first-known allusion to this material. Frieze was a woollen cloth made in several qualities, and priced from sixpence to three shillings a yard.[2] Its heavy nap—usually on one side only —is suggested by similes in *Othello* and *Mother Bombie*,[3] a nap which made it especially suited for gowns, jackets, jerkins, and coats.[4] It was therefore the cloth used by military men, as shown in *Edward I*, though it was worn by both men and women in all classes of society.[5]

FRIZADO

An inventory of the goods of Henry Fitzroy, 1527, included two cloaks, 'oon scarlet and the other frizado'.[6] The latter material was a woollen cloth of high nap, better than frieze, costing from two to six shillings a yard.[7] Though, seemingly, of Spanish origin, it was early made in Holland, but was a product of the Dutch weavers in Stanford by 1567,[8] and fourteen years later was listed among the things to be carried 'for a shewe of' English commodities by Pettle and Jackman on their voyage to discover the North-east Strait.[9]

[1] *Statutes at Large*, 50 Edward III. c. 8.

[2] 1566, *Durham Wills*, ii. 257; 1617, *Shuttleworth Accts*. xxxv. 223–5; 1618, *Eng. Hist. Rev.* vii. 92.

[3] *Othello*, II. i. 126; *Mother Bombie*, IV. ii.

[4] 1569, gowns, *Bury Wills*, 155; *Lancashire and Cheshire Wills*, li. 358; 1590, jerkins, ibid. 118; jackets, 1592, *Durham Wills*, xxxviii, 252; *Westward Hoe*, II. ii. 17, jerkins.

[5] *Edward I*, sc. ii, stage directions; cf. *Durham Wills*, ii. 253; Rabelais, *Gargantua*, bk. i, ch. 21. *Clyomon and Clamydes*, *M.S.R.* (1913), line 1327: 'Frumptons wench in freese.' 1580, *Archaeologia*, xix. 501, used for livery.

[6] *Camden Miscy.* iii. 4.

[7] Florio, 1598, '*gottonato*, a kind of cotton, frizado, penestone or buffin sarge'. 1546, E. 351/3025, 'ij frizado vi s viii d'. 1546, E. 154/2/22, 'fry-seadowe grene, blacke, tawney', 2s. 8d. 1566, *Durham Wills*, ii. 256, 'rede fresaedo ii yds. vs'; 1587, ibid. xxxviii, 290, 'ix yds black fresaedowe', £3; 'xiiij yds. fresaedowe', £3 18s. O. Johnson, a merchant of London, in a letter of 1546 to his brother at Calais refers to frizadoes as light cloths, bringing five shillings a yard, which price did not allow for importer's profit. *Ellis Letters*, II. ii. 174–5.

[8] *C.S.P.D.* xliii. 29. Flanders frizado was among the products at Norwich, 1571, *Walloons and Their Church*, 256.

[9] Hakluyt, *Voyages*, iii. 269. See also Lansdowne MS., 81, art. 51.

Frizado was, until the middle of the sixteenth century, found in the costume of noble persons,[1] but early lost favour, and by the nineties was not worn by fashionable persons. Frizado was used for any garment in which warmth was desired: capes, gowns, jackets,[2] doublets—as in *Anything for a Quiet Life*—and whole suits, as in *What You Will*.[3]

GROGRAIN

An order to a sixteenth-century mercer for grograin would have stated whether the buyer wished hair, silk, or worsted material, for grograin was the name of a taffeta weave with 'gros grains' or cords in the warp; hence one finds allusions to 'changeable sylke grogram', 'damaske silke grogram', 'grogram of goat's hair or wool', and in the testimony given in the Delves *v*. Norwich case a statement that 'the newe stuffe called Grogryn ys all one with the stuffe heretofore called chamlett'.[4] Grograin or 'gros de Naples', as it was sometimes called, was well known in England early in the sixteenth century,[5] coming by way of Antwerp, Turkey, Valencia, Lyons, Ypres, and Lille. Grosgrains of Turkey[6] were of hair, and the most

[1] 1532, L.C. 9/51; 1546, L.R. 2/115, an inventory of the effects of the Earl of Surrey, shows a cape of frizado garded with velvet and 'imbrodered upon with tawney satin'.

[2] Caps and gowns: 1581, *Durham Wills*, xxxviii. 27; 1546–49, E. 351/3025–6; jackets, 1551–8, *Lancashire and Cheshire Wills*, liv. 49.

[3] *Anything for a Quiet Life*, II. ii. 119; *What You Will*, II. i. 185.

[4] Miege, 'grogram, sorte d'éttoffe de poil melé de soie'; Minsheu, 1599, 'gorvaran, grograin'. *Tres Lenguas*, 1644, 'gorvaran, taffetas à gros grain ettoffe de soye, gros de Naples'; 1589, *Chetham Soc. Pub.* xli. 382, 'changeable sylke grogram'; 1579, *Lancashire and Cheshire Wills*, li. 122, silk grograin; also 1567, *Durham Wills* ii. 279; 1595, E. 101/632; 1623, *Household Bk. Howard*, 213, damask silk grograin; 1638, *Merchant's Map of Commerce*,

180; Exch. Dep., Norfolk, 44 Elizabeth, Mich. 1, testimony Delves *v*. Norwich. 'Chamlet groggerine' is noted in 1561, L.C. 9/55; 1561, A.O. 3/1106; 1597, *Durham Wills*, xxxviii. 281.

[5] It is mentioned in the wardrobe of Cardinal Wolsey, 1529, Stowe, *Annales* (Howes), 546. An interesting correspondence concerning grograin for a nightgown desired by Sir William Paget is recorded August–September, 1545, in *Letters and Papers, Henry VIII*, xx. 2. 96, 106, 163. Vaughn, in Antwerp, finally sends twelve yards, but remarks that ten is sufficient, and less than eleven would make one 'to the half leg'.

[6] 1585, *Durham Wills*, xxxviii. 134, Turkey grogram cost 3s. 7d. a yard. In 1618, among twelve overdue 'adventures beyond the sea' belonging to Adrian More, was a ship which had

expensive ranged in price from four to twelve shillings a
yard; those of French cities—of silk—usually cost less
than three shillings a yard.[1] Sometime previous to 1578,
grograin weaving was begun by foreign workers in Norwich, but they did not hold their standard, and by the
first quarter of the seventeenth century grograin was 'for-
raine trash',[2] and a 'poor grogran rascal'[3] was worse than
a fustian one! The change was due to the fact that imported grograin yarn was used in other stuffs variously
named. Roberts, 1638, tells how this yarn which was no
longer 'camels haire as some vainely conceive, being
lately brought into England' had by 'ingenious workmen'
been woven into 'tames and many other stuffes to the
great decay and prejudice of the grograin trade'.[4]

Grograin was made into coats, jackets, breeches,
doublets, cassocks, cloaks, women's kirtles, and gowns,[5]
embroidered, guarded with velvet, and trimmed with lace.
A silk grograin gown is offered by Needle to Mother
Chair as a very desirable gift, in *Magnetic Lady* (IV. i. 9),
and silk grograin as gown material, for which an entire
lining of velvet is appropriate, is mentioned in *Eastward
Hoe*;[6] but badly worn grograin, whose cords were threadbare, was very shabby wear, so that Ford's simile in *Love's*

---

taken English broadcloths to Constantinople to exchange for grograins,
E. 154/4/6. See also 1620, *Household
Bk. Howard*, 161, costing 6s. 6d.;
1623, *Eng. Hist. Rev.* vii. 98, costing
4s. 5d. For other prices varying from
11s. 6d. in 1596 to 12s. 6d. in 1631,
see *Agriculture and Prices*, v. 582, &c.
1620, Lord Howard paid 33s. 4d. for 2
yds. silk grograin, *Household Bk*. 122.

[1] Chaworth wrote in 1621 that
'grograms' were made with great
'facilitie and abundance' in Lisle,
Loseley MSS, 460. 1585–97, *Durham
Wills*, xxxviii. 134, 281, Lyons 'grogram' cost 2s. 8d.; Ypres, 2s. 5d.
'Lisle grogram' is mentioned by Lodge
in *Incarnate Devils*, iv. 27.

[2] Wither, *Works*, ix. 193.

[3] *Cynthia's Revels*, III. ii. 6.

[4] *Merchant's Map of Commerce*,
123. Turkey weavers petitioned an
embargo on grograin yarn in 1630,
so debased had this stuff become in
commerce.

[5] 1551, *Durham Wills*, ii. 134, coat;
1582, ibid. xxxviii. 65, jacket; 1584,
ibid. xxxviii. 95, breeches; 1565, ibid.
ii. 241, doublet; 1561, A.O. 3/1106,
cassock; 1602, Henslowe, *Diary*, i.
183, cloak; 1562, *Durham Wills*, ii.
200, gowns; 1582, ibid. xxxviii. 69,
and 1597, *Lancashire and Cheshire
Wills*, li. 229, gowns. 1629, *Household
Bk. Howard*, 256: 'for making up a
tufted grogarome suite.' *Pride and
Lowliness*, sig. C 2: 'His upper stockes
of silken grogeram.'

[6] I. ii. 20. See also *Every Man In
His Humour*, II. i. 9 (Folio).

Sacrifice (I. ii. 73): 'fretting like an old grograin', suggested a familiar picture to his audience.

KENDAL

The first record of cloth-weaving at Kendal is an Act of 1389 exempting from the required assize of cloths 'Draps in diverses counties d'Engleterre appellez cogware & Kendale cloth'.[1] It was a species of rather coarse[2] cloth worn during the fifteenth century by middle-class persons,[3] but during the sixteenth by the lower class:[4] woodsmen, as in *Downfall of Robert Earl of Huntingdon*;[5] fools in noble families;[6] but according to the author of *Discourse of the Common Weal of England* (fol. 47 *b*) it was scorned by servants. Falstaff's imaginary 'knaves' had dressed true to form, either as robber woodmen, or as low-class thieves.[7]

In spite of its inferiority, Kendal continued to be worn, and was one of the cloths which Parliament, 1610, sought to encourage.[8] Roberts, in 1638, reported Kendal still 'famous for making cloth of wooll'.[9]

KERSEY

Kersey was a light-weight, narrow, wool cloth in many colours,[10] costing from one to three shillings a yard.[11] It was probably manufactured originally at Kersey, Suffolk.

[1] *Rot. Parl.* iii. 271; *Cal. Close Rolls*, Nov. 6, 1391, m. 29, mentions cloth of Kendal. The tradition that John Kempe settled in Kendal in the thirties and started cloth-making is not supported by records.

[2] *Statutes at Large*, 13 Richard II, c. 10, states that Kendal was made of the worst wool in the realm, the kind that could not serve for any other cloth.

[3] 1432, *Somerset Wills*, xix. 333; but it was used for a coat for the King of Scotland, 1497, *Accts. Lord High. Treas.* i. 340.

[4] *Pride and Lowliness*, l. 33.

[5] IV. i; but sometimes by others: *Thoresby Soc. Pub.* xix. 26, 42, 47.

[6] 1502, *P. P. Ex. Elizabeth York*, 24, costing 8*d.* a yard; Rogers, *Agriculture and Prices*, iii. 498, 502, records price of, 9*d.* in 1463; 10*d.* in 1509.

[7] *1 Hen. IV*, II. iv. 250.

[8] *Statutes at Large*, 7 James I, c. 16.

[9] Op. cit. 231.

[10] 'And this vaile in Holland is of a light stuffe or Kersie', Moryson, *Itinerary*, iv. 214. Florio, 1611, 'Drappo basso, narrow cloth as kersie'. By statute of 4 Edward IV, c. 1, each kersey must be 18 yds. long, 1 yd., 1 nail wide. Cf. 1552, 5 & 6 Edward VI, cc. xii, xiii, xl. 1566–71, *Durham Wills*, ii. 256, 363; in the following colours: black, sky, 'flanders dy', yellow, sad green, sheep; 1576, *Richmond Wills*, 276, 'gillcflower'.

[11] *Agriculture and Prices*, vi. 550–4.

It is named, 1315, in an order to the mayor and sheriffs to proclaim that 'No merchant sell canvas . . . cloth . . .before it is measured by Pecok . . . alnager of Kersies . . . and all kinds of cloths of Lincoln, Essex, Norfolk, Suffolk, Kent, Stanford, Beverley, St. Osyth, Devon, and Cornwall'.[1]

In 1537 kersies were made, chiefly for export, in Berks., Oxon., Hants, Surrey, Sussex, and Yorks. In Berkshire the centre of the industry was Newbury,[2] where the kersies of John Winchcombe were famous. The Devonshire kersies, or 'dozens'—so called because they were made in lengths of twelve yards, but tented three more—were hot pressed,[3] and therefore in greater demand than were other cloths. During the fifteenth century, kersey was used by royalty, but was superseded by the 'new draperies' before the seventeenth.[4] 'Of satin changed to kersey hose I sing' is Newcut's way of saying that Frank Plotwell has changed his status,[5] and become poor. Similarly, Grumio pretends to be poor, or to have a contempt for appearance, by wearing kersey boot-hose to Petruchio's wedding.[6]

The reason for the decline in the demand for kersey was the inferior manufacture which characterized this cloth, from the eighties. By 1610 a large number of the broadlist kersies were being made. These cloths, which were only fourteen to seventeen yards long and less than a yard in width, had very wide selvedge or 'list', sometimes one-fifth of the width of the cloth. So wasteful were these kersies that there was little demand for them, and they were held in contempt. The First Gentleman's statement,

[1] *Let. Bk. E*, 54. Stow gives the original date of Devonshire kersies as 1505, when Antony Bonville, an Italian, taught Englishmen how to spin with a distaff, *Annales* (Howes), 870. For other early references to kersies, see *Cal. Close Rolls*, July 18, 1337, m. 17; 1391, *Rot. Parl.* 294, concerning the proper making of kersies; 1428, kersies were being exported to Netherlands and Genoa, *Port Bk. Southampton*, 135.

[2] *V.C.H., Surrey*, ii. 343.

[3] May, *Estate of Clothing*, 32.

[4] 1423, *Rot. Parl.* iv. 234. It was commonly made into boot-hose during the sixteenth and seventeenth centuries. 1599, *Shuttleworth Accts.* xxxv. 117; 1611, ibid. 197; 1614, *Household Bk. Howard*, 12; Hall, *Virgidemiarum*, ii. 18; Greene, *Works*, ix. 265; xi. 251. Kersey was worn by children of wealthy persons: 1624, *Archaeologia*, xlviii. 144.

[5] *City Match*, Dodsley, xiii. 217.

[6] *Tam. Sh.* III. ii. 70.

Measure for Measure: 'I had as lief be a list of an English kersey' (I. ii. 35), may have had these wasteful cloths in mind.

LINSEY-WOOLSEY

Linsey-woolsey, known in England by 1483,[1] was a loosely woven, plain cloth of linen yarn and wool,[2] an excellent example of which survives in the bed curtains of Anne Hathaway's bedchamber at Shottery.

In the drama, this material is always spoken of contemptuously, as in *Lovers' Melancholy* (v. i. 140); sometimes to indicate confused talk as in *All's Well that Ends Well* (IV. i. 13).

MOCKADO

Mockado, often called 'mock velvet', was a piled cloth of silk or wool, or mixed silk and linen, with linen back, worn in England previous to 1543,[3] and manufactured at Norwich before 1560.[4] Mockado was made in a variety of colours, plain, striped, and tufted,[5] costing from ninepence for plain to six shillings for tuft.[6] It was made into garments such as gowns, farthingales, kirtles, stomachers, breeches, and jackets,[7] and was guarded with velvet, embroidered with gold, and trimmed with lace.[8]

[1] *O.E.D.*

[2] *C.S.P.D.* xliii. 30; July 22, 1567, the Dutch weavers at Stanford appealed to the Queen to allow them the exercise of 'mysteries', which 'fit together', namely: 'lynsey, lynsey-wolsey, fresado'. For prices, which varied from 6*d.* to 1*s.* a yard, see 1585, *Durham Wills*, xxxviii. 134; *Household Bk. Howard*, 63.

[3] 1543, *Richmond Wills*, 51. On July 13, 1577, four wardens of the Walloon weavers at Norwich presented a bill to the mayor requesting certain rules for the making of double mocadoes: 'fower threeds in every slae, that is to weete, twoo threedes of flaxe and twoo of saye in the grown of the work.' Moens, *Walloons and their Church, 1565–1832*, 78. 1615, Kempe, *Loseley MSS.* 408: a doublet of black silk mockado.

[4] Reynolde Hothe in the Delves *v.*

Norwich case, 1602–3, said Norwich had made 'says, stamyns, mockadoes, chamlettes, russelles, satins reverse for the space of Sixtie years'. Exch. Bills and Answers, Norfolk, 310; 44 Elizabeth, Mich. 1.

[5] 1558, E. 101/428/10, striped; 1575, A.O. 3/1108, changeable; 1574, E. 101/431/6: 'vii yds blacke tufte mocado to make your lordship a payer of gascoyns 41 s.'

[6] 1582, *Durham Wills*, xxxviii. 67, 1*s.* 3*d.* for plain red; 1584, ibid. ii. 103, 1*s.* 5*d.*; 1574, E. 101/431/6, 3*s.* 4*d.* for crymson tuft; also *supra*.

[7] 1567, *Durham Wills*, ii. 273, gown; 1557–8, L.C. 9/52, farthingales; 1596, A.O. 3/1109, kirtle; *Greene's Vision*, xii. 226, stomachers; 1577, *Durham Wills*, ii. 422, breeches; 1578, *Richmond Wills*, 276, hat.

[8] 1561, L.C. 9/55: 'unius kirtle

Mockado fringe,[1] and mockado crewel, the latter used especially for darning, were also made.

Mockado was used chiefly by persons who could not afford velvet, as in *London Prodigal* and *Lady's Trial*,[2] but during the latter half of the sixteenth century, it is found in Queen Elizabeth's wardrobe. It degenerated under her successor, and did not regain its fashionableness.

MOTLEY

Motley was not originally the parti-coloured costume now known by that name, but a worsted material of mixed or variegated colours worn by persons of wealth, and by the clergy in vestments.[3] It is named, 1371, in an order to the bailiffs of Shoreham to deliver goods pirated at sea from Francis Kempe, merchant of London.[4] Moryson, 1607, shows that it was made in more than one quality.[5] Both single and double worsted motley were manufactured in Norwich before 1602.[6]

Although the expense accounts of Lord North for April 2, 1577, itemized the cost of hose, coat, gascons, and netherstocks of motley for his fool,[7] this cloth does not seem to have been the accepted material for a fool's costume. Since the fifteenth century fools had been dressed in parti-coloured suits, such suits, rather than

---

rotund de tawne mockado cū un gard de velvet nigro cū lace'; 1572, A.O. 3/1108: 'tunicelle de mocado carnation striped cum laqueo aur.' 1578, *Richmond Wills*, 276, lace trimmed.

[1] 1589 E. 154/3/9: 'five pounds crymson and blacke mokadoe frindge at fower shilling the pound.' *Durham Wills*, xxxviii. 69; 'on pound mockadowe croles 16 d': also *Household Bk. Howard*, 123.

[2] *London Prodigal*, III. i. (C 4 verso); *Lady's Trial*, II. i. 44.

[3] 1388, *Thoresby Soc. Pub.* vi. 204, gown of blue motley for Dame Joan Calverley. 1487, *E.E.T.S.* cxxv. 135, 'paide for mendyng of a vestmente of worstede Mottleye'; 1406, will Roger de Wandesford, Yorkshire, 'unam togam de motlay', *Test. Ebor.*, iv. 257.

[4] *Cal. Close Rolls*, Aug. 10, 1371, m. 18.

[5] Writing of the courtiers of the King of Denmark, he says: 'They were all attired in an English cloth, which they call Kentish cloth, we call Motley but much finer than that wherof we make cloakebags, and of purpose made for them costing some two dollers the ell', *Itinerary*, iv. 214. It was used for clothing by persons of small incomes in the sixteenth century. 1558, 1560, *Test. Leod.* xxvii. 281, 298, Robert Clark bequeathed his 'motlay jacket', James Scrivenir, his 'motley jerkin'.

[6] Exch. Bills and Answers, 44 Elizabeth, Mich., Norfolk, 301.

[7] Stowe MS., 774.

those made of the ancient cloth motley, are evidently indicated by the allusions to motley in *As You Like It*, *Bonduca*, *Lover's Progress*, *Wit Without Money*, and other plays.[1]

PENISTONE

Penistone was a fine frieze, or napped cloth,[2] white and in colours,[3] manufactured in the Yorkshire town of that name. In 1520, twenty-three yards of 'broad Penistone black' at twenty pence a yard were purchased for lining 'great coats and bonnets' for revels, an item which probably refers to the original penistone.[4] This cloth came under the Cloth Statute of 1551–2, and the drapers of London reported, 1551, that in the four previous years 'Penystone Whites' had increased from fifteen and sixteen to thirty shillings the piece,[5] which increase seems to indicate a gain in use.

Newcut's threat to 'transform' Frank Potwell's 'plush to pennystone' shows his intent to change his silk to wool, or to make him poorer.[6]

PERPETUANA

Perpetuana, one of the 'new draperies', was probably originated by the foreign weavers at Norwich, and known to England long before its mention in *Cynthia's Revels*,[7] 1599. It was a woollen material, resembling serge, lighter in weight than broadcloth, and possibly, like durance, named for its lasting quality, though the quality was so lowered by 1613 that May declared they were 'not like to continue long' on the market.[8] Perpetuana was

---

[1] In order of mention: II. vii. 13, 43, &c.; II. ii. 31; I. i. 34; II. i. 344.

[2] Florio, 1598, '*Frisetta*, verie fine frize or nappie cloth which we call penistone or cotton'. Smith's statement: 'coarse cloths made in the North Parts as . . . Penistones, etc.' has given editors the idea that all cloth made in Penistone was coarse. Stow, *Survey London*, II. v. xix. 401, *O.E.D.*

[3] *Durham Wills*, xxxviii. 290; Rogers, *Agriculture and Prices*, vi. 551.

[4] *Letters and Papers Henry VIII*, iii. 1. 1552.

[5] Johnson, *Drapers*, ii. 396.

[6] *City Match*, Dodsley, xiii. 217.

[7] III. ii. 30: 'By this heaven, I wonder at nothing more than our gentlemen ushers, that will suffer a piece of serge or perpetuana to come into the presence.'

[8] *Estate of Clothing*, 32: 'There be some merchants that deal in stuffs termed new draperies, especially in

made in many colours, cost from two to four shillings a
yard, and was used for drapery and screens as well as for
clothing[1] of both wealthy and poor folk. The contemptuous references to it in *Cynthia's Revels* and *What You Will*
(II. i. 8) are due probably to the fact that it was an English
cloth and therefore not rated with imported products.

PHILIP AND CHENEY

Thirteen pound... 'Twill put a Lady scarce in Philip and Cheyney,
With three small Bugle Laces like a chambermaid.[2]

This, the earliest noted reference to the material, offers
little help in its identification. Although one is tempted
to associate it with the native English phrase for 'Tom,
Dick, and Harry', its price indicates that it was not the
'common material' defined by the *Oxford English Dictionary*. The wardrobe accounts of Prince Charles, 1618–
23,[3] record purchases of green phillip and cheney for
suits for his 'singing boyes', and 'crymsen' to line a cloak,
each costing three shillings a yard. William Freke, an
Oxford student in 1619, paid £1 19s. 8d. for twelve and
a half yards[4] for a gown; and purchases for the Howard
family show an equal price,[5] which compares with that of
fine cloth and less costly silks.

Its name suggests that it was an English product,[6] but
it is listed among imported goods, 1631, with a duty of

perpetuanas, which are now growne
to great vse and traffique, but not like
to continue long by their falsehood
since their first making which brought
them into estimation: for where at
first their pitch in the loome was
twelve hundreth, but now eight hundreth, yet keepe their breadth and
length.' Perpetuanas are classed as
wool in the Delves *v.* Norwich case,
1602; also 1634, *Foedera*, xix. 538, a
proclamation prohibiting the export
of bays, kersies, and perpetuanas to
Germany except to staple towns of the
Merchant Adventurers.

[1] 1605, *Household Bk. Milton Abbey*,
xli. 388, for a pair of hose of perpetuana
trimmed with gold and silver lace ...

£1 19s. 8d. 1613, Campion, *Queen's
Entertainment*, the Traveller and Cynic
are attired in perpetuana; 1613, *Prog.
James*, ii. 632. 1618, *Household Bk.
Howard*, 101, cost 3s. 4d. a yard;
1618, E. 154/41/6; 1633, *Agriculture
and Prices*, vi. 555; 1621, Kempe,
Loseley MSS. 425, used for the doublet
of Sir George Chaworth's riding suit.

[2] *Wit at Several Weapons*, II. i. 38.

[3] E. 101/435/20; E. 101/436/9.

[4] *Eng. Hist. Rev.* vii. 93.

[5] *Household Bk. Howard*, 213.

[6] *Canterbury Marriage Licences,
1619–1660*, 294, 'Donnaing Peter of
S. Alphage, Cant. Phillipp & Chainey
weaver', Nov. 15, 1641. See also
O.E.D. under 'Cheyney'.

fifty shillings a piece.[1] If English, it may have derived its name from its irregular pattern, but whether it were silk, worsted, or woollen, can only be conjectured.

PUKE

The origin of puke—used in England by 1466[2]—is unknown, but it was a dyed-in-the-wool cloth,[3] made in different qualities,[4] of which the fine was priced higher than serge.

The wardrobe accounts of Edward IV, 1481–3, contain frequent items of puke,[5] and a century later it is listed with scarlet among the very 'fyne clothes' destined for the Levant trade;[6] but accounts at home show it to have been worn chiefly by women of the middle class, gentlemen, attendants on officials, and clerks.[7] Prince Henry's contemptuous application of 'puke stocking' to Falstaff[8] is explicable by the fact that persons of quality were then wearing silk stockings. Cloth stockings, therefore, would indicate the low class.

RASH

"'Tis good stuff indeed, It is silk rash', said Walter Camlet in *Anything for a Quiet Life*.[9] He referred to a twilled fabric made in both silk and wool, similar to saye. From 1575 to 1640, rash is a frequent item in wardrobe and mercers' accounts.[10]

[1] *Booke of Rates.*

[2] *O.E.D.*

[3] *Statutes at Large*, 4 & 5 Philip and Mary, c. 8: no broadcloth or 'clothes called pewkes' to be made 'except the wool therof before it be converted into yarn be first dyed. . . .'

[4] 1567, *Durham Wills*, ii. 251: 'fyne pewke' gown valued at 33s.; 1533, *Richmond Wills*, 86, 3s. a yard; 1566, *Durham Wills*, ii. 257, 7s. 3d. a yard.

[5] pp. 120, 148, 150, &c.

[6] *Eng. Hist. Rev.* xxix. 518.

[7] 1524, 'Churchwardens Accounts St. Mary Hill', J. Nichols, *Ill. Manners, Customs Antient England*, 125; 1533, *Somerset Wills*, xxi. 153; 1540,

Hist. Hengrave, 117; 1545, *Lancashire and Cheshire Wills*, li. 63; 1557, *Test. Leod.* xxvii. 86; 1572, *Prog. Elizabeth*, i. 317: '. . . Burgesses in gownes of puke'; 1603, Stowe MS. 142, fol. 29: 'To Robert Tias, clark for his livery, foure yds. fyne pewke for gowne. 3 yd. black velvett to guard same. . . .'

[8] *1 Hen. IV*, II. iv. 79.

[9] IV. iii. 24. Florio, 1598, defines saetta as 'a kind of fine serge or rash'. For wool rash, see Delves *v.* Norwich case, Exch. Dep. 44 Elizabeth, Mich. 1.

[10] 1575, Egerton MS. 2806, used for a cloak lined with Spanish silk; 1581, Wray Accts. *Antiquary*, xxxii. 117: 'iij yeardes silke rashe xvi s'; 1597,

Woollen rash was formerly made in Florence of English wools, but foreign weavers introduced its manufacture to England before 1578; and by the end of the century, the 'fynest wolls that were wont to be employed in fyne kerseyes' were used in making rashes.[1] Rash was about fifty-four inches wide, woven in pieces twenty-four to twenty-eight yards long. It cost two to eight shillings a yard.[2]

RUGG

Rugg was a hairy or shagged frieze made in England and Ireland from the early sixteenth century.[3] Because of its warmth, it was especially suited for the nightgowns and mantles worn by astrologers, as in *Every Man Out of His Humour*; by watchmen, as in *Albovine* and *Renegado*;[4] and other persons who worked at night. It was also, as described in *Damon and Pithias* (sig. F 1 verso), used for linings. Rugg was used in the wardrobes of royalty and noblemen as well as in that of lesser men, so that the 'leash of German Dukes that walk in rugg' named in *The Just Italian*[5] need not be classed with night watchmen.

RUSSET

Russet, originally homespun, was a coarse woollen cloth, usually in the natural grey of the wool, or reddish-brown, though also in black and colours. It was probably made domestically in Anglo-Saxon times, but accounts of it until the thirteenth century are lacking. Its width was first regulated by statute in 1225.[6] Because russet and

---

Lancashire and Cheshire Wills, li. 229: 'to my servant . . . my silke rashe gowne'; 1597, *Durham Wills*, 281, 2s. a yd.; 1629, *Household Bk. Howard*, 259, wool at 4s. 5d. a yd.

[1] *C.S.P.D.* ccl. 47.

[2] Ibid., undyed cost 2s. to 6s. 8d.; dyed, 5s. to 8s.

[3] 1551, *Statutes at Large*, 5 Edward VI, c. 6: 'All clothes called Manchester rugges otherwise named Manchester frieses.'

[4] *Every Man out of His Humour*, III. vii. 21; *Albovine*, IV. i. 180: 'He looks like a watchman in that rugg'; *Renegado*, v. ii. 6; 1556, *Lancashire and Cheshire Wills*, liv. 143, jacket of rugg.

[5] II. i. 317. See wardrobes of Prince Henry, and Lord Howard: 1607–18, *Archaeologia*, xi. 91; *Household Bk. Howard*, 73. Rugg was priced from 10d. to 2s. a yd.

[6] 9 Henry III, 25: 'Sit . . . una latitudo pannorum tinctorum & Russettorum & Habergetorum, scilicet due Ulne infra listas.' Russets of Oxford are mentioned 1232. *Cal. Close Rolls*, m. 13, p. 41.

blanket were the only cloths allowed husbandmen and poor persons, by statute of 1364—a statute repeated by Henry VIII and James I[1]—'russet coats' usually indicated countrymen, as in *Three Lords and Three Ladies of London*.[2] It was the custom of wealthy persons to provide in their wills for a certain number of russet gowns to be given to the poor who attended their funerals.[3] Since deceit was not practised in weaving or dyeing russets, and they were usually left undressed, this cloth stood for honesty and simplicity. It is therefore used metaphorically in *Hamlet, Love's Labour's Lost, Patient Grissel*.[4]

SAYE

Green and grey saye were purchased in Lincoln for the royal wardrobe in 1182.[5] This material was a soft, light, finely twilled fabric made in both silk and wool.[6] An idea of the colours, uses, and prices of saye between 1514 and 1621 can be gained by the following excerpts: 1514, red saye for tents at Calais; 1522, hangings of green saye; 1525, two yards black saye for doublet; 1542, women of Holland cover their faces with 'theyre mantles of saye'; 1570, 'blew saye' 4*s.* a yard; 1588, 'a paire of greene saye stockings'; 1602, Henslowe lends the Company money to buy saye for a 'wiches gowne'; 1605, on the King's entry into Cambridge, footmen of the mace-bearer were 'tired in wachet saye'; 1617, three yards of embroidered

---

[1] *Statutes at Large*, 37 Edward III, c. xiv; 24 Henry VIII, c. xiii; 1 James, c. 27.

[2] Sig. D.; also 'Courtier and Countryman', *Inedited Tracts*, 196; *No Wit Like a Woman's*, IV. ii. 81, yeomen.

[3] *E.E.T.S.* o.s., lxxviii. 15, 18, 19, 61, 101, &c.

[4] I. i. 166, reference to the colour russet; V. ii. 414; sig. (B 4). Russet cost usually less than 1*s.* per yard: 1571, *Durham Wills*, ii. 363; 1*s.* for grey; 8*d.* for reddish-brown; 1590, *Agriculture and Prices*, vi. 550, 2*s.* 2*d.* —an unusual price.

[5] *Pipe Roll*, 28 Henry II, 50. John Pecok, appointed, Aug. 30, 1315, *Cal. Pat. Rolls*, m. 25, had ulnage of sayes among other cloths of Lincoln, Essex, &c.

[6] 1377, Stowe refers to it as sendal, *Survey*, 79. 1524, *Statutes at Large*, 15 Henry VIII, c. 3: No worsted weaver of Yarmouth to be allowed to weave any 'worsteds, sayes, or stamins' unless he be English born. 1585, *Durham Wills*, xxxviii. 134: 'a remblet of silke saye.' 1595, *Nottingham Rec.* iii. 254: 'kyrtylle of sylke seeay.' 1585, Rider, *Bibliotheca Scholastica*. 1631, *Book Rates*: 'silk say the yd vi s viij d.'

green saye at 4*s*. 9*d*. a yard; 1621, two yards of black 'dutch saye' at 5*s*. 8*d*. a yard for a doublet.[1]

References like that in *Promos and Cassandra*: Both hood and gown of green and yellow saye,[2] give no suggestion as to whether the saye is of silk or wool, but that in *Henry VI* is clear. When Cade addressed Lord Say as: 'Thou say, thou serge, nay, thou buckram lord', he calls him a silk, a wool, a cotton person, each spoken with increasing contempt.

SCARLET

Jonson allows his Red-Hood to appear in stammel because 'Scarlet is too dear'.[3] Although scarlet had been made in England since before 1182—it was purchased in Lincoln at that date for the royal wardrobe[4]—it never became cheap: first, because it was a very fine worsted cloth; second, because the red scarlet was made of wool dyed in the *Coccus ilicus*. When Gertrude of *Eastward Hoe* (I. ii. 20) longs to 'dye rich scarlet black' she is wishing for wealth.

The French *escarlette* from which the English *scarlet* is supposed to have been derived was made in many colours: *vermeille, rouge, verte, peonace* (peacock blue), besides white and black.[5] The use of crimson scarlet was early limited to the use of the royal family, noblemen, and civil officials, and in the twenty-fourth year of Henry VIII was forbidden to servants.[6]

---

[1] In order of their mention: *Letters and Papers of Henry VIII*, I, entry 5172; ibid. III. ii, entry 2968, inventory Lord Monteagle; *Archaeologia*, xxv. 461; *E.E.T.S.* ii. 149; *Durham Wills*, xxxviii. 328; *Diary*, i. 183; *Prog. James*, iii. 86; *Shuttleworth Accts.*, xxxv. 225; Kempe, *Loseley MS.* 426; also *North Country Wills* (1537), cxvi. 146: 'oon new sparver of redde and grene of the beyond the see saye.'

[2] II. iv. ii (sig. Liij); *2 Hen. VI*, iv. vii. 27.

[3] *Love's Welcome at Welbeck* (Gifford ed.), vol. viii. 124.

[4] *Pipe Roll*, 28 Henry II, 50; cost 6*s*. 8*d*. an ell.

[5] Godefroy, *Dictionnaire de l'ancienne Langue Française*.

[6] *Statutes of Realm*, 24 Henry VIII, c. 13. In *Tam. Sh.*, Tranio, disguised as his master, wears a cloak of scarlet, v. i. 68. For scarlet in wardrobe of royal and noble families, see *Wardrobe Accounts Edward IV*, 115, &c., *Archaeologia*, ix. 25; *P. P. Ex. Elizabeth York*, 115, 133, &c.; Great Wardrobe accounts cited throughout this book.

SERGE

> When you love, lanch it out in silks and velvets,
> I'le love in Serge, and will outgo your Sattins
>
> (*Spanish Curate*, II. i. 25–6.)

Serge, purchased in Southampton, 1303,[1] may have been foreign, but it was listed among the English cloths of which John Pecok was to have ulnage in 1315,[2] and 'sarges d'Angleterre' made in Norwich were used by the Duke of Normandy in 1363,[3] and by the Cardinal of Bologna, 1390.[4] Serge is mentioned so frequently in accounts, that any detailed discussion of it is unnecessary. It was used for all outer garments as well as for linings and facings, as in *A Trick to Catch an Old One, Edward II*,[5] and is usually spoken of slightingly as if it were an inferior material;[6] though its price—two to four shillings a yard— was about the same as that for saye, kersey, and other standard English cloths, but less than that for the 'new draperies'.

SHAG

Shag, a thick-piled cloth with a nap of worsted or silk, produced by a double warp and single woof, the latter often of goat's hair, is first noted in a 1592 inventory of a wealthy Darlington tradesman,[7] but it was evidently known some time before that date. Its most common use in the sixteenth century was for lining garments, as Pander in *The Woman Hater*[8] shows, but that with silk nap was made into gloves, gowns, and waistcoats, and other garments in which warmth was especially desired.

1 Rogers, *Agriculture and Prices*, ii. 537.

2 *Cal. Pat. Rolls*, Aug. 30, 1315, m. 25.

3 Gay, *Glossaire archéologique*, ii. 342.

4 *Cal. Close Rolls*, Aug. 15, 1390, m. 31.

5 I. iv. 12, line 750.

6 *Cynthia's Revels*, III. ii. 30; 2 *Hen. VI*, IV. vii. 27.

7 *Durham Wills*, xxxviii. 211, 212, 'Three quarters of black shage 12s. iii payer of shag gloves 3 s 6 d'. 1614,

Household Bk. Howard, 13, 4s. 2d.; 1621, *Shuttleworth Accts.* xl. 252, 5s.; 1627, Rogers, *Agriculture and Prices*, vi. 554.

8 IV. ii. 34, 1594–5, L.C. 9/86, 'shagg for lining shoes and pantoffles'. 1612, 'Wardrobe of Princess Elizabeth', *Archaeologia*, xxvi. 390, used for lining for velvet coats of pages. 1622, stolen from Sir Thomas Merry, 'a silke wastecoate lined with silke shagge worth forty pounds', *Middlesex Sessions Rolls*, ii. 162.

STAMMEL

Stammel or 'bastard scarlet',[1] was a fine woollen cloth, which should not be confused with the expensive 'estamine', though a comparison of the definitions of Palsgrave and Cotgrave may suggest that they are the same.[2] An inventory of the goods of the Archdeacon of Richmond, 1526, mentions 'fine stammell' with scarlet, and sarcenet, but Borde, 1542, classes it with linsey-woolsey, and it appears as 'red russet or stammel' in an inventory of the goods of the Earl of Norfolk, 1546.[3]

It was sometimes guarded with velvet and trimmed with lace,[4] but was less desirable than scarlet as one learns from *Monsieur d'Olive*; and, though superior to durance, was not considered by Gertrude of *Eastward Hoe* as proper material for a lady.[5]

TAMINE

Tamine, presumably the same material as *estamine*,[6] was a thin fine silk and wool cloth,[7] occurring in English accounts from the middle of the sixteenth century.[8] Massinger mentions it in *A New Way to Pay Old Debts* (III. ii. 45).

TAWNY

Tawny, a woollen cloth, usually of yellowish-brown, but also of other colours,[9] is noted in the will of Domine

[1] 1622, Foster, *English Factories in India*, 133.

[2] Palsgrave: 'Stamell fyne worstede, estamine'; Cotgrave: 'estamine, the stuff tamine.' Garland, *Dictionarius*, 1218–9: 'Staminias ab hoc nomine stamin, Gallice estamine.' Both stammel and stamin were made in Norwich, Delves *v.* Norwich case.

[3] 'Inventory Archdeacon', *Letters and Papers Henry VIII*, IV. i. 877; Borde, *E.E.T.S.* i. 249; inventory Norfolk, L.R. 2/115.

[4] 1570, Egerton MS. 2806: 'Itm for making two peire of hoose of red stamell garded with blewe vellat layed with copper golde lace sett on with silke'; 1587, *Durham Wills*, xxxviii.

290, eleven and a half yds. red stammel cost £6 6s. 6d.; 1574, *Mid. MSS.* 450: 'To the Ducheman of Nottingham for dying x yardes of stamell for my Mrs. at ijs the yarde.'

[5] M. d' *Olive*, II. ii. 96; *Eastward Hoe*, I. ii. 15; see also *The Woman Hater*, IV. ii. 10; *Durham Wills*, ii. 273.

[6] Cotgrave, 'estamine, the stuff tamine'.

[7] Florio, 1611, '. . . a thin kind of stuff like Buratto half silk and half wool called Tamine.'

[8] 1552, *Middlesex County Rec.* i. 8, 'Unum par manicarum de serico vocat tawin' (tamin ?).

[9] See Godefroy, op. cit.; 1576, *Lancashire and Cheshire Wills*, li. 86.

William of Newport, 1366.[1] In 1509 twenty-four shillings was the cost of only five yards of tawny for a cloak for Sir Henry Willoughby,[2] but from 1530,[3] its price averaged a shilling a yard, which suggests that it was an inferior cloth. Since allusions in the drama to tawny seem to be to the colour, they have been noted in that section.

[1] *Test. Ebor.* i. 81: 'Unam togam taune, furratam cum grys.'

[2] *Mid. MSS.* 328.

[3] *Durham Household Bk.* xviii. 97.

IV

LINEN CLOTHS

BEFORE Abraham visited Pharaoh, the Egyptians had attained perfection in the fabrication of linen, as early dynastic tombs and Biblical allusions testify. Phoenicia traded with Egypt and gained a knowledge of this textile. Ships of Phoenicia, Carthage, and Sidon carried linen to Athens. By degrees, linen was substituted for wool in Rome; and the conquering Romans carried industrial knowledge to their subdued peoples.

Linen weaving was known to Flanders and Brabant in the tenth century. Ypres, built in that century, became famous for cloth *d'Ypres*, or diaper. Six centuries later, Flanders and the Low Countries were world leaders in linen manufacture.

Either the Belgae or the Romans may have introduced to the Britons the custom of wearing linen. Little is known of the early history of its use in England. Bodies were wrapped in linen—probably homespun—A.D. 500.[1] The Bayeux Tapestry, executed by Queen Matilda in commemoration of the Conquest, is of linen; but it is claimed by both France and England, and the yarn which composed it may have been from either land. It is reasonable to suppose that linen weavers were among the immigrants to England after the Conquest, but neither flax nor hemp appears in the list of titheable products made in the fourth year of William the Conqueror, though both appear in the list of 1175.[2]

In 1253, the sheriffs of Wilts. and Sussex were ordered to buy 'tua mille ulnas Lineas telas pulchrae & delicatae' and send it to the royal wardrobe before next Whitsuntide.[3] This was presumably native product, but the first definite evidence of English manufacture is an account of the purchase of linen 'telae de Aylesham', 1285.[4] A

[1] Macpherson, op. cit. i. 223. (i. 377).
[2] Ibid. i. 348.
[3] Madox, *Hist. Exch.*, ch. 10, xii
[4] Rogers, *Agriculture and Prices*, i. 536.

writ of August 30, 1315, forbade merchants to sell 'lineam telam' unless checked by an alnager,[1] and an order of July 13, 1345, to weavers and all other workers of cloth of Aylesham, 'of linen cloth of Betele and of flannel of linen thread called coverchiefs of Salle, in the county of Norfolk', mentions John de Heythe as 'keeper of the assay of such cloths'.[2] These writs show that the production of linen was sufficient to warrant an alnager.

Testimony given in the Court of Exchequer, 1409, tells that an organization of linen weavers had been formed in London in 1386.[3] Rules for 'English Linen Weavers' were made in 1409, and there are frequent allusions to the guild until 1440, when, presumably, linen weavers re-united with the woollen weavers; for thereafter they are mentioned together.

To encourage the industry, a statute was enacted in 1531 requiring that one rood in every sixty acres of tillable land be sown with flax and hemp.[4] This statute was revived in 1563, but repealed in 1593. Ireland was exporting some linen in 1437, and a statute of 1542 states that 'many strangers, as well of Ireland as of other places within the realme have resorted' to Manchester 'with linen yarn ... for making cloth'.[5] Leland described Liverpool as a place where Manchester merchants bought 'mock Yrish yarn'.[6] In 1572, Irish linen-workers protested against the export of linen yarn to Manchester because Irish linen manufacture was injured thereby.[7]

Dorneck was manufactured in Norfolk by 1552,[8] 'preston' in Lancashire, 1583–1624,[9] sail cloth by 1590;[10] considerable linen-yarn used in the 'new draperies' was

[1] *Let. Bk. E*, 53.
[2] *Cal. Close Rolls*, m. 22.
[3] William Cokenage, a London linen weaver, sued two Sheriffs for seizure of property. Madox, *Firmi Burgi*, 198 ff.
[4] *Statutes at Large*, 24 Henry VIII, c. 4; 5 Elizabeth, c. 5; 35 Elizabeth, c. 7. The statute of 1563 was enacted to ensure sufficient hemp for fish nets rather than yarn for cloth.

[5] *Statutes at Large*, 33 Henry VIII, c. 16. For fifteenth-century conditions, see *Libelle of Englyshe Polycye*, ch. 9.
[6] *Itinerary*, v. 41.
[7] State Papers, Ireland, xxxv. 473, 472, 518.
[8] *Statutes at Large*, 5 & 6 Edward VI, c. 24.
[9] Rogers, op. cit. v. 554.
[10] *Statutes at Large*, 2 James, c. 24, preamble.

made in all the 'stranger' settlements; and the report of
a commission appointed by James I to inquire into the
decline of English trade stated, 1622, that the 'Eastland
merchants did formerly load their ships with undressed
hemp and flax in great quantities which set great numbers
of our people on work in dressing the same, and con-
verting them into linen cloth'.[1] There were linen weavers
in Southwark, 1618, and 'whitsters' or bleachers in several
vicinities of London from 1582 on.[2] Such 'whitsters' were
essential to linen manufacture. But, in spite of this evidence of native manufacture, accounts of trade declare
'much is yearly spent in Linen imported at dear rates'.[3]
Evidently England imported much of the fine linen
which she used.

The term *linen* is used to include all materials of flax
and usually those of hemp, and, since quality is seldom
stated, price lists are not of much value. Table linen[4] cost
from fivepence an ell, up; shirting was slightly higher,
and the finest linen used for neckwear and accessories
cost from two to ten shillings a yard.

LINEN IN THE DRAMA

In the drama the generic term *linen* is not often mentioned. There are allusions to linen stockings[5] and a few
articles of clothing, but for the most part, the specific
terms: bis, canvas, dowlas, holland, lawn, lockram, and
tiffany are used.

Bis

In describing the pageantry which attended the coronation of Anne Boleyn, Hall wrote: 'When she came to
Ludgate, the gate was newly garnished with golde and
byse.'[6] This material does not appear in sixteenth-century

[1] *Foedera*, xvii. 414.

[2] Kirk, op. cit. i. 463, 466; ii. 287,
382.

[3] *Foedera*, xvii, 415; Stowe, *Annales* (Howes), 868; Wheeler, *Treatise
of Commerce*, 28; *Eng. Hist. Rev.* xxix.
516 ff.

[4] The £18 tablecloth mentioned

in *Silent Woman*, III. i. 134, was not
damask linen, but silk. For prices,
see Rogers, *Agriculture and Prices*, ii.
537–42; iii. 472–94; v. 560–2. See
also under holland, lawn, &c.

[5] *Mad World My Masters*, II. i. 8.

[6] *Chronicle*, 802. Bis is also a
colour.

wardrobe accounts. Lexicographers define it as a silky
linen, similar to cypress,[1] and it seems to have been made
in colours as well as in white, and sometimes interwoven
with gold thread.

In literary allusions it is associated with purple and
used to symbolize royal or noble state. Thus Manhood
in *The World and the Child* says:

> I am royal arrayed to reven under the ris,
> I am proudly apparelled in purpur and bis.

and Alfrida in *Knack to Know a Knave* boasts:

> And I will be attired in cloth of biss
> Beset with Orient pearl.[2]

CAMBRIC

Cambric, from Kameryk, the Flemish name of Cam-
bray where the material was first made, was a fine linen,
costing from two to twenty shillings an ell.[3] In stating
that the knowledge and wearing of cambric began in
England in 1562,[4] Howes was misleading. *The Book of
Rates*, July 1507, gives the customs for 'lynenge clothe
caled camerycke' as 26s. 3d. Cambric was purchased for
the Lady of Kent, 1521; for Katherine, Countess of
Devon, 1524; for L'Estrange of Hunstanton, 1525; for
Henry VIII, 1530; for the Countess of Rutland, 1531,
as a present to the King and Queen. The inventory of
goods of Catherine of Aragon, made February 14, 1536,
shows thirteen sheets and a towel of 'camerycke'. In

[1] Calepini, *Dictionarivm* (1598):
'Byssus. Gall.-De crespe, fin lin. Angl.
Silk fine flexe. Tenuissimi lini genus,
proximam ab asbeto dignitatem obti-
nens, ex quo subtilissimae fiunt vestes,
quae mulieribus olim praecipuè in deli-
ciis erant. Plin. circa Elim Achaiae
nasci credidit. Pollux verò ex India
& Aegypto gigni prodidit. . . .' *Voc.
della Crusca* (1612), 'bisso . . . ch'è
panno lino nobilissimo.'

[2] *World and Child*, Dodsley, i. 252;
Knack to Know Knave, sig. F 2.

[3] 1521, *Letters and Papers Henry
VIII*, iii. 1, 420, 4s.; 1530, *P. P. Ex.*

Henry VIII, 84, 6s.; 1573, *Mid. MSS.*
449, 8s.; 1579, *Household Bk. North,
Archaeologia,* xix. 299, 12s.; 1601, *Agriculture and Prices*, vi. 527, 9s.; 1608,
ibid. 529, very fine, 20s.; 1613,
Shuttleworth Accounts, xxxv. 208, 3s.

[4] *Annales*, 867. He says only Dutch
merchants sold it in 1554, and not one
shopkeeper in forty dared buy a whole
piece. Wray's accounts, 1581, *Antiquary*, xxxii. 118, lists only one ell at
10s.; other merchants' accounts seldom
show more than 6 ells, *Durham Wills*,
xxxviii. 283: 'v els of camericke
46s. 8d.'

1542 Lady Russell sent Princess Mary a gift of cambric; and in 1546 Henry VIII granted Peter Walle and his son licence to bring into the realm all manner of silks, 'linen cloth as Holland, cameryke, and damaske worke'.[1] Certainly, from this date, cambric was common in accounts and inventories of royal and noble households. The statement made by Howes may have been applicable to its use by the lower classes, though in Shakespeare's time it was being sold by pedlars such as Autolycus[2] pretended to be.

The frequent references made by dramatists to this material indicate its popularity and the interest of Elizabethans in foreign materials. Shakespeare was presenting a familiar picture when he showed Virgilia making 'spots' on cambric;[3] and he may have been historically correct in his attribution of the use of cambric to the Romans, for Cambrai was under their rule and may have even then been producing the fabric called by its name. Other dramatists mention cambric for shirts, ruffs, or bands, handkerchiefs, and household linen[4]—uses common in Elizabethan times.

CANVAS

Have you none of this striped canvas for doublets?
(1 *Honest Whore*, I. ii. 23.)

Canvas, occurring in English accounts, 1260, designated cloth of *chanvre* or hemp.[5] It was made in several qualities, ranging in price from one to three shillings a yard.[6] It was sometimes trimmed with lace and silk,

[1] 1521, *Letters and Papers Henry VIII*, iii. 1, 420; 1524, ibid. iv. 1, 340; P. P. Ex. *Henry VIII*, 84, 23 ells are used for six shirts; 1536, *Camden Miscy.* iii. 31–2; 1542, P. P. Ex. *Mary*, 97; 1546, *Letters and Papers Henry VIII*, xxi. 1, 680.

[2] *Wint. Tale*, IV. iii. 209.

[3] *Cor.* I. iii. 95.

[4] *The Picture*, IV. ii. 90: 'Cambric shirt perfumed'; 1 *Honest Whore*, I. vii. 3: 'Holland for shirts, cambric for bands'; 1601, *What You Will*, IV. i. 59. Melitza vows she will not marry

until she means to be 'a slave and starch cambrick ruffs'; *Great Duke of Florence*, IV. ii. 191, cambric handkerchief; *Parliament of Love*, III. i. 154, bed linen.

[5] 1605, *Shuttleworth Accts.* xxxv. 161: 'weaving of xx yardes of canves of the hemp that came from Hulle this year.'

[6] Coarse canvas is mentioned in *The Guardian*, I. i. 341; Gascoigne, *Supposes*, III. iii. 24; 1582, *Durham Wills*, xxxviii. 103: 'x elles course canves 10 s'; 1621, *Shuttleworth Accts.* xli.

especially made into doublets,[1] though its chief use was for household linen, shirts, and aprons for workmen.[2]

The coarse was much used in stage costume and properties. Jerkins of canvas were painted to represent mail, and costumes of canvas were made for cupids, satyrs, monsters, giants, and personified abstractions.[3]

DOWLAS

This coarse linen, originally made in Doulas, Brittany, and imported into England by 1300,[4] was used by rich persons for cloak bags and cases, and by the poor for neckwear and clothing.[5] Bakers made sieves of it; hence Falstaff's contemptuous: 'Dowlas, filthy dowlas: I have given them away to bakers' wives, and they have made bolters of them.'[6] In common with lockram, it was early used for amices, albs, surplices, and cost from two to ten pence a yard,[7] though William Freke, an Oxford student, paid three shillings and sixpence for two ells of 'fine Douless' in 1623.[8]

HOLLAND

Holland for shirts, cambrick for bands.
(1 *Honest Whore*, I. vii. 3.)

Holland cloth, a linen fabric first made in Holland,[9] had been used in England by 1423.[10] It was manufactured

250: 'an ell and a qùer fyne browne canves iiij s'; ibid. xxxv. 218, Normandy, 1s. 10d. an ell.

[1] *Antonio and Mellida*, III. ii. 102: 'an elle and a half of taffeta to cover your olde canvas dubblet'; 1584, *Durham Wills*, xxxviii. 107: 'To my godsonne a kanvishe dublett drawen out with tafete'; *London Prodigal*, II. i; *Shuttleworth Accts.* xli. 388: 'making the brown canvass doublet trimmed with blue silk and silver lace £1.16.11.' One trimmed with gold lace cost £1 7s. 10d.

[2] Household linen, 1541, *Lancashire and Cheshire Wills*, xxxii. 127; 1620, *Shuttleworth Accts.* shirts, 1520, *Archaeologia*, xxv. 440; aprons, 1511, *Letters and Papers Henry*

VIII, ii. 2, 1494.

[3] 1551, Feuillerat, *Revels*, 59, 94, 108, 130; 1572, 175; 1521, *C.S.P.V.* iii. 136.

[4] *The Oak Book Southampton*, ii. 16. List of customs rates. (Southampton 1910–11.)

[5] 1578, Egerton MSS. 2806, 'for making of a case of Doulas for the garde of a foreparte'. 1587, *Bristol and Gloucester Wills*, 267, neckwear.

[6] *1 Hen. IV*, III. iii. 79.

[7] 1544, *Agriculture and Prices*, iii. 487, 489, &c.

[8] *Eng. Hist. Rev.* vii. 98.

[9] 1502, Arnold, *Chronicle*: 'Item, a pece of Holland or any other lynnen clothe.' Also *Anything for a Quiet Life*, I. i. 244–6.

[10] *Test. Ebor.* xlv. 72.

in a fine quality used for shirts—as mentioned in *A Mad World My Masters* (1. i. 124) and numerous accounts—for smocks, kerchiefs, and other garments;[1] and a coarser quality which was used for bed linen and linings[2] for clothes; though as *Albumazar* (sig. D 4) suggests, sheets were also made of the finest holland.

Prices of holland varied according to its quality. Four shillings a yard were paid for fine quality in 1467; one to six shillings in 1485; sixpence in 1527; three shillings in 1582; five shillings and sixpence for fine in 1589; one and six for coarse in 1590; five in 1604; thus averaging a shilling a yard for coarse and four for fine.[3] In 1607 holland at thirteen shillings and fourpence an ell was purchased for Prince Henry.[4] Mistress Quickly's price of eight shillings for that of Falstaff's shirts was high for one of her station,[5] but not a royal price.

LAWN

Lawn, possibly from *Laon*, a French city, is named in English accounts in 1415.[6] It was linen of such fineness that it was often called 'cobweb lawn' as in *Scornful Lady*,[7] and its whiteness was the subject of Autolycus' praise.[8] Lawn was sold by the 'plyte',[9] a measure of one and a fourth yards, and though the eighteen shillings a yard asked by Candido of *1 The Honest Whore*[10] was a high

---

[1] Shirts, 1502, *P. P. Ex. Elizabeth York*, 17, at cost 2s. an ell. Among King James's New Year's gifts for 1605 was '1 shirt of fyne holland, the band and cuffs of cutwork', *Prog. James*, i. 589; 1627, *Eng. Hist. Rev.* vii. 99. Smocks, 1559, *Prog. Elizabeth*, iii. 455; kerchiefs, 1583, *Durham Wills*, xxxviii. 74.

[2] Bed linen, 1527–8, E. 101/419/18; 1621, *Bury Wills*, 167. Linings, 1544, E. 101/423/12.

[3] *Paston Letters*, Intro., 110; Wardrobe accounts Henry VII (coronation); 1527, *Letters and Papers Henry VIII*, iv. 2, 1391; 1582, *Durham Wills*, xxxviii. 69; *Agriculture and Prices*, vi. 528; 1604, *Shuttleworth Accts.* xli. 250.

[4] L.C. 9/95.

[5] *1 Hen. IV*, III. iii. 82–3.

[6] *O.E.D.* Lawn is frequent in fifteenth-century accounts; 1423, *Rot. Parl.* iv. 239; 1446, *Test. Ebor.* xlv. 101, an inventory of Thomas Grysop, chapman; 1485, *Somerset Wills*, xvi. 255.

[7] IV. i. 262. 1603, *Eglinton MSS.* 32: '12 yardis cobub lawn to my rufis . . . xij s.'

[8] *Wint. Tale*, IV. iii. 220.

[9] 1502. Arnold, *Chronicle*, see under 'Spicery'.

[10] *Honest Whore*, I. i. 584. See also for prices *Agriculture and Prices*, iv. 555, v. 558; 1597, *Durham Wills*, xxxviii. 283, 6s. 11d. an ell. Lawn was presented to Queen Elizabeth as

price, it seldom sold for less than seven shillings, and was usually ten or more. The value of lawns and cambrics sold in England was declared August 8, 1612, to be greater than that of all the English cloth sold in Flanders.[1]

Lawn was made into frontlets, sleeves, ruffs and bands,[2] doublets, foreparts, and gowns. Bellario's 'printing my thoughts in lawn'[3] probably meant that she was embroidering lawn handkerchiefs or neckwear.

INKLE

Inkle was a linen tape of different qualities and widths,[4] used in England by 1502.[5] It served all purposes for which tape was needed: apron strings, girdles, binding, and in embroidery—as suggested by *Pericles*.[6] It was always to be found in the packs of chapmen and pedlars,[7] and Savil's remark: 'My wife is learning now, sir, to weave inkle', means he will take the road as a pedlar if Elder Loveless turns him out.[8]

LOCKRAM

Lockram, named from the Brittany town, Locronan, or from the German *lock raum*, thick thread, was a loosely woven fabric of hemp, known to England by 1300,[9] and priced from six to eighteen pence a yard.

New Year's gifts, a fact which indicates that it was expensive, *Prog. Elizabeth*, iii. 12. It is coupled with rich network in *Friar Bacon*, xiii. 71.

[1] *C.S.P.D.* lxx. 30.

[2] Frontlets, *Letters and Papers, Henry VIII*, iv. 1, 416. Sleeves, 1583, Egerton MS. 2806, fol. 186, lawn sleeves stitched with black silk and edged with bone lace; 1601, L.C. 9/92, 'slashed and trimmed with spangles and oes'. See also index, 1599, L.R. 2/121, 'a slashed jupe and safeguard of lawn cut in snippes and spangles in the ends of the snippes, lyned with silver chamblet'. Doublet, 1588-9, *Prog. Elizabeth*, iii. 8, lawn cutwork 'flourished with oes'.

[3] *Philaster*, v. i. 557. Lawn was sold by drapers whose sign was a pea-

cock, *Westward Hoe*, II. i. 91.

[4] Florio, 1598: '*Cordicella* . . . an inkle, a tape'; 1559, A.O. 3/1106: 'vii libr. de fyne white Inkle'; 1584, *Durham Wills*, xxxviii. 69: 'vii pound of narrowe inckell . . . 18 s'; 1584, ibid. 103: 'V lbs. brod enkell 13s. 4d.'

[5] Arnold, *Chronicle*, see under 'Spicery'.

[6] v. i. 8. For uses named above see: 1541, *Yatton Churchwardens' Accounts*, 155; 1598, *Shuttleworth Accts.* xxxv. 116; 1619, *Eng. Hist. Rev.* vii. 94.

[7] *Love's L. L.* III. i. 146; *Wint. Tale*, IV. iii. 208.

[8] *The Scornful Lady*, v. i. 344.

[9] *Oak Bk. Southampton*, ii. 16. For prices, *Agriculture and Prices*, iii. 486, 487, 489, 490; vi. 524, 529; L.C. 9/51;

Lockram was used by lower-class persons for ruffs and falling bands, and for coifs, as in *Coriolanus*, *Fool Upon Fool*, *Northern Lass*, and *Spanish Curate*; also for kerchiefs, household linen, and linings for garments.[1] It was always to be found in the packs of pedlars, as in *Three Lords and Three Ladies of London* (sig. H 3 verso), and in the stock of street venders.

TIFFANY

Tiffany is a corrupted form of Epiphany, and the name applied to a thin gauze-like fabric of soft silk and linen,[2] probably originally worn on this festival. It could be had in black, and in fancy weaves;[3] and because of its softness, it was appropriate for the first lining in slashed garments, from the slashes of which such linings puffed.[4] In common with lawn, it was used for neckwear, as in *2 Honest Whore* (I. i. 835), but is classed with velvets and jewels in *Noble Gentleman* (I. i. 91).

&c. In 1529 an Act was passed concerning 'lynnen cloth called dowlas and lockeram', to prevent importation of these from Brittany unless each piece was five ells in length and one yard in breadth. The weavers of Brittany refused to make the cloths according to this requirement, and the statute was repealed 1536. *Statutes at Large*, 21 Henry VIII, c. 14; 28 Henry VIII, c. 4.

[1] *Cor.* II. i. 228; *Fool Upon Fool*, 31; *Northern Lass*, IV. iii. 9; *Spanish Curate*, IV. v. 137; kerchiefs, 1554, *Bury Wills*, 147; *Bristol and Gloucester Wills*, 267; household linen, 1546, L.R. 2/119; linings, *Hist. MSS. Com. 9th Rep.* i. 44. 1594, Greene, *James IV of Scotland*, IV. iii. *Slip[per*, the Cloun]: 'Let my dobblet bee white Northren, fiue groates the yard ... Cut it me like the battlements of a Custerd, ful of round holes: edge me the sleeues with Couentry-blew, and let the lynings bee of tenpenny locorum.'

[2] Florio, 1611, defines *Bombina* as any kind of 'bombasin stuff as tiffanie or cipress'. Holland's 1601 translation of Pliny classes it with fine, thin, silk-like sarcenet. XI. xxii. 1. 323. This is the earliest reference to it noted in English.

[3] 1618, *Household Bk. Howard*, 74, costing 1s. 2d. a yd.; 1620, 188, costing 1s. 3d. a yd.

[4] 1605, *Malone Soc. Coll.* I. iii. 259: 'One dublett of orenge coloured satin drawen out wt white tyffanye.'

V
COTTON CLOTHS

THE history of cotton is almost a history of commerce between Oriental and European countries—a history of voyages, of exploration, of exploitation of the new-found countries, of international contention for monopoly of markets.[1] The history of cotton is inextricably connected with the history of the Renaissance, for European contact with the culture of the Near East, brought about chiefly through market-seeking voyages, was the powerful influence that led to the revival of arts and learning.

Much fiction was interwoven with the facts of the early history of the cotton plant. Not the least interesting of the stories is the myth of the 'vegetable lamb'. Nearchus, officer in the army of Alexander the Great, wrote, about 300 B.C., a brief account of an Indian shrub bearing bunches of wool from which the natives made garments.[2] Theophrastus in his *De Historia Plantarum* (IV. iv. 9) described the plant in detail and unwittingly laid the foundation for the myth of a lamb-like animal growing on bushes in Scythia and Tartary—a myth repeated by writers of several nations during succeeding ages. Du Bartas, for instance, 1578, placed these vegetable lambs or 'bonarets' in Eden. Instead of feet, they had living roots fixed in the ground. They fed upon the surrounding grass and died when they had 'brouz'd the neighbour grass away'.[3] Other imaginative writers, including Sir John Mandeville, took up the myth, elaborating it in prose or verse until the end of the eighteenth century.[4]

The earliest known reference to cotton, which is found in the Rig Veda hymn (CV. 8), written between 2000–1500 B.C., indicates an advanced stage of manufacture in India; but many centuries elapsed before knowledge of

---

[1] Rawlinson, Hugh George, *British Beginnings in Western India*, ch. 2, 3.
[2] Arrian, *Historia Indica*, xvi.
[3] Sylvester trans., 181.

[4] Henry Lee unravels this myth in his interesting book, *The Vegetable Lamb of Tartary*, 1887.

it reached the Western world. Waterways and highways constructed or improved by Alexander the Great enabled the weaving skill of India to become known in Europe.

In spite of the proximity of Egypt to India, cotton seems not to have been raised to any extent in the former until the sixteenth century. The Rosetta Stone contains references to cotton; Herodotus mentions it; Pliny names it, but all Egyptian mummies thus far discovered were wrapped in linen. This fact may be evidence that cotton was not much used, or that linen was considered better suited to that purpose. No definite conclusion can therefore be drawn from it.

From India and Persia, knowledge of cotton had reached Rome by 63 B.C., and Spain about A.D. 712. Spanish towns, especially Seville and Cordova, owing to Saracen influence, became famous for cotton cloths. Portugal, following the successful voyage of da Gama, 1497, opened the rich Indian markets; but Italian merchants were responsible for the widespread use of cotton in Europe. It became a regular article of commerce between Venice and Ulm by 1430. From Germany, skill in cotton-weaving spread to Holland and Flanders, from which countries it was introduced into England.

Cotton-wool had been imported into England since the late fourteenth century, but it had been used for candles, not for cloth. Norwich was making fustian which contained some cotton by 1554. In 1575 Dutch weavers at Norwich 'presented a stuffe callinge it Bombazine',[1] a cotton and linen material; and in 1586 all-cotton fustians were being made, the yarn of which was imported by the Turkey Company. With the foundation of the British East India Company, 1600, England's interest in cotton materials increased. This company established factories in India from which it imported large quantities of calicoes,[2] and was responsible for the later introduction of calico-printing in England. Lancashire led in the manufacture of cotton fustians in 1620, materials which had almost usurped the place of woollen goods in some counties.

---

[1] *Walloons and their Church*, 78.   [2] Foster, *English Factories*, i. 113.

London became the market for both cotton-yarn and cotton materials. Roberts writing, 1642, of the city of Manchester, tells of its weavers buying in London cotton-yarn imported from Cyprus and Smyrna, working it into dimities, fustians, and 'vermillions' and returning it to London where 'the same is vented and sold, and not seldom in foreign parts'.[1]

COTTON CLOTH IN THE DRAMA

The sixteenth century was not the 'age of cotton'. Quantities of cotton-wool were used in bombasting garments, but, since much of the cotton cloth was imported, there are not as many allusions to it as to woollen or linen cloth. The fashion in calicoes is frequently mentioned, and many dramatists noted buckram, dimity, and fustian.

BUCKRAM

Buckram, known to England in the early thirteenth century,[2] probably originated in Boukhara, Tartary. It was formerly a delicate fabric of linen or cotton[3] used exclusively for garments, but in succeeding centuries served not only for hose, shirts, jerkins, and suits, but for hangings, and for stage costume and properties.[4] It was used also for lining rich materials, and seems to have been, in the sixteenth century, a coarse linen, or possibly cotton material resembling canvas. There was also a coarse,

[1] *Treasure Traffic*, 41.

[2] *O.E.D.*

[3] 1611, Florio, 'buckerame'—buckram. Anciently it was taken for the finest linen cloth. 1295, Marco Polo, *Travels*, bk. iii, ch. xxv, writing of the province of Abash, said that the people manufacture very fine buckrams and other cloth of cotton; also that the buckrams of Mutfili looked like spiderwebs. There is not a king or queen in the world but might be glad to wear them. Ibid. ch. xix, but in bk. ii, ch. cxli, he noted that buckrams were worn by the poor of eastern Tibet.

[4] 1522, *Archaeologia*, xxv. 461, 'boke-ram hosen for my master'; 1577, *Durham Wills*, ii. 422, 'one old Jerkine of buckerame with old gardes of velvet'; 1537, *Bury Wills*, xlix. 128, buckram shirt; *1 Hen. IV*, i. ii. 200, suits. 1527, *Lancashire and Cheshire Wills*, xxxii. 36; 'one testr. for bedd of grene buckram'; 1546, L.R. 2/115, 'a wyndowe curteyn of blew and yellow buckeram'; 1600, *Hist. Hengrave*, 25, 'buckram for stools'. Sharp, *Pageants*, xvi. 47, 50; *Letters and Papers Henry VIII*, iii. ii. 1557; Feuillerat, *Revels Ed. VI*, 13, 121; *Annals of Stage*, i. 171; Malone *Soc. Rep.* (1922), 132; Henslowe, *Diary*. i. 147.

stiff buckram, probably starched, which was used in stiffening collars, gowns, tops of sleeves,[1] &c. Judging from Shakespeare's 'Thou say, thou serge, nay, thou buckram lord' this material, in some quality, must have been considered inferior.[2] Possibly this reference is to the quality used in lawyer's bags mentioned in *Downfall of Robert, Earl of Huntingdon, Ram Alley,* and *Chabot.*[3]

CALICO

Calico, a term derived from Calicut, India, the original place of manufacture, designated a class of cotton and cotton-linen fabrics of plain weave, in various textures and colours, some coarse, some white and exceedingly fine like lawn, though lawn was called linen,[4] because the weft was of linen. Calicoes were used in England before 1541, but were worn only by royalty and rich nobility who could afford their price, for they were imported from India by foreign merchants, chiefly Portuguese and Spanish. Among the *Letters and Papers of Henry VIII,* 1541, is one telling of the arrival at Southampton and London of

[1] 1502, L.R. 1/50, to line cloth of gold pall at funeral Prince Arthur; 1547, Kempe, *Loseley MSS.* 157, carpet of needlework in silk and gold lined with buckram; 1517, E. 101/413/10, lining for gown; *Lancashire and Cheshire Wills,* li. 122, lining for cloak. Stiff buckram; 1532, *P. P. Ex. Henry VIII,* 223; 1546, E. 351/3025; 1599, A.O. 3/1106; 1618, *Household Bk. Howard,* 75.

[2] 2 *Hen. VI,* IV. vii. 27.

[3] In order of mention: sig. B 3; Dodsley, x. 357; V. ii. 89. For other uses of buckram, see 1530, *Archaeologia,* xxv. 510; 1558, *Lancashire and Cheshire Wills,* liv. 79: 1617, *Shuttleworth Accts.* xxxv. 225.

[4] Roberts, *Merchant's Map of Commerce,* 188 (ch. 92): 'Callicut famous ... for that cotton cloth that was first hence transported to Europe.' p. 179: 'Cambaia . . . great quantitie of cotton linens are here made, which we terme callicoes of all sorts from the very coursest wherewith they make sayles for shipping to the finest which are by us called by the name of calico Lawnes.' Tavernier, Harris, *Voyages,* i. 811, writes, 1660, that 'white calicuts' so called from Calicut (whence the Portuguese and Dutch first brought them) are woven in Bengal and Mogulistan and carried to Raioxsary and Baroche to be whitened because of large meadows and plenty of lemons there. 'Some calicuts are made so fine you can hardly see them in your hand.' This kind, however, was not exported, for all was sent to the Great Mogul's seraglio to make garments for the sultana and wives of noblemen. For coloured calicoes, see Ellis, *Letters,* III. iv. 102. 1619, letter from Kerridge to the company, says: 'no incarnadine fine callicoes' to be had. Foster, *Factories in India,* i. 51.

merchants from these countries with 'callocowte' cloth expecting 'to sell the same as formerly'.[1]

Because of the monopoly which foreign merchants had on the Indian market, calicoes imported into England were expensive throughout the sixteenth and early seventeenth centuries,[2] and consequently fashionable. In 1599 the British East India Company was founded, and granted a royal charter the following year. Thereafter, British merchants received the profit that had previously gone to those of Portugal, Spain, and Flanders, and by 1621, to quote Thomas Mun, 'touching the Trade of Callicoes of many sorts into whiche the English lately made entrance' these calicoes were lowering the 'excessive prices of cambrickes, Hollands, and other sortes of linen cloth'.[3]

Calicoes were the chosen materials for handkerchiefs, inner sleeves, and such outer garments as doublets, as the apprentice of *1 Honest Whore* assures his customers: 'I can fit you gentlemen with fine callicoes, too, for your doublets; the only sweet fashion now . . . a meek gentle callico, cut upon two double affable taffetas' (i. i. 495). Calicoes and linens vied with silks for popularity, and every merchant catering for gentlemen's trade carried a stock of 'pure callicoes, fine hollands, choice cambrics, neat lawns'.

DIMITY

Go put on
One of thy Temple suits and accompany us
Or else thy dimity breeches will be mortal

is Bright's threat to Frank Plotwell in *The City Match* (i. iv. 89). The breeches in question were made of a fine fustian containing some linen thread and woven in diagonally raised stripes. The origin of this material,

---

[1] xvi. 241. For use of calico among the nobility, see 1546, L.R. 2/115; 1594–5, L.C. 9/86; 1630, L.C. 9/99; 1545, *Somerset Wills*, xxi. 87: a pair of 'shetes of calacowe'; 1553, *Hatfield MSS.* i. 32: Sleeves of cambric and calico cloth for plucking out of French sleeves.

[2] 1583, 2s. 8d. a yd. Rogers, op. cit. iv. 523; 1587, *Wray Accts.* 781, 8s. 9d.; 1598, *Rutland MSS.* iv. 423, 2s.; 1612, Rogers, ibid. v. 531, 4s.

[3] *A Discourse of Trade from England unto the East Indies.* Purchas, v. 266.

known to England by 1440, is obscure. Dimyāṭ, a possible place of manufacture, *dimito*, a coarse linsey-woolsey, and *dimitaque*, meaning 'woven with two threads', have been suggested, but none fully accepted.[1] It had evidently been made in England some time before 1641, when Roberts tells of the manufacture of imported cotton-yarn into dimities, fustians, &c.[2]

FUSTIAN

When Bullen edited *Anything for a Quiet Life*, he had difficulty in explaining Camelet's remark: '. . . one of my neighbours in courtesy to salute me with his musket set afire my fustian and ape's breeches' (i. i. 156). He finally noted: 'Unless the meaning is that the seat of the breeches was threadbare, I cannot understand the mention of the ape.' 'Fustian-a-napes' or fustian of Naples was a velure of cotton, or flax mixed with wool, so silky-looking that it substituted for velvet.[3]

Elizabethan statutes of apparel limiting the use of silk materials to rich nobility made fustian a fashionable sub-stitute for middle-class persons. The masque, *Gesta Grayorum*, given at Gray's Inn, 1594, for the Queen's entertainment, contains among rules of government for the 'Order of Knighthood of the Helmet', one forbidding such knights who 'wear fustian for necessity, to pretend to wear the same for the new fashion';[4] and the statute of 1597 concerning fustian manufacture states that the 'wearing of fustian has lately grown to greater use than ever it was before'.[5] The mode decreed unnapped fustian. In 1597 Philip Gawdy, who kept his family supplied with fashionable wear, sent his brother fustian for a doublet

[1] *O.E.D.*

[2] *Treasure of Traffic*, 41.

[3] Lebrixa, op. cit. 'fustani, pannus, gossipinus.' Baret, 1573, 'of cotton, pannus xilinus fustiā'. 'fustian anapes, heteromallum', i.e. friezed on one side only. Nicot, 1573, 'de la fustaine, du bombasin and toute autre chose faicte du coton'. Florio, 1598, '*Tripa*, a kind of tripe velvet that they make

women's saddles with called fustian of Naples'. The patent of 1594 granted Delves and Fitzwilliam as alnagers mentions 'bays, rash, fustian of Naples . . . and new stuffs made of wool only or most part of wool'. *C.S.P.D.* ccxlix. 20.

[4] *Prog. Elizabeth*, iii. 286.

[5] *Statutes at Large*, 39 Elizabeth, c. 13.

with taffeta, silk, and buttons for trimming, informing him that the Lord Admiral had 'suites' of the same 'trymmed in same kynde'. The fustian was not 'napte because that is saruingman lyke, and you shall fynde that it will weare as softe and as well as velvet, or sattin'.[1]

Until the sixteenth century, fustian had been imported into England,[2] and was consequently expensive, and worn by royal and noble persons. The earliest known reference to fustian is in an inventory of vestments of St. Paul's Cathedral, 1295, when a *casula* of fustian is listed.[3] During succeeding centuries it was made into socks, waistcoats, coats, caps, aprons, doublets, gowns, linings for various garments,[4] even for royalty.

Of the imported fustians, 'Holmes' or Ulm was the coarsest and cheapest, usually 1*s.* to 1*s.* 5*d.* a yard; Milan, the most expensive, 3*s.* to 5*s.*, and Naples, 'Jean' or Genoa, 'osbrow' or 'osborough' from Antwerp, 1*s.* to 4*s.*[5]

Fustians had been made in England previous to 1554. In that year weavers at Norwich who had been making 'fustian-a-napes' petitioned to be allowed to call their product 'Norwich fustian', such fustians to be fifteen yards long and half an ell wide in the loom.[6] In 1589 they

[1] Letters of Philip Gawdy, 1579–1616, Egerton MS. 2804, fol. 121.

[2] *Statutes at Large*, 11 Henry VI, c. xxvii, states that fustians were brought from beyond the sea unshorn, and were greatly used for doublets among the common people of the realm. By 3 Edward IV, c. 5, fustian had been forbidden to persons with income less than forty shillings a year.

[3] Dugdale, *History St. Paul's Cathedral*, 323.

[4] Socks, 1480, *Wardrobe Accts. Edward IV*, 118; 1502, *P. P. Ex. Elizabeth York*, 16; 1605, *Household Bk. Milton Abbey*, xli. 388. Waistcoats, 1619, *Eng. Hist. Rev.* vii. 94. Caps, 1620, *Household Bk. Lord Howard*, 121. Aprons, 1598, *Shuttleworth Accts.* xxxv. 114. Doublets, 1530, *P. P. Ex. Henry VIII*, 23, 87; 1554–8, *Testamen-*

ta Leodiensia, 16, 38, 74, 82, 89, 103, 249; 1581, *Durham Wills*, xxxviii. 27; 1588, *Household Bk. Milton Abbey*, 379. Gowns, 1605, ibid. 387.

[5] Holmes, 1571, 10*d.*, *Durham Wills*, ii. 362; 1583, 1*s.* 4*d.*, *Agriculture and Prices*, vi. 550; 1617, ibid. 554; 1623, 1*s.*, *Eng. Hist. Rev.* vii. 99. Milan, 1592, 3*s.* 2*d.*, *Agriculture and Prices*, vi. 551; 1597, 4*s.* 6*d.*, *Durham Wills*, xxxviii. 282. Osborough, 1597, 1*s.*, *Antiquary*, xxxii. 79; 1*s.* 1*d.*, *Durham Wills*, xxxviii. 282. Jean, 1597, 2*s.*, ibid. 282; 1612, 1*s.*, *Shuttleworth Accts.* xxxv. 208, 251; 1615, 10*d.*, *Hutton Accts.* xvii. 215. Naples, 1571, 3*s.* 2*d.*, *Durham Wills*, ii. 362.

[6] *Statutes at Large*, 1 & 2 Philip and Mary, c. 14; *Selected Rec. City Norwich*, ii. 409.

requested the Court to grant eight articles concerning 'vellues or fustians', article seven requiring that the linen crewel used in their making be well dressed; and article eight, that all work be examined before being 'glossed'.[1]

The cotton used in their manufacture was of course imported, chiefly by the Turkey Company. A letter from this company to the Aleppo Factors, June 3, 1586, contains the earliest noted reference to cotton fustian manufacture in England: 'For cotton yarne we would have you send us 60 baggs at the least, wearof some 20 or 30 may be of the bigest you can gett, and the other the fynest you can gett for the great serveth for candells, and the smaulest for fustians.'[2] By 1620 Lancashire led in the fabrication of England's yearly output of 40,000 pieces of cotton fustian, which also contained some linen yarn, but no wool.[3] But even at the beginning of the century, English fustian manufactures, as May wrote, had declined because they had failed to keep up to standard;[4] and a review of France's new manufactures, presented to King Henry, 1604, told the same story:

'Les fustaines d'Angleterre sont ainsi appellées combien qu'elles soient manufacturées en France, en Italie, et en Allemagne, en bien plus grande perfection qu'audit pays d'Angleterre, où il ne s'en fait quasi point; mais elles y sont toutes portées pour un secret qu'ils avoient seuls au pays d'Angleterre, de les sçavoir teindre, apprester et friser en perfection, mais ce secret est descouvert et introduit en France.'[5]

In the drama of this period, fustian is treated with small respect. It is mentioned in connexion with the costume of low-class persons and servants.[6] From its substitution

---

[1] *Walloons and Their Church*, 78.

[2] Lansdowne MS., 241, fol. 392*b*.

[3] Price, *Quarterly Journal Economics*, xx. 612, quoting *Petitions and Parliamentary Matters*, vol. *Beta*, no. 16, Guildhall Library, London. The petitions state that fustians were made of: 'a kind of bombast or down, being fruit of the earth growing upon little shrubs, brought into this kingdom by the Turkey Merchants from Smyrna, Cyprus, Acra and Sydon, but commonly called cotton wool; and also of linen yarn most part brought out of Scotland and othersome made in England, and no part of same fustians of any wool at all.'

[4] *Estate of Clothing*, 33–24.

[5] *Archives curieuses de l'histoire de France*, sér. I, xiv. 232.

[6] *Tam. Sh.* IV. i. 49; *Anything for a Quiet Life*, I. i. 156.

for silk materials, grew the figurative meaning of false-
ness, pretence, or bombast; hence such allusions as
'fustian lord', in *Gentleman Usher*; 'fustian book', *Alchemist*; 'fustian country', *Cynthia's Revels*; fustian talk,
Every Man out of His Humour.[1]

[1] *Gentleman Usher*, I. i. 108; *Al-* *Humour*, III. iv. 7; 'fustian rascal',
chemist, IV. i. 318; *Cynthia's Revels*, 2 *Hen. IV*, II. iv. 203.
'Induction'; *Every Man Out of His*

VI

SILKS

By the soft winde of whispering silkes.
(*Satiro-mastix*, i. 209.)

SILK, the fine thread spun by the *Bombyx mori* at its entrance into the chrysalis stage, was known in China from 2689 B.C., but was not used in costume before 1100 B.C.[1] Towards the beginning of the Christian era, Roman traders found silk at ports on the Indus and Ganges rivers where it had been exported from north-western China. Allusions to silk are common in classical literature. To Aristotle we owe the earliest account of silk production.[2] It was introduced into Egypt by the Persians, and during the Ptolemaic period was one of the chief articles of commerce in Alexander. Lucan's description of the silken garments of Cleopatra[3] shows that Shakespeare was not historically wrong in his picture of that queen's luxurious appointments.[4]

The story of Justinian's introduction of silkworm culture at Constantinople in the sixth century is too familiar to need reviewing. His successors guarded the secret for five hundred years; but the conquering Saracens spread the knowledge as far west as Sicily, where King Roger developed it in Palermo from 1146.[5] The bloody episode of the Sicilian Vespers 1282 scattered the Arabic and Grecian workers of that city, who went to various cities in Italy. Silk-weaving flourished in Lucca during the thirteenth century, and when the Florentines took possession of Lucca in 1315 they carried weavers back to Florence. Between 1300 and 1450, silk culture and weaving spread throughout Italy, but silks of 'Lukes', 'Jeans', Venice, and Florence remained the most famous in commerce for many centuries. In the middle fifteenth century the silk-weaving industry was given a new im-

---

[1] Cox, *Les soieries d'art*, 2 ff.
[2] *Hist. Anim.* V. xix. 11.
[3] *Pharsalia*, x. 142.
[4] *Ant. & Cleop.* II. ii. 201, 207, 217.
[5] Muratori, *Rerum Italicarum Scriptores* (1725), vi. 668, ch. xxxiii.

petus by Louis XI, who set up looms in Lyons and
Tours. Since the weavers were Italians and therefore
favoured Italian patterns, the product of these cities did
not express French taste until over a century later.

The history of silk patterning may be divided into four
periods: the Byzantine, from the sixth to the eighth
centuries; the Mussulman, to the late thirteenth; the
Italian, which reached its greatest development in the
fifteenth, declining in the sixteenth; the French, which
predominated under Louis XIV.

Up to the sixth century, Coptic materials contained no
silk, being made of wool or linen. Byzantine fabrics are
decorated by a special pattern composed of two-headed
eagles, winged horses, griffins, lions. The decadence of
the Byzantine Empire was hastened by the Mussulman
conquest which prepared the way for the spread of Arabic
influence. Arabic silks were characterized by inscriptions
and hieratic animals and birds: gazelle, eagle, parrot.
The invasion conducted by Gengis-Khan in the thirteenth
century, followed by the domination of Tamberlane, who
brought Persia and China under his rule, introduced new
elements into the decorative art of the Mussulman. In
contact with extreme Eastern civilization, decorators
turned to Nature for their inspiration, and flowers which
were appropriate to conventional treatment: the tulip,
eglantine, carnation, hyacinth were patterned in silk.

During the Middle Ages Venice, establishing broader
commercial relations with the Orient, recognized the beauty
of Eastern fabrics which her ships brought from Constantinople and Levantian parts. Each Italian centre specialized
in a pattern or type. Florence produced damasks decorated
in motif on small scale; Lucca and Siena used religious
subjects; Genoa made embossed velvets; and Venice all
kinds of cut velvets and brocades in symmetrical flowers.

The twelfth-century designs in velvets and other silks
consist of symmetrically placed animals in geometric
frames which show Byzantine influence. The thirteenth
and fourteenth show a naturalistic movement of running
animals, birds on the wing. In the fourteenth, European

animals replaced those influenced by Chinese of the thirteenth. Branches which enclosed the motifs became thicker.
The large pomegranate and artichoke patterns were
evolved in Italy during the next century, which was a
period of remarkable sumptuousness, symmetry of design,
and harmony of colour. Velvets with satin or cloth-of-
gold ground, two-pile velvet decorated with 'purls' of gold,
were designed by eminent artists. The decadence of
Italian silks began in the early seventeenth century with
the introduction of a clever and complicated medley of
conventional floral and mullion designs.

England imported most of her supply of silk by the
piece, but some raw silk was imported even in the fifteenth
century.[1] In 1592–3 over 20,000 of organzine, long raw,
short raw, and silk nubs were brought into the port of
London alone,[2] the total subsidy being over £2,250.

Silk-weaving in England had, since the mid-fourteenth
century,[3] been in the hands of women, but it had been
confined to small articles; no piece silk was made. By
the sixties, alien silk-weavers were working in England.
In 1569 Peter le Roye was summoned to court for
unauthorized silk-weaving in Bermondsey[4] and the list
of foreigners in Southwark fourteen years later shows
one Burgundian, one French, and thirteen Dutch silk-
weavers.[5] Weavers at Norwich used silk in their satins
and tabines, as was brought out in their case against Delves
in 1602.[6] By that year the Queen was said to be losing
much revenue because the strangers were making 'tuft-

[1] *Port Bk. Southampton*, 136 ff.

[2] *Hatfield MSS.* iv. 575. Thrown
silk is formed of two or more singles
being twisted together in a direction
contrary to that in which the singles
of which it is composed are twisted.
This process is called organzining, and
the silk so twisted, organzined.

[3] Cf. 37 Edward III, cc. 5, 6.
Artificers are restricted to one trade.
Exception made in case of women
weavers, spinsters upon works in wool,
linen, silk, embroidery. 33 Henry VI,
c. 5. Such women are protected against

importation of small silk wares. Also
3 Edward VI, c. 4; 19 Henry VII,
c. 21. In 1536 Sir A. Guidotti offered
to bring Messina silk weavers to England, but there seems no record of the
project, Cot. MSS. Vit. B. xiv. 33.

[4] Exch. K. R. Mem. Rolls, Easter,
11 Elizabeth, 151.

[5] Kirk, *Returns of Aliens*, ii. 287–
93, 328–33. One finds allusions to
'London silk' in accounts as early as
1558, L.C. 2/4.

[6] Exch. Dep. Norfolk, 44 Elizabeth, Mich. 1: Francis Smalpeece

taffetas, velvets, figured satins' and other silk and wool goods.[1] Silk-weaving was not confined to London. The Corporation Records of St. Albans show the purchase for Hertford, 1588, of a 'new great loom and two flayes one for silk and the other for cruell; two little looms one for silk and the other for cruell'.[2] There were silk-weavers at Lewes, also, in 1601.[3]

Raw silk for weaving had to be imported, for none was produced in England. King James, ever ready to adopt schemes which promised curtailment of importation, sent letters, 1609, to the lords lieutenant of all shires giving instructions for the planting of mulberry-trees and the rearing of silkworms.[4] The climate was unsuitable, and, in spite of royal urging, the project languished until from the settlement of Virginia, 1622, the report of wild mulberry-trees again raised hopes of producing all the silk England needed. The King recommended that the Virginia Company breed silkworms in preference to cultivating tobacco,[5] but the attempt failed, and silk-weaving had to continue on imported raw silk. In 1629 the silk-throwsters of London formed a corporation,[6] and thirty-two years later 40,000 men and women were employed in silk manufacture.

SILK CLOTH IN THE DRAMA

The drama reflected Tudor love of silks. Sarcenet and cypress, taffeta in many colours, the floral damask, the gorgeous cloths of gold and silver, tabine, tinsel and tissue, the chamlets and sayes, and, most beautiful of all, the pile-silks, as velvet and plush, merely by their names created the atmosphere which the dramatists desired; or through the 'mystery of the needle and thimble' enabled actors to appear royal.

mentions 'Russelles & Russells Satyns, Norwich Satynes, Spanishe Satyns, wherof the greatest parte ys sylke . . . Tobynes, half sylke'.

[1] *Hatfield MSS.* xiv. 190. Thirty-two foreign silk-weavers were in London in 1618, one a tuft-taffeta weaver, 'Foreign Residents in England', *Cam-*

den Soc. Pub. o.s. lxxxii. 89–99.

[2] Gibbs, *Corporation Rec. St. Albans*, 28.

[3] *Sussex Rec. Soc. Pub.* i. 37.

[4] *Harl. Miscy.* iii. 80 ff.

[5] *C.S.P.D.* cxxxii. 26.

[6] *Statutes at Large*, 13 & 14 Charles II, c. 15.

Cloth of Gold and Silver

'And they did beat the gold into thin plates, and cut it into wires to work it in the blue, and in the purple, and in the scarlet, and in the fine linen, with cunning work.' This quotation from Exodus (xxxix. 3) describes one method of making cloth of gold, and shows how ancient is the practice. Another method mentioned by Pliny is that of spinning gold thread without silk or wool; while a third, much practised in the sixteenth century, was that of using a warp of coloured silk and a weft of gold thread. Cyprus and Venice each perfected a process of enwinding silk or hemp threads with gold, which was used in making cloth as well as lace. The gold thread of Cyprus had an unbroken gold appearance, but that of Venice showed the foundation.

An inventory of cloth remaining in the royal wardrobe when Queen Mary came to the throne lists: purple cloth of gold damask, yellow cloth of gold tissue, crimson cloth of gold 'wyth workes', blue cloth of gold striped, russet cloth of gold plain, tawny cloth of gold baudkin;[1] and cloth of gold or silver design, upon satin ground, or velvet patterned upon cloth of gold were the gorgeous fabrics of copes and royal costume,[2] beautiful specimens of which are preserved in the Musée Historique, Lyons, and the Victoria and Albert Museum, London. One to three pounds a yard, depending upon its elaborateness, was the price of cloth of gold. Cloth of silver was slightly less expensive.[3]

In the drama, cloth of gold and silver symbolize wealth or extravagance in dress, as in *Much Ado*, *Anything for a Quiet Life*, and *Wit Without Money*.[4] Bodkin, tinsel, and tissue, so frequently named by dramatists, were varieties of cloth of gold and silver. Tinsel later degenerated into a cloth containing threads of any kind of shining metal—

[1] E. 101/602/6.

[2] 1480, Wardrobe Accts. Edward IV, 116; 1546, E. 351/3023; 1560, L.C. 9/54; 1587-8 L.C. 9/79, &c. Much cloth of gold and silver was used in revels, Feuillerat, op. cit., see index.

[3] 1540, *P. P. Ex. Prin. Mary*, 87, £2 a yd.

[4] *Much Ado*, III. iv. 19; *Anything for a Quiet Life*, II. ii. 152; *Wit Without Money*, III. i. 330.

chiefly copper—but bodkin and tissue retained their
association with royal purple and rich jewels.

BAUDKIN OR BODKIN

Cloth of bodkin or tissue must be embroidered;
As if no face were fair that were not powdered.

Bagdad, famous for weaving damasked and brocaded
cloths of gold, originated the 'raised work' upon cloth of
gold or tissue, known as bodkin work, described in *Philaster* as 'branched cloth of bodkin' (v. i. 252). It was, seemingly, an ancient fabric. Gay notes an allusion to it in
1197, and it is mentioned in the *Calendar of Close Rolls* in
1232.[1] It was characterized by raised designs of animals,
plants, branches, and geometric figures, and made in
many colours: azure, blue, perse, purple, green, vermillion, murrey, &c. Until the fourteenth century bodkin
was a product made almost exclusively in Bagdad, Damascus, Cyprus, and Palermo; but during that century its
manufacture extended to France, and later to England.
Bodkin work was then not limited to silk material. 'Baude-
quin de laine', 'baudekyn de serico mixto', 'baudekin of
cotton stuff'[2] appear in accounts of subsequent centuries.
It is therefore difficult to determine whether allusions to
bodkin indicate the original handsome silk material or an
inferior cloth in raised pattern; but references in *The Fatal
Dowry*, *The City Madam*, and *Philaster* are to the cloth of
gold.[3]

TABINE

Cloth-of-tissue or tabine
That like beaten gold will shine
In your amorous ladies' eyne

sang George Cressingham in an apprentice's 'What do
you lack?' style.[4] His description is almost sufficient, for

[1] M. 9 (p. 71): 'Mandatum est
venerabili patri W. Carleolensi episcopo thesaurario quod emi faciat ad
opus domini regis quinque baudekinos
cum auro.' Also 1232, m. 13 (p. 46).

[2] In order of their mention: 1462,
Gay, i. 136; 1513, Dart, *Hist. Canter-*

bury Cathedral, xvi; 1545, *Archaeologia*, xliii. 234, 236, 237.

[3] *Fatal Dowry*, v. i. 30; *City Madam*,
II. i. 75; also *Cynthia's Revels*, V. iii.
91; *Philaster*, v. i. 270.

[4] *Anything for a Quiet Life*, II. ii. 6.

the shine was the chief attraction of tabine. This material, used by Henry VII in 1487[1] for carriage awnings, was a thick silk of taffeta weave with a slight nap, calendered by passing in folds under a hot cylinder, which produced an uneven or moire effect on the surface of the material, causing portions to reflect a different light from that of the remainder, thus giving the whole a suggestion of change-able colour which it did not have. Some tabine was en-riched by threads of gold or silver.[2] It was a Norwich product by 1602.[3] It was indeed much desired by ladies. Queen Elizabeth's New Year gifts, 1599–1600, included many articles of tabine.[4] Thirty-one shillings a yard was paid for sixteen yards of 'white fringed Tabine' bought by Sir Nicholas Bacon in 1591, probably destined for one of the Bacon family.[5] Although that was unusually ex-pensive, its price ranged from ten to twenty shillings a yard.

TINSEL

Tinsel was a silk interwoven with gold or silver thread like brocatel.[6] In 1244 a standard was ordered by Henry III for the Church of St. Peter, Westminster. It was to be of 'rubeo samitto qui ubique sit auro extencellatus',[7] a description which probably refers to tinsel which glistened like sparkles of fire.

'Tynsell saten' was purchased for Elizabeth of York, 1502;[8] and in 1515 Sir Christopher Garneys, writing to Henry VIII, spoke of the Queen of Scotland's inordinate love of clothes, especially her interest in a gown of 'tyn-

---

[1] G.W.A., 'ii carriage-awnings whit tab'.

[2] *Book of Rates*, 1631: 'Tabines of silk, v s a yd.; Tabin tinceled xiij s iii d.' 1597, *Hatfield MSS.* vii. 259, 'tabines branched', the ground 'gold and silver tinsel'.

[3] Exch. Bills and Answers, 44 Eliz., Mich., Norfolk, no. 301.

[4] *Prog. Elizabeth*, iii. 446, 'silver tabyne', 454, 'gold tabyne', &c.

[5] Bacon MSS. Univ. Chicago.

[6] Cotgrave, 1611. *Brocatel*, tinsel or thin cloth of gold or silver thread. Brocatel, known A.D. 943 (Gay, op. cit. i. 222), was originally entirely of gold, then of silk interwoven with gold, finally of silk enriched by cer-tain floral and arabesque designs.

[7] *Cal. Close Rolls*, 28 Henry III, m. 7.

[8] *P. P. Ex.* 9. See also *Statutes at Large*, 1 Henry VIII, c. 14. 1597, *Hatfield MSS.* vii. 259, 'tafatas tin-selled'.

sen'.[1] Daughter of Henry VII, she shared the Tudor love of rich materials! Queen Elizabeth possessed many garments of tinsel in silver and colours,[2] and a reader of her wardrobe accounts realizes that Shakespeare probably found at Court his inspiration for the Duchess of Milan's gown 'that they praise so' vividly described as of 'cloth of gold, and cuts', laced with silver, set with pearl, and worn over bluish tinsel[3]—a beautiful combination of colours. Marston had in mind a sumptuous costume when he dressed the merchant of *What You Will* in a black beaver hat with ash-coloured band, and a cloth of silk jerkin with sleeves of white satin cut on tinsel.[4]

TISSUE

When Sir Simon de Montacute was buried in 1317, King Edward II ordered two pieces of gold and silk tissue to be laid upon his body.[5] This rich fabric, much used for altar cloths and church vestments,[6] was made of precious metals, or of these metals and silk, and was invented, according to Pliny, by Alexander.[7]

It was a favourite material of royalty, occurring in the wardrobe accounts of all sovereigns from Edward II to Charles II. Costume accounts of Henry VIII, his wives, and Court ladies, are full of references to it: white, russet, silver, &c.[8] Galleries were hung with it, and it was used in abundance at the coronation of Anne Boleyn.[9] It was always carefully distinguished from the plain weave of cloth of gold, for both warp and woof of tissue were

[1] *Letters and Papers Henry VIII*, ii. 1, entry 1350. See goods of Anne Hungerford, 1530, *Archaeologia*, xxxviii. 369, for other references to this material.

[2] 1574, A.O. 3/1108; 1599, *Prog. Elizabeth*, iii. 447.

[3] *Much Ado*, III. iv. 19–22.

[4] I. i. 151. For uses of tinsel in masques, &c., see: Kempe, *Loseley MSS*. 49; Feuillerat, *Office of Revels*, 22, 30, 38, 43, 45, 286, 299.

[5] *Archaeologia*, xxvi. 339. A piece of gold and crimson tissue of the early

fourteenth century is in the Victoria and Albert Museum, London.

[6] 1508–69, *Churchwardens' Accounts St. Mary the Great*, 11, 167, 189; 1537, *North Country Wills*, cxvi. 146.

[7] (1601, Holland), bk. VII. xlviii. 228.

[8] 1519, *Letters and Papers Henry VIII*, iii, 1548; 1529, *P. P. Ex. Henry VIII*, 6, &c.; 1531, *Rutland MSS*. iv. 526, purchased at £2 a yd.; 1537, *Archaeologia*, xliii. 230.

[9] Hall, *Chronicle*, 801.

composed of twisted threads. In the royal wardrobe, 1533, are 'purple cloth of golde playne', 'purple cloth of golde with workes', i.e. embroidered, 'white cloth of gold rased with silver tissue', i.e. a brocaded pattern of tissue weave in silver on a ground of plain weave white silk and gold, 'russet cloth of gold tissue rased with gold'.[1]

Naturally, references to it were made on the stage, for it was synonymous with wealth. Cleopatra's pavilion was of tissue;[2] Laverdure frets for his tissue suit;[3] Noval's tailor has made him look like an angel in a 'cloth of tissue doublet', and Lord Cressingham spends fifteen hundred pounds for tissue, cloth of gold, velvets and silks for his wedding[4]—a conservative sum, with tissue at two pounds a yard; and there are briefer references to it in *The City Madam*, *The Maid of Honour*, and *Unnatural Combat*, *New Way to Pay Old Debts*, *White Devil*.[5]

CYPRESS

Cypress, a light, transparent material of silk and linen,[6] bears the name of the place of its origin. It was made in plain and crepe weaves, the latter often called 'crespe', crespin, or creppin,[7] and was used for partlets, foresleeves, and neckwear.[8] Cypress could be had in white, black,

---

[1] E. 101/602/6. Rased, i.e. brocaded.

[2] *Ant. & Cleop.* II. ii. 207.

[3] *What You Will*, II. i. 85.

[4] *Anything for a Quiet Life*, I. i. 101; II. ii. 5.

[5] In order of mention: II. i. 96; I. ii.; III. iii. 89; *New Way to Pay Old Debts*, II. ii. 199: 'Tissues matched with scarlet suit but ill', a statement which means that silks are not appropriately placed with woollen materials. *White Devil*, II. i. 57; *Cynthia's Revels*, v. iii. 91; *Maid in the Mill*, v. ii. 224.

[6] Minsheu, 1599, '*Gaca*, a kind of silke stuffe lyke cypers'. Florio, 1598, '*Velitta*, also a kind of fine lawne or cypresse'. 1611, '*bauero*, a stuffe made of raw silk as curled cipers'. 'Curled' indicated crepe. 1557, A.O. 3/1109, 'curled cipers', 'plain cipers'; 1581,

Egerton MS. 2806, 168 b, 'silk sipers, smothed and curled'; 1588, L.C. 9/79, 'Pro 77 virg. Sipers de serico plan et rigid'; 1590, *Prog. Elizabeth*, iii. 458, 'one mantell of white curled cypress'. Known in England, 1398, *Test. Ebor.* iv. 240.

[7] Florio, 1598, '*crispare*, to curle, crispe'; 1578, Thynne, *Animadversions*, 41; Hollyband, 'crespe, cendall, cipres'; 1611, Cotgrave, 'crespe, cipers'. Palsgrave, 1530, 'crespin, a cypress lynyn clothe'; Florio, 1611, '*crespine*, curled sipres'.

[8] 1533, *Hatfield MSS.* i. 131, 'Eight collars of crypens wrought with gold'; 132, 'Two crypen partletts of cypress wrought with gold'; 1559, A.O. 1/1106, 'Pro translatiō unius par crippen sleves'; 1565, A.O. 1/1106, 'Pro une partellet de crippin alb'.

and colours.[1] The black was used for mourning, as *The Staple of News*[2] shows.

Because of its transparency, cypress was frequently used to veil other materials, especially embroidery of gold, to lend it a charm through partial concealment. Hall tells of an entertainment given in 1521, in which the participants wore Turkish bonnets of cloth of gold and silver 'rolled in cypress',[3] and Jonson in *Every Man in His Humour* (I. ii. 107) refers to the milliner's wife concealing her wrought stomacher in cypress. Its transparency explains Olivia's 'a cypress, not a bosom, Hideth my heart', meaning that her affection is as visible as if her heart were exposed.[4]

Its transparency rendered it suitable for bongraces, tires,[5] and partlets; so frequently was it used for bongraces that the name was applied to the article itself in *The Four PP*: 'Sipers, swathbands, ribbons and sleeve laces.'[6] The popularity of cypress did not last beyond James's reign. Dean Corbet's description of the 'newe dress' of 1633 explained that

> Ladies that weare blacke Cypress vailes
> Turned lately to white linnen railes.[7]

DAMASK

'Shalt give his worship a new damask suit.
(*The Alchemist*, II. I.)

Damask, deriving its name from Damascus, the city of its original manufacture, was a rich silk of floral or conventional geometric pattern. The geographic position of

[1] *Letters and Papers Henry VIII*, ii. 2, 1517, cypress of various colours. 1565, A.O. 3/1106, 'vi virg. de Sipers alb'; 1591, L.C. 9/83, 'Pro una zona de sipß alb ij yds. long'; 1599, L.R. 2/121, 'black stitched Sipers', 'white curled Sipers', 'white striped Sipers'; 1560–1, L.C. 9/54, 'Sipers black & russet'.

[2] II. ii. 200. Autolycus carried black cypress, *Wint. Tale*, IV. iii. 221.

[3] *Chronicle*, 619.

[4] *Tw. N.* III. i. 134.

[5] 1512, *Annals of Stage*, i. 66; 1524, *Letters and Papers Henry VIII*, iv. 1, 419.

[6] p. 36. Also Florio, *velaregli*, 'shadowes, vailes, lawnes, scarfes, sipers or Bongraces that women used to weare on their forheads to keep them from the sun'.

[7] *Camden Soc. Pub.* lxvi. 71.

Damascus early made it an active centre of commerce and industry, and its products were taken to all parts of the civilized world. Damask probably came to England early in the fifteenth century. Lydgate mentions it in the *Story of Thebes*,[1] 1430, and it was bequeathed in wills of the sixties.[2] In an Act of 1474 it is named with 'bawdkin, velvet, satin, sarcenet, and chamlet' as 'brought in by merchant strangers'.[3]

By a sumptuary law of 1463, the use of damask was confined to esquires and yeomen in the king's household, sergeants, esquires and gentlemen having possessions of a yearly value of forty shillings,[4] and until Elizabeth's reign it is found only in wardrobe accounts of royalty, nobility, and clergy;[5] for a statute of the twenty-fourth year of Henry VIII forbade its use to persons of estates under the value of £100.[6]

Damask was an expensive silk, partly because of its complicated weaving—'Les fleurs ont le grain de satin et le fonds a un grain de taffetas'—partly because of the high import duties imposed upon silks. Its price of three to sixteen shillings[7] placed it out of the reach of many persons to whom sumptuary laws allowed its use, but the eighteen pounds which Mrs. Otter boasts of having paid for her damask table-cloth[8] seems exaggerated, unless it were embroidered with gold, in which case four pounds a yard would have not been unusual. Various plays contained brief allusions to damask, as that in *The Alchemist*,[9] which was necessary for Subtle's suit.

[1] III. iv. The testament of Henry, Lord le Scrope, 1415, names '1 vestimentum de albo Damask'. *Foedera*, ix. 273.

[2] *Bury Wills*, xlix. 9, 88.

[3] *Statutes at Large*, 12 Edward IV, c. 3.

[4] *Rot. Parl.* v. 504; also vi. 221. Damask was one of the favoured materials of Edward IV. See his Wardrobe Accounts, 115, 129, 134, 146, &c.

[5] *P. P. Ex. Prin. Mary*, 62, 68, 85, 96, 149; 1530, *P. P. Ex. Henry VIII*, 87, 223; 1562, *Durham Wills*, ii. 200; 1526, *Somerset Wills*, xix. 252; 1558, *Lancashire and Cheshire Wills*, xxxiii. 178; 1567, *Richmond Wills*, 210.

[6] *Statutes of the Realm*, 24 Henry VIII, c. 13.

[7] *P. P. Ex. Prin. Mary*, 149, &c.; Rogers, *Agriculture and Prices*, iv. 572; vi. 553.

[8] *Silent Woman*, III. i. 135.

[9] IV. iv. 174; *Shoemaker's Holiday*, vol. i, p. 31 (II. i.).

PLUSH

Plush was an expensive silk fabric with nap longer and softer than velvet. Jonson in *The Devil is An Ass*[1] refers to it as costing £3 10s. a yard. In 1629, it was 23s; in 1630, 13s. 6d.; in 1631, 10s.; in 1633, 12s.[2] In *The Guardian*, its cost is vividly expressed by the statement:

> When two Heirs quarrel,
> The Swordmen of the city shortly after
> Appear in Plush, for their grave consultations
> In taking up the difference. (i. i. 275.)

Sarcenet

Sarcenet, a fine, thin,[3] soft silk fabric of taffeta weave, was originally made by the Saracens. The will of Agnes Pickerell, April 9, 1373, bequeaths a 'cloth of sarzinet' to be embroidered with 'W & A' and used for covering the Holy Sepulchre at Easter,[4] a use which suggests that it was then an expensive material. References to it show that it was made 'beyond the see',[5] and as late as 1477 sumptuary laws denied its use to persons of certain incomes.[6] Its price was not low: seldom less than four shillings a yard, and frequently as much as seven;[7] so that any contemptuous references to it on the stage are to its thinness rather than to its cheapness.

Sarcenet was made in both 'single, and double' quality, that is, thin, and heavy;[8] and in many colours, as well as

[1] I. ii. 158. Mentioned, 1594. *O.E.D.*

[2] Rogers, *Agriculture and Prices*, vi. 555, 556, &c.

[3] *2 Promos and Cassandra*, I. i: Polina enters in a 'Blewe Gowne shadowed with blacke sarcenet'. In 1514 this material was used for face-veils for mummers, a use which indicates its thinness, *Letters and Papers Henry VIII*, II. 2, 1501. Also Florio's definition, 1598.

[4] *Hustings Wills*, ii. 155. *Cal. Close Rolls*, Jan. 27, 1378, m. 10: 'Three curtyns of red sarsinet.'

[5] *Rot. Parl.* vi. 155 a.

[6] Ibid. 189 a.

[7] 1464, *Agriculture and Prices*, iii. 498–9, 4s. 5d.; 1488, Wardrobe Accts. Edward IV, 117, 3s. 4d.; 1502, *P. P. Ex. Elizabeth York*, 54, 2s.; 1530, *Rutland MSS.* ii. 269, 4s.; 1576, Lord North Accts., Stowe MS. 744, 6s. 9d.; 1605, *Household Bk. Milton Abbey*, 388, 8s.; 1616, *Shuttleworth Accts.* xxxv. 218, 4s. 3d.; 1619, *Household Bk. Howard*, 122, 7s.; 1624, *Eng. Hist. Rev.* vii. 99, 7s. 6d.

[8] 'Thou slight prince of single sarcenet', *Philaster*, v. i. 318; 1535, *Philobiblon Soc. Pub.* vii. 14, mentions double sarcenet.

changeable.[1] The softness and semi-transparency of single sarcenet is shown by Mammon of *The Alchemist*, who plans a wardrobe having shirts of taffeta-sarcenet as soft and light as cobwebs (II. i. 228), but in *Troilus and Cressida* (v. i. 36), and *1 Henry IV* (III. i. 255), sarcenet is used metaphorically to suggest contemptuous slightness.

Sarcenet had many uses: drapery, hats, doublets, tippets, shirts, garters, children's frocks, stage costume, and lining for all kinds of garments.[2]

SATIN

Branch me his skin in flowers like a satin.
(*Philaster*, v. i. 290.)

Satin of the sixteenth century was a glossy silk, woven upon a loom with at least five healds and as many corresponding treadles. 'These are so mounted as to rise and fall four at a time, raising and depressing alternately four yarns of the warp, across the whole of which the weft is thrown by the shuttle, so as to produce uniform smooth texture, instead of the chequered work resulting from intermediate decussations as in common webs.' Satin is woven with the glossy side undermost.

Satin is first noted in English accounts among silks given by Bishop Grandison to the Cathedral at Exeter, 1340, but must have been fairly common in England before the end of the century, since Chaucer names it among the goods sent far and wide by the 'compagnie of chapmen' of Surrey.[3]

[1] *Supra*; also 1531, *Archaeologia*, ix. 244, 247.

[2] Drapery: 1463, *Bury Wills*, 41; 1552, *Archaeologia*, xliii. 236; 1588, *Lancashire and Cheshire Wills*, liv. 135. Hats and doublets: 1536, *Archaeologia*, ix. 244, 247. Tippets: 1502, *P. P. Ex. Elizabeth York*, 9. Shirts: 1483, *Ant. Rep.* ii. 250. Garters: 1527, *Letters and Papers Henry VIII*, iv. 2, 1620. Children's frocks: 1620, *Household Bk. Howard*, 122. Stage costume: 1547–53, Feuillerat, *Revels*, 169, 182,

183, 252, 338. In 1601 Henslowe loaned the Company 14s. for a pair of hose of 'taffty sasnet' for 'mycke to tumbell in before the quen', *Diary*, ii. 152. Lining of garments: 1541, E. 154/2/20; 1547, L.C. 2/3; 1553, E. 154/2/41; 1576, Stowe MS. 774. The above are merely suggestive; references to this material are almost unlimited.

[3] *Tale of Man of Law*, line 137. For description of weaving of satin, see Hooper, *Handloom Weaving*, 1910.

Satin was made in all colours, plain, figured, branched, 'pirled',[1] i.e. decorated with purls or tiny loops of gold thread, and was one of the most expensive and desired of sixteenth-century silks. It was most valued for its gloss, and 'mirror' satin was a frequent item in Queen Elizabeth's wardrobe accounts.[2] The price of 11s. 3½d. a yard for crimson satin mentioned in *Antonio and Mellida* (II. i. 82) was not an unusual price. Satin cost from three to fourteen shillings a yard.[3] Any work, such as embroidery or purls, on satin of course increased the price.

The manufacture of russels satin and satin reverse, i.e. wrought or stitched, flourished in Norfolk, 1554;[4] and by 1603 the weavers of this city were making not only these, but satin of Cyprus and Spanish satin.[5]

TAFFETA

Beauties no richer than rich taffeta.
(*Love's L. L.* v. ii. 159.)

Taffeta, from the Persian *taftah*, presumably the onomatopoeic representation of the sound produced by movement of the material, was a thin, fine silk fabric of even texture, made in many colours and changeable.

[1] Blush colour, *Every Man Out of His Humour*, III. v. 2; primrose, *What You Will*, II. i. 36; peach, *Meas. for M.* IV. iii. 12; crimson, *Silent Woman*, III. i. 144; figured, *Household Bk. Howard*, 293; 1536-7, E. 315/455: 'satin tawney of Bruges pirled.'

[2] 1581-90, A.O. 3/1110; *Anything for a Quiet Life*, II. ii. 93, indicates the desirability of this gloss; *Tu Quoque*, sig. F 3. Much satin was used in Court revels: *Letters and Papers Henry VIII*, ii. 1, 1517; Feuillerat, *Revels*, Edward VI, Elizabeth, *passim*. It is found in wardrobe accounts of nobles and persons of the middle class. 1541, E. 154/2/70: 'hose of crymsen satten cutt'; 1546, L.C. 2/115, inventory Earl Surrey: 'gowne blacke saten embroydered and lyned with golde sarco-

nett'; 1593, L.C. 9/85: 'Unus par. manucarum pendent de satten colour Isabelle sciss . . . lin. cum tinsell'; 1599, L.R. 2/121: 'dublett of Sea water grene Satten cutt and embrod. wt flowers of Venice golde drawne oute, wt cobbwebbe lawne'; 1591, *Middlesex Sessions Rolls*, i. 191: 'sea water greene satin breeches.'

[3] 1524, *Letters and Papers Henry VIII*, iv. 1, 341, 8s. 1d.; *Household Bk. Howard*, 162, 13s. See also Index, *Agriculture and Prices*.

[4] *Statutes at Large*, 1 & 2 Philip & Mary, c. 14.

[5] Exch. Bills and Answers, 44 Elizabeth, Mich., Norfolk, 301. Russels possibly means Ryssel, Flemish name for Lille.

In the early fourteenth century it was classed with the most expensive materials; for instance, in 1317, Edward II ordered two pieces of taffeta with cloth of gold to be laid upon the body of his favourite, Sir Simon de Montacute.[1] Even in the sixteenth century it was priced as high as fifteen shillings a yard.[2] It was used for every kind of garment in the wardrobe of both men and women.[3]

But plain taffeta was not rich enough for Elizabethan taste. It must be 'tufted', i.e. woven with raised stripes or spots. These stripes, upon being cut, left a pile like velvet, and, since the tufted parts were always a different colour from the ground, beautiful colour combinations were possible. A farthingale in Queen Elizabeth's accounts of 1570–1 was of 'tuft-taffata de colour orrenge-tawnie tuft en serico virid'; a gown of 1587 had a ground of silver with tawny tufts; a Dutch cloak of 1599 had yellow ground with black tufts; a petticoat had silver ground with murrey tufts; and one of changeable taffeta had tufts of carnation, plunket, and silver.[4] Tuft-taffeta was used for hats for both men and women, and for men's hose, jerkins, cloaks, and jackets, as in *Roaring Girl*.[5]

Deceit in finishing taffeta was practised by unscrupulous persons. Inferior and defectively woven material was gummed and glossed to give an attractive appearance;

---

[1] *Archaeologia*, xxvi. 339.

[2] 1572, *Mid. MSS.* 422, Tuft-taffeta 12s. a yd.; 1585, *Durham Wills*, xxxviii. 134, 'levens taffetie', 1s.; 1592, 211, 'chaingeable taffetye', 10s. 6d.; 1594, Bacon MSS. Univ. Chicago, 'ij ydes., d. qr. russet tuftafeta ... xxvi s'; 1612, *Shuttleworth Accts.* xxxv. 202, 17s. an ell; 1617, 225, 1 ell changeable 15s.; *Household Bk. Howard*, lxviii. 296, Florence taffeta, 14s. Ell broad taffeta was a shilling more a yard. For other references to price, see *Agriculture and Prices*, v. 581.

[3] Hats, doublets, farthingales, jerkins, hose, petticoats, cloaks, &c.:

1530, *P. P. Ex. Henry VIII*, 87; 1548, E. 351/3026; 1560, L.C. 9/79; 1588–9, *Prog. Elizabeth*, iii. 13; 1612, *Archaeologia*, xxvi. 386; 1629, *Household Bk. Howard*, lxviii. 292.

[4] 1570, A.O. 3/1180; 1587, L.C. 9/79; 1599, L.C. 2/121. *Eastward Hoe*, I. ii. 16: 'buffin gown with tuft-taffeta cape.' Tuft taffeta was used 1559–60, L.C. 9/53: 'fflanders gowne de Taffata purple tufte.'

[5] 1587, *Lancashire and Cheshire Wills*, liv. 34; jerkins and cloaks, ibid. 139; jackets, *Roaring Girl*, III. i. 14.

but upon becoming wet or warm, this taffeta showed its defects; hence, the numerous allusions to gummed or 'fretted' taffeta.[1]

VELVET

Velvet, a closely woven silk material having on the right side a short pile or nap, is believed to have been a product of the twelfth century. The velvet-weavers of Florence had their guild by 1247. Joinville mentions velvets in 1277 and chasubles of velvet are inventoried among vestments of St. Paul's, London, 1295.[2]

Italian velvets were the best. England imported her supply, which was limited at first to ecclesiastical and royal use, from Genoa, Lucca, and Florence. As early as 1303 she was importing from Genoa, as one learns from the petition of two Genoese merchants against persons of Flanders who had robbed of cloth-of-gold and velvet a ship bound for Dover.[3]

Italy during the fifteenth and early sixteenth centuries produced velvets of the greatest beauty. Artists expressed their religious fervour in designs for ecclesiastical vestments. Copes, such as those in the Musée, Lyons, the Victoria and Albert Museum, London, the Boston Museum of Fine Arts, and the Metropolitan Museum, will thrill even an unimaginative mind by the exquisite grace of their patterns and the glory of their colours.

The wardrobe accounts of English royalty especially appeal to a lover of beauty of colour combinations in velvets. The accounts of Edward IV show items of black velvet 'speckled with white', blue 'figured with tawney', checkered velvet, green changeable, velvet 'russet figury', 'crymsyn figured with white', 'motley' velvet, and the incomparable 'velvet upon velvet', in many colours (116,

---

[1] The following are representative: *Malcontent*, I. i. 22; *The Ball*, IV. i. 30; 'Quip Upstart Courtier', Greene, *Works*, xi. 287. Since taffeta was often given as reward to whores, they were called 'taffeta punks', 'taffeta girls', &c., *Spanish Gipsy*, IV. iii. 70.

[2] Dugdale, *Hist. St. Paul's*, 318.

[3] *Cal. Close Rolls*, June 4, 1303, m. 10. In 1403 Henry IV forbade any person below the rank of 'banneret' to wear cloth of gold, crimson cloth, or velvet.

&c.). The last is a pattern which shows itself in a double pile, one pile higher than the other, and of the same shade, though crimson velvet upon velvet assumes marvellous variations of shade according to the direction from which the light falls upon it.[1] Velvet was made also in two piles upon a ground of satin. Since this makes three heights, if the satin ground be counted as one, it is probably the 'three pile velvet' mentioned in *Westward Hoe, Winter's Tale*,[2] and many other plays, and used as a figure of perfection in *Measure for Measure*.[3] No specimen of three-pile velvet of these centuries has ever been found.

In some velvets, the tiny loops which, cut, would form the pile, were left uncut. Such velvet was known as 'uncut' or 'unshorn' velvet, of which some very beautiful pieces and copes are preserved in museums. In 1599 Queen Elizabeth received a New Year's gift of a lapmantle 'of ash-coloured and heare-coloured unshorne velvet lozenwise, lyned with crimson unshorne velvet'.[4] It was used especially for lining cloaks, as in *What You Will* (v. i. 57). A beautiful variation was made in patterns of cut velvet, outlined by uncut, frequently in two colours upon a background of white or gold. One of Queen Elizabeth's New Year gifts of 1600 was a 'juppe and safegard of orenge-colour vellat, cut and uncut'.[5]

Not satisfied with the beauty of pattern in the velvet itself, embroiderers sought to make it more sumptuous by adding tiny loops of gold thread in patterns over the surface—the 'pirled' velvet of accounts.[6] Velvet was also embroidered in flowers, or 'branched', sometimes called 'wrought'. In such a gown, the Earl of Essex went to his

---

[1] Velvet upon velvet is frequent in sixteenth-century accounts: 1523, L.C. 9/51; 1531, L.R. 416/5; 1532, *P. P. Ex. Henry VIII*, 189; 1546, L.R. 2/119, &c.

[2] *Westward Hoe*, I. i. 67; *Wint. Tale*, IV. ii. 14: *A Mad World My Masters*, I. i. 216.

[3] I. ii. 34.

[4] *Prog. Elizabeth*, iii. 450. See also, 1605, *Household Bk. Milton Abbey*,

388; 1623, E. 101/436/9, describing a suit for Prince Charles, consisting of hose, cassock, and cloak of tawny uncut velvet; 1628, *Eng. Hist. Rev.* vii. 99: William Freke, an Oxford student, paid 31s. a yard for unshorn velvet.

[5] *Prog. Elizabeth*, iii. 510.

[6] The wardrobe and revels accounts of Henry VIII offer many examples: 1530, *Letters and Papers Henry VIII*, iv. 3, 3040; E. 351/3024, &c.

execution.[1] Malvolio's dream of power includes a branched velvet gown,[2] and the cloak by which Somerton of *The Witch of Edmonton* is to be recognized is of this material.[3]

[1] Stowe (Howes), *Annales*, 792. 'Murrey vellvet embroidered' is inventoried in the goods of the Duke of Norfolk, 1546, L.R. 2/119. Also wardrobe account, Henry VIII, 1546, *Archaeologia*, xliii. 230.

[2] II. v. 43. 1602, Henslowe, *Diary*, i. 180: 'Lent . . . for a gowne of branshed velluet and a doublet . . .' £6.

[3] III. iii. 115. *Philaster*, v. i. 190, in which Dion's wish that the moths 'branch their velvets' means that he hopes moths will eat the pile and so ruin it.

VII

LACE

'SHE was, indeed, a pedler's daughter and sold many laces', said Dick, of Jack Cade's wife.[1] Lace is found in every pedler's pack exhibited on the stage of this century.[2] The term 'lace' was used of two products; a braid or cord, and an ornamental openwork fabric, both products being composed of linen, cotton, wool, or metal threads. The braid lace was used during the sixteenth century for fastening[3] garments, binding the hair, or trimming garments by sewing flat along seams or in decorative design all over the article. The openwork fabric was used for ornamenting the edges of every kind of garment from ruffs to pantofles, and all accessories from handkerchiefs to footcloths.

The origin of the openwork fabric and the country of its invention have ever been the subjects of dispute. It may have had an ancestor in the drawn or plaited thread work of which the cloths found in Egyptian tombs offer an example. The discoveries of Dr. Juliano Tello, Director of the Lima Museum of Archaeology, show lace to have been of pre-Inca antiquity. A lace gown was taken from the mummy of a woman of the Parakas culture, at least 3,000 years old. But Egyptian and Parakan arts were lost in the night of time, and openwork lace, according to the modern use of the term, was, as far as is known, a Renaissance invention or revival, probably having its inception during the first quarter of the sixteenth century. Pattern books for embroidery suggestive of those later used by lace-workers appeared in several countries 1525–50. Both Flanders and Italy claim to have originated

---

[1] 2 *Hen. VI*, IV. ii. 49–50.

[2] *Wint. Tale*, IV. iii. 325; *Tu Quoque*, I. i. 19; *The Four PP*, p. 36; *Downfall Robert Earl Huntingdon*, F. 4 verso.

[3] Mantel lace, shoe lace, sleeve lace, points, &c.

Renaissance lace. Italy seems to have the better claim. A pattern book by 'R.M.' published at Zürich, 1550, states that lace was introduced into Germany from Italy in 1526.[1] On the other hand, a pattern-book for needlework containing designs similar to those later used for lace was published by Jorg Gastel at Zwickau in 1525, and its title-page indicates that there had been previous editions.[2]

Lace-making as an industry came to England comparatively late, the work at Honiton being founded by Flemish refugees escaping from the Alva persecutions, 1568–70. The first pattern-book in English, *A newe tretys*, was published at Antwerp by William Vorsterman. The fact of its being in English is interesting evidence of the close commercial relation between the Netherlands and England. The first British pattern-book was not published until 1591: *New and singular patterns and works of linen*, by Adrian Poyntz.[3] William Barley's *A Booke of curious and strange inventions, called the first part of Needleworkes, containing many singular and fine sortes of cut-workes raisdeworkes, Stitches, and open cut-works*, 1596, had previously been printed at Venice and was newly printed 'in more exquisite sort for the profit and delight of the gentlewomen of England'. The most famous of British pattern-books is, of course, Richard Shorleyker's *A Scholehouse for the Needle*, 1624, and his second part, *Here foloweth certain patterns of Cut-workes: newly invented and never published before, Also sundry sorts of spots as flowers, Birdes and Fishes*

[1] '. . . die kunst de Dentelscheren. Dañ dieselbigen im jar 1526 erstmals durch die Kauffleit vas Vendig uñ Italien ins Tuechland bracht worden'. Ilg, *Geschichte und Terminologie der alten Spitzen*, Wein, Lehmann & Wentzel, 31.

[2] Haussmann, Nicolaus. *Eyn new Modelbuch, auff aussnehen vnd borten wircken yn der Laden vñ langen gestell, Gemert vnd gebessert mitt 105 andern modeln*. In 1527, at Cologne, two pattern-books were published: *Eyn new Künstlick Modelbuch*, Peter Quentell;

and *Liure nouveau et subtil touchant l'art et sciëce tant de brouderie fronssures, tapïsseries cõme aultres mestiers quo fait alesquilles*. . . . by P. Quinty. The same year, A. Paganino published a pattern-book at Venice: *De richami p elquale se impara in diversi modi lordine e il modo de recamare*, &c.

[3] Published by J. Wolfe and Edward White. For a complete list of pattern-books see A. Lotz, *Bibliographie der Modelbücher*, Hiersemann, 1933.

& and will fitly serve to be wrought, some with Gould, some wyth silke, and some with crewell in coullers: or otherwise at your pleasure, is indicative of the kind of lace fashionable at the time. The 'spots'[1] had been the mode since the late years of the previous century. Although England had not produced any pattern-books until late, she had evidently not been without them. An item occurring in the inventory of the effects of Edward VI: 'A Booke of parchment containing diverse patrons' offers interesting speculation as to its source and purpose.[2] But the publication of pattern-books is not an indication of priority of knowledge of the art of lace-making. Workers would naturally guard their patterns jealously and publish them only after they had long been used. All that can be said is that Italy *seems* to have been the inventor, with France, Flanders, and Germany following. How early was it known in England?

After careful examination of evidence produced to show fifteenth and early sixteenth century use of lace in England, one is forced to admit that such evidence is very weak. The quotations usually cited from fifteenth-century inventories and accounts to prove the early existence of lace in England are too indefinite to support such conclusion. They suggest the lace-braid rather than the openwork fabric.[3] Lace does not appear in the portraits until the second half of the sixteenth century. The yard of lace mentioned in connexion with a shirt in *The Accounts of Lestrange of Hunstanton* does not indicate 'laced linen' as Mrs. Pallisser[4] states, but merely the fastening of the shirt. The 'viij peces yelowe lace for the Kings Grace' purchased 1530, were probably braid laces, for these existed throughout the sixteenth and seventeenth centu-

---

[1] *Oth.* III. iii. 435.

[2] Harl. MS. 1419*b*, 474. This book may, of course, have been one for costume rather than for lace and embroidery.

[3] *Statutes at Large,* 3 Edward IV, c. iv. Merchandise not lawful to be brought into England: '. . . de file laces, laces dor.' Also Wardrobe Edward IV, 1480: 'To Alice Claver silkewoman laces & tassels for garnysshing of diverse Books', 117. Also 'a mantell lace of blue silk with butons of the same', 'laces of riben of silk'. Ibid. 149.

[4] *History of Lace,* 265.

ries, in many colours.[1] The edge of purl purchased for
Mary Neville's wedding clothes was seemingly lace,[2]
though that may have been an *habillement* of pearl.

The introduction of lace into England probably re-
sulted from an order of Henry VIII, made 1545–6, which
allowed

'Guydo and Stratte Cavalcanti merchants of Florence to bring into
this our Realm of England from the Partes beyond the See during
the space of three yerys next . . . all manner clothes of Tyssue Gold,
Silver, Tinsell, Velvet and silk of whatsoever making faccon or kind
they be, all maner sorts of Fringys and Passamentys wrought with
Gold and Silver or otherwise, and all other Gentlenesses of what
facyon and value soever . . . as he or they shall think best for the
pleasure of Us, our derest Wyef the Quene, our nobles, Gentlemen
and others'.[3]

Passements, the French term for braids, ribbons, lace, are
found frequently in the royal and noble wardrobe accounts,
thereafter,[4] and passement lace is used through the century, which, since it serves to edge articles,[5] suggests the
openwork fabric. From 1545 on, the term lace is con-

[1] *P. P. Ex. Henry VIII.* 69. Also,
1536, Wardrobe Henry VIII, *Archaeologia*, ix. 245: 'Coatys of grene clothe
garded with brade gardes of grene
velvette sette on with foure laces of
grene silke.' Hose 'inbrotheryd wt
redd Lace', 'dublett stryped doune wt
white lace', occur in 'An Indenture of
goods received by John from John
Gale', 1541, E. 154/2/20; 'hollowe
lace of divers collors' is used in preparation for coronation of Elizabeth, L.C.
2/4 (3). Also *Shuttleworth Accts.* xxxv.
216.

[2] See discussion of purl-lace.

[3] *Foedera*, xv. 105. Reference to
Italian lace is found in manuscripts of
this time. Such items as 'Venice lace
for toga', A.O. 3/1106 (1559), are
common.

[4] 1545, E. 101/42/4: 'Articles delivered to the Queens Wardrobe' are
'pasmens of gold'. 1546, E. 101/424/7:
'Apparel for my Lady Mary's Grace'
includes 'xxxvi oz. of passment of

gold spent upon gowne'. 1545,
E. 101/429/4: 'ii yards of passman
of gold and crimson silk.' 1546, Lord
Chamberlain's account expenses, coronation Edward VI, L.C. 2/3: 'Passamaine riband.' 1553, L.C. 5/84:
'passmeyn lace' of bone work of gold.
1556, *Satire on Toun Ladyes, Percy
Soc. Pub.* xxvii. 92: 'coits . . . Brodrit
braid, with pasments.'

[5] 1546, 'short pair of hose of purple
silk of Venice and gold, woven like a
caul, edged with passamaine lace of
purple silk and gold, worked at Milan',
Harl. MS. 1419*a*; 1546, 'a partlet of
lawn edged with passement lace of
gold', effects Mrs. Holland, retainer
of attainted Duke of Norfolk, L.C.
2/115. Passement lace is used also for
a cloak, L.C. 2/3; for 'garnyshing the
pylors of the chariot' at burial of
Edward VI, L.C. 2/4 (2); to 'garnishe
the litter' of Elizabeth at her coronation, L.C. 2/4 (2).

stantly met: Spanish lace,[1] braided lace,[2] 'fyne whipped lace',[3] twisted lace of gold and silver,[4] bobbin lace, needlework-lace,[5] seaming lace,[6] parchment lace, purl lace, bone lace, bride lace, galoon lace, statute lace, tawdry lace, gold and silver lace, cutwork, and drawnwork.

The openwork lace was made in two ways: 1, with a needle in fabric, or parchment; 2, with bobbins on a cushion. Lace was made in fabric by withdrawing threads of the material to form open spaces, and buttonholing the remaining threads into designs. On parchment, it was built up stitch by stitch over a pattern outlined on the parchment. The cushions for bobbin lace were various shapes, according to the width and design of the lace to be made. Whatever their shape, they were firmly stuffed, and covered with a dark material. A parchment or paper pattern containing a pricked or inked design was stretched over the cushion. Pins were used to outline the design. Bobbins containing the thread were interlaced, twisting the thread around the pins and so making the lace, the pins in the completed work being removed and inserted farther along the design, as required.

Designs for lace, at first geometric, producing a wiry, ungraceful result, became more intricate and ornamental by the end of the sixteenth century; and some patterns, following the curious fashion in embroideries and tissues, showed human figures, animals, flowers, and insects.[7]

Lace made with the needle included purl, drawnwork, and cutwork; bone lace, billiment lace,[8] and some bride

[1] L.C. 2/3, for a doublet. 1572, Feuillerat, op. cit. 156.

[2] Of silk for 'embrawdering a jerkin withe', L.C. 2/3.

[3] Ibid. Also will of Breton, 1557: 'doublet of black sattin wt whypped Lace', *Works*, I. xvii.

[4] L.C. 2/3; 1552, L.C. 3/84.

[5] 1558, L.C. 2/4 (2); E. 154/2/19. 1559, A.O. 3/1106, for six white smocks edged 'cum white nedlework lace'; 1561, Add. MS. 35328: 'cxxiij ydes. white nedlework lace.' Gremio's 'Valance of Venice gold in needle-work' refers probably to embroidery, *Tam. Sh.* II. i. 348.

[6] *Devil is an Ass*, II. i. 492: 'lace to her smocks, broad seaming lace.'

[7] The portrait of Mary, Countess of Pembroke, Walpole, *Royal and Noble Authors*, shows an exquisite pattern of swans in the lace of her whisk.

[8] In list of robes of Edward VI was a jerkin bound with billiment lace of Venice silver and black silk, L.R. 2/12; 1571, among aliens, is mentioned William Crutall, 'Maker of byllament

lace were made with bobbins. The cheaper tawdry, galoon, hair, and statute laces were woven. Lace-looms were used in Elizabeth's day. In a pageant presented at a reception accorded her at Norwich, 1579, pictured looms, with weavers before them, were mounted on platforms. Above the looms were names of materials being woven. These included fringe and lace.[1] In 1621, complaint was made of aliens in London who kept their 'mysteries' to themselves and 'have been bould of late to devise engines for the workinge of tape, lace, ribbin, and such, wherin one man doth more than 7 Englishe men can do'.[2] The nature of these engines must be left to the imagination; no description of them is given. Machines for weaving openwork lace in imitation of the hand product were not invented until 1768.[3]

LACE IN THE DRAMA

Much has been said in the previous pages concerning the mention of lace in the drama. This section will discuss details of the kinds of lace, as they originated, and as they were used both in life and on the stage.

Gold and Silver Lace

Gold and silver lace, gold and silver bonework lace, gold and silver parchment lace were frequently listed in the same documents during the sixteenth century.[4] Whether these are two, or three, classes, the first being a generic name, is impossible to decide, for no contemporary definitions of the terms have been found. The early metal laces were plaited cords used to fasten articles of clothing;[5]

lace', *State Papers Dom.* lxxxiv, Dec. 2, 1571. See also Wray's inventory, *Antiquary*, xxxii. 117; and wills, as *Lancashire and Cheshire Wills*, 1588, liv. 139; also, 1594–5, L.C. 9/86: 'pro ii doz. de laquoe vocat billiment lace'; 1602–3, L.C. 9/83: 'vi virg. tenia de serico nigro vocat billiment lace.'

[1] Holinshed, *Chronicle*, iv. 381. 1579, Egerton MS. 2806, 142: 'Loome

lace'; 1579, A.O. 3/1109: 'loome lace aur venice et argent.'

[2] *Camden Soc. Pub.*, 1862, Intro., v.

[3] For history of machine laces, see Fekin, *Machine-wrought Hosiery and Lace Manufacture*.

[4] 1558–61, L.C. 5/84, &c.

[5] Hall, *Chronicle*, 526: 'A mantell lace of blew silke and Venys gold'; 1526, E. 101/419/18; 1558, L.R. 2/4 (2).

later, a flat braid, also called 'lace' was applied in designs over garments.[1] 'Clinquant' was a thin plate lace of
gold or silver, but the term came to mean glittering with
precious metal. The French troops outshone the English,
as described by Shakespeare in *Henry VIII*, through the
glitter of their gold laces.[2]

Parchment lace of gold is mentioned as a trimming for
a sleeve in 1542.[3] Authorities on lace have ever disputed
the definition of this lace. Lace made of metal thread
wound on thin threads of parchment is extant. The term
may also refer to the lace made with needle and thread
over patterns inked in parchment. Parchment lace is
mentioned in accounts during the entire sixteenth century. It garnished many garments: Spanish leather jerkins, velvet coats, satin doublets, cassocks, hats, and
handkerchiefs.[4]

All the gold lace of this century was not cords or braids.
Openwork bobbin lace was also made of the precious
metals. The 'shurt duble cufted and edged with silver
lace' inventoried among the goods of Richard Bretreton,
1558,[5] was evidently trimmed with the openwork lace
such as is seen on gloves and caps of this period.

Metal laces were in demand by gallants both for their

For process of making gold thread,
see Binet, op. cit. 211–12. Sept.
1604, a patent was granted to
Richard Dike and others to make
Venice gold and silver thread for 20
years, *C.S.P.D.* ix. 48.

[1] Hall describes a coat worn by
Henry VIII, 1540, as 'embrodered
with flatte golde of Dammaske with
small lace myxed between of the same
golde, and other laces of the same
so going traverse wyse, that the
grounde lyttle appered', *Chronicle*,
239. See description of cassock belonging to Earl of Surrey, 1543, L.R.
2/115. 'Braded lace for the King's
garments' is mentioned 1543, E.
101/423/12. The More (?) portrait
of Edward VI in the Louvre shows his
doublet, cassock, and hose braided in
an all-over design of gold.

[2] *Hen. VIII*, I. i. 19.

[3] *P. P. Ex. Prin. Mary*, 93, 143;
1545, *Lancashire and Cheshire Wills*,
li. 64: 'cappe withe parchement lace.'

[4] Jerkins: 1555, L.R. 2/119. 1558,
L.C. 5/84, 'parchement lace playne
red silke & golde'; 1571, *Durham
Wills*, ii. 362: 'greane p'chment lace'
is mentioned. 1572, Feuillerat, *Revels*,
156, parchment lace of watchet and
silver. 1580–85, *Antiquary*, xxxii. 81,
parchment lace is valued at only two
pence a yd. Cassocks, 1572, *Debate
Between Pride and Lowliness*, 19.
Hats, livery for footmen of Prince
Charles, 1623, E. 435/20. Parchment
lace may also have been painted
threads of parchment.

[5] *Lancashire and Cheshire Wills*,
xxxii. 178.

own garments and those of their servants. Such a custom
was not extravagant, since the servants could rip it off
and pawn it when they lacked food.[1] But gallants found
gold lace quite an expenditure,[2] and, with other luxuries,
sometimes the cause of their clothes being in pawn.[3]
Naturally, dishonest milliners took advantage of 'heirs',
selling them counterfeit gold for genuine.

Women shared men's desire for gold and silver lace.
It appeared on all parts of their costume: gowns, petticoats, ruffs, caps, and was worn by all classes of society,
from the poor maids to court ladies.[4]

Gold lace was even more fashionable in the seventeenth
than in the previous century. Howes wrote that all the
shops in London during the first dozen years of Elizabeth's reign had not as much lace as was to be found in
Cheapside fifty years later.[5] So much money was being
spent for foreign lace that James I gave Sir Giles Mom-
pesson a patent for its exclusive production in England;
whereupon, £10,000 worth of bullion and silver a month
was spent 'to make this unprofitable stuffe'.[6] In spite of
its extensive use, little of this lace survives. A few garments, such as caps, gloves, bodices, retain their gold
trimming, but most of them show broken threads where
the lace was formerly sewed. Lack of surviving lace is
due chiefly to an eighteenth-century custom of gold-
gathering, a fad for collecting gold laces, unravelling them
and selling the gold of which they were made.[7]

BONE LACE

Buy some coifs, handkerchiefs, or very good bonelace,
Mistress? (*Tu Quoque*, I. i. 19.)

The origin of bone lace, which was an openwork lace
of gold, silver—later of linen thread also—is not known,

[1] *Every Man Out of His Humour*, I.
ii. 101.
[2] *Anything for a Quiet Life*, I. i. 198.
[3] *Devil is an Ass*, III. i. 120.
[4] *Prog. Elizabeth*, iii. 6. In the
gallery of the Ashmolean Museum
is a portrait of an unknown lady,
who wears a ruff made entirely of gold
lace.
[5] P. 1039.
[6] Birch, *Court and Times James*,
ii. 239.
[7] De Genlis, *Mémoires*, iii. 174.
See M. Jourdain, *History of Old Lace*.

but the term seems to have been derived from bone bobbins or pins used in its making. Fuller's statement that
this lace was so named because it was first 'made with
bone bobbins (since wooden)'[1] is supported by numerous
references in royal wardrobe accounts to laces worked
over bone.[2] Shakespeare's picture of the maids 'who
weave their thread with bones' is probably descriptive of
bone lace.[3] This lace was made on a cushion, as were
other bobbin laces.[4]

The earliest reference to bone lace which the writer has
found is in the Great Wardrobe accounts of Henry VIII,
in September, 1545, when it is used for garnishing 'bon-
nittes'.[5] Fairholt, quoting Stowe, mentioned the hat of
Wyatt, which was 'edged with broad bone work lace',
attributing the costume to the elder Wyatt, who died in
1542. It was, however, the younger Wyatt who wore the
hat in 1554.[6] Even the oft-quoted references in early
Italian documents to *punto a spina* as bone lace are
questionable, since this phrase referred to a certain stitch
known as the 'through stitch'.[7]

Bone lace was made chiefly of 'venys golde', and 'bon-
nie silver' thread,[8] but also of white and black silk;[9] and

[1] *Worthies of England* (1662), 246–7.

[2] 1563, L.C. 9/57; 1579, A.O.
3/1109; 1587–8, L.C. 9/79; 1601–2,
L.C. 9/92. In 1559–60, L.C. 9/53,
occurs an item of 'vi virge Laquoi
Glauc. de Granado opat. sup. bobbins'; but laces made 'sup. oss.' are
far more numerous. For other references to bobbin laces, see, 1553, E.
154/2/39; 1561, A.O. 3/1106; 1565,
A.O. 1/1106; 1614, *Household Bk.
Howard*, 13; &c. Florio, *World of
Words*, 1598: '*ossoli*, bobbins to winde
silk upon.'

[3] *Tw. N.* II. iv. 45.

[4] 1574, 'What a pleasure it is . . . to
see her . . . take her cushion for bone
lace, or her rock to spinne', Hellowes,
*The Familiar Epistles of Sir Anthonie
of Guevara*, 512. 'Herring-bone lace'
is frequent in accounts of this period:
Durham Wills, xxxviii, 211, inventory

of a merchant, 1592; 1614, *Household
Bk. Howard*, 11; also Marston's
Scourge of Villanie, II. vii. 20, though
this term probably referred not to the
lace-implements, but to the pattern.

[5] E. 351/3025. Also 1546, E.
351/325.

[6] Kempe, *Loseley MSS.* 129.

[7] Florio, *World of Words*, 1611.

[8] 1546, E. 351/3025; 1547, L.C.
2/3; 1552, L.C. 5/84; 1553, E.
154/2/39; 1560–6, L.C. 9/54; 1566,
E. 154/2/39; 1573, Egerton MS. 2806;
1611, L.R. 2/121; 1612, *Archaeologia*, xxvi. 386. That it was expensive
is shown by the allowance, 1633, of
£1,000 a year for King Charles's linen
and bone lace, *C.S.P.D.* ccxxxiv. 83.

[9] 1559–60, L.C. 9/53; 1558, Egerton MS. 2806; 1598–9, L.C. 9/89;
1578, *Prog. Elizabeth*, ii. 255.

in Fuller's time, thread[1] was also used. In 1578, 'xj yards pirlye bone lace' is valued at 3s. 8d.,[2] which may indicate edging lace. Bone lace trimmed not only bonnets but cuffs of gloves, sleeves, scarves, night-rails, cuffs and ruffs, stomachers, aprons, cloaks, and even such linen as pillow-cases and sheets.[3]

The making of bone lace was considered one of the ac-complishments of a thrifty housewife,[4] though it could be purchased from any pedlar.[5] One bone lace seller, pre-sumably a merchant rather than a pedlar, has a memorial tablet erected by Honiton townsmen. On a wall of the older church in that borough is the inscription: 'Here lyeth ye Body of James Rodge of Honiton in ye County of Devon-shire Bone lace seller who hath given the poor of Honiton P'she the benefitte of 100 l for ever who deceased ye 27 July A D 1617 aetatis suae 50.'

BRIDE-LACE

Bride-lace was bobbin-made lace, buckram or silk rib-bon used to tie on the wedding-cup or on nosegays of flowers—especially scented rosemary—at weddings. Bride-laces possibly originated in the lover's custom of wearing laces in his hat as a symbol of love.[6] Machyn mentions

[1] *Worthies*, 247. Bone lace of black is priced at one shilling a yard in 1626. *Household Bk. Howard*, 239.

[2] *Richmond Wills*, 279. Lady Bacon bought 9 yds. for a ruff at 18d. a yd. in 1597, Bacon MSS. Univ. Chicago.

[3] Gloves, 1605, *Prog. James*, i. 589; sleeves, 1553, E. 154/2/39; scarves, 1566, Add. MS. 35328: 'Silver bone lase to edge Skarfes of oringe tawney sarcenet rounde aboute'; night-rails, 1599, A.O. 3/1106; 1560–1, L.C. 9/53; *Crudities*, i. 399; 1623, E. 101/436/9: 300 yds. were used for 22 ruffs and 24 pair cuffs; stomacher, 1595, L.C. 9/87; aprons, 1566, Add. MS. 35328; cloaks, 1557, *Lancashire and Cheshire Wills*, xxxii. 178; 1575, Egerton MS. 2806; 1599, L.R. 2/121; pillow-cases and sheets, 1612, E. 154/3/40; 1559, L.C. 9/539; *Prog. Elizabeth*, ii. 255.

[4] 'She cuts cambric at a thread, weaves bone lace', *Scornful Lady*, v. i. 296, which indicates that she can make cutwork as well as bone lace. Henslowe paid £5 on June 5, 1595, to a certain 'john gryges when I put mery henslow to him to learne al maner of workes & to learne bonelace', *Diary* i. 192. A curious item which probably repre-sented the lace production of one woman occurs in an 'Inventory of Goods at Hackney', 1601. It is: 'a pillow-bere with bonelase, cutwork, falling bandes, squares of bonelase and network and cuffs', E. 154/3/24.

[5] Accounts of Bacons, Shuttle-worths, and other families, have numerous items of lace purchased from pedlars who came to their estates.

[6] The curious *Pleasant Dialogue or Disputation Between the Cap and the*

bride-laces in 1560,[1] but the custom is probably much older.

The wearing of bride-laces is noted in literature as a custom of country folk and the lower class, though it may not have been confined to them. When Queen Elizabeth visited Kenilworth in 1575, a country wedding was arranged for her entertainment and all 'the lusty lads and bold bachelors' were marshalled, 'euery wight with hiz blu buckeram bridelace vpon a braunch of green broom (cauz rozemary iz skant thear) tyed on hiz leaft arme (for that syde lyez the heart)'.[2] Jonson's *Love's Welcome at Welbeck*[3] depicts a similar wedding. The six maids attending the bride were 'attired with buckram bride laces-begilt'.

A scene in Jonson's *Tale of a Tub* shows that bride-laces were a gift of the bride to the attendants on her husband. Turfe, seeing the maids enter with 'ribands, rosemary, and bay', remarked: 'We shall all ha' bride-laces or points.' (I. ii. 158.) Dorothea Target of *2 The Honest Whore*[4] threatened the constable with the furious words: '. . . the bride-laces that I give at my wedding shall serve to tie rosemary to both your coffins.'

Before the wedding, the lace-tied rosemary was worn on the left arm, but after the ceremony the nosegay was placed in the hat. After the marriage of Master John Frankford, of *Woman Killed With Kindness*, all the

> mad lads
> And country-lasses, every mother's child
> With nosegays and bride laces in their hats
> Dance all their country measures . . .[5]

Head, printed by Henry Benham, 1564, gives the cap's complaint that the head makes it wear among other objectionable ornament, 'Read, Yellow, and Blew laces'. The Head informs the Cap that 'he that weareth thee so hath a lusty lovers heart and is courtlike'.

[1] *Diary*, 240.

[2] *Prog. Elizabeth*, i. 442. In *Jack of Newbury* the bride is led to church 'betweene two sweete boyes, with Bride-laces and Rosemary tied about their silken sleeves', Deloney, *Works*, 22, 23.

[3] Gifford ed., viii. 127. Also *Custom of the Country*, v. i. 515. *2 If You Know Not Me*, I. i. 240: 'The horning busk and silken bride laces are in good repute with the parsons wife.'

[4] v. ii. 316. In *The Broken Heart*, IV. ii. 127, Penthea indicated a future wedding by the remark, 'We shall have points and bride-laces'.

[5] I. i. 87. See also *Two Angry Women of Abington*, line 495.

CUTWORK

Cutwork was of Italian origin.[1] Limited at first, as were other kinds of needlework, to decoration of ecclesiastical vestments, it was used during Shakespeare's age for trimming handkerchiefs, caps, bands, ruffs, stomachers, sleeves, smocks, and articles of household furnishing, as both drama and accounts show.[2]

Italian cutwork had appeared in England before 1577, since many New Year gifts of the Queen for that year were ornamented with it.[3] It was made by cutting away the material in squares, and filling the spaces with geometric designs of needlework. The cutting required skill; hence Elder Loveless's praise of a good wife: 'She cuts cambric at a thread.'[4] Filling the cut-out spaces was accomplished by working threads from one side or corner to the other, fastening these in the centre, and working over and around them with button-hole stitch, forming bars. 'Purls' also were a usual part of cutwork, and when this work was done in gold 'a pound a purl' was not a greatly exaggerated price.[5]

DRAWN-WORK

Drawn-work of a kind was practised by the Egyptians, as mummy cloths preserved in the British Museum testify. The material of one of these cloths is loosely woven linen

[1] L.C. 9/87; Add. MS. 5751.

[2] Handkerchiefs, *Bartholomew Fair*, IV. i. 216; bands: *Every Man Out of His Humour*, IV. vi. 90; 1584, A.O. 1/2341; *Prog. James*, i. 598: 'one shirt fyne holland, the band and cuffs of cutwork'; stomachers: 1587, E. 351/3061; smocks: 1595, L.C. 9/87; smocks: *Parliament of Love*, II. i. 49; *Four Plays In One*, Time, sc. i; *Prog. Elizabeth*, iii. 11. There are numerous references in drama to cutwork whose use is not specified.

[3] *Prog. Elizabeth*, ii. 68, 70, 76, 77, &c. The term cutwork applied to garments in the reign of Richard II, by John Hardyng, *Chronicle*, fol. cxiiii, indicated designs cut from fabrics and sewed on. The term was so used in the sixteenth century; 1510: 'For hemming and cutworks for the ladies kirtles and gowns', *Letters and Papers Henry VIII*, ii. 2, 1491; 1536–6, E. 315/45.

[4] *Scornful Lady*, v. i. 296; *City Match*, Dodsley, xiii. 273: 'and you return to cutwork,' i.e. to her former occupation as a lace-maker. *Devil is an Ass*, III. i. 133.

[5] *Devil's Law Case*, II. i. 179. Cf. 1601–2, A.O. 1/2344/29: one yard Flanders cutwork with Italian purl, cost 33s. 4d.; Add. MS. 5451, fols. 33–4.

from which the weft threads have been drawn out, forming designs. Instead of being cut off, these threads are worked back through the material around the edges of the designs, causing the parts there to appear thicker and more closely woven than does the remainder. Coloured wool worked through the design supplied the missing threads. In the sixteenth century, coloured silk often supplied the missing threads, though much of the Italian work was done with linen thread.

Known to England by the fifties, drawn-work was used for smocks, ruffs, rails, and other neckwear, besides such household decorations as cushion-cloths of the kind which Bianca of *Women Beware Women* desires for the furnishing of her chamber.[1]

Galoon Lace

'Oh, for a whip to make him galoon laces!'[2] is almost a definition, for galoon was a tape or braid, sometimes of silk,[3] used for binding and trimming. The *Oxford English Dictionary* suggests an origin in the French *galon*, with a possible connexion with gallant, and states that the substantive first appears in the seventeenth century.

Braids resembling galoon have been found in Egyptian tombs,[4] but there is no means of knowing how old the name is. An inventory made in 1589 of the goods of John Marston, mercer, lists eight pounds of 'Galowne and curtoe lace'.[5] Since it was valued by weight, it was probably enriched by metal, for silk galoon usually sold by pieces of a dozen yards.[6] In 1600, Philip Gawdy, who had been requested to purchase tawny velvet, tawny and gold

[1] III. i. 19. 1559, A.O. 3/1106: 'alteringe bande de smocke alb de ope tract.; . . . pro iiij smocks de drawne worke le manic. ruffe wristband & coller de blacke worke'. 1585, Egerton MS., 2806: 'for drawing and working with blak silke drawnework sixe smockes of fine holland clothe.' 1579–80, L.C. 9/72, 'ruff de tel holland with drawne work de blacke silke'; 1582–3, L.C. 9/74: 'Pro ij Qwoyfes nocturn et ij rayles nocturn de tel holland bon

opat cum opē. tract. de serico nigro.'
[2] *Philaster*, v. i. 393.
[3] 1606–7, L.C. 9/95, 'galoone of silk', 'galowne de serico carnation'. 1617, A.O. 1/2348, 'Crimsen in grain galoon lace'. 1630–31, L.C. 9/99, 'Gallowne de crimsen ingraine'.
[4] Fig. 7, E. Jackson, *History of Handmade Lace*, London, 1900.
[5] E. 154/3/19.
[6] 1619, *Shuttleworth Accts.* xli. 236, 1s. 10d. a doz. yds.

galoon lace, and metal buttons for cloaks of his brother's men, wrote of his purchases. Going to St, Martin's for the lace, he found that 'bynding and gallowne laces' were 'stale' (fol. 127), and decided to purchase another kind. Galoon lace, therefore, must have been used many years before that date.

HAIR LACE

A hair lace was a braid or ribbon used before the invention of hairpins for tying about the head to bind up the hair.[1] It was not a lace made of hair, as is often stated. Hair laces were placed about the head in bandeau fashion, or entwined in the hair for decoration.[2]

Though ribbon was often the material for these laces,[3] the pedlar's pack of *The Four PP* contained 'laces round and flat for women's heads' (p. 36), showing that the cord, as well as the braid, variety was used, and the former was evidently the kind to which Middleton referred in *The Family of Love*, as suggestive of whip thongs (I. ii. 42).

PURL

Purl lace was a narrow, needle-made lace of silk, silver, or gold frequently having deep scallops or 'peakes', as they are termed. The minute loops which characterized the patterns gave the name *purl* to such laces.[4]

The earliest reference which the author has noted to purl is in the expenses for the wedding clothes of Mary Neville, 1530.[5] This may have indicated pearl, as may also Queen Mary's gown of black velvet with 'an edge of purle and pipes of gold',[6] though one of Queen Eliza-

---

[1] 1524, *Letters and Papers Henry VIII*, iii. 146: 'i oz. reband for hair laces.' Florio, 1598: '*Tenia*, a woman's head-band, fillet, or lace to tye up the haire.'

[2] 1530, *Calisto and Melibaea*, A iij: 'Hair which is so goodly crisped to her heels tied with fine lace.'

[3] 1575, Egerton MS. 2806: 'Heare-lasing Rebande of sundry coloures.'

[4] Florio, 1611: '*rosette*, rose purles or work on bone lace'; '*rotelle*, little wheeles or round purles in bone lace'; '*ingasiare*, to work purle or stitch work.' Add. MS. 35328: 'Three yards of black hollowe lace of Jean silke purled on both sides.' 1594-5, L.C. 9/86: 'j virge laqu. fact. de crine braided cum purles de crine.'

[5] 'eyge of purle', printed 'pearl', in *Surtees Soc. Pub.* xli. 362.

[6] L.R. 2/121.

beth's New Year gifts, 1561–62, of 'creppens of lawne garnished with gold and silver purle'[1] is unmistakable. Purl lace is noted in the Lord Chamberlain's accounts of 1559–60[2] and 1582–3, and 'fayre peake' purl is provided for ruffs and cuffs for Prince Charles, 1617–18.[3]

Purl was probably of Italian origin; early references to it are to 'Italian purl'. Flanders cutwork with Italian purl is noted quite frequently in the Queen's[4] accounts from 1587. 'Tom of all Trades' advises parents not to allow girls to learn 'curious Italiã purles, or French borders, but only plaine workes of all kinds'.[5] Naturally, lacemakers of other nations invented their purls. Tales's boast that Goosecap can 'work you needlework edgings, French purls from an angel to four angels a pound',[6] shows the usual price of such work. William Freke, a student at Oxford, paid over two shillings an ounce for purl lace in 1623; Lord Howard paid six shillings an ounce for 'gould and silver purle' in 1620.

The importation of foreign 'purles, cutworks and Bone-laces' was forbidden in 1635 as protection for the lace-makers of England and Wales.[7] The consumption of bullion was so large, however, that five months later a proclamation was issued charging that 'no coin, Plate, Bullion shall be hereafter used in the making of Gold and Silver Thread, Copper guilt or silvered Gold and silver foliat, Purles, Oaes, Spangles, Wire . . . but what shall be imported'.[8]

STATUTE LACE

Statute lace was made of yarn whose weight was regulated by statute. It was woven, rather than made by bob-

---

[1] *Prog. Elizabeth*, i. 113, 1577; ii. 67: 'kyrtill . . . embraudered with purles of gold like cloudes' means the embroidery was characterized by the purl stitch.

[2] L.C. 9/53: 'Pro v virg. purle lace de auro et arg. venice'; L.R. 9/74.

[3] E. 101/434/9.

[4] Add. MS. 5751 offers examples.

[5] *Tom of all Trades or the plaine*

Pathway to Preferment, London, 1631, p. 47.

[6] *Sir Giles Goosecap*, II. i. 312. Cf. *Eng. Hist. Rev.* vii. 98. *Household Bk. Howard*, 145.

[7] *Foedera*, xix. 690–1. This included 'commodities laced or edged therewith'.

[8] Ibid. xix. 718.

bin or needle.[1] It was much cheaper than other lace,[2] and was worn by the lower class of persons.

TAWDRY LACE

Tawdry lace was a braid, supposed to have been named from St. Etheldreda, A.D. 630–679, a princess of East Anglia and founder of the cathedral and monastery of Ely, of which she was first abbess. According to a story told by Bede, she was accustomed to wear a carcanet of jewels which caused a swelling in her neck.[3] Two conjectural origins for the lace have been offered: that she substituted a silk necklace for the jewels in order to conceal her neck, or that a lace was offered at fairs[4] held in her honour many years after her death. Such lace was called Audry or tawdry lace, a shortened form of St. Audry. Whether or not the entire legend is correct, the lace seems to have been named after her. The earliest reference which the writer has found calls it 'Awdre lace', 1526,[5] and Palsgrave refers to it as 'Seynt Audries lace'.

Spenser mentions it in *The Shepherds' Calender*,[6] Shakespeare in *The Winter's Tale* (IV. iii. 252), and Fletcher in *The Faithful Shepherdess* (IV. i. 42).

---

[1] *Passamanio d' accio*, statute lace. *Accio* is defined by Florio, 1598, as 'any yarne that is to be woven, spining crewel or statute'.

[2] 1578, *Richmond Wills*, 279, valued at 7s. 10d. a gross. This is the earliest known reference to the lace. 1588, *Antiquary*, xxxii. 54, 4s.; 1597, *Durham Wills*, xxxviii. 282, 3 gross cost 30s.; *Shuttleworth Accts.* 1599, xxv. 117, cost 11d. a doz. See also Greene,

Works, xiv. 34.

[3] *Ecclesiastical History*, IV. ix.

[4] Southey, *Omniana*, i. 9; also *O.E.D.*

[5] *Letters and Papers Henry VIII*, iv. 1, entry 1906: '3 bundles of Audre laces.' But it is called Tawdry lace by 1561: see *A Declaration of Edmonde Bonner's Articles*, fol. 80: 'holy tawdrye laces.'

[6] 'April', i. 135.

VIII

EMBROIDERY AND ORNAMENT

THE earliest known work which may be called embroidery
—but which was made by the tapestry process—is that
discovered by Mr. Howard Carter in the tomb of a
Pharaoh at Thebes. This work, executed about 1500 B.C.,
is now in the Cairo Museum. No embroidery from ancient Assyrian civilization has survived, but portions of
garments found in a grave in the Crimea, evidently of the
fourth century before Christ, show woollen embroidery.[1]
Owing to dominance of Byzantine art, no national styles
of embroidery arose in Europe until after the Latin sack
of Constantinople in 1204; and all early English embroidery up to the Tudor period must be judged by
ecclesiastical vestments, for no domestic articles of these
centuries are extant.

Documentary evidence of Anglo-Saxon skill in needlework is not wanting, and it is not unreasonable to suppose
that the noble ladies executed embroidery prior to the
seventh century, for embroidery began with evangeliza-
tion.[2] Edith, queen of Edward the Confessor, embroidered his robes.[3] Young girls taught by Ædelswitha are
said to have embroidered for St. Hilda's Abbey.[4] Aldwid,
according to The Doomsday Survey of Buckinghamshire,
taught Sheriff Godric's daughter 'aurifrisium operari', and
was given in payment a half hide.[5] The only known surviving embroidery of this period is a stole and maniple
worked by order of Queen Ælflaeda for Fridestan, Bishop
of Winchester, early in the tenth century. These pieces,
found in the tomb of St. Cuthbert, are thought to have
been placed there by Æthelstan, step-son of Ælflaeda,
when he visited the shrine in 936. Their identity is un-

---

[1] Kendrick, *A Book of Old Embroidery*, 3; also A. S. Cole, 'Some Aspects
of Ancient and Modern Embroidery',
Jour. Soc. of Arts, l. 958.

[2] *Archaeologia*, xvii. 93.

[3] Jourdain, *English Secular Embroidery*, 8.

[4] A. F. Kendrick, *English Needlework*, 8 ff.

[5] *V.C.H. Bucks.* i. 221.

mistakable because they contain the inscription: 'Ælfflæd fieri precepit Pio episcopo Fridestano.' They are now in the Cathedral Library at Durham.

When William the Conqueror returned to Normandy after the Battle of Hastings, the beauty of his embroidered robes astonished his countrymen. Thus the fame of English needlework spread. Much of it was executed in convents for ecclesiastical use. Scenes from the life of Our Lord and the Virgin, legends concerning St. Dunstan, St. Thomas Becket, St. Etheldreda or Audrey, St. Ethelbert, Edward the Confessor, and others were pictured in gold thread on vestments and church goods. Pope Innocent IV in 1246 sent to the Cistercian Order in England for embroideries, and thereafter many English-made vestments went to Rome, for 'opus anglicanum'[1] had become famous in all the Christian world, and its fame lasted until the middle of the fourteenth century. One splendid example of thirteenth-century work is preserved in the Victoria and Albert Museum. It is the Syon Cope, which represents the Coronation of the Virgin, the Crucifixion, Christ's meeting with Mary Magdalene in the garden, the death and burial of the Virgin, the hierarchies of angels, and the archangel Michael killing the Dragon.

Thirteenth-century embroideries, writes Kendrick, 'have a venerableness and dignity in figures and genuine religious spirit which the later and more correctly designed work does not always possess'.[2] The fourteenth century, which brought an increasing secular demand for embroidery, saw the beginning of decadence in the ecclesiastical work. Embroidery was used on costume of all who could afford it—kings or squires alike—in household decoration—even on beds, screens, and hangings; and King Edward's attempt in 1362 to limit its use to persons having an income of 400 marks a year was not wholly effective. A law passed in 1363[3] forbade any artificer to

[1] Fragments of metallic embroidery removed from the tomb of Bishop Walter de Cantelupe (1237–66) are preserved in the Victoria and Albert, and British Museums.
[2] *English Embroidery*, 26.
[3] *Rot. Parl.* ii. 279 a.

exercise more than one 'mistery', but excepted 'silk-women',
who were allowed to carry on the work of embroidery in
addition to any other trade in which they were engaged![1]
Such a law seemed designed to increase production. Few
traces of medieval embroidery survive. Gone are the
king's robes and the squire's gown 'embrouded—as it
were a mede'. One interesting example, however, is still
to be seen in Canterbury Cathedral—the surcoat of the
Black Prince. This faded, disintegrating garment of once
splendid blue and red velvet, embroidered in gold with
the Royal Arms of England, hangs above the tomb on
which lies his effigy represented as clad in a surcoat—its
counterpart, even to a half fleur-de-lis, occurring in the
design.

The decadence of embroidery in the late fourteenth
century was not entirely due to its secular use. England's
commercial relations were extending to more and more
of the known world, and she was importing luxuries such
as damasks, brocades, and velvets, whose sumptuousness
and beauty of design discouraged superior needlework,
which was necessarily slow. From the fifteenth century
the 'Wardens of Brauderie' waged a fight against 'un-
sufficient stuff undewly wrought', securing Royal writs
to prevent deceitful workmanship and materials.[2] But
gold embroidery was demanded, and economy dictated
the use of small amounts of the precious metal to make a
great show. Gilded parchment and thin strips of gold
wire spun upon silk were substituted for pure gold thread.
Thin spangles were added to increase the glitter. Designs,
however, to the credit of the fifteenth century, became
simpler.

The sixteenth century was predominantly the age of
embroidered costume. Every article, from pantofles to
caps, was 'wrought' or 'spotted' with gold or silver thread,
coloured silks, metal plate, spangles and 'owes'. At first,
embroidery decorated accessories only such as bands,
ruffs, guards; but, with the manufacture of needles in

---

[1] *Rot. Parl.* ii. 278.
[2] Ibid. *2 Hen. VI*, c. x; *4 Hen. VII*, c. 22.

England,[1] came the increased use of garments covered by embroidery. This rage for 'all-over' work cannot be credited to the abundance of needles alone; Spanish influence was partly responsible. Numerous are allusions in wardrobe accounts to 'Spanish workes'. Fine imported linens offered excellent ground for designs in coloured silks and metal thread, and especially for 'black-work', which remained in favour for nearly a century, though Bacon observed in his essay on Adversity: 'We see in needleworks and embroideries, it is more pleasing to have a lively work upon a sad and solemn ground than to have a dark and melancholy work upon a lightsome ground.'

A full discussion of embroidery stitches would occupy a volume. Only a few are noted in the drama: 'the tent stitch' named in *City Match*[2] was, of course, *petit point*; the 'broad stitch' of *Mother Bombie*, and the 'through stitch' of *Magnetic Lady*,[3] are self-explanatory; the 'true stitch' is best described by Jonson's: 'What, true stitch, sister! both your sides alike!'[4] There were also the cope stitch or 'cope work',[5] which may have been the split stitch so common in ecclesiastical embroidery, the high stitch, the purl stitch, back stitch, cypher stitch, Irish stitch, and the fool's stitch—so called because it was easy to make— besides 'black work', 'white work', and 'laid work', the last of which differed from couching in that the mass of silk thread was first laid on the surface, and the auxiliary stitches added afterwards.[6] Such stitches are of great interest to the embroidery artist or collector, but any attempt at their

[1] According to Howes, *Annales*, 1038, a negro attempted the manufacture of fine Spanish needles, during Mary's reign, but the art was lost at his death, and was reintroduced in the village of Long Crendon, 1560, by Christopher Greening. See also *V.C.H. Bucks*. ii. 117.

[2] Dodsley, xiii. 273.

[3] *Mother Bombie*, I. iii. 86; *Magnetic Lady*, IV. i. 9.

[4] *Case is Altered*, II. iii. 16. True

stitch is frequently mentioned in the Queen's wardrobe accounts during the nineties and thereafter.

[5] 1551–60, Hall, *Elizabethan Society*, 151: 'a tester of blewe and white velvett, paynd & embrodered with cope worcke of gould.'

[6] Laid work was used for flat effects, couching for outlines. In 1546, 'vi laid workes' were purchased for the 'frowes paste' of Princess Elizabeth, E. 351/3045.

full exposition would cause a student of the drama to beg with Valeria: 'Come, lay aside your stitchery.'

The Reformation in England had affected the production of ecclesiastical embroideries; the destruction of the monasteries and the wholesale confiscation of church goods caused a cessation of needlework for the enrichment of vestments. The immense wealth of embroidery possessed by churches until the middle of the Reformation had, by Elizabeth's reign, passed into private hands to be used for household decoration, or had been destroyed for the sake of the gold it contained.[1] Some idea of this destruction can be gained from the following items of 1571: 'Thoms Homes upholster for thaltering of certain coapes into Quisshion chairs . . . xi li. viij s vij d'; 'To Mr. Creme goldsmyth for a silver pott parcell guylt . . . waing li oz. Toward wch charge ther went xxxiij oz iij qrts sylver that cam of biring' (burning) 'of certen coapes at v s the oz amounting to viij li xviij s ix d. To the goldsmyth in regard for burnyng the said coapes vj s viij d.' Surely posterity is indebted to those Orders who, like the owners of the Syon Cope, carried some of their vestments into exile with them and lovingly preserved these treasures until they could be safely returned to England.

Possibly this appropriation of sacred embroidery influenced the Elizabethan tendency to emblems, as it had to 'ecclesiastical stitches', and led to the 'religious petticoats', 'holy embroideries' on smocks, and 'historical shirts' satirized in the next century. Towards the end of the century, flowers, insects, and animals entered the designs. Gowns of black velvet were embroidered all over 'with wormes of silk of sundrie colours'; gowns of white cloth of silver in 'workes of yellow silke like flies, wormes, and snailes'; gownes of lawn, with 'fountaines, snakes, swordes, and other devises'; mantles of ash-colour were 'flourished w^t oaken leaves of gold and silver'; petticoats were covered 'w^t roses of gould'.[2] The geometric symmetry

[1] Kendrick, *English Embroidery*, 67. *The History of English Secular Embroidery*, by M. Jourdain, contains excellent discussion of Tudor and Stuart embroidery.

[2] *Prog. Elizabeth*, ii. 255, 504;

of the designs was probably copied from woven fabrics, and their elaborateness was due partly to the influence of highly skilled embroiderers retained in the households of royal and noble families.[1] Others depended upon the commercial work of such embroiderers as are satirized in *Sir Giles Goosecap*: 'He will work you any flower to the life, as like it as if it grew in the very place, and being a delicate perfumer, he will give it you his perfect and natural savour. . . . He will make you flies and worms of all sorts, most lively, and is now working a whole bed embroidered with nothing but glow-worms; whose lights 'a has so perfectly done, that you may go to bed in the chamber, . . . without a candle' (ii. i. 317–25).

Elizabethan patterns occupied embroiderers of the Jacobean period, but they were less effective, lacking the grace and something of the harmony of colour combinations which characterized the work of the former period. 'Spots' of small flowers and fruits like those of Othello's handkerchief continued until the reign of Charles I. A certain stiffness in the Stuart presentation, together with the extensive use of spangles, 'owes', jewels, pearls, and various metal plate and wire—including the coiled-spring type—served to give much of the embroidery of this period a rigid and clogged appearance, which, in spite of its technical cleverness, is far from satisfying.

BLACK-WORK

Nay, if you will needs be starching of ruffs, and sewing of black-work, . . . I will become a tyrant. (*Love's Cure*, ii. i. 150.)

The black-work waistcoat in *Amends for Ladies* (iii. i. 33), and the name wrought in black-work mentioned in *Westward Hoe* (ii. i. 142), have puzzled editors. It was an embroidery of black silk characterized by an all-over pattern of slender stems and leaves in continuous scrolling, which originated possibly in Spain; though black-work

L.R. 2/121. Stubbes, in his *Anatomy*, inveighs against this 'clogging' of garments with embroidery. See Plate I.
[1] *P. P. Ex. Henry VIII*, 103, 124, 128, &c.; *Cal. Pat. Rolls*, June 9, 1547, m. 33; *Prog. Elizabeth*, i. 271; A.O. 1/2339–44.

and black Spanish work are distinguished in accounts. For instance, in 1545, 'vi virg de laques hispani nigr pro edginge 1 smocke' is charged in the Great Wardrobe accounts;[1] and, in 1561, an item of 'una Interula cum le collar manir. et wrestband opat cu. ope. nigr.'[2] Queen Elizabeth's New Year's gifts, 1577–9, included 'pillow-beres', handkerchiefs, 'cusshen cloths', collars and cuffs 'wrought' with black-work.[3] In 1577 Sir Philip Sidney gave her a smock of cambric whose sleeves and collar were of black-work. Men showed a preference for this embroidery on their shirts and night-caps,[4] and at the height of its fashion, i.e. 1570–90, it decorated not only garments, but tooth-cloths, table covers, book-binding. Its popularity declined during the reign of James I, and by 1630 it was out of fashion.

MISCELLANEOUS TRIMMING AND ORNA-MENTATION

In addition to lace and embroidery, other ornamentation of costume was practised. The most favoured trimming was the guard, both plain, and embroidered. Oes and spangles were used extensively in embroidery; and pinking and slashing were fashionable until the Puritan régime.

GUARD

A guard was a band or border placed on a garment for ornament. The material of guards was, of course, different from that of the garment which they ornamented; usually also, the colours contrasted; for instance, bonnets guarded

[1] E. 351/3025. 1561, A.O. 3/1106: 'xvi virg. op. hispan. pro ruff.' 1578, *Prog. Elizabeth*, ii. 259, 'sixe faire handkerchiefs of camebrake of blake Spanish worke edged with a brode bone lace'. 1598–9, L.C. 9/89, Spanish work of divers colours.

[2] A.O. 3/1106.

[3] *Prog. Elizabeth*, ii. 76, 255, 259, 260. See also, 1601, E. 154/3/24; 1618,

E. 154/4/6, &c., for 'blacke-worke night rayl', doublets, &c.

[4] The portrait of the Earl of Surrey at Hampton Court illustrates this work on men's shirts. William Freke, an Oxford student, purchased in 1629 a 'blackeworke and gold cappe' for the high price of 17s. 6d., *Eng. Hist. Rev.* vii. 99.

with sarcenet, great-coats with broad guards of russet velvet and white kersey hose with yellow guards were provided for revels 1514–27, and the dramatic records of Queen's College, 1546, show woollen coats guarded with 'fustian à Napes'.[1] In the early sixteenth century, royalty, nobles, and their attendants favoured guards, but by the end of the century guards had become the mark of footmen and other servants.[2]

Plain guards, or the mere 'laying cloath upon cloath', were not ornamental enough for royalty, and embroidered guards were introduced, some time before 1547. An inventory of the wardrobe of Henry VIII, made 9 September of that year, includes a 'Coate of purple clothe of silver with knottes having a garde of purple vellat embraudered with veanice golde', and among the 'Stuffe remaynning at Westm̃.' November 12, 1549—some of which had belonged to King Henry—was a 'gowne wth a square Cape of crymsen vellat and crymsen Satten . . . wth a garde of crymsen vellat embrauthered wth damask golde'.[3] The Lord Chamberlain's accounts for the coronation of Edward VI record the expense of 'embrouderinge the gowne with wreathes of venyse golde upon the gardes and forevent', but by that time nobles also were wearing embroidered guards.[4]

The Lord of Misrule for the Christmas celebration at Court 1552 wore a robe of white 'baudkyn garded w^t a greet embrothered garde of cloth of goulde wrought in knotts' and a 'cote' of 'fyne flatt silver' with 'an embrothered garde of leves of goulde' and coloured silke.[5]

[1] 1514, *Letters and Papers Henry VIII*, i. 719; 1520, iii. 2, 719: 1527, IV. ii. 1528. 1546, *Malone Soc. Coll.* II. ii. 195.

[2] The wardrobes of Henry VIII, Edward VI, and Elizabeth show many guards. See L.R. 2/121; 1564, *Prog. Elizabeth*, i. 191; 1578, ii. 259, iii. 503. When the Princess Elizabeth passed through London in 1556, she was attended by a great company of men in red coats guarded with black velvet. Machyn, *Diary*, 120. There are numerous allusions in plays to the guards on costume of servants, *Merch. of V.* II. ii. 170; *Meas. for M.* III. i. 95; *Albumazar*, III. v. 79.

[3] Coat, Harl. MS. 1419 A, fol. 91 verso; gown, Harl. MS. 1419 B, fol. 151.

[4] Lord Chamberlain 2/3 (2); also L.R. 2/115, inventory of effects of Earl of Surrey, 'a Doblet of crymsen sattin guarded with small gardes of vellut embradered with lace of golde'— the lace indicating narrow braid.

[5] Kempe, *Loseley MSS.* 45.

From the fifties until the reign of Charles I, embroidered guards are found in the wardrobe accounts of the middle and lower classes,[1] though they were worn also by ladies at court.[2] They could not, however, be counted a 'new' fashion at Court, especially for royalty. The question of date of *Cambises* needs to be reconsidered. In spite of external and internal evidence thus far produced, it seems probable that the queen bade her first farewell to court, 'to brodered gards and all these fashions new',[3] before 1569.

OES

In 1575 a patent was granted Robert Sharp giving him the right to manufacture spangles and oes of gold.[4] Oes were eyelets fastened to the material in design such as squares, 'esses', wheat ears, or powdered over the whole surface.[5] They were worn at Court in 1579[6] and were probably then a fairly new style, for they appear in the royal wardrobe frequently after the seventies; bodices, doublets, foreparts, gowns, petticoats, rails, and all costume accessories were trimmed with oes. This trimming was very effective on the stage, and was much used in masques. Gowns embroidered with oes of gold and silver were used at the Oxford performance on the occasion of the visit of King James in August 1605, in Chapman's *Masque of the Inns of Court*, 1613, Honour wore a 'vaile of net lawne embroiderd wth Oes' and spangles, and the lords who took part in Jonson's *Masque of Hymen*, 1616,

---

[1] 1557, Breton, *Works*, I. xvii: '. . . my best damaske gowne wth the Imbrodered gard.'

[2] 1568, Egerton MS. 2806; 1578, *Prog. Elizabeth*, ii. 255. Heywood rails against 'braudered gardes' as one of the extravagances of his age. 1562, *Fifth Hundred of Epigrams*, 19. A will of 1638 leaves a petticoat with an 'embroydred gard about it', *Lancashire and Cheshire Wills*, liv. 205. (Its age is not given.)

[3] F. 3. Sisammes, the judge, also suggests that the embroidered guard was peculiar to Court:

'Even now the king hath me extoll'd, and set me up aloft, Now may I weare the bordred gard, and lie in downe-bed soft'   (A 4). For a more complete discussion, see *P.M.L.A.* xlix. 459–61.

[4] D'Ewes, *Jour. House Commons*, 650.

[5] See the Lord Chamberlain's accounts between 1580–1600; also my more complete discussion of this subject in *Rev. Eng. Studies*, vii. 198–200. For many references to oes as trimming see index.

[6] Egerton MSS. 2805, 149. See also *Prog. Elizabeth*, iii. 5, 6, 7, 9, 456, &c.

wore mantels embroidered with oes.[1] Lord Howard paid
six shillings an ounce for gold and silver 'oese' in 1620.
Oes continued to be used throughout the reign of Charles I.

PINKING

'O, he lookt somwhat like a spunge in that pinckt yellow
doublet, me thought'[2] is a very good description, for pinking was a term applied to the cutting of small holes or
slits, one-sixteenth to three-fourths of an inch in length,
either in the materials[3] or in the finished garment. Cutting longer slits was known as 'scissoring', slashing, or
'jagging', and should be distinguished from pinking.
Both were practised early in the sixteenth century, but
the latter became especially fashionable after 1545.[4]
Gowns, suits, partlets, sleeves, doublets, hose, hats, and
shoes were pinked, the last of which plays an important
part in *The Shoemaker's Holiday*.[5] It was not uncommon
for a gown to have from one to nine thousand 'pinks'.[6]

Mercers and tailors contrived new styles in pinking.

[1] In order of their mention: *Malone Soc. Coll.* I. iii. 258-9; Pearson ed. Chapman, *Works*, iii. 94; Gifford ed. Jonson, *Works*, vii. 71. Oes were made also in copper. *Household Bk. Howard*, 114, 145, 206, 232 mentions oes in several metals. See discussion of *purl.* 1623, L.C. 5/5/38: 'Imbroder-inge two yards of satten in borders for roses wth silver twist and oes.'

[2] *Every Man Out of His Humour*, II. iii. 15.

[3] 1577, A.O. 3/1109: 'pro sciss. et pinking satin'; also Middleton, *Works*, viii. 23. In leather, only the grain was cut.

[4] 1509, *Accts. Lord High Treas. Scotland*, ii. 221: 'for pynking of the sleffis' of a gown; 1548, Starkey, *Eng-land under Henry VIII*, 80, discusses the beginning of pinking. Gowns, 1581, Egerton MS. 2806: 'for making of the nether partes of a frenche gowne of blacke pinked sattin embr. wth leaves of heare colord sattin'; 1599, L.R. 2/121: 'one ffrenche gowne of

blacke Sattin cut and pinkd allouer.' Partlet, 1553, L.R. 2/19: 'a partlett of blacke vellet pinked, tuffed and lozened.' Sleeves, 1562, A.O. 3/1106: 'pro manicarum de Sattin alb sciss. et pinkt.' Doublet, 1546, L.C. 2/3: 'cut-tinge rasinge and pynkinge of the saide doblett of blacke Sattin wth dyvers busy workes.' Hose, 1546, L.C. 2/3; 1551, E. 351/3026. Hats, *infra*, also *Henry VIII*, v. iv. 52.

[5] Vol. i, p. 16; also *Friar Bacon's Prophecy*, iv. 282; *Tam. Sh.* IV. i. 136; *Ham.* III. ii. 288. Holme, *Academie of Armourie*: 'That is termed the pinking of a Shooe, when the grain of leather is raised by a sharp-pointed Tool, that the inner part is seen; which is done in a certain order and also into roses & flowers as they fancy.'

[6] 1573, Egerton MS. 2806: 'Itm for weltinge and pinkinge of a french Gowne of vellat wth nyne thousande pinkes'; 1580, ibid.: 'for one thou-sande and a halfe pynkes' for a 'kyr-tell', 'circoate', and 'Whodde'.

Extant garments of the sixteenth and early seventeenth centuries show a progression from the straight pink of the fifties through the chevron design of the eighties and nine-ties,[1] to the saw-tooth style of the next century. The style of one's 'pinks' was as important as the style of one's gown, doublet, or cloak. In a letter to his brother, 1597, Philip Gawdy, who kept his family informed of the latest modes, wrote that he had sent a hat and feather, the hat 'pinked of the newest fashion' (fol. 121). To prevent ravelling, pinking was done on the bias of the material, and the designs were governed by the pinker's imagination. Since pinked garments were usually lined with material of con-trasting colour, such garments offered rich possibilities for colour effects.

[1] 1599, L.R. 2/121: 'blacke Taphata pinkt shevronwise.'

COSTUME

IX

NECKWEAR

'All manners of attire came first into the City and Countrey from the Court, which being once receiued by the common people, and by the very Stage-players themselues, the Courtiers iustly cast off, and take new fashions . . . and whosoeuer weares the old, men looke vpon him as vpon a picture in Arras hangings. For it is prouerbially said that we may eate according to our owne appetite, but in our apparell must follow the fashion of the multitude with whom we liue.' (Moryson, *Itinerary*, i. 199.)

The Band

A BAND was a collar of holland, lawn, cambric, or other linen, worn about the neck of the shirt or bodice.[1] Henry VIII, said Peacham, was the first English person to wear a band and 'that very plaine, without lace, about an inch or two in depth'.[2]

According to their size, ornamentation, and style, bands were known as: 1. plain, worn until the advent of the ruff, *circa* 1550; 2. the falling band, *rabat* or French fall, introduced about 1580, so called because it was normally turned down, and in the reign of King Charles I extended out over the shoulders; 3. the ruff or ruff-band, which was multi-pleated and stiff. The plain band was only an upright collar, embroidered or edged with a narrow ruffle. The falling band, Plate II, consisted of a 'stock' or strip fastened to the shirt by pins,[3] a straight collar made to fit the neck by darts or 'clocks', and strings to tie it in front.[4] From the eighties the band as well as

---

[1] 1592, L.C. 9/82, 4 falling bands of stitched cambric; ruffs of holland cloth. 1626, *Household Bk. Howard,* lxviii. 239, 'for 20 ells of hollin for sherts for my Lord, and lawne and cambrick for bands'. 1631, E. 352/3097, 'cuffs & bands of cobwebbe laune'.

[2] *Truth of our Times,* 61.

[3] *Satiro-mastix,* i. 186; *Christ's Tears,* 161.

[4] Band strings appear in portraits of the period, Plate VIII, and are mentioned in the drama: *Duchess of Malfi,*

the ruff increased in width, and the well-dressed man
usually wore both band and ruff. Marston, 1599, ridicules
this fashion in his 'Scourge of Villanie':

> Under that fayre ruffe so sprucely set.
> Appears a fall, a falling band forsooth.[1]

At the beginning of the seventeenth century, the latest
fashion was that of multiple pleated ruffs or 'three falls',
mentioned in *1 Honest Whore* (III. i. 44). Rowlands, 1604,
said that a band and a ruff was the dress of gentlewomen;[2]
and a bandless person, according to the *Return from Parnassus*, was a ruffian. Ladies had worn a large band open
in front and supported by a rebato since the seventies.
By 1610 the straight falling band worn by men was also
erected by a starched or wired supporting collar, called
a pickadill.

Bands acquired more and more ornamentation and
consequent expense, those of Italian cutwork or purl-
trimmed being most in demand.[3] Cutwork bands with
the fashionable tiered cuffs cost six or seven pounds a set,[4]
and a courtier needed many sets to appear correctly attired. The fastidious courtier was as exacting as a lady
over his bands, a fact ridiculed on the stage. The gallant
was presented as discomfited if one of his purls fell out
of place,[5] and he always maintained a stiff neck to prevent
such disaster!

In the last half of the sixteenth century, probably soon
after the fashion of starching began, coloured starches
were used on bands. Stubbes mentions red, blue, and

II, 1, 5; *Cynthia's Revels*, v. iv. 158;
Loyal Subject, III. ii. 131.

[1] *Satire*, iii. *Your Five Gallants*, I.
i. 81. Portraits of the Earl of Essex
between 1595–1600 illustrate the mode.
Florio, *Second Frvtes*, 1591, p. 9:
'falling bands (2 doz.), 8 ruff bands
with hand cuffs.'

[2] Rowlands, *Look To It*, i. 28. *Return from Parnassus*, sig. B 2.

[3] *Fair Maid of Exchange*, III. i.
sig. F; *Every Man Out of His Humour*,
IV. vi. 90: 'takes me away six purles
of an Italian cut-worke band I wore

. . . (cost me three pounds in the exchange.)' Flanders work, Plate II, was
also in demand, 1561–2, L.C. 9/55:
'4 bands white flanders work.' 1605–
6, L.C. 9/94: 'Falling bands . . . edg.
current. cum purles curious de opē.
auro.'

[4] 1613, Birch, *Court and Times
James I*, i. 264: 'His father told me
he had a hundred pounds worth of
such ware.'

[5] *Fatal Dowry*, II. ii. 87; *Amends
for Ladies*, III. iii. 112.

purple; Jonson, goose-green; but allusions to yellow are
the most frequent in the drama. The following are representative: *The Alchemist, Love's Cure, More Dissemblers
Besides Women, Queen of Corinth, The Widow, Albumazar*.[1]
Mrs. Turner is credited by D'Ewes with having originated the fashion of yellow bands, but this fashion did not
lapse at her execution. Fitzgeffrey wrote in 1617 that an
Englishman could be known in any country by his yellow
band.[2] In 1620 the Dean of Westminster forbade ladies
wearing yellow bands to be admitted to the abbey,[3] and
D'Ewes tells of the King's disgust over the yellow bands
worn by ladies who stood watching his progress to Westminster, 1621, to open Parliament.[4] In fact, yellow bands
did not go out of fashion completely until 1630.[5]

RUFF

'Ces beaux Mignons portoient . . . leurs fraises de
chemises de toiles d'alour empezées et longues de demi-
pied, de façon qu'à voir leur teste dessus leur fraize, il
semblait que ce fust le chef Saint-Jean dans un plat.'[6]
This description of French ruffs recalls a similar one in
The Alchemist: 'He looks in that deep ruff like a head on
a platter.'[7] Not only the carefulness which the wearer of

[1] *Alchemist*, IV. ii. 54; *Love's Cure*,
I. ii. 2 (blue); *More Dissemblers*, V. i.
106; *Queen Corinth*, IV. i. 104; *The
Widow*, V. i. 53; *Albumazar*, II. i. 21.
Goose-green, *Bartholomew Fair*, II. i.
290. Stowe (Howes), *Annales*, 869,
wrote that Mrs. Dingham brought to
England the fashion of starching
bands in 1554. Stubbes, *Anatomy of
Abuses*, 35–6, shows that the practice
of coloured-starching was common.
In 1597, 'blue pother starch' was
valued at 2s. 1d. a pound, *Durham
Wills*, xxxviii. 282; but a penny an
ounce, in 1610, *Shuttleworth Accts.*
xxxv. 193. White starch was only 2d.
to 4d. a pound: 1593, *Antiquary*,
xxxii. 369; 1620, *Household Bk.
Howard*, 145.

[2] *Notes from the Blackfryers*, 16
(B 4); D'Ewes, *Autobiography*, i. 79.

[3] *C.S.P.D.* cxiii. 18.

[4] Op. cit. i. 170. The King objected
not only to the yellow bands, but to
the mannish apparel of the ladies.

[5] Holme, *Academy of Armoury*, bk.
iii, ch. 1, said they were much used 'in
the beginning of the reigne of King
Charles the first', but ladies of the
Court did not wear them after 1625,
for they are absent from wardrobe
accounts.

[6] Pierre de l'Estoile, *Registre-Jour-
nal, juillet 1576*, i. 143.

[7] IV. i. 368. See *Roaring Girl*, IV.
i. 20, which describes the face of Gos-
hawk in a shag ruff band as resembling
'an agate set in a cramp ring'; also
Woman Is a Weathercock, I. ii. 27:
'Is 't he that looks like an Italian tailor
out of the laced wheel?'

ruffs exercised to prevent rumpling,[1] but the size of that neckwear gave the head-on-a-platter appearance. Stowe tells how certain noble Englishmen, wearing ruffs a fourth of a yard deep and twelve lengths to a ruff, under the impression that they were mirroring a French fashion, came to Paris early in Elizabeth's reign. There they learned that the French did not know such a ruff and called it 'the English monster'.[2] Whatever the English may have added to the size of the ruff, historians agree that the fashion was introduced into England from France, whither it had been brought by Catherine de Medici about 1530. The full-length portrait of Henry VIII, dated 1538—School of Holbein—shows a narrow pleated ruffle at the top of his shirt collar. Such a ruffle seems to have been the origin of the ruff mode in England.

The royal wardrobe accounts of 1548 contain the first mention of ruffs which the author has been able to find: 'pro viij camisiis de tela holland bon cum bands et Ruffs.'[3] During the next twenty years, they are constantly named in accounts as accessories to 'togas' and 'upper-bodyes'.[4] By the sixties they had acquired supreme importance, and were extravagantly ornamented, edged with 'loome lase', 'nedelworke', 'laqueo aur. opat. sup. oss.', 'damaske golde purle', and were 'wrought' with 'blak' and 'blewe spanyshe worke',[5] for lace and embroidery were in full favour. New Year gifts to the Queen 1577–1600 show ruffs of lawn cutwork, cambric, holland, and lace. One set given by Philip Sidney, 1577, was of 'cutwork flourished with golde and silver and set with span-

---

[1] *White Devil*, III. i. 78: 'He carries his face in's ruff as I have seen a serving-man carry glasses in a cypress hatband, monstrous steady for fear of breaking.'

[2] *Annales* (Howes), 869.

[3] E. 351/3026. Taylor, *The Prayse of Clean Linnen*, writes of the ruff that its 'antiquitie is here but small. Within these eighty years not one at all,' and credits Henry VIII with wearing only a plain band with a hem. (1630), 167.

[4] 1559, L.C. 9/53; A.O. 3/1106, &c.

[5] 1555. *Mid. MSS.* 408: 'For loome lase to make . . . a payer of ruffes.' 1561–2, L.C. 9/55; 1565, A.O. 3/1106: 'pro una virg. ruffing de Tinsell arg. Lin cum camerick edged cum Laqueo aur. opat sup. oss.'; 1556, Add. MS. 35328: 'Cameryk Ruffes wrought with blak spanyshe worke xxiij yardes of Damaske golde purle to edge the same ruffs. Vij ydes lawne Ruffes wrought with blewe spanyshe worke.'

gills'.[1] Matching hand ruffs were usually included, and the set was called a 'suit' of ruffs;[2] the hand ruffs alone were called a 'pair'.[3]

Although the proclamation of the sumptuary Act of 1562 had forbidden 'greet ruffs',[4] English coins of that year showed the Queen in quite a broad one. If Stowe's account of the Queen's attempt, 1571, to limit ruffs by setting 'grave citizens' at every gate to cut off ruffs that exceeded 'a nayle of a yard in depth',[5] were true, the cutting was not effective, for the 'quarter deep measured by the yard', named in *Dumb Knight*,[6] was not a fictitious measure for the deepest. As they increased in size, they increased also in complexity of pleating, varying from the cartwheel of 'many organ pipes'[7] to the 'labyrinthian set . . . Whose thousand double turnings never met', the latter representing the 'calves chitterlings' ruff of *Like Will to Like*.[8] In writing of foreign fashions, 1576, Gascoigne said that the English 'doo not onlye reteyne them, but do farre exceed them: that of a Spanish Codpeece, we make an English football . . . of a French ruffe, an English chytterling'.[9] Some idea of the size and intricate pleating of ruffs can be gained from the amount of material required to make them. The Great Wardrobe accounts for 1617–18 list the following materials for a dozen 'suits' of ruffs: '27 elnes very fyne cambricke; ccclxix yardes lace; 11 1/2 elnes holland stocke' (i.e. neckbands); two dozen strings.[10] In 1623, 300 yards of bone lace was purchased for twenty-two ruffs and twenty-four pairs of cuffs,

[1] *Prog. Elizabeth*, ii. 76, 78, 256; III. 11, 456, &c., 1592, L.C. 9/184.

[2] *Fair Maid of Exchange*, I. i. 23: 'Stay, Ursula, have you those sutes of Ruffs?' 1602–3, L.C. 9/93: 'Pro iij suites de les ruffes de lawne op. sciss., edg. cum tenia bob. opat sup. oss.'

[3] 1564, *Durham Wills*, ii. 224: 'four pare of roffes'; 1582, ibid. xxxviii. 66; 1600–1, L.C. 9/91.

[4] Machyn, *Diary*, 281.

[5] *Chronicle*, 869. The shag ruff of *Roaring Girl*, II. i. 20, and 'shagged ragged Ruffe' of *Knave of Harts*, 13, indicated deep points.

[6] Dodsley, x. 123.

[7] T. Randolph, *Hey for Honestie* (1651), sig. E 2. Because of their size, food was often spilled upon the ruffs. *Westward Hoe*, I. ii.

[8] 1565, I. i. 24; Estienne, *Deux Dialogues*, 'Dialogue Premier', 177.

[9] *A delicate Diet for daintie-mouthde Droonkardes*, London, Jones, 1576.

[10] A.O. 3/3248/45.

at a cost of £35.[1] A 'suit' of ruffs costing from thirteen to fifty shillings was not therefore unusual.

The pleats of ruffs were maintained by lining the ruffs with pasteboard,[2] or by stiffening them with starch. While the ruff was still wet with starch, the pleats or 'sets' were put in, by folding each pleat over a poking-stick until it dried. The size of the 'sets' depended upon the size of the stick. The smallest sticks were used by Puritans, the largest by chambermaids and waiting women, as *Antonio and Mellida* and *If You Know Not Me* explain.[3] Setting with bone or wooden poking-sticks was naturally difficult; but after 1573, when steel sticks were introduced,[4] the laundress heated the stick in a pan of coals or the fireplace and quickly dried each pleat, but, of course, the sticks then needed 'fair and long handles'.[5] To maintain a 'spruce ruff'[6] or one 'starched in print' the wearer must carry his head straight and avoid damp.[7]

By 1600 the multiple ruff, or 'French fall', was *the* fashion. This was a deep ruff, which, instead of extending at right angles to the neck, hung down from the top of a high stock which was fastened up to the chin. The 'fall' was double,[8] treble,[9] or, according to *What You Will*,[10] quadruple, 'ay in the summertime'!

Ruffs were pinned to the support, pickadil or rebato, which, in turn, was pinned to the neck of the doublet or gown. They were, consequently, 'armed with pins',[11]

[1] E. 101/436/9. In the same account, 72 yds. of bone lace were purchased for 36 falling bands, *Hutton Accts.* 215; *Shuttleworth Accts.* xli. 239.

[2] 1570, A.O. 3/1108: 'pro new pasting ruffes'; 1580, L.C. 9/72: 'xxiij ydes. sattin pro toga french . . . the ruffes lined with pastbord.'

[3] Induction 135; 2 *If You Know Not Me*, I. i. 70: 'Your huge poking-stick with chambermaids and waiting women. A long slender poking-stick is all in all with your Suffolke Puritaine.' *Dumb Knight*, I. i: 'You have a pretty set too! How big is the steel you set with?'

[4] Stowe (Howes), *Annales*, 1038.

[5] *Blurt, Master Constable*, III. iii. 106.

[6] *Great Duke of Florence*, III. i. 425; *Night Walker*, III. ii. 339.

[7] *Every Man Out of His Humour* III. iv. 114: 'Thy breath will thaw my ruff.' See chapter on bands.

[8] *Sea Voyage*, I. i. 270. Cf. Breton, *Works*, I. xxxiii b; Rowlands, *Dr. Merrie Man*, II. 7; *Whole Crew of Gossips*, I. 70.

[9] *Your Five Gallants*, I. i. 81.

[10] IV. i. 91, 'three-pild ruffe', *Every Man Out of His Humour*, 'second sounding', line 111.

[11] *Pleasant Quippes for Upstart Gentlewomen*, 13.

a

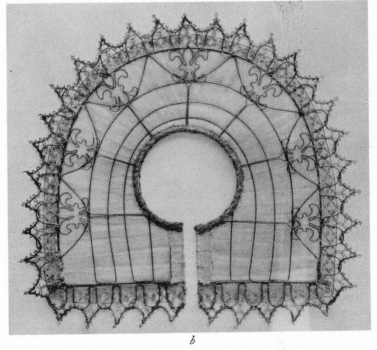

b

II. *a.* Gentleman's falling band, Flanders lace. *Circa* 1630

Photograph by Archives Photographiques, Paris

b. Pickadil on a linen band edged by gold lace. *Circa* 1610

Metropolitan Museum of Art, New York

and hours were spent in pinning one's neckwear in place. To keep ruffs and falling bands stiff and fresh, a special 'band-box' was made for them. In *A Match at Midnight*,[1] the maid informs the audience that the bandbox carried by the chamberlain contains her mistress's ruffs just come from, the seamstress. When a lady travelled, a servant, whose sole charge was the bandbox, always accompanied her.[2]

After 1610 the whisk, or standing band, open front, was the chosen style for women;[3] though a modification of the Spanish ruff, very broad at the sides but narrow in front, was used as late as 1630.[4] By this date, however, the younger set was wearing the fallen whisk, i.e. a broad band covering the shoulders, which began a little to the front, of the shoulder seam. A portrait of a member of the Eldred Family, 1620, shows that older men were still using the organ-pipe ruff of the sixteenth century, especially the open front variety, so common to the seventies.[5] Indeed, the ruff was not completely displaced by the broad shoulder band until the late thirties.

CHINCLOUT OR MUFFLER

A chinclout was a muffler, or large square of material worn over the chin, usually by women of the lower class. Seeking a complete disguise, Follywit, of *A Mad World, My Masters* (III. iii. 85), calls for a woman's kirtle, mask, and chinclout; and when Falstaff desires to escape, a hat, a muffler for his chin, and a kerchief are suggested to disguise him.[6]

KERCHIEF

Kerchief originated in a *couvre-chef* or veil covering the head, sides of the face, and neck. The term was early

[1] IV. i, sig. H. Also Hazlitt, *Inedited Tracts*, 1868, 151.

[2] *Servingman's Comfort*, 151.

[3] Clifford, *Diary*, 71, June 1617: 'The 13th I sayed on my sea-water green satin gown and my damaske embroidered with gold, both which gowns the Tailor made fit for me to wear with open ruffs after the French fashion.'

[4] A portrait of the Duchess of Devonshire with her children shows this type. A copy of the portrait is reproduced in Kelly and Schwabe, *Historic Costume*, pl. xxxii.

[5] Portrait reproduced in *Archaeologia*, xv. 403.

[6] *Merry Wives of Windsor*, IV. ii. 76.

applied to the veil of St. Veronica.[1] Kerchiefs were used by Anglo-Saxon and Norman women of every rank, but from the fourteenth to the late seventeenth century they were worn only by the lower classes.[2] They were made of cambric, cypress, holland, or other soft fine linen,[3] and according to Baret were embroidered. Shakespeare uses the word in *Julius Caesar* to indicate sickness (II. i. 315), because kerchiefs were worn to bind the heads of the sufferers.

PARTLET

Partlet, or patlet,[4] was originally a short jacket worn by men,[5] but from the late fifteenth century,[6] the term was applied to a garment covering the upper part of the chest and neck only.[7] Partlets were worn by men as well as by women throughout the reign of Henry VIII, for the fashion of low-cut doublet demanded them. Wardrobe accounts of His Majesty from 1511 to his death, and inventories of many classes of men mention this garment.[8] Detachable sleeves of the doublet usually matched the partlet in material and trimming, so that many accounts note partlets *with* sleeves,[9] a description which has much confused lexicographers.

[1] *Coventry Mysteries*, xxxii, Shakespeare Soc. Pub. (1841), 318.

[2] *Merry Wives*, III. iii. 62; IV. ii. 74.

[3] *Durham Wills*, xxxviii. 74.

[4] Godefroy gives its origin as OF. *patelet*, a band of stuff. But see *Sex Lingua*: 'Fr. *collet*, Eng. collar, Ger. *partlet*.'

[5] 1523, Inventory good Lord Monteagle, *Letters and Papers Henry VIII*, iii. 2, 1254: 'A strait sleeveless jacket made like a partlett of black satin furred with martins.'

[6] *O.E.D.*

[7] Hollyband, *Dictionarie*: 'Un collet ou gorgias de quoy les femmes couvrent leurs poictrines, a partlet.' Minsheu, *Guide into Tongues*, 1617: 'Partlet mentioned in the Statute Anno 24 Henry 8 cap. 13 seemeth to be some part of a mans attire . . . as some loose collar of a doublet, to be set on or taken

off by itselfe, without a bodies, as the Pickadilles now adaies, or as mens bands, or as womens neckerchifs which are in some places called Partlets.'

[8] 1511, E. 101/417/4: A yd. black satin for a partlet. White fustian to line the partlet. Harl. MS. 1419, 406, containing an inventory of the King's goods, shows such items as: 'Partlett crimesen vellat wᵗ oute sleves all over embrawdered with Venice golde and silver stiched wᵗ purple silke, lined with crimsen.' 1519, Harl. MS. 2284, 42: 'x yerds russet satten for a Jaquet and partlet for the kinges grace'; 1520, *Test. Ebor.* lxxix. 114; 1541, E. 154/2/20: 'A partlet of black satten furred wᵗ black conaye and faced with Sabuls.'

[9] Feuillerat, *Revels Ed. VI*, 43, 44, &c.; also *infra*.

Partlets worn by women were more elaborate than were those of men. In 1511, a partlet of white satin garnished with damask gold was provided for the Princess of Castile,[1] and the Duchess of Northumberland had partlets with sleeves made of black satin edged with swan; of black velvet 'pinked, tufted, and lozenged'.[2] Partlets of cobweb lawn edged with gold lace, of linen, of cypress, of holland, of network,[3] and of cloth of gold and silver,[4] elaborately embroidered, are common in accounts until about 1580, when partlets went out of fashion. From 1530 until the last quarter of the century, partlets were made with standing collars[5] having ruffles at the top.[6] By 1551, the ruffles had become ruffs, were lace-trimmed,[7] and acquired such importance that partlets, by the nineties, were old-fashioned, or as Valerius expressed it, had turned 'into rebatoes'.[8] Partlets are one of the long list of accessories worn by women which makes Tactus of *Lingua* complain that a 'ship is sooner rigged than a gentlewoman made ready'.[9]

PICKADIL

'Men must guess they have traveled (for there is no other way) by a Legge, or a piccadell, or a Pickadevant, or a new block, or a mangled sute.' Thus the author of *Horae Subsecivae* characterized the English Traveller of

---

[1] *Letters and Papers Henry VIII*, ii. 2, 1498. Also accounts of materials furnished Anne Boleyn, 1535, *Philobiblon Soc. Miscy*. vii. 9.

[2] 1553, L.R. 2/119; 1590, L.C. 2/82.

[3] 1546, L.R. 2/115, gold lace; *Arcadia*, iii. 274, linen; 1586, L.C. 9/77: 'un partlet francio de cobweb sips.' 1584, L.C. 9/75: 'un ptlett de serico Sips. nigr edged cum seric. nigr.' For numerous allusions, see wardrobe accounts from 1564, especially A.O. 3/1106, &c.; 1545, E. 351/3025, holland; 1577, *Prog. Elizabeth*, ii. 73, network.

[4] 1544, *P. P. Ex. Prin. Mary*, 145; 1559, L.C. 9/53; 1582, Egerton MS.

2806, 175. One yard of cloth of silver was required for a partlet.

[5] 1533, *Letters and Papers Henry VIII*, vi. 563: 'He cannot make a standing collar for a partlet without the measurement for her neck.' 1543, 'ii high collar ptlets', *P. P. Ex. Prin. Mary*, 144.

[6] Ellis, *Letters*, II. ii. 215: 'vi highe collered patletts and ruffes to same.'

[7] 1559, A.O. 3/1106: 'ij ells fyne white lace pro ruffes pro partlettes.'

[8] *Rape of Lucrece*, III. iv. References to partlets through the eighties are frequent: 1580, *Lancashire and Cheshire Wills*, li. 162; 1585, *Durham Wills*, xxxviii. 114.

[9] Sig. I 2 verso.

the Jacobean period, who returned to his native country with foreign styles in hose, band-support, beard, hat, and pinked or slashed suit.[1] Pickadil was a synecdochical term for a wired or stiffened support of an erected band or broad collar worn in England from 1590 until about 1630.

Minsheu, 1617, gave its origin as the Dutch *pickadilli-kins*, a jagged hem, and it was originally a border of scallops or tabs placed about the tops of gamashes, around the armseye of a doublet, at the edge of sleeve-hands, or at the top of a collar. Such uses are noted in France from the middle of the sixteenth century; for instance, 'des picadelles au bout des dits aellerons au collet et aux manches' occurs in a description of a page's robes, 1560. In 1593 is mentioned a 'cote d'armes' of which 'la bastine et les espaulettes' were 'decoupées a ces grandes picadelles'; also 'une paire de cullottes de veloux . . . avec des picadelles'.[2] But the pickadil of the seventeenth century evolved from such an ornamental border placed at the top of a doublet collar. The stiffened tabs set out at right angles to the collar, supporting the small ruff, but, as the ruff grew broader and deeper, men's doublets were made without high collars, and the ruff was starched so stiffly that its many folds enabled it to stand alone.

In the early nineties the French fashion of erected broad collar or band was introduced. To hold this band erect, a frame containing a lining of stiffened linen or buckram—and for the lace or cobweb lawn band, a silk-wrapped frame—was made. (Plate II.) The frame retained the tab-border of former days, and was called by the French a *peccadelle*, but Englished 'picadilly, picadell, pickadil'.[3] Blount's definition, 1661, of a kind 'of stiff

[1] Ed. Blount, London, 1620, 33; the tract is anonymous.

[2] Gay, op. cit. i. 757. Godefroy, *Dictionnaire l'ancienne langue française*. Cotgrave defines *piccadilles* as 'the severall divisions or peeces fastened about the brimme of a collar of a doublet'; and Oudin, *Le Tresor des trois langues*, 1617, defines *brasoneras*

as 'picadilles des manches'. Bruyn, *Omnium Pene Europae, Asiae, Aphricae, Atque Americae Gentium Habitus*, 1581, shows pickadils on sleeves, hose, gamashes. See also Ketel's portrait of Frobisher, 1577.

[3] 1616, No apprentice shall 'weare any pickadelly or other support in, with, or about the collar of his doub-

collar made in fashion of a band'[1] has misled editors and lexicographers into thinking that the band itself was called a pickadil; but expense accounts, which are the best lexicons of costume, show that pickadil was a support, not a band. The Lord Chamberlain's accounts for 1606 show items such as one-fourth yard of carnation taffeta 'pro collat and pickadill' for a 'tunica'; a 'collar and Pickadill de taffeta pro tunica de velvett poppingay greene'.[2] And Fitzgeffrey's *Certaine Elegies*, 1617, presents the fastidiousness of the coxcomb concerning the set of his clothes, especially his care to see

> How his Band jumpeth with his Piccadilly,
> Whether his band-strings ballance equally.[3]

The band, erected by a pickadil, stood up from the neck like a corbel or cartouche.[4] Either the pasteboard used in the collar, or the fancied resemblance of the erected band to the architectural support, explains the speech of the taylor of *Northward Hoe* who informs Doll that the fashion to produce the 'best bodie' is a 'short dutch wast with a round Catherine wheele fardingale, a close sleeve with a cartoose collar and a pickadell' (III. i. 60). Since the band set close around the head, one can understand the care that Novall's barber, in *Fatal Dowry*, had to exercise in cutting hair, for truly, 'with a hair's breadth's error', there would have been 'a shoulder piece cut, and the base of a pickadelle in puncto'.[5] For this reason also, a halter is designated a 'French Pickadel' by the outlaw in *The Pilgrim* (II. ii. 178).

---

let', Heath, *Grocers*, 91. 1688, Holme, *Academie of Armourie*, iii. 15: 'In the begining of the reign of King Charles the first, yellow bands were much used, which were Dyed with Safron and Supported round the neck by a Picadill.'

[1] *Glossographia*.

[2] L.C. 9/95; 1612, *Archaeologia*, xxvi. 389, 390, &c. Also 1614–15, L.C. 9/97, 'pickadells de satin alb'.

[3] Sig. F 6. 1615, Stephens, *Essays*, 225, description of country bride-

groom; Overbury, *Characters*, 117, description of lawyer.

[4] Cotgrave, '*modillon*, a cartridge or cartoose, a folding bracket or corbel'. We are so familiar with the sculptured tablet and escutcheon by the name of *cartouche* that we do not realize it also indicated a corbel.

[5] IV. i. 29. Other references in *Woman Is a Weathercock*, I. i. 12, *Devil is an Ass*, II. i. 371; in both of which the pickadil represents the best fashion in clothes.

Both bands and pickadils soon reached excessive size and height.[1] Before the King visited Cambridge in February 1614, orders had to be issued to the Vice-Chancellor and heads of the colleges to forbid the graduates and students 'to wear strange pikadivelas, vast bands, huge cuffs, shoe roses . . . during the tyme of His Majesties abode in the towne'.[2] Bands continued to increase in size until they could no longer be held upright. They were then allowed to lie gracefully on the shoulders. This fashion, introduced at court soon after the accession of King Charles, gradually superseded all other modes in neckwear, so that when Peacham in 1638 listed 'French monstrosities' which had previously found favour in England, i.e. 'slashed doublets, half-skirts, long breeches, spangled garters pendant to the shooe, perfumed perrukes, pickadilles', he observed the last were 'now out of request'.[3]

RAIL

The Willoughby accounts for 1526 list the cost of 'iij yelse (ells) cloth for rayles for Mrs. Alice and Mrs. Jane'.[4] The sixteenth-century rail, a possible survival of the Anglo-Saxon *rægel*, was of linen, lawn, cypress, cambric, network, or other fine material. It was made, according to its use, into: 1. a square kerchief to be folded shawl-fashion for the neck and shoulders; 2. a veil worn over the back of the head, and bowed out with wire at the shoulders; 3. a cape which hung below the shoulders, to be worn at night.[5] The kerchief does not appear in por-

[1] Drayton satirized women of his time in *Mooncalf in Agincourt*, 489:
In everything she must be monstrous:
Her Picadell above her crowne upbears;
Her fardingale is set above her ears.

[2] Cooper, *Annals of Cambridge*, III. 69. In 1588, Lord Burghley had addressed the heads of the colleges of Cambridge on the subject of large bands. Bands and ruffs of all students except sons of noblemen were limited to the width of one and a half inches and all 'colour other than white' was prohibited. Ellis, *Letters*, III. i. 26.

[3] *Truth of Our Times*, 78.

[4] *Mid. MSS.* i. 386.

[5] Palsgrave, 'rayle for a woman's necke, crevechief en quattre doubles'. 1554, Machyn, *Diary*, 245, head rails. 1588, Egerton MS. 2806: 'for mendinge washinge and starchinge of a heade raille of fine sipers edged rounde aboute with white thred bone lase.' *Prog. Elizabeth*, iii. 9: 'a network head rail flourished with venis gold, silver, and owes.' Rails are frequently mentioned in sixteenth-century bequests,

traits of noble persons; so that it was evidently limited to the lower classes, of whose use there are numerous illustrations. The head rail was much used from the sixties, and night rails are bequeathed in wills and are named in the royal accounts from the fifties.[1] They are made of drawn work, edged with lace or ruffles, or elaborately decorated with gold.[2] One in the royal wardrobe in 1588 cost £5, but the price of Lady Frugal's[3] night rails was, judging by actual accounts, a stage price only.

REBATO

'If your ladiships want embroidered gownes, tires of any fashion, rebatu's . . .' began Asotus of *Cynthia's Revels*.[4] After 1570, ladies' closed ruffs gave place to those open in front and set up fanwise from the low-cut neck-line, or as expressed later in *Your Five Gallants*: 'Gentlewomen's falls stand upright now.' (I. i. 87.) This style was worn especially by unmarried women. The open ruff was supported by a linen-covered, wire frame, called rebato, and, since the style took the place of a partlet, Valerius of *The Rape of Lucrece*, sings: 'Your partlets turne into rebatoes.'[5]

---

inventories, &c.: 1526, *Lancashire and Cheshire Wills*, xxxii. 14; 1543, *Test. Leod.* xix. 106, 156; 1545, E. 351/3025; 1551, Ellis, *Letters*, II. ii. 205, 'double railes'; 1551, *Middlesex Sessions Rolls*, i. 13: John Evans stole 'a pece of linen called woman's rayll'; 1556-60, *Test. Leod.* xxvii, 79, 239, 317, 325, 326; 1562, *Lancashire and Cheshire Wills*, xxxii. 164; 1562-65, *Durham Wills*, ii. 201, 277.

[1] 1554, *Bury Wills*, 146.

[2] 1559, A.O. 3/1106: 'pro ouercasting & edginge unus nighte rayle cum bone lase'; 1560, L.C. 9/53; 1581-82, L.C. 9/73: 'pro ij railes nocturne de cambrick ^pat. cum opere tract. de serico'; 1594, L.C. 9/85; 1598-99, L.C. 9/89: 'Un rayle nocturn. de camerack opat. cum serico nigro tract. et edged cum bonea de serico nigro et alb.'

[3] *City Madam*, IV. iv. 132; *Rape of Lucrece*, III. iv: 'Your frontlet lay by and your rails'; *Wit of Woman*, line 1067.

[4] IV. iii. 410; *Dumb Knight*, Dodsley, x. 122; *Antonio and Mellida*, II. i. 37; *Woman Killed with Kindness*, V. ii. 8; *Much Ado*, III. iv. 6.

[5] III. iv. Cotgrave, '*porte fraise*, A rebato, or supporter for a Ruffe, wrought or embroidered and cut into panes'. Minsheu, 1599, *A Dictionarie in Spanish and English*, '*Avandelas*, rebatoes, supporters for womans ruffs'. Moryson, *Itinerary*, iv. 206: 'I observed them to wear long ruffs, with rebatoes of wire to bear them up, as our women use.' *Household Bk. Howard*, 110: 'a rebatoe wyer for Mrs Mary viiid.' In 1595, 4 rebatoes were purchased for Dorothy Bacon's trousseau at a cost of 3s. 2d. Bacon MSS. Univ. Chicago. The earliest reference noted to rebatoes is 1588 when the Countess of Dudley

Ruffs were pinned to the rebatoes, and the latter to the neck of the kirtle, and then bent back to make the most becoming frame for the face; hence the many allusions to time consumed in adjusting the 'set' of the rebato and pinning it in place. The five hours mentioned in *Lingua* as necessary to dress a lady to her girdle was not greatly exaggerated, for the 'pinning and unpinning, setting and unsetting, forming and unforming of tires, ruffs, and rebatoes', to say nothing of the required cosmetic artistry, naturally made dressing a long process.[1]

SCARF

A scarf was a band of silk, lawn, cypress,[2] or other light material worn by both men and women; the former wearing them diagonally across their chests and knotted at the waistline, the latter casting them about their faces to keep from sunburning.[3] Elder Loveless of *The Scornful Lady* expressed his relief at his freedom from his former lady's extravagance in the words:

Now can I keep my money in my purse
That still was gadding out for scarves and waistcoats (IV. i. 204).

Scarves were given by ladies as favours to their lovers, as in *Every Man Out of His Humour* and *The Lady's Trial*, and by bridegrooms to wedding guests, as in *Silent Woman*.[4]

STANDING COLLAR

The standing collar was a high, straight collar fastened in front. It was of two types, the first worn from about 1530 to 1570, the second, a new French fashion until

gave Queen Elizabeth 'two ruffes with rabatines of tawne cut-work'. *Prog. Elizabeth*, iii. 7.

[1] *Lingua*, IV. vi. 23; *Law Tricks*, II. i. 85.

[2] 1561, L.C. 9/55, 'scarf of sipers black edged with ffringe of venice golde'; 1562, A.O. 3/1106: 'skarff de Sipers nigr garn. cu. Buttons et Tassells de serico nigr. et auro.' 1592, *Durham Wills*, xxxviii. 224, 'black silke scarfe tipped with silver', 1593, L.C.

9/85, 'scarf de Taffata color orrenge Tawney et watchet changeable'; 1599, *Prog. Elizabeth*, iii. 450, 'one skarfe of lawne cutwork florished with silver and silke of sundry colours'.

[3] Stubbes's *Anatomy of Abuses*, 76; Machyn, *Diary*, 180. See portrait King Charles, Plate XVII.

[4] *Every Man Out of His Humour*, II. iii. 200; *Silent Woman*, III. ii. 253; *Lady's Trial*, II. i. 47.

about 1616. The first type was used on the high-collared partlets and kirtle bodies, and on men's doublets; the second on women's gowns, and in place of the doublet collar inside the band. With the lace or fine lawn band, a pickadil was worn. Wardrobe accounts from the fifties contain many references to the former, which was fastened only in one place, at or below the base of the throat, and allowed to fall open. Since these collars were a part of the kirtle, they were embroidered or decorated.[1] This is the type of standing collar mentioned in *Jeronimo* (III. i. 43).

Early in the seventeenth century, all became 'a stiffe necke generation',[2] i.e. both men and women wore the second type which attracted the attention of the authors of *Northward Hoe, Family of Love, Dutch Courtezan, Ram Alley, Roaring Girl*,[3] &c.

TIPPET

A tippet was a strip of material of varying length and width worn pendant on hoods as a 'liripipe' from the twelfth to the late fifteenth centuries, surviving in mourning or official robes thereafter; on sleeves as a decorative band above the elbow, during the reign of Edward III; and as a scarf after the fifteenth century.[4] In *New Custom*, religious persons are presented in such scarfs.[5] Because a tippet was, during the sixteenth century, worn around

[1] 1559, A.O. 3/1106: 'pro embraudr̄ unus standing collr̄.pro una Toga de velvett nigr.', 1561, 'pro Sciss. & pinking unis kirtle cōpor et manche.cum un standing coller.'

[2] 1612, *Knave of Harts*, ii. 13:
Let us have standing collers in the fashion,
All are become a stiffe-necke generation.
Rose hat-bands, with the shagged-ragged ruffe,
Great cabbage shoe-strings.

[3] *Northward Hoe*, II. i. 198: 'I bidde him measure how hie hee would make the standing coller of my new Taffetie Gowne'; *Family of Love*, II. iii. 47: 'If she wear but the standing collar

and her things in fashion'; *Dutch Courtezan*, III. i; *Ram Alley*, Dodsley, x. 340, 'what we use about our hips to keep our coats from dabbling, He wears about his neck—a farthingale! A standing collar to keep his neat band clean'; *Roaring Girl*, III. iii. 32: 'You shall take them both' (i.e. men and women) 'with standing collars.' Also *Seven Deadly Sins* (Arber), 36: 'so for the same reason are women men's she-apes. . . . If we get up French standing collars, women will have French standing collars, too.'

[4] 1440, *Promp. Parv.* 492, 'Typett, liripum'; *Paston Letters*, Intro., 139.

[5] Dodsley, iii. 28. 1572, *Durham Wills*, ii. 380.

the neck, a hangman's rope was frequently termed a 'hempen' or 'Tyburn tippet', as in *Jew of Malta*.[1]

WIMPLE

So much material on the word wimple is given in the *Oxford English Dictionary* that nothing important can be added. It was a square or rectangle of linen—not a veil —worn by women in mourning, so folded as to envelop the head, chin, sides of the face, and neck. It is retained in modern times in the costume of nuns of certain religious orders. The word, wimpled, occurs in *Three Lords and Three Ladies of London* (sig. C verso), and *Love's Labour's Lost* (III. i. 189), in the former indicating a mask worn over the face; in the latter, the traditional blindness of Cupid. Wimple has been confused with veil, because one side of it was usually worn hanging over the forehead, and could be used, if the owner desired, to conceal the eyes; hence Virginia's request before her father strikes: 'Let first my wimple bind my eyes.'[2]

[1] IV. iv. 28. Crowley, 'Epigrams', E.E.T.S. (1872), 30; Latimer, *Sermons*, i. 119, 180; Taylor, *Works*, fol. 287.

[2] *Appius and Virginia*, Dodsley, iv. 146.

XX

SLEEVES.

Sᴌᴇᴇᴠᴇs of the period 1530–1630, in England, were influenced in turn by fashions of France, Germany, Spain,
Italy, and finally by France, again. The chief characteristics of French sleeves were graceful cut and fit; of German, slashing, shortness, and puffing; of Spanish, padding
and stiffness; of Italian, length. These were, of course, only
general characteristics; French sleeves, as well as German,
were puffed; Italian sleeves, as well as those of French
mode, were sometimes very graceful.

Men's sleeves from the beginning of the century were
full—so wide, according to 'Courtly Abusyon' of *Magnificence* (ii. xiv. 902 ff.), that they would hide a person. A
Venetian visitor of 1527 was much impressed by the
length and ornamentation of English women's sleeves.[1]
The long bell sleeve which he admired was similar to that
of Anglo-Saxon times, except that it was narrow at the
hand; the widest part, lined with fur or contrasting material,
was turned back to the elbow. A separate 'foresleeve',
open at the back, and caught together every few inches
with laces or gems over an inner sleeve, was worn over
the forearm, this foresleeve[2] forming puffs between the
caught parts. Sleeve-laces, used to tie the sleeves, are
named in the Pedlar's pack of *The Four PP* (p. 36). A
variation of foresleeve in masculine and feminine attire
was made of strips of rich material fastened together at
intervals over the under sleeve, by gems, and worn with
the short puffed German sleeve of cassocks.

By 1545 the Spanish fashions were manifest in England,
lasting until their exaggeration in the eighties brought a
decline in popularity and the introduction of French

[1] *C.S.P.V.* iv. 60.

[2] These sleeves were considered suitable gifts for royalty, 1542–4, *P. P.
Ex. Prin. Mary*, 97, 143, &c.; 1599–
1600, *Prog. Elizabeth*, iii. 455. Knit

sleeves were worn from the forties,
1545, E. 351/3025; 1551, Ellis, *Letters,*
ii. ii. 215. They were manufactured
in Norfolk from the seventies.

styles. Men's sleeves in the forties were padded at the top, producing width of shoulder similar to that of the sleeves of a century previous. The trunk or farthingale sleeve and the puffed, padded sleeve were Spanish contributions, and were worn by both sexes. The trunk sleeve was often accompanied, especially in women's gowns, by a 'side sleeve', i.e. a long, open sleeve hanging to the knee or foot. Sleeves of the latter length, an Italian fashion, were called hanging or pendant sleeves. They were lined with material in colour contrasting to that of the gown, and were attached all around the armhole, meeting in front, where they were allowed to fall open from the shoulder. The shoulder seam was hidden by a 'wing' of the same material as that of the gown. These sleeves were in favour from the eighties until about 1620. The padded trunk sleeve was preceded in the sixties by a tight sleeve with a roll or shoulder puff, the latter paned. The sleeve was gathered into a tight cuff which fitted the upper arm midway between shoulder and elbow.

Men's doublets and women's gowns showed, from the eighties, the short, tight, hanging sleeve, and the long or 'down sleeve' sometimes tied along the front closing by points, sometimes open, sometimes buttoned from wrist to shoulder; hence Butler's statement: 'They have not wit to button their sleeves without teaching.'[1] The fashion lasted until the early seventeenth century.

Another sleeve introduced from France about 1574 was made in 'rising panes', or puffs. It consisted of two pieces, cut much longer than the arm, slashed perpendicularly at regular spaces, and drawn in, between the slashed portions, by a shorter, tightly fitting foundation sleeve, thus puffing the slashed portions.[2] By the early seventeenth century, all suggestion of padding and whalebone in sleeves was old-fashioned.[3] Sleeves then fitted the

[1] *Miseries of Enforced Marriage*, sig. F 2 verso.

[2] 1575, Egerton MS. 2806, 80: 'Item, for making of a French Gowne wᵗʰ a long treine of ashe colour sipers wᵗʰ a sleve made very longe to stande in ruffes alonge the arme'; 1586, L.C. 9/77: 'pro factr̃. unus par. manicarum de Satten sciss. en le₃ rising panes . . . lined cum satten colour crimsen.' Also 1581, A.O. 3/1110.

[3] Moryson, *Itinerary*, iv. 235, de-

arms like stockings,[1] with 'wings' at the armhole. These sleeves were seamed up back and front, or, in the case of women's sleeves, buttoned or left open in front to show the pleated inner sleeve of lawn, cypress, or cambric.

By 1610, the falling band and matching cuff had largely replaced the ruff and hand-ruffle. Sleeves were finished by exquisite detachable cuffs in lace and sheer lawn. Women still wore the pendant and 'down' sleeves, with cuffs matching their bands.

From the reign of Charles I, masculine sleeves consisted of a full, paned and puffed upper sleeve gathered into a tightly fitting cuff reaching to the elbow; a turned-back short cuff, matching the band, completed the sleeve. Women's sleeves became shorter, reaching only the middle forearm, and were made in two puffs, usually paned, tied between by ribbon. These puffs were often padded and lined by contrasting material, such as pink taffeta in blue velvet sleeves, white satin in crimson cloth-of-gold sleeves. The sleeve was finished by a cuff of tiers of lace.

SLEEVES IN THE DRAMA

DOWN-SLEEVES AND SIDE-SLEEVES

Margaret's description of the Duchess of Milan's gown as having 'down sleeves, side sleeves'[2] is not as difficult of explanation as some editors think. The down-sleeves were long sleeves to the wrist; the side-sleeve, the hanging or pendant sleeve, open from the shoulder. This fashion of sleeve was French and accompanied the French farthingale, introduced in the seventies.[3] These side-sleeves were the 'dragon-wing sleves' of *The Pilgrim* (III. iv. 56).

scription of England: 'All in general weare gownes hanging loose at the backe, with kirtle and close upper body of silke and light stuffe, but have lately left the French sleeves borne out with hoopes.'

[1] *The Cruel Brother,* I. I, 394; *Blurt, Master Constable,* II. ii. 209: 'Eel skin sleeves.'

[2] *Much Ado,* III. iv. 20–1.

[3] 1573, A.O. 3/1108; 1575–81, Egerton MS. 2806; 1577–8, *Prog. Elizabeth,* II. 66; 1580, L.C. 9/72, 'xxiij yards satten for a french toga with great hanging sleeves cut in works and scallops'; 1593, L.C. 9/85, 'pendant sleves Isabelle colour satten snipped' lined with tinsel, worked with black silk and gold.

Foresleeve

In his dictionary of 1538, Elyot defined *cubitale* as 'a foresleve of a garment which keuereth the arme from the elbowe downward'.[1] Since sleeves of the sixteenth century were made in two or three parts, consisting of a fitted under-sleeve and an upper ornamental sleeve, the upper-most sleeve was usually pendant from the shoulder or from the elbow. The under-sleeve was attached to the shoulder, but only the lower part was visible. This lower part, or 'half-sleeve' as it is called in *Ram Alley*,[2] was known as the foresleeve. It was made of material contrasting with that of the gown and was often embroidered or trimmed with buttons or gems.[3]

Foresleeves showed to best advantage with the bell-shaped sleeves of the 1525–60 period, but they were worn throughout the sixteenth century[4] and until the three-quarter sleeves of the reign of Charles became fashion-able. Foresleeves are mentioned in *The Dumb Knight* and *Death of Robert, Earl of Huntingdon*.[5]

Trunk-sleeves

Petruchio describes a trunk-sleeve of the late sixteenth century in his interview with Katherina's tailor:

What's this? a sleeve? 'tis like a demi-cannon:
What! up and down, carv'd like an apple-tart?
Here's snip and nip and cut and slish and slash.
(*Taming of the Shrew*, IV. iii. 88.)

Trunk-sleeves were fashionable at the time of the prob-able writing of this play. Philip Gawdy, who knew all the newest fashions at Court, sent his sister a pair of trunk

[1] Foresleeves are mentioned in *Piers Plowman*, A. v. 64.

[2] Dodsley, x. 378. Cotgrave, '*man-cheron*, halfe sleeve, a sleeve that couers the arme from the elbow to the wrist'. A coat with 'demi sleves' occurs among the robes of Edward VI. *Prog. Elizabeth*, III. 501. 1584, A.O. 3/1110, half sleeves.

[3] The inventory of Mrs. Holland's goods, 1546, lists: '1 paire of fforsleves

of Venice gold and silver wrought with silk' and a pair of 'crymsen satten fore-sleves trimmed with twenty rounde gold buttons', L.R. 2/119.

[4] 1526, *Letters and Papers Henry VIII*, iv. 1, entry 1888; 1557–8, L.C. 9/52: 'Foresleves of a loose gown'; 1566, *Richmond Wills*, 183; 1574, *Durham Wills*, ii. 400; 1576, ibid. xxxviii. 317.

[5] Dodsley, x. 124; sig. C.

III. Lady Elizabeth Paulet (?). Costume 1615–20. White kirtle embroidered in coloured silks; rose-coloured cloak; French band, erected; matching cuffs. Cut-work lace apron. Lace roses on shoes

Ashmolean Museum, Oxford

sleeves in 1589.[1] This type of sleeve was large and cannon-shaped, i.e. tapering from shoulder to wrist, and was held out stiffly by wire, reed, or whalebone.[2] It was decorated by pinking or slashing. The under, or foundation sleeve, because of its wire, reed, or whalebone foundation, was known as a farthingale sleeve. It was made of fustian, holland, and similar materials.[3] Such sleeves were used by country folk by 1600.

Sleeves belled out at the shoulders were worn during the reign of Edward VI, and were probably the trunk-sleeves noted in inventories of that time,[4] but they did not resemble the later 'demi-cannon sleeves'.

Two parts of sleeves are frequently mentioned in the drama: sleeve-hands, and wings.

SLEEVE-HAND

'Sleeve-hand' has been the subject of considerable comment, but its meaning is very simple. It was not a separate cuff, or even a wristband as it is commonly defined, but a term applied to the part of the sleeve nearest the hand, sometimes a ruffle formed by a band of gathering at the wrist, as suggested by Cotgrave's definition of *poignet de la chemise* as 'wristband or gathering at the sleeve hand of a shirt'; sometimes the circular flare pendant over the hand. These ruffles or circular flares were usually embroidered or lined.[5] Autolycus was therefore chanting to an object of beauty whose embroidery on 'sleeve-hand' and 'square' was worthy of praise.[6]

[1] Egerton MS. 2804, fol. 62.

[2] 1603, Florio, *Montaigne's Essays*, II. xii. 310; 1632, 'They make trunk sleeves of wyre'. 1573, A.O. 3/1108, 'rolls of bente in sleeves of toga'. 1577, Egerton MS. 2806, describes a gown for Mary Sidney with 'rolls of bente' in the sleeves.

[3] 1587, L.C. 9/79, 'farthingale sleeves of whalebone covered with fustian'; 1590, L.C. 2/82, 'verthingale sleves de Telo holland bented cum oss. cart. et coopt. cum reban'; 1593, L.C. 9/985; 1600, L.C. 9/91; 1613, Cam-

pion's entertainment for the Queen at Caversham House showed Robin Hood's men with wide sleeves shaped 'farthingale-wise at the shoulders', *Prog. James*, ii. 633. 1606, *The Fawn*, IV. i. 84, shows trunk-sleeves used by a country woman.

[4] 1546, L.C. 2/115, inventory of effects of Mrs. Holland.

[5] 1559–60, L.C. 9/53, describes a drawn-work smock with 'collar, wrist-band and ruffe' of black-work. See discussion of smocks.

[6] *Wint. Tale*, IV. iii. 212.

'Sleeve-hands' were a part of outer garments as well as of shirts and smocks. The Great Wardrobe accounts of 1546 itemize the expense of a riding costume of green cloth guarded 'in the vents and sleve-hands' with velvet,[1] and an account of 1548–9 describes such a costume of scarlet, the 'skirte and sleve hands' lined with three and three-fourths yards of crimson taffeta.[2]

WINGS

When the detachable outer sleeve became fashionable during the early years of the reign of Elizabeth, various methods of attaching them to the armhole were practised. They were buttoned in or tied in by points and, since some disguising of the juncture was desirable, rolls or wings were invented. The former were rolls of stiffened buckram covered by the material of the garment and fastened around the armhole. This outer covering was slashed and trimmed. By 1555 the fashion of wings was introduced. Wings were flat tabs lined with buckram[3] placed around the armhole side by side and joined by visible stitches, so that the whole extended out from the shoulder widest at the top of the arm and narrowing towards the under side. The apprentice's list of his accomplishments in *Like Will to Like*: 'I learned to make gowns with long sleeves and wings....',[4] showed he was quite skilled. Wings decreased in size until they were by 1604 'as little and diminutive as a puritan's ruff'.[5]

---

[1] E. 351/3025.
[2] Ibid. Leland, *Collectanea*, iv. 323; Holland trans. *Loves of the Emperors*, by Gaius Suetonius Tranquillus, 18.
[3] 1562, L.C. 9/56, 'buceram to line wings of doubblet'.
[4] I. i. 24; *Every Man Out of His Humour*, III. v. 5; 1575, Egerton MS. 2806.
[5] 'Father Hubburds Tales', viii. 69. Cf. this statement with Peacham's concerning the 'high bolstered wings' of Queen Elizabeth's time, *Truth of Our Times*, 67.

XI

GARMENTS FOR WOMEN

APRON

THE earliest record of aprons in England was in the thirteenth century, when they were worn by working persons as a protection for other garments. *Sloane MSS.* 346 and 2983 show a man's leather apron with a bib, and a woman's waist-apron. In the sixteenth century, aprons were worn by mechanics, carpenters, armourers,[1] &c., as a protective garment; but by women, as an ornament.[2] During the second half of the sixteenth century aprons were a part of the costume of royalty and all fashionable women, a fashion lasting until about 1640. These aprons 'so quaintly cut, so richly wrought', were made of finest cambric, silks, and trimmed with lace[3]—sometimes made entirely of lace, of which a beautiful example is shown in the portrait of Lady Elizabeth Paulet, Plate III.

Although mechanics and artisans wore aprons, the term 'apron husband' in the *Roaring Girl* (III. ii. 33) is a contemptuous one for a man who tries to usurp woman's place.

BODY

'Layd out for the company of my lord admeralles men for to by tafetie tinsell to make a payer of bodyes for a womanes gowne to playe allece perce in . . . xx s' is one of Henslowe's records for 1597.[4] He indicated the 'upper bodies' or bodice of a kirtle or gown. Since the bodice was made in two parts, a back and a front, joined together at the sides, it was called a pair.[5]

[1] *Cor.* IV. vi. 97; *Ant. & Cleop.* v. ii. 209; *Jul. Caes.* I. i. 7; *2 Henry VI,* II, iii. 75, &c.

[2] 1524, *Letters and Papers Henry VIII,* iv. 1, 340; 1545–55, *Somerset Rec. Soc. Pub.* xl. 89, 143, 207, 213, 230, 242, 245, 248; 1585, *Durham Wills,* xxxviii. 114; 1596, ibid. ii. 305, &c.

[3] Gosson, *Pleasant Quips,* 29, gives a description of the rich aprons; *Shoemaker's Holiday,* II. i, mentions aprons of cambric; 1556, Add. MS. 35328 lists expense of 13 oz. of 'brode bone lace of golde and silver' to edge an apron and one towel.

[4] *Diary,* i. 70.

[5] 1574, Egerton MS. 2806, 'Itm for making a payer of kyrtle bodies

Beginning in the eighties, the bodies were made so much like the masculine doublet, that distinguishing them was difficult. Preachers and prose writers criticized the style and dramatists for many years created scenes with the apparent intention of ridiculing it. When Follywit disguised himself in a woman's skirt, mask, and muffler, Mawworm asked him: 'What shift will you make for upperbodies?' He replied: 'Why the doublet serves as well as the best, and is most in fashion.'[1]

Under the upper body of the kirtle was worn another, corresponding to a corset, stiffened by stays of wood or whalebone, and fastidious men, as well as ladies, wore these 'whalebone bodyes for the better grace'.[2] The stays, called 'busks',[3] were often carved and richly ornamented. They were inserted in casings in the bodies and tied there by laces or 'busk-points'.[4] Ladies gave their busk-points to their lovers, who wore them about their wrists or in other conspicuous places, and made sonnets to them, much to the envy of less fortunate suitors.[5] 'I was once like thee', said a lover in *How to Choose a Good Wife from a Bad:*

the forepart being of tyssue and the back of white Satten . . . '. This use of 'forepart' must not be confused with the detachable front of the kirtle skirt. Ibid. 1575, 'for alteringe of a frenche gowne of blak wrought vellat & makinge of a peire of bodies wth a highe coller and ruffes to it cutt downe thicke wth longe cuttes . . . wth two peire of hanginge sleves . . . the bodies ruffes & hanginge sleves lyned wth black sarcenet'. Also 1581-5, L.C. 9/73; L.C. 9/76. For more complete discussion of bodies, see discussion of kirtle, &c.

[1] *Mad World, My Masters*, III. iii. 112. *White Devil*, IV. i. 60. 'An Orient gown . . . of cloth of tissue . . . a curious body with embroidered flowers', *Maid in the Mill*, V. ii. 223.

[2] Fitzgeffrey, *Certaine Elegies*, sig. F 6. Also *Loyal Subject*, II. i. 383: 'If the bones want setting in her old

bodies.' These bodies cost five to nine shillings, *Household Bk. Howard*, 9; 1620, *Shuttleworth Accts.* xli. 242.

[3] *Antonio & Mellida*, Ind. 55: 'Sirrah you must seem now as glib and straight in outward semblance as a lady's busk.' 1583, Egerton MS. 2806, 'twelve payer busks of whales bone'. 1586, L.C. 9/77: 'pro fcūr 11 doz Buske de oss caet et wyer cōpt. cum sarcenet quilted.' *Incarnate Devils*, 15: 'And since busk came into request, horne is growne to such scarcity that Leuiathan hath cast his owne beakes of late to serve the market.' Busks were usually part of a pedlar's wares, *Downfall Robert Earl of Huntingdon*, sig. F 4 verso.

[4] *Malcontent*, IV. i. 23.

[5] Wither, *Juvenilia*, ix. 36; Rowlands, *Dr. Merrie Man*, ii. 22; Fitzgeffrey, *Satires*, sig. B 8; *Lingua*, IV. vi. 22.

IV. Child's embroidered kirtle and gown. Spanish late 16th century.
Spanish farthingale belled the skirt at the bottom. Hanging sleeves, wing
at shoulder

Metropolitan Museum of Art, New York

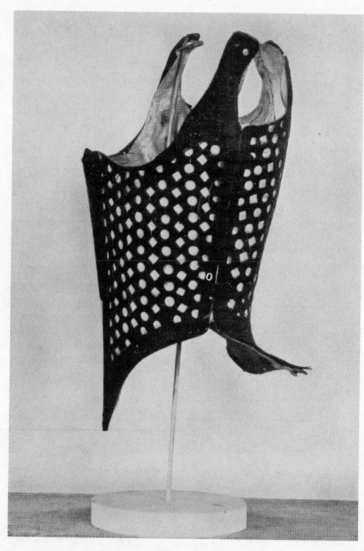

V. Iron 'body'. Late 16th century
Victoria and Albert Museum

A sighing, melancholy humorist,
A crosser of arms, a goer without garters,
A hatband-hater, a busk-point wearer.
(Sig. B 3 verso.)

But even busks did not give sufficient stiffness. 'Bodies
for women and children of whalebone or leather' are listed
in the *Book of Customs Rates* for 1631; and 'iron bodyes',
according to *Wit in a Constable*, 1639 (IV. ii. 378), were
worn by women, a fact attested by extant models.[1]

FARTHINGALE

What compass will you wear your farthingale?
(*Two Gentlemen of Verona*, II. vii. 51.)

Farthingales were stiff accessories used to hold out the
skirts of women's kirtles.[2] The date of the introduction
of farthingales into England can be only conjectured.
Hall tells of a masque at Greenwich, March 7, 1519, in
which eight participants dressed in black velvet gowns
'with hoopes from the wast douneward',[3] and a contemporary note to Latimer's sermon before King Edward, 1552,
states that 'vardingales are learned from players that
decked giants after that manner', a statement supported
by Bansley's 'Wyth a double fardyngale and a caped cassock, Much like a player's gowne' (p. 239). It is not unreasonable to suppose that, in seeking unusual devices for
Court masques, the costumier may have seized upon this
foreign mode, and thus introduced it to the Court. A
ballad credits Eleanor, wife of Edward I, with the introduction of Spanish tailors into England, and says that
they 'brought in fashions strange and new. . . . The

[1] Plate V.

[2] Apparently derived from the
Spanish *verdugado*, possibly so named
because *verduguillos* or withes were
used in their construction, possibly because the garment resembled the bell-
shaped growth of twigs on a truncated
tree. Lebrija, 1631, defines *cycla funi-
culata* as 'Propiamente es el verdugado
que vsan aora las mugeres de nuestros
tiempos con los verduguillos de espar-
to'. Minsheu, 1617, seized upon the
popular association of their origin with
whores, and derived the word from
vertus, galle. Cf. Gosson, *Pleasant
Quippes for Upstart Gentlewomen*, 26;
Duchess of Malfi, II. ii. 163; Estienne,
Apologie pour Herodote, i. 288.

[3] *Chronicles*, 597.

farthingale and mighty ruff',[1] but gives no date for these fashions.

The first occurrence of farthingales in the royal wardrobe accounts seems to be in 1545, when 'vii virg. Satten de bruges crimsen pro una verdingale' are itemized for the Princess Elizabeth.[2] The following year 'supplies for my Lady Mary's Grace' included an item, 'ffor making a vardingale of crimsen sattin'.[3] If these were the first farthingales worn, noble and lesser ladies must have immediately adopted them. An inventory of the effects of Mrs. Holland, one of the household of the Duke of Norfolk, taken 1546, lists 'ij vertingales redde bridges Satten',[4] and the undated play of *Ralph Roister Doister*[5] shows that within a decade or less farthingales were worn by the common people. Farthingales were of two chief types, the Spanish and the French. The Spanish, or 'round' farthingale was a circular skirt, made small at the waist and very wide at the feet, stiffened by hoops of 'bents' or rushes, wood, wire, or whalebone inserted in casings, so that it resembled a large bell. Thus Infidel tells Mary Magdalene: 'With wiers and houpes, your garments must be made' (sig. D 1). Every kind of woollen and all expensive silks, including velvet, were used in farthingales.[6]

The Spanish farthingale continued to be worn until the end of the century, but declined, as the French type—

[1] Peele, *Works*, i. 78.

[2] E. 351/3025.

[3] E. 101/424/7.

[4] L.R. 2/119; 1551, *Mid. MSS.* 404; Ellis, *Letters*, II. ii. 215.

[5] II. iii. 43. See *Library*, British Bibliographical Soc., 1928, for possible date. Also 'Dialogue of Robin Conscience', *Early Popular Poetry*, iii. 238, for reference to round farthingale.

[6] 1557, L.C. 9/52, 'verdugado de Sattin', also of 'Mockdowe'; 1559, A.O. 3/1106, 'de Sarcenett crimsen le bents coopt cum kersie'; 1560, L.C. 9/52, 5 yds. purple taffeta for farthingale, 7¾ yds. purple velvet for border, 7½ yds. kersey for the 'ropes' i.e. the casings; 1574, Egerton MS. 2806,

'verthingale de carnacion Satten', the 'bents' covered with green velvet, trimmed with carnation lace 'purled'; 1566, Add. MS. 35328, to John Bate, 'verthingale maker', payment for a farthingale of 'crymsen tuft taffeta edged cum crymsen vellat', also for a hamper to carry 'two verthingales in'; 1583, A.E. 3/1110, 'of peach colour mirror Satten'. 1587–9, L.C. 9/79, 157 yards of whalebone were used for three farthingales, 214 yards for seven farthingales; 1595, L.R. 9/87, 'ij verthingals de taffata coloris strawnibus, cum oss. caet. pro ead' (i.e. whalebone). To produce greater stiffness, the bents were covered with buckram.

found in Queen Elizabeth's accounts 1561—gained favour.[1] (Plate VI.) The French type was a roll resembling an automobile tire, stiffened by wire, or stuffed with cotton.[2] This roll was placed around the hips and the pleated skirt of the kirtle allowed to fall over it. A variation of this roll was used by 1580. Instead of a complete roll, a half roll, made by stuffing only part of it, was placed behind 'like a rudder to the body', leaving the front straight. It was called a 'half-', 'demi-', or 'semi-circled' farthingale, the kind which Falstaff assured Mrs. Ford that she could wear gracefully.[3]

An Italian mode was a wheel fastened about the waist and extending out eight to forty-eight inches, at right angles. The harsh line made by this farthingale was softened by adding to the kirtle at the waist a circle of soft pleats reaching to the outer edge of the wheel. This mode was designated in the allusion to 'farthingales and frounces' of *Monsieur Thomas* (III. ii. 3). Because of their resemblance to St. Catherine's wheel, these 'frounced' farthingales were given the name of Catherine-wheel farthingales. They were worn at Court in the sixties,[4] and were still used there in 1617,[5] though they were then considered the best style for citizens' wives who sought to imitate court fashions.[6] Scotch farthingales are not named in wardrobe accounts. The allusion to these in *Eastward Hoe*[7] was evidently not to a style, but to a small farthingale which

---

[1] A.O. 3/1106, 'pro fcura unus varthingale de Buckeram nigr de fcura ffrancio'. Two rolls of buckram were needed.

[2] Cotgrave, *Hausse-cul*, 'a French Vardingale, or . . . the kind of roll used by such women as weare no Vardingale'; 1617, Minsheu, *Ductor*, 'a role to weare under womens gownes, a French verdingale'; 1573, *Mid. MSS.* 439: 'iij Yardes of cotton for rowles'; 1585, A.O. 3/1111: 'rotulorum de Bent coop. cū fust.', bents meaning here the rushes which stiffened the roll; also 'ij rotulorum de tele holland cum wyar'. These rolls were vulgarly called 'bums' or 'bum-rolls'. *Michaelmas Term*, I. ii. 15; *Westward Hoe*, II. ii. 37; *Women Beware Women*, II. ii. 133; *Poetaster*, II. i. 67.

[3] *M. Wives*, III. iii. 68; 2 *If You Know Not Me*, I. i. 271.

[4] L.C. 9/55.

[5] Horatio Busino describes the Queen's costume in December 1617 as of 'pink and gold, with so expansive a farthingale that I do not exaggerate when I say that it was four feet wide at the hips'. *C.S.P.V.* xv. 80.

[6] *Northward Hoe*, III. i. 60.

[7] I. ii. 49; *Westward Hoe*, II. ii. 40: 'Scotch bum.'

suggested to the dramatist the supposed miserliness of the Scots.

Farthingales so increased in size that difficulty in seating ladies at gatherings caused an order to be issued, 1613, that no ladies wearing them would be admitted to Court masques,[1] but the order was not wholly effective, for an Italian witness of Jonson's *Vision of Delight*, 1617, wrote that most of the ladies were wearing loose gowns, but that there were some farthingales.[2] Lady Anne Clifford, however, recorded in her diary for November, 1617, that while she was at Court she wore no farthingale.[3] The ladies of King Charles's Court, following the French fashion of full-gathered skirts, which hung in soft folds, soon set the fashion for farthingale-less costume, and by the late twenties only country folk were wearing farthingales.

GOWN

A gown was a long garment open in front, somewhat resembling the modern top-coat. It was worn over other garments except the cloak, for which it often served. The night-gown differed from the usual gown in being less elaborate, warmer, and unconfined at the waist. Gowns were worn by women from Norman times; by men, from the fourteenth century.[4] Sixteenth-century gowns, which required six to twelve yards of material in addition to linings, were very expensive; for they were not only made of costly cloths, but guarded, embroidered, trimmed with lace, pinked and jagged.[5] An inventory of the goods of

---

[1] Birch, *Court and Times James I*, i. 228.

[2] *C.S.P.V.* xv. 112. They were ridiculed on the stage, *Ram Alley*, Dodsley, x. 323.

[3] *Diary*, 79–80.

[4] Camden describes the original gowns in his *Remains Concerning Britain* (ed. 1614), 233: '. . . some in a garment reaching to their heeles, close before and strowting out on the sides, so that on the backe, they make men seeme women, and this they call by a ridiculous name, Gowne.' The

fifteenth-century gowns were furred, without sleeves, lined or unlined, made of woollen, silk, cloth of gold, tissue, and velvet. See *Fifty Early English Wills*, lxxviii. 15, 17, 34, 50, 78, &c.; *Paston Letters*, i. 101, 134, iii. 215, 437, 465, &c.; *Archaeologia*, xxi. 252.

[5] 1546, L.R. 2/121; 1553, E. 154/2/41; 1564, *Durham Wills*, ii. 220; 1581, L.C. 9/93. See also Stubbes's description, *Anatomy*, 69. *Ram Alley*, Dodsley, x. 344: 'red taffeta gown Bound with a silver lace.' See also index.

VI. French farthingales, petticoat, French sleeves in 'rising panes', 'demi-cannon' sleeves.
Note mask, fan, purse. Costume 1590–1600

Photograph by F. Bruckmann, Munich

VII. Loose gown, late 16th century. Italian brocade slashed
saw-tooth fashion. Cream ground, gold pattern, touches of red,
blue, and green

Victoria and Albert Museum

Margaret Gascoigne, made 1567, values a 'goune of changeable taffatie laid w^t gold lace' at 66s. 8d.; 'a goune of silk grogram laid w^t silke lace' at 46s. 8d.,[1] not a mean price for old clothes in those days!

The chief fashions of sixteenth-century gowns were the Dutch or 'round gown', which was 'made round without any trayne';[2] the Flanders, which had a fitted bodice and stiff collar;[3] the Italian, usually trainless, which had double bodices,[4] of which the outer was slashed; and the much admired French, which had full skirts, rolls or wings at the sleeves, usually hanging sleeves, and was much welted or pinked.[5] The 'loose-bodied' gown has been much maligned by editors of sixteenth-century drama, who have based their statements upon the puns of drama-tists. An Italian spectator at Jonson's masque, *The Vision of Delight*, given at Court, Christmas 1617, describes the loose gown then worn: 'The dress hangs behind well nigh from the neck down to the ground, with long close sleeves and no waist. There are no folds so that any deformity, however monstrous, remains hidden.'[6] The Victoria and Albert Museum has an excellent example of such a gown. (Plate VII.) Queen Elizabeth had nearly a hundred loose gowns, some of which had been presented as New Year's gifts.[7] In the drama, however, they are usually mentioned with innuendo.[8]

Young men did not wear gowns as outer garments—except, of course, occasionally the night-gown for daytime costume; but gowns were the usual wear of old men. Members of professions as lawyers, justices, scriveners, clergymen, and civil officials naturally wore their profes-sional gowns.[9]

[1] *Durham Wills*, ii. 273.

[2] 1540, Hall, *Chronicle*, 835; 1566, Add. MS. 35328; 1578, A.O. 3/1108.

[3] 1561, A.O. 3/1106; 1575, Egerton MS. 2806.

[4] Ibid.

[5] 1546, E. 101/424/7; L.R. 2/119; 1559, A.O. 3/1106. See also references under 'Farthingale', 'Pink'.

[6] *C.S.P.V.* xv. 112.

[7] 1556–7, E. 101/428/5; 1559, A.O. 3/1106; 1561, L.C. 9/55, 1599, L.C. 2/121 (an inventory of the Queen's gowns). *Prog. Elizabeth*, iii. 13, 450, 452, &c.

[8] *1 Honest Whore*, I. viii. 28; *Michaelmas Term*, I. ii. 13; *1 Henry IV*, III. iii. 37; *Witch of Edmonton*, I. ii. 46; *Virgin Martyr*, III. iii. 89.

[9] *M. d'Olive*, IV. ii. 52; *Magnetic*

NIGHT-GOWN

A night-gown was an ankle-length gown with long
sleeves and collar varying in size from the shawl-collar of
the men's modern dressing-gown to the fur collar on
ladies' coats. It was worn for warmth both indoors and
out. Previous to the reign of Henry VIII, it was frequently of worsted or woollen materials, sometimes made
with a hood.[1] Many of those of the later sixteenth century
were made of grograin, fine puke, shag, satin, taffeta, velvet, embroidered with gold and silver, trimmed with martin, lamb, cony, and other fur, and lined with expensive
material.[2] After the sixties, profuse use of buttons on
night-gowns as well as on other garments became the
mode. The following is a typical description: 'a nyght
Gowne of blak wrought vellat with lace of golde silver and
murrey and blak silke and eight dozen buttons and loupes
of like lace lyned with murrey sarcenet with fryse in the
ruffs lyned in the skyrtes and collar with buckeram.'[3] Six
yards of material were required for a man's night-gown,
and seven to nine for a woman's. This estimate did not
include lining or trimming.[4] One for Anne Boleyn, 1532,
required eight yards of black satin, eight of black taffeta
for lining, three of velvet for borders, two of buckram to
line the upper parts of the sleeves. The gown cost
£10 5s. 8d.[5]

In order to explain Lady Macbeth's: 'Get on your
night-gown, lest occasion call us',[6] editors have tried to
prove that night-gowns were for night wear in one's

Lady, I. i. 388; Measure for Measure,
II. ii. 44; Lear, IV. vi. 170.

[1] 1500, Ill. Ant. Man. England, 241.
1599, made of buffin, Durham Wills,
xxxviii. 233.

[2] 1541, E. 154/2/20; 1546, L.R.
2/119; 1553, L.R. 2/118, inventory
Duke Northumberland, russet taffeta
faced with martin; 1564, L.C. 9/58,
tuft-taffeta embroidered with silver;
1574, silk grograin, lace, trimmed with
cony; 1581, L.C. 9/73, carnation velvet; 1593, Durham Wills, xxxviii. 227,

tuft-taffeta; 1591, L.C. 9/83, drake
colour satin embroidered with silver,
body lined with fustian; 1615, Loseley
MSS. 408. Earl Somerset's effects,
tawny velvet embroidered with gold,
lined with unshorn velvet.

[3] 1570, Egerton MS. 2806.

[4] 1564, L.C. 2/58; 1572, Egerton
MS. 2806.

[5] P. P. Ex. Henry VIII, 223. Philobiblon Soc. Miscy. vii.

[6] Macbeth, II. ii. 71.

chamber. Many accounts show the error of this assumption. In *Sir Thomas Wyat* (sig. G 2), Lady Jane is presented as wearing a night-gown on the scaffold. At his execut:on in 1568, Count Egmont was 'attired in a black velvet doublet, wide black velvet breeches, white Spanish boots. Over this, he wore a red damask night robe and an ordinary black cloak, both edged with gold braid. He also wore a hat with black and white plumes thereon.'[1] But the best proof of daytime wear is to be found in the *Diary* of Lady Anne Clifford. On December 28, 1617, she wrote: 'I went to Church in my rich night gown.'

KIRTLE

Few words in costume nomenclature have been the object of so much misinformation as the kirtle, and its accessory, forepart—misinformation due partly to the fact that the kirtle changed its fashion and purpose through the ages. In Anglo-Saxon times, a knee-length tunic of fairly loose fit, worn by men, was called a *cyrtel*; during the latter part of the reign of Henry IV, a tightly fitting, long-sleeved garment of knee-length for men, but ground-length for women was known as kirtle. By 1460 ladies had adopted a kirtle which had a square décolletage and fitted the body closely to the mid-thigh, falling in folds about the feet, but men continued to call their short tunic a kirtle, even in the sixteenth century.[2]

The sixteenth-century kirtle worn by women was used over petticoats and farthingale as an outside dress, but a gown or cloak was worn over it.[3] It consisted of a separable bodice, called a 'pair of bodies', and a skirt. Over the bodice was worn the partlet—when this was in fashion—but the bodice took the place of doublet or waistcoat. The kirtle was open in front from neck to feet, the stomacher filling in the opening of the bodice. The Spanish kirtle needed a triangular accessory for the opening in the skirt.

[1] Fugger, *News Letters*, 4. *Pleasant Conceits of Old Hobson*, ix. 15: 'In a night gown, a buttoned cap, and a pair of slippers tooke shippinge.'

[2] See robes of Edward VI, L.R.

2/121; L.C. 2/3⁽²⁾.

[3] 1556, *Lancashire and Cheshire Wills*, li. 15, 'ij Damaske gowns garded wᵗʰ velvet and Kyrtels thair unto belongynge'. Plates IV, VIII.

This accessory was known as a 'forepart'. Since the Catherine-wheel farthingale required a closed kirtle, no forepart was worn with this style. The accessories were usually considered together, and often given as presents; thus a reader of the Lord Chamberlain's accounts and of records of New Year's presents given Queen Elizabeth finds such items as: 'Unius forepte de velvet Russet opat. cum dutche bodies pro eadem', 'a foreparte, boddies and partlett of sipers', 'a foreparte and a peir of boddys of a Frenche kyrtill of blewe cloth of silver'.[1] About seven yards of yard-wide material were required for a kirtle, of which two or three were needed for the bodice.[2] The skirt of the kirtle was called a 'half-kirtle'. Doll's exclamation that she will forswear half-kirtles if her statement be untrue,[3] means that she will give up a necessary part of woman's dress.

'What stuff wilt have a kirtle of?' Falstaff asks Doll.[4] She had many materials from which to choose: mockado, worsted, lawn, saye, or the expensive silks as damask, satin, taffeta, velvet, tissue, tabine.[5]

Forepart

The *Oxford English Dictionary* erroneously defines the forepart as a stomacher, i.e. placard. The following items will show that the two are different articles: 'It'm one forepart wth a plackard of crimsen satten striped with gold

[1] 1559, L.C. 9/53; 1557, *Prog. Elizabeth*, ii. 75, 70.

[2] 1511, E. 101/417/4; 1546, E. 101/423/12, 'vij yeardes of clothe of silver for a kirtle for my Lady Mary's Grace'; 1530, *Chetham Soc. Pub.* xli. 365. 1511, E. 101/417/4, 'vij yeards sattin fore a kyrtle 3 elles lynyn cloth to lin upper boddies'; 1546, E. 351/3025, 'ij verg. sattin nigr pro upper-bodying a kirtle'.

[3] 2 *Hen. IV*, v. iv. 24; *Westward Hoe*, IV. i. 111; 1568, *Durham Wills*, ii. 281: 'One old sathan halfe kirtle gairded wth veluet.'

[4] 2 *Hen. IV*, II. iv. 297.

[5] Mocado, 1561, L.C. 9/55; worsted, 1526, *Lancashire and Cheshire Wills*, xxxiii. 13; lawn, 1588, L.C. 9/88: 'Unius kirtle rotund de lawne.' Round kirtles were circular skirted without trains. Saye, 1519, *Nottingham Rec.* iii. 354 a; damask, 1558, *Richmond Wills*, 122; satin, 1540, *P. P. Ex. Prin. Mary*, 90; taffeta, 1600, *Prog. Elizabeth*, iii. 507: 'rounde kirtle of heare-colour tufte taphata'; velvet, 1547, Harl. MS. 1419 a, 162: 'One kertle of Orrenge Tawney Vellat embrawdered with silver'; 2 *If You Know Not Me*, I. i. 354: 'I will take up French commodities, velvet kirtles and taffety foreparts'; tissue, *Prog, Elizabeth*, iii. 502; tabine, ibid. 466.

VIII. Mary Sidney. Gown over kirtle. 'Shadow' with matching cuffs.
'Organ-pipe ruff', plain gloves, embroidered kirtle body

National Portrait Gallery

raised velvet and lined with changeable sarconet'; 'for lyninge of a forepart and placarde of nedleworke'.[1] The forepart was the elaborate accessory worn with the kirtle to fill the triangular opening in front. It was usually embroidered, 'pinked', or 'raised', furred, flourished with oes and spangles, or trimmed with lace.[2] Since foreparts seldom matched the material of the kirtle, were detachable, and easily changed, their changeability was the target for the wit of dramatists.[3]

PETTICOAT

Petticoat, once the name for a short coat worn by men —as the 'petticotes of lynen clothe stoffyd with flokys . . . withought slyves' which are named in the wardrobe of Sir John Fastolfe,[4] 1459—was, by the middle of the sixteenth century, used almost exclusively to designate a woman's underskirt, usually tied by points—though sometimes attached permanently—to the body.[5] 'A cliquant petticoat of some rich stuff to catch the eye', an expression from *The Maid in the Mill*, is a good description, for, since the long skirts were sometimes lifted gracefully to facilitate walking, the petticoat was exposed, and was therefore made of material as rich and ornamental as the wearer could afford. *The Malcontent, The City Madam, The New Inn, Your Five Gallants*[6] named women's petticoats made of velvet, pinked, lined with contrasting material, and guarded with expensive lace. Petticoats given Queen

[1] 1611, L.R. 2/121; 1572, Egerton MS. 2806.

[2] Embroidered, 1599, L.R. 2/121; *Prog. Elizabeth*, ii. 73; iii. 7; pinked or cut (razed), with a pun, *Northward Hoe*, I. i. 492; furred, 1553, L.R. 2/119; oes, 1589, A.O. 3/1111; lace-trimmed, 1572, Egerton MS. 2806; *Westward Hoe*, I. i. 73 (pun).

[3] *Your Five Gallants*, I. i. 30.

[4] *Archaeologia*, xxi. 253. The name was used to designate a similar garment for men during the first sixty years of the sixteenth century: 1536, *Archaeologia*, ix. 244, 246; 1546, L.R. 2/115; 1549, *Test. Ebor.* cvi. 294;

1552, *Bury Wills*, 49; 1563, *Durham Wills*, ii. 209.

[5] Egerton MS. 2806 offers numerous excellent examples: 'for making two petycoates one red cloth the other stanell fryzado upperbodied with mockado' . . . 'for alteringe and enlarging of a peire of bodies for a Petycoate of white sattin.' *Prog. Elizabeth*, iii. 447 (New Year's gift, 1599), 'one pettycoatte without bodyes, of silver tynsell wrought in squares, with a border of trees of grene sylke nedleworke'.

[6] In order of their mention: v. ii. 230; I. i. 154; IV. iii. 33; I. i. 75.

Elizabeth for New Year's gifts were covered by gold and silver lace, with eight to ten yards of heavy gold passement around the hem.[1] Since petticoats were lined, and, according to a description in *Anything for a Quiet Life*, were two and a half yards in circumference,[2] the weight must have been burdensome, especially as two or more were worn.[3] They were, of course, put on over the head.

SAFEGUARD

Seven yards of velvet or three and a half yards of satin were required to make a woman's safeguard.[4] This amount of material shows how voluminous or thickly gathered[5] was this skirt worn with a short coat or cloak as a riding-costume. Its name probably arose from its purpose: to protect the lady's costume from dust and soiling by the horse; and it may have been originally made of inexpensive materials, but the safeguards of the sixteenth century —the earliest noted being 1546[6]—were of velvet, taffeta, plush, rash, satin, stammel, and even lawn, many of them elaborately embroidered and trimmed with lace.[7] Pre-

[1] *Prog. Elizabeth*, i. 114; ii. 78; iii. 2, 6, 78, &c.

[2] II. ii. 197: 'a yard and a quarter broad, which is just the depth of a woman's petticoat.'

[3] Kiechel in 1585 said the women of England wore 'three cloth gowns or petticoats one over the other'. Rye, op. cit., 90. They put on a smock next the skin; then a boned body or corset, then petticoats, at least one of which had a boned body; then a farthingale, usually covered by a light-weight petticoat; then the kirtle which had a boned body, a stomacher, and a heavy forepart.

[4] 1591, L.C. 9/83; 1587, L.C. 9/79; 1589, A.O. 3/1111.

[5] 1620, *Hic Mulier*: '. . . exchanging the side thick gathered sauegards to short bases.' Florio, *Fadella*, 'used for a sauegard that women wear in riding'.

[6] *State Papers, Henry VIII*, 245, fol. 209 (Royal wardrobe).

[7] Velvet, 1588, L.C. 9/79; 1588,

Prog. Elizabeth, iii. 9, trimmed with 'passamaine lace of venice gold and silver'. Taffeta, 1566, Add. MS. 35328; 1570, Egerton MS. 2806, 'a cloake and saufegarde of russet tufte taphata striped wth golde layed wth bone lace, buttons and lase of silver carnation and russet the cloake and Safegarde bordered wth carnation taphata'; 1599, L.C. 2/121, 'a cloake and saufegarde of orenge colō. Taphata cut set wth doble owes striped allouer wth a lace of silver and purple silke'; 1600 *Prog. Elizabeth*, iii. 509, 'safe-garde of gozelinge colour taphata'. Plush, 1588, L.C. 9/85, 'Jupp' (coat) of peach colour satin. 'Safegarde', white plush. Stammel, 1573, Egerton MS. 2806. Satin, 1588, *Prog. Eliza-beth*, iii. 3; 1601–2, L.C. 9/92, 'safegard Satten colour blush'. Rash, 1577, A.O. 3/1108. Lawn, 1601–2, L.C. 9/92, slashed and set with oes, silver plate, and spangles.

sumably, poorer women used cheaper materials. Allusions to safeguards occur in *The Roaring Girl*, *Ram Alley*, *The Noble Gentleman*,[1] and other plays.

SMOCK

'I have heard that you have threescore smocks that cost three pounds a smock', said Birdlime in *Westward Hoe* (I. i. 87). He refers to a shirt-like garment worn as underwear, and as a sleeping gown by sixteenth-century women. The former use is indicated in *The Dumb Knight*; the latter, in *Much Ado*, *Othello*, and numerous plays.[2] The smock's resemblance to a shirt is characteristically noted in *Every Man In His Humour* and *More Dissemblers Besides Women*.[3] It is, indeed, difficult to distinguish between extant specimens of shirts and smocks; for both were straight two-piece garments, thirty to forty inches long, with collar and sleeve-hands, usually lace-trimmed, and both had a front slit or opening at the neck.

Since Chaucer's days,[4] smocks had been embroidered, and those of the sixteenth century were especially elaborate. Of three 'smokis of fyne holland' in the royal wardrobe, 1535, two were 'wrought aboute the collers with golde and the thirde wrought aboute the coller and handis with silke'.[5] Those in Queen Elizabeth's wardrobe were embroidered in blackwork, gold, silver, and needlework, some with standing collars edged with lace.[6] Sir Fulke Greville, in 1577, presented her with a smock of 'camerick wrought about the coller and sleeves with Spanishe worke of roses and trees, with a night coif and a forhed clothe of the same worke'.[7] Such descriptions call to mind the

---

[1] *Roaring Girl*, III. iii. 29; *Ram Alley*, Dodsley, x. 227; *Noble Gentleman*, II. i. 120.

[2] In order of mention: Dodsley, II. 149; II. iii. 147; V. ii. 271.

[3] III. vi. 54 (Folio); I. iv. 64–5.

[4] *Miller's Tale*, 52.

[5] Royal MSS. 7 F, xvi. 136 b. A smock collar in 1524 required a yard of material, *Letters and Papers of Henry VIII*, iv. 1. 340.

[6] 1559, A.O. 3/1106: 'pro fčur. vi white smocks edged cum white needleworke'; 1561, ibid. 'pro una interula cum le coller manica. et wristband opat. cu. ope. nigr.' See her New Year's gifts for 1577–88, *Prog. Elizabeth*, i. 113; ii. 67, 73, 77; iii. 12.

[7] Ibid. ii. 78. The forehead cloth was a band worn at night to prevent wrinkles.

'cambric smocks . . . Wrought and perfumed' which Sir Frugal censures.[1] Cut-work smocks, named in *The Devil is an Ass*, *Parliament of Love*, and *Triumph of Time*,[2] and those of drawn-work[3] were especially desirable. Plate IX shows an embroidered smock with standing collar.

One form of embroidery, square-work,[4] was much used for ornamenting the fronts of the bodices of gowns, smocks, &c. An inventory of the apparel of the Duchess of Norfolk, 1546, noted 'a square for a gown of crimsen vellut embroidered with golde',[5] and an account of expenses in the household of Anne of Denmark, 1611, itemizes among accessories for dress: 'three squares wrought with silk of divers colours, some holland, some Lawne.'[6] In 1577 Sir Gawen Carewe gave the Queen a New Year's gift of a 'camerick smock wrought with black silke in the collor and sleves, the square and ruffs wrought with venice golde, and edged with a small bone lace of Venice golde',[7] and her wardrobe accounts of 1594–5 showed the cost of 'vi Interula de tella holland the squares et ruffs edged cum laquois opis acui et laqueo opat. sup. oss de serico nigro'.[8] If the square and sleeve-hands of the smock of which Autolycus chanted resembled in beauty those in the Queen's wardrobe, one can understand the enthusiasm of his salesmanship.[9] But square-work declined in royal favour before the end of the sixteenth century and was out of style before 1614. In January of that year Jean Ruthvaine wrote to the Countess

[1] *City Madam*, II. i. 115; *Friar Bacon*, I. i. 104: 'fair wrought smocks'; perfumed smocks, *Malcontent*, I. iii. 40; 1559, *Proud Wyves Pater Noster*, 145: 'With smockes wel wrought.'

[2] In order of mention: I. i. 135; II. i. 50; I. i. 42.

[3] 1559, L.C. 9/53; 1602, L.C. 2/93: 'Pro fčura iij interula Telo holland cum ope.tract.de serico nigro, ruffe et wristband edged cum tenia.'

[4] 1560–1, L.C. 9/54, lists 'square-worke, billiament worke, blacke-worke'.

[5] L.R. 2/115. Cf. 1578, Hake, *Newes Out of Powles Churchyarde*, D,

iv. a: 'She must have Partlet, Square & Lace with chaine about her neck'; also Fairfax, trans. *Tasso*, XII. lxiv: 'Betweene her brests the cruell weapon riues Her curious square embost with swelling gold.'

[6] L.R. 2/121. These were evidently old. Square-work was out of fashion for persons of her status.

[7] *Prog. Elizabeth*, ii. 74.

[8] L.C. 9/81, that is '6 smocks of holland whose squares and neck-ruffs were edged with needlework and bone-lace'.

[9] *Wint. Tale*, IV. iii. 212.

IX. Girl's smock. Italian, late 16th century. Linen embroidered in
coloured silks on collar, skirt, and sleeve-hands

Metropolitan Museum of Art, New York

of Eglinton, concerning purchases which he had evidently been asked to make: 'As for the piccadaill I have boght it of the best fashon; and as for lace to be a band and cuffs and square with long peakes, please your ladyship know that it is not the fashon to weare such now.'[1]

STOMACHER OR PLACARD

'Golden quoifs and stomachers' were acceptable gifts from sixteenth-century lads to their 'dears', as Autolycus sings.[2] The stomacher or placard, originating in a piece of armour to protect the chest, never lost its stiffness, though it became an ornamental, detachable shield worn over the abdomen under the doublet or kirtle body to fill the front opening in these garments. It was made over a foundation of pasteboard,[3] or was stiffened by busks.

Stomachers for men were noted in 1450;[4] for women in 1510.[5]

Although women continued to wear stomachers to the end of the eighteenth century, men gave them up when stiff doublets went out of fashion, i.e. about 1605. The stomacher, which might or might not, according to the preference of the wearer, match the remainder of the costume,[6] though it matched the forepart[7] of the woman's kirtle, required five-sixths to a yard of material.[8] Whether the stomacher were of scarlet, velvet, tissue, or satin trimmed with lace, cut-work, or purl,[9] it was usually veiled to

[1] *Eglinton MSS.* 43.

[2] *Wint. Tale,* IV. iii. 226.

[3] 1578, Egerton MS. 2806: 'Itm for making of foure stomachers of paste bourde covered with taphata.'

[4] *Coventry Mysteries,* 241. An unusual stomacher is described in the private expenses of Henry VII, 1494: 'For an estryche skinne for a stomacher . . . £14', Add. MS. 7099.

[5] *Letters and Papers Henry VIII,* ii. 2, 1491; 1513, 1500; 1520, iii. 2, 1554.

[6] *Philobiblon Soc. Miscy.* vii. 15: 1553, 'sattin for a plackard of a gowne of whyt sattin 11s'; see also references below.

[7] 1611, L.R. 2/121: 'Itm one fore-part wᵗ a placard of crimsen satten striped with golde raised velvet and lined with changeable sarconet.'

[8] 1545–6, E. 351/3025: '26 virg. satten cremsen for 29 stomachers'; 1546, L.R. 2/119, 'one yard blacke cloth of tissue for a plackarde to the best kirtell'.

[9] 1556, L.R. 2/119, stomacher of black 'vellet embroidered with purles'; 1551, Ellis, *Letters,* II. ii. 215, of scarlet; 1575, Egerton MS. 2806: 'Itm for making of six stomachers of white Satten layed at the topps with bone lase of venice golde and silver lyned wᵗ white fustian'; 1600, L.C. 9/91: 'Pro vi pectoral de op.sciss.fact.de Italic.et flando purle.'

enhance its richness—'shadow their glorie as a Millaners wife doth her wrought stomacher, with a smoakie lawne,[1] or a blacke cipresse', said Edward Knowell in *Every Man in His Humour* (I. ii. 105–7).

PLACKET

A placket was a short opening or 'vent' at the top of a woman's petticoat or kirtle skirt, usually in front.[2] It was necessary to enable the wearer to put the garment on and off. In the drama placket is frequently used with indelicate suggestion. This term should not be confused with 'placard' or stomacher.

---

[1] 1601–2, L.C. 9/92: 'Pro fcur ij pectoral de opat.sciss., cum Lawne et edg cum tenia bon opat.sup.oss.'

[2] *King Lear*, III. iv. 98; *Little French Lawyer*, v. i. 359; *Downfall of the Earl of Huntingdon*, II. ii; *Love's L. L.* III. i. 194; *Friar Bacon*, I. i. 110; *Roaring Girl*, III. iii. 29; *Troilus*, II. iii. 22, &c.

XII

GARMENTS FOR MEN

Cloak

The sixteenth-century cloak was a revival, with some changes, of the Norman *manteau*. Early sixteenth-century ladies used a long, semicircular, sleeved cloak, requiring seven to twelve yards of material.[1]

Gentlemen during these early years wore the Spanish cape, a hooded cloak of hip-length whose circular edge was ornamented by lace, or guards of taffeta, velvet, and other silk.[2] Worn at first over the coats, Spanish capes were, by the sixties, shortened and used with the trunk-hose and doublet. Only footmen, tapsters, and a low class of persons went without cloaks;[3] gentlemen wore them except in their chambers.

In the late seventies the long French cloak was introduced, and in 1594 Philip Gawdy—who was a fashion reporter for his family—wrote that 'all men are settled into long cloaks';[4] indeed, so long did they become that Queen Elizabeth forbade any courtier wearing a cloak beneath the knee to come into her presence. These cloaks were made in two ways: circular, or 'compass', and semicircular, or 'half compass',[5] and sometimes had small

---

[1] 1502, *P. P. Ex. Elizabeth York*, 19; 1532, *P. P. Ex. Henry VIII*, 222; a cloak for Anne Boleyn required 12 yds. satin, 3 yds. velvet for collar and facing; 2 yds. satin to line the sleeves, 11 yds to line the cloak, the total costing £12 5s. 10d.

[2] Baret, 1583: 'A Spanishe cape, a cloake with a hoode.' 1527, Breton, *Works*, i. xvi. The wardrobe of Henry VIII, *Archaeologia*, ix. 247, &c.

[3] An Italian visitor in England, 1557, observed that gentlemen's servants wore 'doublets without cloaks'. *C.S.P.V.*, p. 1670. Rowlands, *Knave of Harts* (ii. 12):

'Because we walk in jerkins, and in hose
Without an upper garment, cloak or gown,
We must be tapsters running up and down.'

[4] Egerton MS. 2804, fol. 109. Florio, *Second Frutes*, London, 1591, gives as part of a gentleman's wardrobe, shirts with falling bands (p. 5), cut fustian suit, long gown furr'd with martin, nightgown of chamlet, rugg gown, cloak lined with bays, cape cloak of fine cloth, riding cloak of broadcloth, two doublets, one coat, velvet jerkin, Spanish leather jerkin, breeches, stockings, beaver and felt hats, velvet caps, p. 7.

[5] *The Noble Gentleman*, v. i. 76.

shoulder capes. They were of taffeta, velvet, scarlet, rash, &c., lace-trimmed, embroidered[1] with bugles, pearls, jewels, and so richly lined 'that the inner side standeth almost as much as the outside'.[2] The long cloak was draped over the left shoulder half-falling,[3] and would 'ne'er keep on',[4] so that the gentleman who went to Black-friars and rose between the acts could, gracefully and without apparent intention, let fall his cloak from his shoulders displaying his rich suit.[5]

The cloak fashion was, of course, not confined to men. Women wore cloaks over caped dresses. Stubbes anato-mizes women's gowns which 'haue capes reachyng downe to the middest of their backes, faced with veluet, or els with some fine wrought silke taffatie',[6] which probably resembled Katharina's 'small compassed cape'.[7] The cloaks of court ladies were singularly beautiful in colour combinations: cloaks of 'blewe chaungeable Taphata, lyned with strawe colour'; of 'Skarlett lyned with carnation Taphata pinked'; trimmed with gold lace and buttons; shoulder cloaks of carnation satin furred with mink; and the 1599 inventory of the royal wardrobe includes among sump-tuous cloaks, one of perfumed leather 'striped downright and laide w^t a lace of Venice golde and silver set with small buttons . . . lyned w^t aishe colō satten'.[8]

---

[1] *What You Will*, IV. i. 89. 'Then there's the cape-cloaked courtier.' When Lord Hay went as ambassador to France, 1616, he had a cloak em-broidered within and without up to the cape, *Prog. James*, iii. 183.

[2] Stubbes, *Anatomy of Abuses*, 52. Taffeta cloak, *Spanish Gipsy*, II. i. 118; velvet, II. ii. 199; 1578, Egerton MS. 2806, 'for making of a cloake of blak rashe layed with bone lase of venice silver with buttons & loopes, lyned with spanishe taphata striped & tufte with white silke'; 1558, *Lancashire and Cheshire Wills*, xxxiii. 178; bugles, Henslowe, *Diary*, i. 81; pearls, *Patient Grissel*, III. ii; also portrait of Sir Wal-ter Raleigh, National Portrait Gallery, London. These long cloaks were very

expensive. One for Prince Charles required 9¾ yds. three pile velvet; 9¼ Florence plush to line it, 40 yds. of lace, and 1½ yds. of ribbon, E. 101/434/9.

[3] *Cynthia's Revels*, V. iii. 87.

[4] *Love's Cure*, II. ii. 14.

[5] *Devil is an Ass*, I. iii. 68.

[6] *Anatomy of Abuses*, 69.

[7] *Tam. Sh.* IV. iii. 139. *Eastward Hoe*, I. ii. 17, Gertrude mentions as an inappropriate combination a buffin gown with a tuft-taffeta cape. The will of Ralph Mainwaring, 1588, leaves his wife 'blacke velvet to lyne her a cape of a gowne', *Lancashire and Cheshire Wills*, liv. 12.

[8] L.R. 2/121; Egerton MS. 2806; *Prog. Elizabeth*, iii. 12, &c.

In addition to the long and the shoulder cloak the much guarded and sleeved Dutch cloak[1] was worn by men and women until about 1620, when men altered the fashion slightly, wearing the cloak in a variety of ways: hanging from the shoulder, wrapped across the chest or back with the right-hand corner flung over the left shoulder—never on straight, with the arms in the sleeves!

Rich cloaks had to have protective covering when not in use. Cloak-bags were therefore invented which were as rich as their owners could afford, and which, like the band- or ruff-box, were taken on journeys, for ladies and gentlemen must have morning, afternoon, and evening cloaks.[2]

CASSOCK

The masculine cassock was a loose, wide-sleeved coat of knee or thigh length[3]—chiefly the latter, after the fifties —mentioned in *Every Man In His Humour*, and *All's Well that Ends Well*,[4] as the coat of a soldier; in *Scornful Lady*, as that of a curate; in *Mucedorus*,[5] as that of a shepherd; in *A Trick to Catch the Old One*, as that of a gentleman; and in many expense accounts of gentlemen as one of the necessities for a journey.[6] The cassock fashion originated in France and reached the English Court by the late

[1] 1574, *Richmond Wills*, 246; 1588, *Lancashire and Cheshire Wills*, li. 199, 'a Duche damaske cloake garded wth three guards of velvet and faced with tuftafta'. The Dutch cloak differed from the mandilion in length, reaching only to the waist, and in fullness of sleeves. 1593, *Durham Wills*, xxxviii. 233: 'Dutche cloke garded with velvett, 20 s.'

[2] Wardrobe accounts provide many cloak-bags, and the drama contains numerous allusions to them. Cf. Wardrobe, *Henry VIII, Archaeologia*, ix. 247: 'Itm for making of syxe half cases of yelowe cotten for clene keping of syxe of oure riche clookys.' 1572, Egerton MS. 2806, 'cloake bagge of blak vellat striped with blak silke lase lyned w^t russet satten'. *1 Henry IV*,

II. iv. 103; *Every Man In His Humour*, IV. viii. 11 (Folio).

[3] 1593, Hollyband, '*Casaque*, a man's cassock, a short garment as men of warre or Lackies doe use'; 1611, Cotgrave, '*Casaque*, a cassocke, mandilion, long coat'.

[4] *Every Man In His Humour*, II. v. 143 (Folio); *All's Well*, IV. iii. 193; Holinshed, *Chronicle*, iii. 1317.

[5] *Scornful Lady*, II. i. 30; *Mucedorus*, Dodsley, vii. 207.

[6] *Trick to Catch the Old One*, IV. iv. 15; 1621, Kempe, *Loseley MSS.* 424, Sir George Chaworth provided for a journey a riding suit consisting of a 'cassock, breeches and cloak of black cloth, . . . a stiff doublet of black perpetuana'. This reference is typical of many.

thirties. Elaborate cassocks of velvet, silk, grograin, and
taffeta, embroidered and braided, are described in accounts.[1] The gorgeous costume of the Earl of Surrey
presented in his famous portrait at Hampton Court shows
an excellent example of the early cassock.

WOMEN'S CASSOCKS

The cassock fashion early appealed to women and
gowns made 'cassock-wise' of black velvet embroidered
in gold, cassocks of black damask guarded with velvet,
and even cassocks with hoods are inventoried between
1546 and 1553.[2] They appear in items of stage apparel;
writers satirize the 'brave apparel' of 'fardingale and a
caped cassock, Moche like a players gowne',[3] and the
rich 'silke cassocks' which Tibet Talkapace longs to
wear every day.[4] By 1554 there were 'worky day' cassocks as well as 'best cassocks'.[5] After the eighties
women's cassocks were little worn: country pedlars carried them among their wares[6]—a sign that they were out
of fashion in the city; and except for travelling or cam-
paigning they were not used by fashionable men. They
were then the accustomed wear of misers, usurers, grave
old men, councillors, and rustic folk.

COAT

The coat was an outer garment, worn instead of a
cloak. It was lined, had sleeves, and skirts reaching to the
knees, was fitted at the waistline or confined by a belt, and

[1] 1546, Inventories of Earls of
Northumberland and Surrey, L.R.
2/115, L.R. 2/119: cassocks of crimson
velvet embroidered with gold, trimmed
with lace and lined with crimson
sarcenet; 1563, Durham Wills, ii. 145;
1567, Richmond Wills, 210. Branched
cassock, Magnetic Lady, I. i. 267.

[2] 1546, L.R. 2/119; E. 351/3025;
1551, E. 351/3060, gown made 'cas-
sockwise of black vellat with gard of
blacke satten, 36 links of golde upon
the same'. Cassock of velvet laid with
'passamayn virid et lignat cum cotton,
hoode de velvett russet cum buttons';

1553, L.R. 2/120; 1550, Somerset
Wills, xxi. 117: a cassock of 'unwatered
chamlet'.

[3] Bansley, Pride and Abuse of
Women, 239; 1547, Feuillerat, Revels,
16.

[4] Ralph Roister Doister, II. iii. 49.

[5] 1554, Camden Soc. Pub. o.s. xlix.
145: 'To my sister my best cassocke
gawded wt velvet, to my mayde my
worky day cassocke'; 1564, Durham
Wills, ii. 224; 1569, ibid. 303; 1582,
ibid. xxxviii. 65. Celestina, ix. 163:
'a cassocke is good wear after winter.'

[6] Pedler's Prophecy, sig. B 2.

required four or more yards of material.[1] Coats for women were longer than those for men and could hardly be distinguished from gowns.

Rich folk wore coats of velvet and silk, embroidered and lace trimmed;[2] poorer folk, of russet and skins; and soldiers, of buff leather; servants, coats of cloth, usually blue; and retainers of church dignitaries, usually of tawny cloth. Fools wore long coats,[3] often with hanging sleeves, i.e. 'a coat with four elbows', and facings or guards on the front and sleeves; hence Monsieur d'Olive's remark to his Pages: 'for wit's as suitable to garded coats as wisdom is to welted gowns' (IV. ii. 52), i.e. to lawyers.

DOUBLET

The doublet, probably originating from 'gambeson', was a closely fitting garment with detachable sleeves, which was used in England early in the fourteenth century. To the doublet was fastened by points the detachable hose of men and skirts of women:

> Some women a doublet of fyne lynnen use to weare
> Unto the which they tye theyr other nether geare.[4]

The doublet harmonized in colour with the remainder of the costume but often was of different material, so that a person had more doublets than hose. Henry VIII wore doublets of silver brocade, satin, taffeta, rash, velvet,[5] with hose of contrasting materials; Prince Charles, son of James I, had a green satin doublet and scarlet hose;[6] and students of the drama are familiar with such descriptions as that in the *Witch of Edmonton* (III. ii. 125), of a white doublet, crimson lined, worn with black hose and cloak of scarlet.

---

[1] Coats were mentioned in accounts by 1300, *O.E.D.* The *Witch*, I. ii. 30, mentions lined coats. For amounts of material required, see *Shuttleworth Accts.* xxxv. 184; xli. 246, and references below.

[2] 1546, Hall, *Chronicle*, 834.

[3] 'A Fooles Bolt', Rowlands, *Works*, ii. 25.

[4] *Repentance of Mary Magdalene*,

sig. D 1.

[5] *Archaeologia*, ix. 244. Such materials were used for doublets throughout the century. Cf. 1525, *Archaeologia*, xxv. 461; 1577, Breton, *Works*, I. xxii; 1588, *Lancashire and Cheshire Wills*, liv. 12; 1587, *Durham Wills*, xxxviii. 233; 1596, 262; also see under different materials.

[6] E. 101/434/9.

From the forties the doublet was slashed or pinked, braided, or embroidered and lace-trimmed. Wardrobe accounts have numerous items as 'a doublet of white Sattin cut stryped down wth white lace lyned wth black velvet', 'a doublet of Crimsen Sattin allover embroidered wth venice golde cut and pulled oute wth tinsell Sarcenet wth a paire of hose of crimsen Sattin embroidered wth venice golde',[1] and later accounts show how well founded was the ridicule of Stubbes and Harrison concerning doublets with 'brests full of iags and cuts and sleeves of sundry colours',[2] for the detachable sleeves were seldom of the colour or even of the material of the doublet. Wings at the armholes hid the points which tied the sleeves[3] to the doublet and accentuated both the width of the shoulder and, later in the century, the shortness of the bases or skirts and the narrow waist.

Few garments underwent so many changes as did the doublet. From the straight-bodied, full, long-skirted doublet of the reign of Henry VIII evolved the 'Peascod' or Dutch 'doublets with great belly and small skirt',[4] so familiar from the seventies. (Plate X.) This garment was long in front, overhanging the girdle like the end of a peas-cod. It was sometimes worn with the French hose, the short Spanish cloak, and the copatain hat, but more often Iniquitie's description in *The Devil is an Ass*, of a Lusty Juventus, accurately presented the costume:

> In a cloak to thy heel, and a hat like a pent-house.
> Thy breeches three fingers, and thy doublet all belly . . .
>
> (1. i. 54.)

The doublet was fastened up the front to the top of the collar, sometimes with buttons, sometimes with hooks and eyes. When buttons were used, fourteen to thirty-four were needed for the front, and a dozen for each sleeve, so that the courtier's criticism in *The Old Law* of a doublet

---

[1] 1541, E. 154/2/20; L.R. 2/121. For later times see such descriptions as that given by Stubbes, *Anatomy of Abuses*, 1583, 45; Henslowe, *Diary*, i. 99, &c.

[2] 1577, *Des. Eng.*, bk. iii, ch. 2.

[3] *Cupid's Revenge*, II. i. 335. See discussion of wings.

[4] Rowlands, *Martin Mark-all*, ii. 27; Stubbes, *Anatomy Abuses*, 44. Portraits such as Ketel's Frobisher well illustrate the fashion. Cf. *The White Devil*, I. ii. 31.

X. Earl of Nottingham. Costume 1570–90. Peas-cod doublet; trunks
'slopwise', paned, with codpiece; long hose; embroidered 'night-cap';
corked shoes; French hat with plumes and jewelled band

On loan to National Portrait Gallery, by permission of the Baroness Lucas

XI. Gentleman's doublet of cut and uncut velvet, green. 1610–15.
Divided bases, eyelet holes for points at the waistline. Front closed by 32
buttons; each sleeve by 6

Victoria and Albert Museum

that was 'three hours a buttoning' (IV. i. 160) was not
grossly exaggerated. The French doublet, mentioned in
Northward Hoe (II. i. 59), was characterized by the sleeves
which in the late sixteenth century were cut in 'rising
panes'. These gave place to the straight sleeves which
were arm-fitting. (Plate XI.) So great was the variety in
shape, trimming, and sleeve design that a young man who
wished to impress his lady might well *need* to 'lie ten nights
awake, carving the fashion of a new doublet';[1] for though
he needed only two and a half to three yards of material
for the outside, the lining, the lace, the pattern of embroidery or pinking, and the elaborately wrought buttons, all
required planning; and the cost of six pounds for a single
doublet was not unusual. Unfortunately for the purse of
young men of Shakespeare's days, fashion was so ephemeral that even one of the middle class would have found
useless a bequest such as that of John Fulwood in 1549:
'To my brother my best dublett for the terme of his lif and
after his deceasse to remayne to John Fulwood his sone.'[2]

The peas-cod front—to which jerkins and even armour
had conformed—disappeared by 1610, and the doublet
became form-fitting—but was worn over a stiff lining—with
a small waist decorated by points. The skirts were short.
Matching sleeves took the place of the detachable sleeves,
but wings at the shoulders persisted, even broadened.
With the accession of Charles I doublet sleeves changed
their shape. The upper part was full and cut into panes
which hung loosely, displaying contrasting lining; and
the lower part was a tightly fitted cuff reaching almost to
the elbow. (Plate XVII.) The skirts were pointed in front,
usually in six to eight pieces, and were longer than those
of previous years. From 1630 the waist became shorter
and the skirts longer, until the doublet was, in the forties,
cut in one piece with a curve to indicate the waistline.

WOMEN'S DOUBLETS

Women's doublets served as kirtle bodies when the
latter were not worn. In the early sixteenth century they

[1] *Much Ado*, II. iii. 19.   [2] *Test. Ebor*. cvi. 294.

were form-fitting, but in Elizabeth's reign conformed to
the style preferred by men, except that the front had an
acute point instead of the peas-cod shape. 'What are
they? Women?' asks Gascoigne, in *Steele Glas*, 1574,
'masking in men's weedes? With Dutchkin dublets and
with Jerkins iagged?'[1] And Stubbes condemns women's
doublets 'buttoned up the brests and made with winges,
welts, and pinions on the shoulder poynts as mans apparel
is'. Like the men's, the women's doublets were pinked
or slashed, embroidered, and lace-trimmed. All through
the latter part of the century the searcher finds in wardrobe accounts descriptions of doublets of 'pfumed fustian
layed wth lase of venice golde & grene silke lyned w^{th}
grene taphata', of 'lawne wrought wth venice golde, silver;
purple silke layed wth golde lase lyned wth canvas & white
sarcenet, with buttons, hookes and eyes', of 'sattin nig^{r}
siss. in rising panes', of 'cloth of tyssue in flowers w^{th}
gold silv. & colourd silke . . . for canuas, stiffenyng whalebone cutting & scissering',[2] not to mention numerous ones
of less expensive materials. The woman's doublet continued form-fitting in spite of Stuart changes. The pointed
front, so pronounced in 1600, was blunted and not so long
by 1615, but it survived in the thirties, though the natural
waistline was marked by a sash or girdle from 1625.

GABERDINE

You call me misbeliever, cut-throat dog,
And spet upon my Jewish gaberdine . . .
(*Merch. of V.* i. iii. 112–13.)

Shylock's accusation of Antonio coupled with Cotgrave's definition of gaberdine as 'a long coat, or cassock,
of coarse, and for the most part motley or partie-coloured
stuffe' has always given editors of Shakespeare an erro-
neous impression of this garment. The gaberdine was not
a *compulsory* garment for Jews, nor was it originally worn
only by poor persons. Proof of the first of these state-

[1] Arber Reprint, 83.
[2] 1574, *Prog. Elizabeth*, i. 412, iii.
68; 1575, Egerton MS. 2806; 1599,

L.R. 2/121; 1612, Add. MS. 2751,
fol. 106, &c.

ments is given elsewhere;[1] proof of the second can be easily summarized here.

The gaberdine was a long coat, worn loose or girdled, with long sleeves—a useful garment for soldiers, horsemen, or travellers, whatever their status.[2] The earliest reference which the author has found to the English gaberdine is in 1511, when a Great Wardrobe account gives the cost for eight yards of scarlet for two gaberdines, with four yards of black satin to line one, the other to be unlined.[3] In 1514 a 'gawbdyne of russet veluett . . . gardytt with greene clothe of golde, and lyned with black sarcenett' was part of the wardrobe of Henry, Earl of Northumberland.[4] A yard of velvet and six yards of other material for lining were used for a gaberdine for Sir Henry Willoughby in 1523.[5] Hall tells that the King's archers were dressed in white gaberdines on June 5, 1514;[6] and noblemen's trumpeters in gaberdines of black damaske, blue, and yellow satin, trimmed with gold and silver lace, were seen at a tournament in Madrid, 1623.[7]

Lesser folk—yeomen, mercers, fishmongers—and women of several classes of society wore gaberdines of tawny, medley, and other cloths,[8] up to the sixties. Seemingly they went out of fashion before the end of the century, for they are absent from wills and accounts. Some Jews, as orthodox persons, may have continued the cos-

[1] *P.M.L.A.* xliii. 757–66 discusses dress of Jews in several lands. Illustrated.

[2] *Vocabolario degli Accademici della Crusca* (1612): 'Feltro si dice anche a mantello o gabbano fatto de feltro da far viaggio. E gabbano è mantello ma con maniche.' Minsheu, 'a horseman's coat'. Palsgrave (1530), 'gaberdyne to ride in, gauerdine'. Marcello, *Vocabolario Italiano e Spagnuolo*, 1637, states it was used by soldiers.

[3] E. 101/417/4.

[4] *Antiq. Rep.* iv. 357.

[5] *Mid. MSS.* 360.

[6] *Chronicle*, 539.

[7] *Prog. James*, iii. 892, 893, 895.

[8] 1523, *Archaeologia*, xxxviii. 371,

inventory of goods of Dame Agnes Hungerford, gaberdine of scarlet, guarded with velvet. 1525, *Lincoln Wills*, i. 150, will of a fishmonger, gaberdine of tawny, unlined. 1530, ibid. iii. 53, will of E. Hobson, mercer—of tawny medley; 1530, ibid. 118, status of person or material not named. 1531, *E.E.T.S.*, ser. 1, cxlix, 246, faced with sarcenet. 1545, *Med. Wills Wells*, xl. 123. 1557, *Test. Leod.* xxvii. 96, yeoman leaves his gaberdine to woman. 1562, *Durham Wills*, ii. 209, Florence Porter leaves sons a gaberdine. For other references to gaberdines see, 1551, *Test. Leod.* xxvii. 179; 1553, *Somerset Wills*, xxi. 153.

tume of their fathers, and so worn gaberdines, but others
wore long cloaks, doublets, and hose as Ferdinando Bertilli
illustrates in his *Omnium fere gentium nostrae aetatis habitus,
nunquam ante hac editi*, 1563.

JACKETS

In contrast to the coat the jacket was a form-fitting,
lined, waist-length garment worn for warmth.[1] Jackets
were made with or without sleeves, usually of silken stuffs,
guarded, trimmed with lace, or embroidered.[2] Jackets
were usually worn under the doublet or outer garment, but
lackeys wore them as outer garments.[3] Sir Lionel's remark: 'I will give over my citie coat and betake myself
to the court jacket',[4] means that he will become a courtier.

JERKIN

Jerkin, a term of unknown origin, designated a short
coat[5] with a collar, sometimes sleeveless, but usually
sleeved.[6] It was worn over a doublet or when worn alone,
as in *The Two Gentlemen of Verona*,[7] the 'jerkin is a doublet', that is, it takes the place of both; but Robert Sydney's
doublet, 'made jerkinwise',[8] was a doublet made with long
skirts, high collar, and sleeves, which were not detachable,

[1] *Archaeologia*, xxi. 253, inventory
of Sir John Fastolfe's wardrobe shows
a jacket of black velvet, the body lined
with blanket, the sleeves with black
cloth.

[2] 1512, *Somerset Wills*, xix. 150,
jackets with, and without, sleeves.
Archaeologia, ix. 245; 1541, E. 154/2/20;
1546, L.R. 2/115; 1580, *Durham Wills*,
ii. 436, shows various silks used in
jackets; *Durham Wills*, xxxviii, 68,
262; Breton, *Works*, I. xvii; L.R. 2/121,
lace-trimmed and embroidered jackets.

[3] 1503, *P. P. Ex. Elizabeth York*,
93; 1553, *Viaje de Filipe Segundo á
Inglaterra*, 25, describes Spanish lackeys as wearing 'cueras de terciopelo
morado aforradas en raso amarillo,
con fajas de tela de oro por guarni-
cion'; 1625, *Prog. James*, iii. 895:
'Laqueyes . . . with tawny hose and
jackets laid with silver lace.'

[4] *Tu Quoque*, I. i. sig. (A 5 verso).

[5] Elyot, *Bibliotheca*, 1548, 'Cincti-
culus*, a shorte cote called a jerkin.'
Mentioned in English 1519, *O.E.D.*

[6] 1558, *Lancashire and Cheshire
Wills*, liv. 139: 'old tuftafita jerkin
wthoutsleves'; 1590, ibid. li. 118; Breton,
Works, i. 62: 'make poore men weare
their Jerkins without sleeves'; *Prog.
James*, i. 105: 'their liveries blew coates
with sleeves parted in the middest,
buttoned behinde jerkin fashion.'

[7] II. iv. 20. Editors of Shakespeare
have wasted much energy trying to
prove from this quotation that jerkins
and doublets were the same. Thurio
merely says that he is wearing a jerkin
to take the place of a doublet, thus
making it do double duty. His remark
gives Valentine opportunity for further punning.

[8] 1577, *De l'Isle MSS.* 270.

XII. Sir Philip Sidney. Costume of 1585–1600. Note mandilion, scarf, embroidered girdle, band and cuffs. The hose is Spanish

National Portrait Gallery

as doublet sleeves usually were. A jerkin required three yards of material such as frieze or velvet,[1] more of narrower materials. This was half a yard more than was required for a doublet but half as much as that required for a cloak; therefore 'an old cloak' easily made 'a new jerkin' as Falstaff said in *Merry Wives of Windsor* (I. iii. 17).

Jerkins, like doublets, were made of satin, cloth of silver, velvet, russet, frieze, as one notes in *What You Will*, *Bartholomew Fair*, *The Prophetess*, *The Roaring Girl*,[2] and wardrobes of Elizabethan and Jacobean times. Leather jerkins, which were reversible,[3] especially those of buff, were worn by officers,[4] military men, and gentlemen attendants. Jerkins were embroidered; lace trimmed as in *Patient Grissel* and *What You Will*;[5] and 'pinked'.[6]

The high-collared, short jerkin lost favour by 1611. As Lord Thomas Howard in a letter to Sir John Harington, advising him concerning the clothes he must wear to Court, describes the 'new jerkin', it was 'well bordered and not too short', for the 'King liketh a flowing garment. . . . It must be diversely coloured, the collar falling somewhat downe.'[7]

MANDILION

On August 16, 1578, upon the occasion of Queen Elizabeth's progress through Norwich, certain 'batchelours', appointed to wait upon the mayor and aldermen of that city, were ordered to 'apparel themselves in Mandelion cotes, hattes in one suite and one fashion'.[8]

---

[1] 1592-3, L.C. 9/84-5: '6 yds. ffreze', for 2 jerkins; 'xxiiij virge velvett crimsen pro viij Jerkins'.

[2] In order of mention: I. i. 145-50, Florentine cloth of silver jerkin, sleeve˘ cut on tinsel; III. i. 21, velvet; V. iii. 37, russet jerkin with blue buttons; I. i. 177. See also 1522, *Archaeologia*, xxv. 461; 1553, robes of Edward VI, *Prog. Elizabeth*, iii. 501; 1548, E. 351/3026, striped with silver, guarded with velvet, lined with velvet, with 2 doz. buttons of silk and silver; Breton, *Works*, i. 8; 1594, *Nugae Antiquae*, i. 167, of frieze. Jerkins were bombasted during the eighties, E. 154/3/20.

[3] 1539, Wriothesley, *Chronicle*, i. 96; *Troilus*, III. iii. 268.

[4] *1 Hen. IV*, I. ii. 48. See discussion of 'Leather'.

[5] Line 1313; V. i. 20. Also 1599, L.R. 2/121.

[6] 1565, Hakluyt, *Voyages*, iii. 504: 'They iagge their flesh . . . as a Jerkinmaker with us pinketh a jerkin.'

[7] *Nugae Antiquae*, i. 391.

[8] Blomefield, *County of Norfolk*, ii. 227. See *O.E.D.* for mention of mandilions, 1577, the earliest reference noted.

Accordingly they wore black satin doublets, black hose, black taffeta hats, yellow bands, and mandilions of purple taffeta laid with silver lace. The description is interesting because it shows the costume of gentlemen attendants.

The mandilion was a short, loose coat with hanging sleeves, worn with one sleeve hanging over the chest and one at the back, or as Harrison so admirably describes it, 'worne to Collie-westonward'.[1] (Plate XII.) This coat was at first a garment worn exclusively by soldiers and gentlemen,[2] but by 1620 was used by grooms and lackeys.[3]

HOSE

Sixteenth-century hose consisted of two parts: upper or trunk hose; and lower, which may refer to canons, long hose, or even, at times, the netherstocks. The term hose, therefore, may refer to any of these parts. Thus 'a paire of red hose wth breeches of red velvet' is named in the will of Richard Breton, 1558;[4] a 'paire of round hose' in the inventory of William Carey's effects, 1593;[5] while 'honester men than thou go in their hose and doublets', of 2 *Henry VI* (IV. vii. 56) suggested the entire hose. The upperstocks were, however, usually called breeches, a term used alike for the 'devil's breeches' of the reign of Henry VIII, the puffed and paned hose of 1540–55, the trunks, venetians, galligaskins of the ages of Elizabeth and James I, and the 'little breeches'.

With the form-fitting 'devil's breeches' the Swiss fashion of cod-piece, a bag-like appendage attached by points[6] to the front, was universal.[7] These appendages, of

[1] 1577, *Des. Eng.*, bk. iii, ch. 2.

[2] 1593, *Durham Wills*, xxxviii, 227, made of 'grogram', and of 'lawnge clothe'; 1597, *Hatfield MSS.* vii. 518, warrant to Chamberlain to export 6,000 suits of apparel to the King's soldiers, consisting of 'mandyllons', breeches, and stockings. *Prog. Elizabeth*, iii. 520; 1602, *Blurt, Master Constable*, IV. iii. 96.

[3] *Prog. James*, iv. 895.

[4] *Lancashire and Cheshire Wills*, xxxii. 178.

[5] *Durham Wills*, xxxviii. 232.

[6] *Amends for Ladies*, IV. i. (sig. G 2 verso); '*Tis Pity She's a Whore*, III. i. 15.

[7] *Unfortunate Traveller*, ii. 223: 'The cod-piece in his devil's breeches, for they were then in fashion . . . plainly was a case for a pistol.' Early mention of cod-piece is in *Towneley Mysteries* (c. 1460), 313; 1521, *C.S.P.V.* iii. 382.

various shapes and sizes,[1] such as a padded cushion, ornamented by pins, a linen bag used as a pocket,[2] or a large bow of silk or ribbon, remained in fashion with the puffed and paned breeches of the reigns of Edward VI and Mary, and until the loosely fitting Venetians of the eighties caused their discard. *The Two Gentlemen of Verona*, *1 Honest Whore*, and *The White Devil*[3] show that the style had passed, and Rowlands' *Knave of Harts* states that they were so far forgotten by 1612 that 'no tailor can avouch the troth [thereof] without he prove it with old painted cloth' (ii. 30).

The trunk, or round or French breeches, 'not unlike Saint Omer's onions', or as Fulwell describes them, 'big as good barrells',[4] were fashionable by 1558.[5] They were usually mid-thigh length, shaped like pumpkins, and stuffed with hair, flocks, or bombast. They were made in panes, i.e. strips, or in pleats which parted slightly, showing a rich lining.[6] These paned hose, embroidered with goldsmith's work, are the subject of much stage satire: *Cynthia's Revels*, *Old Law*, *Witch of Edmonton*, *What You Will*,[7] &c. The short padded rolls, or 'blistered breeches', anachronously mentioned in *Henry VIII*,[8] and the trunk slops, or the short trunks which were allowed to fall in folds without bombast, were also worn, particularly by gallants, from the seventies. The 'round hose bumbasted close to the breech' continued to be worn by the lower class until 1620, though the 'brewers hops sacks' or slops, and the full Venetians largely displaced them after 1603.

In addition to the round hose, Venetians, slops, and the

---

[1] Fitzgeffrey, *A Moral Satyre*, ii. b. 5.

[2] *Winter's Tale*, IV. iii. 625; *Duchess of Malfi*, II. ii. 40, &c.

[3] In order of their mention: II. vii. 56; I. x. 72; V. v. 99; also 1577, Harrison, *Des. Eng.*, bk. iii, ch. 2.

[4] *Like Will to Like*, I. i. 26.

[5] *Lancashire and Cheshire Wills*, liv. 139: 'One paire of round hose panes of blacke rashe laid on wth a

billymt lace lyned wth tuftafita.'

[6] 1592–93, L.C. 9/84, 'pro f̄cur unius par̄ caligarum rotund de rashe serico lin cum fustian ac pro cotton bumbast et rugg pro eisdem'. Three yards of rashe were required.

[7] In order of their mention: IV. iii. 197; II. i. 56; IV. i. 237; I. i. 152.

[8] I. iii. 31; also *Gull's Horn Book*, 30. The puffed breeches of Edward VI were said to be 'blistered'.

Spanish breeches, loose, tubular, and unconfined at the
knee, resembling the modern 'shorts', were worn from the
eighties to about 1607. All of these styles were succeeded
c. 1618 by what is called in *The Queen of Corinth*[1] 'little
breeches', which were little only in comparison with the
previous huge slops or galligaskins. They were full, but
not pleated, tapering somewhat towards the knee, ending
in a fitted band about three inches above the knee, where
they were finished by a circle of points with dangling
aglets. Broad ribbon or silk garters tied in soft bows
below the knee were worn with this type of breeches.

After 1625 breeches became longer, reaching below
the knees. They were finished by a band with a six- or
seven-inch placket, left unbuttoned above the knee to
show the lining of the breeches. Over the bands below
the knees were worn the broad garters fastened by
rosettes of ribbon or lace. This style, with the shoe-roses
to match, was in fashion for boys of noble families as late
as 1642.

CANONS

'French hose', wrote Stubbes in 1583, 'are two divers
makings, for the common french-hose contayneth length,
bredth and sideness sufficient, and is made very round.
The other contayneth neither length, bredth or sideness,
whereof some be paned, cut and drawn out with costly
ornaments, with canions annexed reaching down beneath
their knees.'[2] The second part of this apparently confus-
ing description refers to the short hose, cut in panes, with
tubular extensions below the knee-cap. The name *canons*
was probably derived from *canon*, or great bone of the
leg. The description by Stubbes can be matched from
wardrobe accounts of his age; for instance the following
from an account written eight years before *The Anatomy*
is typical: 'for making a payer of round hose of watchett
kersey . . . with canyons of carnacon taphata the panes

---

[1] II. iv. 160: 'minikin breeches' of
Scornful Lady, I. i. 340, may refer to
the little breeches, but more probably
to the material of which they were

made, i.e. minikin bays. Also *Wild
Goose Chase*, III. i. 545, 'pin-buttocked
breeches'.

[2] *Anatomy of Abuses*, 156.

lyned with bayes hose lyned wth lynen wollen canvas and heare, with knitt stockings.'[1]

One half to two yards of material, depending upon its width and the length of the canons required, were needed for this garment. In 1573, 'a yarde of russet sattyn to make canyons'[2] was purchased for a person of Queen Elizabeth's household, but only a half yard of 'jeans' fustian is used for lining 'canyons' for Lord Willoughby.[3]

The canons were usually made of material contrasting in colour or fabric with that of the hose as 'the slope hose of yellow Shaunveys lased with grene lase with canions of grene satten' made for Robert Sidney, 1576,[4] or the round hose 'of blacke brode billmĕt panes lyned wth satten and the kenyons of tuftaffita's[5] mentioned in the will of William Glaseor, 1588, or the 'payer of Rownd hosse of paynes of sylke layd wth sylver lace & caneyanes of clothe of silver' for which Henslowe loaned 'the company' money in 1598.[6]

The use of canons began when the long stocking became *démodé*, i.e. about 1565,[7] and continued in fashion until the coming of the knee-length slop hose of 1610. They are not frequently mentioned on the stage. In *Patient Grissel*, Emilo, describing his battle with Sir Owen, manages, like Fastidious Brisk, to give an excellent inventory of his costume, including the 'pair of very imperial cloth of gold hose' which was cut 'thwart the cannon'. Dondolo uses the expression 'a pair of canions' (l. 1371) to represent masculinity in *More Dissemblers*

---

[1] Egerton MS. 2806, 92. They were paned in carnation velvet, bordered by silk and silver lace.

[2] E. 101/431/6.

[3] *Mid. MSS.* 436; see also 450.

[4] *De l'Isle and Dudley MSS.* 270.

[5] *Lancashire and Cheshire Wills*, liv. 139.

[6] *Diary*, i. 101. But canons were sometimes made of the same material as the hose. See *Diary* i. 86. For other references to canons, see: 1573, *Mid. MSS.* 444; 1587, *North Country Wills*, cxxi. 133; 1593, *Durham Wills*,

xxxviii. 233; 1595, E. 101/632/46.

[7] Gay, op. cit. i. 353, quotes from the 1570 wardrobe account of Charles IX of France: '2 aulnes et demie de thoille pour doubler une paire de chausses de vellours noir à la garguesse avec les canons', the latter of black taffeta. The earliest English reference which the author of this discussion has noted is 1572: 'Item for making a peire of canyons lyned with canvas for hoyden the foole.' Egerton MS. 2806.

Besides Women;[1] and there are other general references as in *Northward Hoe* (II. i. 30), &c.

GALLIGASCONS

Galligascons, called also 'gaskins', 'galligaskins', 'gally slops', 'gally breeches',[2] were wide breeches made like shipman's hose, except that they reached to the knee only.[3] According to Minsheu, 1617, the Gascons first used them, but Nashe's question: 'From Spaine what bringeth our traveller? A wide paire of gascoynes which ungatherd wold make a couple of womens ryding kirtles', leads one to think that other countries had also adopted them. Those which fitted the hips, but were full at the knee were known as 'venetian galligascoignes', or 'straight gaskins'.[4] They must have been worn in England previous to the sixties,[5] though no previous reference to them has been noted. They were evidently a comparatively new style for gentlemen then, for they are very common in accounts. In 1573 at the Queen's reception at Sandwich, three hundred men wore white doublets and black gascoyne hose.[6] Harrison's *Description of England*,[7] 1577, credits women with wearing them, but there is no stage record of their use by women except as a disguise in *The Pilgrim*, or in caricaturing the mannish woman, as in *The Roaring Girl*.[8]

Galligaskins were usually loose slops, but some followed the bombast style. A pair made for the Court fool in 1575 were short, for they needed stocks. They required six yards of changeable mockado and were trimmed with 'billemēt lace wth lyninge of lynen, woolen, cotton, heare, canvas' and had 'psocketts, poyntes & and a peire of nether-

---

[1] I. iv. 60: 'tis pity that thou wast ever bred to be thrust through a pair of canions; thou wouldst have made a pretty foolish waiting maid.'

[2] *Tw. N.* I. v. 27; 1561, Harman, *Caveat*, 35; Drout, *Pytiful Historie of Gaulfrido and Barnardo*, 1570, sig. D 1; *Gull's Horn Booke* (Grosart), ii. 210.

[3] Stubbes, *Anatomy of Abuses*, 45.

[4] Rowlands, 'Martin Mark-all', ii.

[5] 27; *Knight of the Burning Pestle*, II. i. 93.

[5] Note 2.

[6] *Prog. Elizabeth*, i. 337; Stowe, *Annales*, 1143.

[7] Bk. iii, ch. 2.

[8] *The Pilgrim*, III. iii. 93; *Roaring Girl*, V. ii. 23. 'Gascoyne bride', one who wears galligaskin breeches, or who has authority over her husband.

stockes to them'.[1] This bombasting, standing for pride, explains the expressions: 'Much in my gascoins . . . more in my round hose', 'much in my gaskins . . . nothing in my netherstocks', of *Mother Bombie*, and *Shoemaker's Holiday*,[2] for the round hose were padded more than were the galligaskins, but the netherstocks had no padding. Taken literally it meant that more material was needed for round hose than for galligaskins, and when one wore the knee-length gaskin one needed very little material in the netherstocks. Thus a person seemed great or fine in bombasted clothes, but was small without such bombast.

SLOP

And what said Master Dombledon about the satin for my short cloak and my slops? (2 *Hen. IV*, I. ii. 33.)

Chaucer applied the term, slop, to a loose tunic-like garment,[3] and such a garment[4] was worn in mourning by women even in the sixteenth century. From the reign of Henry VIII, however, 'slops or slop hosen', as they were sometimes called, designated wide or bagging breeches of knee length or shorter. The Switzer's and German slops, the wide Venetians, the trunk or round hose, and the galligaskins are all included in the designation. The Switzer's and German slops were paned with grotesquely full lining in contrasting colour which hung between panes in limp puffs; hence, Don Pedro's description, 'a German from the waist downward, all slops'.[5] Such 'pan'd slops' are named in *Cynthia's Revels*,[6] and *Scornful Lady*.[7]

---

[1] Egerton MS. 2806, 84; also 107, for a pair made of tuft-taffeta, 'bumbasted wth cotton woll'. 'Gaskin points', *Tw. N.* i. v. 25, indicate the laces which tied the breeches to the doublet.

[2] *Mother Bombie*, IV. ii. 39; *Shoemaker's Holiday*, II. i (vol. i. 18).

[3] *Parson's Tale*, 422.

[4] 1524, *Letters and Papers Henry VIII*, iv. 1, 341; 1542, *Test. Ebor.*, cvi.

168.

[5] *Much Ado*, III. ii. 36.

[6] IV. i. 197. Slops occur frequently in costume accounts for stage and revels: 1515, *Annals of Stage*, i. 67; 1521, *Letters and Papers Henry VIII*, III. ii. 1556; 1546, *M.S.R., Coll.* II. 2; *Archaeologia*, xviii. 320; 1546–53, Feuillerat, *Revels*, 12, 13, 65; 1558–60, 19, 21, 23.

[7] I. i. 226: 'dangling slops.'

The round slops of *Faustus* and the French slops of *Romeo and Juliet*[1] are the trunk hose, but the 'great slops' of *The Alchemist*[2] and the Dutch slops of the *Roaring Girl*,[3] were the loose type that would hold a 'bushell of wheate'.[4] The 'swaggering slop' increased in favour until every gallant, according to Rowlands, 1600, was wearing Tarleton's clownish hose.[5] Made of cloth of gold and silver, velvet, and rich silk, and trimmed with lace or gold embroidery,[6] slops often, as Stubbes wrote,[7] cost from ten to a hundred pounds. Slops were not definitely out of fashion until the Puritan period, though the tendency towards narrower breeches began in 1625.

TROUSERS

Trousers, or strossers, were straight-fitting under-hose of ankle length, worn by the early Britons, but disappearing during Roman domination though they seemed to have survived in the Irish garment by that name. Wither's review of the kinds of hose that had been fashionable in England stated: 'Some we have seene in Irish trouzers go,'[8] and the Dolphin in *King Henry V* answered the Constable's comparison between horses and mistresses with: 'and you rode, like a kern of Ireland, your French hose off and in your straight strossers.'[9] In the *Staple of News*,[10] Pennyboy Junior 'walks up and down in his gown, waistcoat, and trowsers' expecting a tailor who is to bring his

---

[1] In order of mention: I. iv. 69; II. iv. 49.

[2] III. ii. 192–6: 'a don of Spain . . . brought . . . six great slops . . . bigger than three Dutch hoys.'

[3] II. ii. 86.

[4] Wright, *Passions of the Mind*, 330. In 1562, the 'great hose' were limited to '1¾ yds. of broadest kersey', *Tudor and Stuart Proc.*, 562.

[5] *Epigrams*, 30.

[6] 1532, *P. P. Ex. Henry VIII*, 274; 1544, E. 101/423/12, made of cloth of silver; 1545–6, E. 351/30/25, of crimson satin and velvet; 1546, L.R. 2/115, of black velvet; 1553, E.

154/2/34, 'furred with shankes'; 1576, *Lord De l'Isle MSS.* 270: 'of yellow Shaunveys lased all over in waves with greene lase, with canons of grene satten, for Mr. Roberte Sydney.' Slops made of fustian or leather were used by servants, fools, &c. 1545, E. 351/3025; 1566, Add. MS. 3528; 1565, A.O. 3/1106; 1571, *Knaresborough Wills*, civ. 133; 1598, L.C. 9/89.

[7] *Anatomy of Abuses*, 57.

[8] 'Juvenilia', *Works*, ix. 188.

[9] III. vii. 60. Cf. *No Wit Like a Woman's*, II. i. 39.

[10] I. i. 4; *The Coxcomb*, II. i. 348, 'trossers to tumble in'.

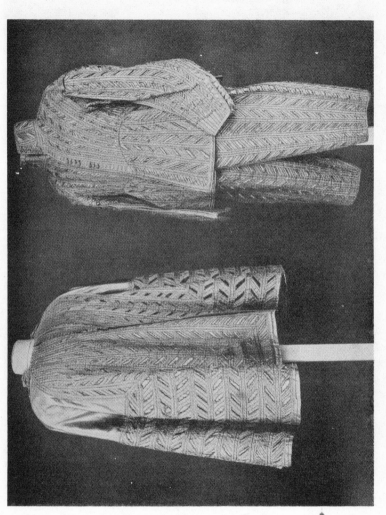

XIII. Gentleman's suit, satin, trimmed with silk braid. English

Victoria and Albert Museum

XIV. Gentleman's shirt. Drawn-work and embroidery. Bobbin lace at collar.
Late 16th century

Victoria and Albert Museum

suit. Holmes describes 'Spanish breeches' as 'those that are stret and close to the Thigh, and are buttoned up the sides from the knee with about ten or twelve buttons, anciently called Trowsers'.[1]

VENETIANS

And brought three yards of velvet and three quarters
To make Venetians down below the garters.

Thus Harington epigrammatized (B 120) on the most popular style of breeches of the eighties. Stubbes included them in his *Anatomy of Abuses* (1 58), 1583, calling attention to the fact that they reached 'the gartering place of the legge, where thay are tyed finely with silke poyntes or some such like, and layde on also with rewes of lace or gardes'. Their length was a distinct characteristic of the Venetians, for other kinds of breeches such as the galligaskins reached only to the knee. Therefore Simony's story of the tailor who stole an apron for his wife from material brought for a customer's doublet and hose would have seemed humorous to an Elizabethan audience, for the doublet was 'three fingers too short', and the 'venetians came nothing neare the knee'.[2] Three styles of Venetians were worn: the close-fitting, 1560–70; the bombasted, 1570–95; the pleated or bellows-shaped[3] mode to about 1620. The servants' Venetians rivalled in width those of their masters. 'Yf thay will not holde a bushell a breetch, thay are not saleable in Berchen lane' was 'W.W.'s' comment in *A Health to the Gentlemanly Profession of Servingmen*.[4]

The portrait of James I as a child, 1574,[5] shows a good example of the full Venetians. Descriptions of entertain-

---

[1] *Academy of Armoury*, III. iii. 96.
[2] *Three Ladies of London*, sig. C ii verso.
[3] Cotgrave, '*Chausse à la gigotte*, a fashion of very close venetians; old-fashioned venetians'. 1592, L.C. 9/84: 'pro fcūr iij pare de venetians de panno fustian . . . pro cotton, bombast.'

Three yards of fustian were used. Minsheu, *Vocabularium Hispanico Latinum et Anglicum*, 1617, '*Follado*, Venetian hose so-called because they are like a paire of bellowes.'
[4] *Inedited Tracts Illustrating Manners*, 138.
[5] National Portrait Gallery.

ment for Queen Elizabeth, such as the 'Devices at Tilt Yard', 1581, and accounts of both private and stage wardrobes show Venetians to have been much in favour in the eighties and nineties,[1] in spite of Greene's statement in 1592 that they were 'stale';[2] although he may have indicated Court styles only.

SUIT

A man's suit consisted of an ensemble of harmonizing or matching garments: doublet, hose, coat, jerkin, mandilion, or cloak. A suit provided for Prince Charles in 1617 required $19\frac{1}{2}$ yards 'blacke fflorence satten', $8\frac{3}{4}$ ells carnation taffeta, $11\frac{1}{4}$ ells changeable taffeta, 50 yards 'blacke embroidered lace', 7 yards black ribbon; 19 ounces sewing silk, $1\frac{1}{2}$ ounces 'bynding lace'.[3] One in 1623 required 8 yards of black Florence satin for hose and doublet, $11\frac{1}{4}$ ells taffeta to line and face them, $8\frac{1}{2}$ yards black uncut velvet for a cloak, $20\frac{3}{4}$ yards black French plush for lining.[4] Though a cloak was part of a gentleman's suit, he sometimes spoke of his cloak *and* suit.[5]

A servant's 'three suits a year'[6] did not include cloaks, for servants wore coats or jackets, or only doublet and hose.

Allusions to suits are too numerous to list. Those in *The Comedy of Errors*, *As You Like It*, *1 Henry IV*, *Every Man Out of His Humour*, *Woman is a Weathercock*, *The Sea Voyage*,[7] are representative.

[1] *Prog. Elizabeth*, ii. 315; 1588, *Durham Wills*, xxxviii. 328; 1592, 277 (made of black velvet with tawny and gold lace, cost 30s.); 1601, *Surrey Rec. Soc. Pub.* xiv. 113; Henslowe, *Diary*, i. 29, 166, &c.; Feuillerat, *Revels*, 350, &c.

[2] *Works*, xi. 95: 'The venetian and the gallogaskin is stale and the trunke slop out of use.'

[3] E. 101/434/9.

[4] E. 101/326/9.

[5] *Woman Never Vexed*, II. i. 109, Plate XIII.

[6] *Lear*, II. ii. 16; *Silent Woman*, II. i.

The Shuttleworth Accts. show materials for servants' suits. In April, 1611, the following were provided for the suits of two servants: 'fyve y'des of fustian', for doublets, 'four y'des and three quarters of blue clothe for briches, thre y'des of linnen clothe for lyninges to the doublettes, two y'des and a half of clothe to lyne the briches, fyve dozen buttons and thride to the button holes, black, and wth thrid', and 'a sheepe skine for pockettes.' xxxv. 194.

[7] In order of their mention: IV. iii. 26; II. ii. 232; I. ii. 81; II. ii. 90; I. i. sig. E 3; I. i. 277.

SHIRT

Shirts were garments with high necks and long sleeves, made of linen and silk, and worn by men as early as 1000. Sixteenth-century shirts were about a yard long—as extant examples show—requiring two and a half to three yards of cambric or holland.[1] Until the age of ruffs, shirts were finished at the neck by a straight collar band, often with a small ruffle—the forerunner of the ruff—at the top. Later they had higher bands, at the tops of which ruffs were worn. The band, the front and the sleeve-hands of shirts were elaborately embroidered with gold, silver, and coloured silks. Between 1526 and 1546, one finds descriptions of shirts 'wrought' with silk in 'freres knots', or the 'collar and hands' wrought like 'jeloflers'; or 'wrought wth damask golde and silv^r on the coler, brest, and foresleves';[2] and, indeed, throughout the century, 'wrought with a thousand devices, all of needlework', as Areusa describes in *Celestina*.[3]

With the coming of lace the neck-band, front and sleeves were usually of drawn-work, or cut-work edged with bobbin lace[4] as in Plate XIV. Jacobean embroidery followed the vogue of tapestry making, and women then worked 'neat historical shirts'.[5]

ROBE

Shakespeare well illustrates in his drama the three meanings of robes as sixteenth-century England knew the word: 1. a generic term for clothes in general, in *Romeo and Juliet, Henry V, Love's Labour's Lost, The Winter's Tale*;[6] 2. an ensemble of garments for a special use as 'riding robes', in *King John* (I. iv. 217); 3. the gown and accessories worn as official insignia, i.e. emperor's robes,

---

[1] 1511, E. 101/74/4; *Shuttleworth Accts.* xxxv. 196; *Hutton Accounts*, 239. Florio, 1578, *First Fruits*, sig. b, gives the price of shirts of the 'finest cloth there is' at 20s. each.

[2] *Letters and Papers Henry VIII*, iv. 1, entry 1906; *P. P. Ex. Henry VIII*, 17, 78, 97, 101, 136, &c.; E. 351/3025;

Kempe, *Loseley MSS.* 78; *Hatfield House MSS.* i. 129.

[3] Mabbe translation, xv. 234.

[4] See also chapters on lace, and *Prog. James*, i. 598.

[5] *Custom of the Country*, II. i. 270.

[6] In order of mention: III. ii. 30; IV. iii. 117; IV. i. 84; III. iii. 21.

Titus Andronicus (I. i. 189), *Antony and Cleopatra* (v. ii. 281), 'robe Pontifical', *I Henry IV* (III. ii. 56), judge's robe, *Measure for Measure, King Lear*;[1] 'sober robes' of school-master, *Taming of the Shrew* (I. ii. 135).

WAISTCOAT

A waistcoat was a waist-length under-garment,[2] with or without sleeves, usually quilted or bombasted.[3] A doublet was always worn over the waistcoat unless the wearer were in dishabille, as in *Cynthia's Revels, Loyal Subject*, or not completely dressed as Pennyboy of *Staple of News*,[4] who, in waistcoat, trousers, and gown, awaited the arrival of his suit. Thus Essex went to his execution dressed in a scarlet waistcoat, a black satin suit and a wrought velvet gown.[5] A woman did not appear in waistcoat unless she were a strumpet, as the reader learns from *Woman Hater, City Madam*, and *Love's Cure*.[6] Unlike other garments, the waistcoat had no front placket, but was loose enough to put on over the head.[7]

Waistcoats for both men and women were made of chamlet, flannel, velvet, damask, sarcenet, taffeta, holland, or other linen,[8] and were 'wrought' or embroidered with silk, gold, and silver.[9] Howes wrote that at the beginning

[1] II. ii. 61; *Lear*, III. vi. 38. Interesting observations on robes of judges, sergeants-at-law, &c., are in *Archaeologia*, xxxviii. 357; *Journal Society Antiquaries*, III, ser. ii. 414.

[2] 1574, A.E. 3/1108: 'Pro fĉur. iij par manicarum pro wascoats de sarcenet.' 1585, Higins, Junius, *Nomenclature*: '*Indusium*, a waistcoat or woollen peticoat.'

[3] 1565, A.E. 2/1106: 'Pro embraudering unius waistcoate de Taffta Sarceñt alb. Pro Bumbast pro dict. wastcoate'; 1614, *Household Bk. Howard*, 9: 'ij yards iij qrs. of stuff bought of Mrs. Jane at 3 s 8 d for my Ladie's stuffe wastecoate.' 1617, Moryson, *Itinerary*, i. 68: 'I having for the cold at Dantzke, in the beginning of September, put on a wollen wastcoat.'

[4] In order of their mention: II. i. 42;

iii. 6, 92; I. i.

[5] Birch, *Memoirs Queen Elizabeth*, ii. 483.

[6] In order of mention: II. i. 252; III. i. 43; III. i. 19.

[7] Breton, *Bower of Delights*, 37: 'He puts on his armour over his ears like a waistcoat.'

[8] Chamlet, 1553, L.R. 2/119; E. 154/2/39; flannel, 1580, L.C. 9/72; 1585, L.C. 9/77; velvet, 1515, Ellis, *Letters*, II. ii. 215; damask, 1346, E. 351/3025, lined with Milan fustian; sarcenet, 1564-5; L.C. 2/58; 1562, A.E. 3/1106, of satin lined with sarcenet and holland wrought with silk and silver; taffeta, L.C. 9/95; Holland, L.C. 9/79.

[9] *Loyal Subject*, III. vi. 78; *Triumph of Time*, I. i. 42; *What You Will*, II. i. 14; *Patient Grissel*, line 1166. Also

of Elizabeth's reign no one knew how to make a wrought waistcoat worth five pounds, but before the end of the reign of her successor, milliners' shops were 'stored with rich and curious imbroydered Waistcoats of the full value of tenne pound apiece, twentie, and some forty pound'.[1] The ten pound waistcoat mentioned by Livia in *Woman's Prize* (I. iv. 60) was, therefore, only modestly priced.

NIGHT CLOTHES

Women of the upper class wore smocks in bed, and men of the nobility, shirts. Malory describes how Sir Lamorak in surprise 'leapt out of bedde in his shirte',[2] and medieval MSS. illustrate bed garments which seem to correspond to the wrought night shirts mentioned in the wardrobe accounts of Henry VIII.[3]

Hieronimo's direction to the painter to 'Bring me forth in my shirte and my gowne vnder myne arme'[4] evidently refers to his night shirt.

Seventeenth-century illustrations of the night shirt show it as a long-sleeved, straight garment with a V-shaped neck, or gathered in closely about the neck by a cord. The latter style is shown in Brathwaite's 'Ar't Asleepe, Husband?' (1640).

When a woman arose from bed, she put on a short, sleeveless, circular cape, i.e. 'a thin night mantle to hide part' of her smock.[5] A man put a night gown over his shirt. On the morning after the wedding of Sir Philip Herbert and Lady Susan, 1605, King James came to their chamber 'in his shirt and night-gown' and gave them *reveille matin* before they were up'.[6]

1585, *Prog. Elizabeth*, iii. 6, 8; 1618, *Household Bk. Howard*, lxviii. 9, 74; *How a Man may Choose a Good Wife from a Bad*, sig. B 3 verso.
[1] Stowe, *Annales* (Howes), 1039.
[2] 1470–85 *Le Morte D'Arthur*, x. xxiv. 452. Also *Troilus & Criseyde*, III, 1372.

[3] 1546, *Letters and Papers Henry VIII*, IV. I, entry 1906.
[4] *Spanish Tragedy*, III. xii. 132.
[5] *The Guardian*, III. iv. 19; III. vi. III. For illustration see Racinet, *Le Costume historique* (1886) Dutch, Pl. F., fig. 2.
[6] *Prog. James*, I. 471

XIII

HEAD ATTIRE

Song of Head-gear

THOMAS HEYWOOD

The Turk in Linnen wraps his head,
The Persian his in Lawne too.
The Russe with sables furres his Cap,
And change will not be drawne to:
The Spaniard constant to his blocke;
The French inconstant ever,
But of all felts that can be felt,
Give me your English Beaver.
The German loves his Coney-wooll:
The Irishman his Shagge too,
The Welsh his Monmouth loves to weare
And of the same will bragge too.
Some love the rough, and some th' smooth,
Some great, and others small things,
But Oh your lecherous Englishman:
He loves to deale in all things.

A SURVEY OF FASHIONS IN HEAD ATTIRE

ACCORDING to shape, headwear of sixteenth-century England may be grouped under four heads:

I. Closely fitting caps such as biggins and cauls, which covered the back and top of the head; caps with flat crowns and brims such as the flat caps or statute caps; and high-crowned, brimless caps as the Monmouth variety.

II. Hats having brims with crowns of varying heights, covering only the top of the head, as the Milan bonnet and copatain.

III. Hoods as the French hood, which covered the head and neck.

IV. Decorative bands or accessories, as bongrace, fillet, paste, worn usually with other headgear.

Caps have the longest history. As Dekker says, they were first worn

> By the Romans; for when any bondman's turn
> Came to be made a freeman, thus 'twas said
> He to the cap was call'd, that is, was made
> Of Rome a freeman.[1]

They continued in fashion until the late twelfth century when low-crowned hats resembling dish-tops and inverted basins became the vogue, lost favour, and were revived four centuries later. During these early centuries, feminine head-gear had consisted of the coverchief or kerchief, the wimple, introduced about 1200, and, in the late twelfth century a close-fitting cap with the chinclout or *barbette*. The earliest illustration of hats on ladies is in a thirteenth-century French manuscript in the Bibliothèque Nationale and they seem not to have come to England until Chaucer's age. In the reign of Henry III the coif, with or without other head covering, became fashionable for men. It was worn out-of-doors under the hood—a type of headgear known since Norman times.

As the hood was the most desired by fourteenth- and fifteenth-century men, so was it favoured by sixteenth-century women. There were two chief styles: the English or gable hood and the French hood; the former mode ending for the nobility by 1535–40 and the middle class by 1560, the latter mode declining during Elizabeth's reign and definitely passing out of fashion for all classes by 1630. Under these hoods, ladies wore cauls and creppins confining the hair; and, as a protection from the sun's rays, the bongrace. Ornamental borders as billiments, frontlets, and pastes served as trimming. During the first fifty years of the sixteenth century men wore various types of brimmed caps especially the Milan bonnet, consisting of a crown pleated into a headband with a high turned-up brim fastened at the side with aglets, a jewel, or a medal.[2]

---

[1] *2 Honest Whore*, I. i. 438.

[2] 'It was the custom at that epoch to wear little golden medals upon which every nobleman or man of quality had some device or fancy of his own engraved, and these were worn in the cap.' *Autobiography of Cellini* (Symonds), 66.

The Milan bonnet had been introduced from Italy about 1455, but was most frequently named in expense accounts from 1511 on.[1] The German bonnet alluded to by Portia as part of the costume of Falconbridge had a béret-like crown, lower than that of the Milan and a slightly up-turned but less graceful brim.[2]

The flat cap, a round, flat-crowned, narrow-brimmed cap, was introduced by Henry VIII, but by 1570 had be-come the exclusive wear of citizens and apprentices. Small hats had been used by the higher classes from the begin-ning of Elizabeth's reign, but from 1570 until the death of James the high-crowned hat with various types of brim was worn by both men and women. Stubbes thus describes the styles of 1583:

'Sometymes they vse them sharpe on the croune peaking vp like the spere, or shaft of a steeple standyng a quarter of a yarde aboue the crowne of their heades. Othersome be flat and broad on the croune like the battlementes of a house. And other sorte have rounde crownes . . . some are of silk,[3] some of ueluet, some of taffata, some of sarcenet, some of wooll,[4] some of a certain kinde of fine haire . . . bever hattes of xx, xxx, or xL shillings price fetched from beyonde the seas. . . . He is of no . . . estimation amongst men if he haue not a ueluet or taffatie hat, and that must be pincked and cunnyngly carued of the beste fashion. . . . Of late there is a new fashion of wearyng their hattes sprong vp, which they father vpon the Frenchman, namely, to weare them without bandes, . . . other sort are content with no kind of hat without a great bunche of feathers of diuers colours peakyng on top of their heads.'[5]

Interest in Spain[6] was responsible for the small skull-fitting, narrow-brimmed barber's basin or porringer style which Stubbes describes. These hats 'scarce pipkin high', whose trimming was often an elaborate brooch and a

---

[1] *Letters and Papers Henry VIII*, ii. 2, 1496; 1516, ibid. 1509; 1530, iii. 3071; 1530, *Chetham Soc. Pub.* xli. 362; 1530, *P. P. Ex. Henry VIII*, 15, 99, &c.; 1536, *P. P. Ex. Prin. Mary*, 9.

[2] *Merch. of V.* I. ii. 80.

[3] Cf. also, *Durham Wills*, ii. 262.

[4] 1563, L.C. 9/57; 1617, A.C. 1/2348/45.

[5] *Anatomy of Abuses*, 50.

[6] Peacham, *Truth of Our Times*, 67: 'those close to the head like barber's basons with narrow brimmes we were at that time' (i.e. Elizabeth's reign) 'beholden to Cadiz in Spain.' Nashe, *Unfortunate Traveller*, ii. 300: 'From Spain what bringeth our traueller? A scull crown'd hat of the fashion of an old deepe porringer.'

bunch of feathers, covered only a small part of the head. An Elizabethan audience therefore would delight in Shakespeare's description of the haberdasher's wife who 'railed upon' the porter's man 'until her pinked porringer fell off'.[1] Probably they did not even object to his placing this Elizabethan style of hat in the age of her father.

These small caplike hats were frequently ridiculed in the drama. 'Our great heads never were in safety since our wives wore these little caps', said Kitely in *Every Man In His Humour* (III. ii. 37). Petruchio abuses Katharina's as 'a velvet dish, a cockle, a walnut shell, a custard coffin, a silken pie',[2]—a description which recalls Waspe's taunt that Quarlous' wife would display her anger 'fine as she is—for all her velvet custard on her head',[3] and the more vivid picture of Ploydenist 'mounted on a trapt Palfrey, with a round Velvet dish on his head'.[4]

But the style had disappeared with the coming of broad-brimmed hats before 1625; hence Gertrude's scorn of 'taffata pipkins'.[5]

Women are described as wearing a great variety of head-dress at King James's court in 1617:

'Some wear on their heads worked bands with fine lace which falling over the forehead, form what our Venetian dames term the "mush-rooms"...others wear hats of various shapes.... Some wear a moderate sized silk kerchief surmounted by a bit of crepe.... Others have black velvet hoods turned over from the back of the neck to the forehead. Others wear embroidered caps covering the whole head, whilst others wear their auburn hair uncovered and curled all over... on which they place a chaplet of silk and gold.'[6]

The copintank, sugar-loaf, or steeple hat worn by both sexes lost favour with the advent of the small hat; for the English Court came more and more under the dominance of French styles in which the broad-brimmed hat was prominent. *Hic Mulier* shows the latter to have been known in England by 1620, though Walter Carey,

[1] *Hen. VIII*, v. iv. 51.
[2] *Tam. Sh.* IV. iii. 64–6, 82.
[3] *Bartholomew Fair*, I. i. 326.
[4] *Return from Parnassus*, IV. ii (sig. G); *Jests of George Peele*, vol. ii. 398:

'There he found George . . . in a Spanish platter-fashioned hat.'
[5] *Eastward Hoe*, I. ii. 23.
[6] *C.S.P.V.* xv. 270.

writing seven years later, on the *Present State of England*,
observed:

'of late the broad-brimmed hat came suddenly in fashion, and put
all the others out of contenance and request and happy were they
that could get them soonest, and be the first seen in that fashion; so
that, a computation being made, there is at the least three thousand
pounds or much more, in England only, bestowed in broad-brimmed
hats, within one year and an half. As for others, either beauer or
felts, they were on the sudden of no reckoning at all . . . in so much
that my self . . . bought a beaver hat for five shillings which the year
before could not be had under thirty shillings.'[1]

Fashions in hat-trimming, bands, and blocks were followed in detail by Elizabethan dramatists. Gold embroidery was in demand especially on hats of dark colours, of
which Brisk's murrey French hat, thickly embroidered
with gold twist and spangles, and having a cable band of
'massy goldsmith's work',[2] is a good example. Embroidered hats were, of course, not 'new come up' as was the
cable hat-band. Maitland had satirized the velvet hats
'Broudit about with golden threidis' worn by 'toun ladyes',[3]
and such hats were made for Elizabeth's coronation:[4]
'1¾ yards velvett crimsen Lukes for one hatte Embraudered all over with Venice gold and Purles of Damaske
Gold. 1 yard crimsen sattin for Lyminge Tassells and
band of silke and gold with buttons. Caule for the same
hat.' This description of buttons on hatbands agrees with
Stowe's observation that 'about the first year of Elizabeth's
reign many very honourable personages and others, as well
women as men did weare borders of great cristall buttons
about their cappes as hatbands, as a worthy garment to
distinguish betweene the Gentry and others.'[5] About the
tenth year this crystal button-wearing was transferred to
doublets, jerkins, &c., and ceased on hats, but gold buttons
did not lose favour. In 1589 the Earl of Worcester gave
Queen Elizabeth a 'hatt of tyffany garnished with 28 buttons of golde of one sorte, and eight buttones of another

---

[1] *Harl. Miscy.* (1808), 556.

[2] *Every Man Out of His Humour*,
IV. vi. 84.

[3] 1556, 'Satire on Toun ladyes',

Percy Soc. Pub. xxvii. 92.

[4] L.C. 2/4 (3).

[5] *Annales*, 1039.

sorte about the band and upp the feather'.[1] But a more common ornament worn at the base of feathers or in a conspicuous place on the hat was of jewels exquisitely set. King James appeared at Theobalds, 1613, wearing in his hat a magnificent jewel with three large precious stones one above the other set in gold.[2] In 1623 he wrote to his son at Madrid: 'I send you for youre wearing the Three Brethren that ye knowe full well, but newlie sette, and the mirroure of Fraunc the fellowe of the Portugall dyamont, whiche I wolde wishe you to weare alone in your hatte with a little blakke feather.' Characters in *Timon of Athens, Edward II, Tragedy of Dido*, and *The Guardian*[3] allude to hats so decorated; while poor John Clay, who could not afford a jewell, turned his hat up with a silver clasp.[4]

Feathers 'peakyng on top of their heads' were desired by both men and women. When Queen Elizabeth visited Cambridge in 1564, she wore a hat that was spangled with gold and trimmed with a 'bush of feathers'.[5] So many feathers were worn on a hat that they were termed a 'forest of feathers' by Hamlet and Monsieur d'Olive.[6] A hat with a feather, and a sword were named as the requisites of a gallant in *What You Will* (III. i. 26). In the early seventeenth-century rage for gold decoration, feathers were of gold or spangled with gold.[7]

Hatbands were of ribbon, cypress, pearls, gold, or silver, which might be plain, engraved, or twisted into a cable as in *Law Tricks, Antonio and Mellida*, and *Every Man Out of His Humour*.[8] But embroidery, jewels, and expensive hatbands were not sufficient decoration for all tastes. Hats

---

[1] *Prog. Elizabeth*, iii. 446.

[2] Rye, op. cit. 150.

[3] *Timon*, III. vi. 124; *Edward II*, line 708; *Dido*, I. i. 47; *Guardian*, v. ii. 108.

[4] *Tale of a Tub*, II. ii. 127.

[5] *Prog. Elizabeth*, i. 160.

[6] *Haml*. III. ii. 291; *Monsieur d'Olive*, III. ii. 173.

[7] A velvet hat with a gold band and a gold feather at a cost of forty shillings were purchased, 1576, for Robert Sidney, then only a school boy. *Mid. MSS*. 270. Spangled feathers are mentioned in *The Roaring Girl*, II. i. 156.

[8] *Law Tricks*, IV. i. 126; *Antonio and Mellida*, II. i. 37; *Every Man Out of His Humour*, IV. vi. 84. Ribbon hatbands, *Cynthia's Revels*, V. ii. 34; cypress, *White Devil*, III. i. 77. Cypress hatbands were out of use by 1638, *Truth of Our Times*, 69.

were frequently 'pincked and cunnyngly carued', even to
the extent of having like Grumio's a 'humour of forty
fancies pricked in it for a feather'.[1]

Velvet and silk hats were supported by buckram frames,
and, in the case of ladies' hats, partly by the wire rolls worn
under the hair, but felts and beavers were moulded on a
wooden block 'cleft out' according to measurement for
the wearer's head, the Spanish, French, and Flemish
blocks giving the desired shapes for 1570–1620, and the
French thereafter predominating. Jonson, Shakespeare,
Beaumont and Fletcher were quick to note changes in
block fashions, and lost no opportunity of punning on
block and blockhead.[2]

The elaborateness of hats was probably responsible for
their continual wear—in doors and out—so that a hatless
man was considered mentally unsound, as one may judge
from Ophelia's description of Hamlet.[3]

BIGGIN

Derived from the French, *béguin*, the biggin was a
closely fitting child's cap,[4] and therefore indicated child-
hood, as in *Silent Woman*[5] and *Unnatural Combat*,[6] or poor
old age, as in *Henry IV*.[7] The Sergeant's coif, from its
resemblance to the biggin, was also called by that term in
City Match.[8] Biggins are in the pedlar's pack of *Pedler's
Prophecy* (sig. D 3).

BUTTONED CAP

The buttoned cap was round, with a slight brim turned
up and fastened by buttons, said to be the kind always
worn by Tarleton.[9] Buttoned caps were fashionable during the twenties to fifties,[10] but were replaced by hats in

[1] *Tam. Sh.* III. ii. 71.

[2] *Staple of News*, I. i. 190; *Much
Ado*, I. i. 78; *Love's Cure*, II. i. 150.

[3] *Haml.* II. i. 79.

[4] Palsgrave, 'Byggen for a chyldes
heed, beguyne'.

[5] III. ii. 245: 'been a courtier from
the biggin to the night-cap.'

[6] IV. ii. 94: 'Would you have me

Transform my hat to double clouts and
biggins.'

[7] *2 Hen. IV*, IV. v. 26.

[8] Dodsley, xiii. 288.

[9] A likeness of Tarleton, in such a
cap, is to be found in Harl. MS. 3885.

[10] *Richmond Wills*, xxvi. 126; *Durham Wills*, ii. 308. 1525, *Archaeologia*,
472.

the seventies, though worn thereafter by old persons. Thus, in *The Pilgrim* (v. iv. 53), it is part of a disguise, and it was probably the old-fashioned 'tucked-up cap' of *What You Will* (ii. i. 185). The *Book of Rates* for 1631 gives export rate for 'buttoned caps of English making', so that they were still known at that date.

CAUL

A caul was a closely fitting hair net worn by English women from the early fourteenth century. Cauls were made of gold thread or of hair,[1] decorated with gold or pearls, and lined with taffeta, cloth of gold, or tissue, in order that 'a man that seeth them', i.e. the ladies, 'would think them to have golden hair'. Lyly mentions them in *Mydas* among 'purtances' for the head (i. ii. 77). Cauls continued the mode until the fashion of fringed hair and curls, *c.* 1625, took the place of smoothed hair dressed upon rolls. Gold cauls were 'quite out of use' by 1638, Peacham writes in *Truth of Our Times* (p. 67).

COIF

A coif was a small cap covering the back and sides of the head, worn as an indoor head-dress.[2] The Venetian ambassador to England, 1531, gives a good picture of this style for women: 'They wear a sort of coif of white linen, from under which a few tresses are visible over the forehead, but the coif fits close behind so that toward the ears everything is covered, the coif concealing their hair.'[3] Plate XV shows a linen coif embroidered in gold.

Coifs were made of linen,[4] embroidered,[5] and edged with lace or made of drawn work.[6] Strings usually tied under the chin, though coifs were sometimes pinned to the hair.

[1] 1528, Hall, *Chronicle*, 732; 1587, L.C. 9/79; 1589, A.O. 3/1111; 1591, L.C. 9/83; 1602, L.C. 9/93: 'caules de crine curiously façt.'

[2] This discussion does not treat the plain linen coif used by men as insignia of offices such as that of sergeant, justices, Lord Treasurer, &c.

[3] *C.S.P.V.* iv. 288.

[4] 1587, L.C. 9/79; 1603, *Eglinton MS.* 31, cambric at 4s. a yd. used for 'quoifs'.

[5] *Prog. Elizabeth*, ii. 259; *Tu Quoque*, i. i. 16. The 'golden quoifs' of the *Wint. Tale* were probably of linen embroidered in gold and trimmed with gold lace, IV. iii. 226.

[6] 1620, *Household Bk. Howard*, 124.

Gertrude of *Eastward Hoe* felt that London lace or string—
she called it 'licket'—was not desirable for a lady's coif.[1]

CREPPIN

Creppin or crespin was a French term applied to a fine
linen material of which partlets[2] were made; and also to
a caul of velvet, cobweb lawn, or of network made from
gold or silver thread.[3]

Creppins, first used by ladies of the thirteenth century,
developed into the reticulated head-dress of the next century. After a short decadence, they reappeared under the
horn-shaped head-dress in the reign of Henry IV and became preposterous in that of Henry VI. During the sixteenth century, they were merely graceful, closely fitting
caps or nets covering the top or back of the head, and
worn to confine the hair under the French hood or hat.
They are therefore mentioned by Lyly among the 'purtances for the head'.[4]

Philip Gawdy, writing to his younger sister, 1589, of
fashions at Court, shows a masculine impatience over the
change and variety of the styles of head-dress:

'For the manner of their hoodes at the courte, some weare cripins
some weare none. Some weare sattin of all collors with their upper
border and some weare none. Some of them weare this daye all
these fashions, and the nexte without. So that I fynd nothing more
certayne than their uncertaynte, which makes me forbeare to sende
you anything further of myne owne devise.'[5]

FLAT CAPS

Though editors of sixteenth-century drama speak slightingly of flat caps, this head-gear was originally worn by

[1] I. ii. 15. *Mydas*, I. ii. 77, mentions coif.

[2] See Cypress. Partlets were sometimes called creppins: 1611, L.R.
2/121: 'two creppins of lawne wrought
about the collars.'

[3] *Pasquil's Mad-cappe* (Breton,
Works, I. 9 b): 'creppin or her caule.'
Cotgrave: 'crespe de chaperon a crepine, the crepine of a French-hood
most commonly of Cobweb Lawne or
white cipres'; 1577–8, *Prog. Elizabeth*,

ii. 73: 'five creppins of lawne, garnished with golde and silver purle.'
1580, *Lancashire and Cheshire Wills*,
li. 162: '1 creppyne ould of velvett.'
1545, E. 351/2023, among clothes for
Princess Elizabeth were 'creppins of
gold'; 1546, L.R. 2/119: '111 crepins
of silver and gold'; 1586–9, L.C.
9/177–9, &c.

[4] *Mydas*, I. ii. 80.

[5] Egerton MS. 2804, fol. 62.

XV. Lady's coif. White linen embroidered in gold and silks. A gathering lace
was used in the hem. Spanish. Late 16th century

Metropolitan Museum of Art, New York

royalty. In his *Survey of London*, Stowe describes the beginning of this fashion:

'Henry the eight (towards his latter raigne) wore a round, flat cap of scarlet or of velvet, with a broch or jewell, and a feather; diuers Gentlemen, courtiers and others did the like. The Youthfull citti-zens also tooke them to the new fashion of flatte caps, knit of woollen yearne blacke, but so light that they were forced to tye them under their chins, for else the wind would be maister ouer them. The use of these flat round cappes so far increased (being of lesse price then the French Bonet) that in a short time some yong Aldermen tooke ⟨to⟩ the wearing of them.' (ii. 194.)

The last statement explains Dekker's 'Flat caps as proper are to Citty Gownes', as to 'Kings their Crownes'.[1] In 1571, in order to save the cap-workers of England who five years before had been declared 'impoverished because of the excessive use of hats and felts',[2] a law was passed compelling all persons to wear English-made caps upon Sundays and holidays,[3] a law in force for twenty-six years.

In 1582 regulations for the apparel of London appren-tices were made. These regulations forbade apprentices to wear hats, allowing them only woollen caps, without 'any silk in or about the same'.[4] These were the flat caps by which apprentices were thereafter known, both in life and on the stage.[5]

LETTICE CAP

The lettice cap was of grey fur, resembling ermine, the ladies' style having three corners 'like the forked cappes of Popishe Priestes'.[6] In *Monsieur Thomas* (III. i. 12), and *Thierry and Theodoret* (v. i. 123), the lettice cap does not refer to this headdress but to a salad of lettuce eaten just before retiring, to produce somnolence.[7]

[1] *2 Honest Whore*, I. i. 461. Also *Eastward Hoe*, I. i. 101.
[2] *Statutes at Large*, 8 Elizabeth, xi.
[3] Ibid. 13 Elizabeth, xix; repealed 39 Elizabeth, xviii.
[4] *Prog. Elizabeth*, ii. 393.
[5] *Edward IV*, IV. i; *Match Me in London*, II. i. 12; *Eastward Hoe*, II. i.

87; *Dutch Courtezan*, II. ii. 35.
[6] Stubbes, *Anatomy of Abuses*, p. 63. The wearing of lettice was forbidden in 1402 to any one below the state of 'banneret'. *Rot. Parl.* iii. 506.
[7] 1614, *Tu Quoque*, sig. L. 3 b. 'Did I eate any Lettice last night that I am so sleepie?'

MINIVER

The 'dainty miniver caps' which Luke Frugal names among the extravagances of Lady Frugal in *The City Madam* (IV. iv. 84) were made of the fur of 'ermines mixed or spotted with the furre of the Weesell caled Gris', according to Cotgrave.[1] These caps, mentioned in *Shoemaker's Holiday*,[2] were old-fashioned in the twelfth year of Elizabeth's reign. They were tri-cornered and three or four inches high. They seem not to have been worn by persons above the rank of gentlewoman.[3] Lady Frugal must have been represented as old, or *The City Madam* must have been written earlier than is generally supposed. Reference to a miniver cap would have puzzled an audience of the reign of King Charles. Other references to costume in this play indicate that it was written previous to 1625.

MONMOUTH

The Monmouth was a round, brimless cap with high, tapering crown, worn by sailors, as mentioned in *Eastward Hoe*,[4] and by soldiers, especially the Welsh, as in *Henry V*.[5]

NIGHT CAPS

Shakespeare's allusion to night caps in *Julius Caesar* (I. ii. 246) has never been supported by evidence that this

[1] See *Menu Vair*; but Holmes, *Armorie*, III. iii. 50, 2, refers to miniver as 'plain white fur'.

[2] V. iv. 54: 'Vanish, Mother Minivercap', i.e. wife of the shoemaker.

[3] Stowe, *Annales* (Howes), 1039: 'At which time (tenth or twelfth year, Elizabeth's reign) and for three or foure yeares after, all citizens wives in general, were constrayned to weare white knit Caps of woolen yarne, unlesse their husbands were of good value in the Queenes booke, or could proue themselues.Gentlemen by descent, and then ceased the womens wearing of Minevor caps . . . which formerly was the usual wearing of all graue Mat-

rons. These Minivor Caps were white, and three square, and the peakes therof were full three or foure inches from their head, but the Aldermens wiues . . . made them Bonnets of Velvet after the Minevor Cappe fashion, but larger, which made a great show vpon their heads, all which are already quite forgotten.'

[4] IV. ii. 8: 'hurl away a brown dozen of Monmouth caps in a sea ceremony to your *bon voyage*.' 'The seaman has his cap par'd without brim', *2 Honest Whore*, I. i. 425.

[5] IV. vii. 105. *Roxburghe Ballads* (ed. J. P. Collier, 1847), 5: 'The soldiers that the Monmouth wear.'

kind of head covering was wőrn by the Romans, but its use can be traced as far as Chaucer's age.[1] Sixteenth-century night caps were exclusively masculine wear. Women wore coifs, kerchiefs, rails, pastes, &c. Velvet night caps of *Westward Hoe*,[2] and 'wrought' linen ones of *Sir Giles Goosecap* (v. i. 51) and *What You Will*[3] were the usual wear. Though the early sixteenth-century night caps were tied under the chin by ribbon and laces,[4] those of the last quarter changed their coif cut; they became round, fitted caps with turned-up brims. These caps were sometimes worn by old men on the street,[5] but a 'day worn night-cap' usually indicated that the wearer was in ill health.[6]

STATUTE CAPS

In 1571 a law to benefit cappers was enacted, requiring that every person above seven years of age should wear on 'sabbath and holyday upon their head a cap of wool knit thicked and dressed in England . . . upon pain to forfeit for every day not wearing, three shillings fourpence: except maids, ladies, gentlewomen, noble personages and every lord, knight and gentleman of twenty marks land and their heirs and such as have born office of worship in any city, borough, town, hamlet or shire'.[7] Such knitted caps were known as statute caps. Rosaline's 'better wits have worn plain statute caps'[8] means that Katharine's remarks show poor wit, and better wit is to be found even among citizens' wives[9] and such as are required to wear the caps. The law was repealed in 1597.[10]

---

[1] 1378, *Let. Bk.* F, fol. ccxxii.

[2] I. i. 224. Nightcaps were made of scarlet, Borde, *Dietary*, 247.

[3] II. i. 14. See also 1615, *Prog. James*, i. 598.

[4] 1555, Waterman, *Fardle of facions*, ch. x; Stowe, *Annales*, 546.

[5] *Silent Women*, I. i. 145. Raleigh wore one on the scaffold, Birch, *Court and Times James I*, ii. 100.

[6] *Match Me in London*, I. i (vol. iv.

146); *In Praise of Clean Linen*, 168.

[7] *Statutes at Large*, 13 Elizabeth, c. 19.

[8] *Love's Labour's Lost*, V. ii. 283.

[9] *Dutch Courtezan*, III. iii. 27. 'Nay, though my husband be a citizen, and 's cap's made of wool, yet I ha' wit.'

[10] *Statutes at Large*, 39 Elizabeth, c. 18.

COPINTANK

Copintank, or copatain, was a high, conical, or sugar-loaf hat,[1] whose original name may have been derived partly from the word 'copped', meaning sharp and high. The cost of '8 coppet hats of black velvet fringed with venice gold'[2] is part of costume expenses for Court revels, 1518. Also for the revels of 1550 'longe coppintanckes of felt covered with silver Lawne spangled and tufted with black gowld sarcenett the frontlets turned up with blewe satten' are provided for characters impersonating Turkish women.[3] Gascoigne's review of English fashions stated that: 'Of a Turkie bonnet . . . (we make) a copentank.'[4] Men of Tartary were said by travellers to wear 'shallowe copintanckes', and North, 1580, wrote of 'copped tanke' hats after the fashion of the Medes.[5] The fashion was therefore probably of Eastern origin, altered to suit English taste.

Copintanks were a favoured style from the beginning to the end of Elizabeth's reign, and were not definitely out of fashion until the low-crowned, beplumed hats of Cavalier days usurped their place. The copintank was trimmed by a band, a small plume, or a large jewelled ornament, usually placed in front, sometimes against the turned-up brim. Sometimes the hat was trimmed only by a cable hat-band, and the brim was rolled up a little on each side. Although copantank or copatain, as in *Taming of the Shrew* (v. i. 69), was the usual name for this hat, it was also, as in *Soliman and Perseda*, *Westward Hoe*,[6] and other plays, called 'sugar-loaf', because of its shape.

BEAVER

The fine, silky fur of the amphibious rodent, beaver, periodically returned to fashion as a hat material. Such hats 'fetched from beyond the seas' were worn in Chau-

[1] Junius, 1585: 'Apex—a sugar-loafe hat; a copped hat.'

[2] *Letters and Papers Henry VIII*, ii. 2, 1517.

[3] Feuillerat, *Revels*, 186.

[4] *Delicate Diet*, 18. Barclay mentions the fashion in *Ship of Fools*, 1508. See *O.E.D.*

[5] Plutarch, *Lives* (ed. 1595), 994.

[6] *Soliman and Perseda*, IV. i. 2; *Westward Hoe*, IV. i. 248.

cer's age; Elizabethan desire for rich materials again brought them into fashion; and their favour at Court continued until the reign of Charles I. Stubbes, 1583, is outraged at their prices of twenty to forty shillings,[1] the latter price corresponding to that of Asotus's exclamation: 'Ile assure you tis a beaver, it cost me eight crownes but this morning.'[2] Neither the £3 beaver of *Tu Quoque*,[3] nor the £4 one of *Magnetic Lady*[4] showed an exaggerated price, for a beaver with a 'curled silke band' purchased by William Freke,[5] a student at Oxford, cost £3 6s. Accounts of King James, 1605, and of his son, Henry, 1608, show items of beavers of many colours, lined, and ornamented with satin or taffeta,[6] costing three to six pounds, with separate purchases of bands of equal prices.

At such prices, beavers naturally became symbolic of wealth, not to be worn by any below a gentleman. A part of a 'gentleman's suit' in *Your Five Gallants* was a 'fine white beaver, pearl band';[7] though even a 'currier's son' could wear one if he had the price. Those who did not have the price of such 'casters' wore the 'demi-casters', which were made of beaver and cony wool, scorned in Roderique's: 'I durst venture the price of your gilt cony's wool.'[8]

From the reign of King Charles I, the followers of Court fashions favoured the large velvet hat rather than the beaver, though the latter was still worn by persons who did not desire 'the latest'.

FELT HATS

Stowe says that the making of Spanish felts in England by Spaniards and Dutchmen began in the first part of the

[1] *Anatomy*, 39. *Hist. Hengrave*, 39, shows an item of 1583 for a tawny beaver hat costing 30s.; while a black silk and gold band for it cost 20s.

[2] *Cynthia's Revels*, I. iv. 151.

[3] Sig. K verso.

[4] v. ii. 20, a woman's hat.

[5] *Eng. Hist. Rev.* vii. 99. The import duty on hats of beaver wool was 26s. 8d. in 1631, *Book of Rates*.

[6] L.C. 9/94; *Archaeologia*, xi. 95.

[7] I. i. 81; *Fatal Dowry*, v. ii. 285; Overbury, *Characters*, 128.

[8] *M. d'Olive*, I. i. 360. A proclamation of Dec. 14, 1639, prohibited the making and wearing of demi-casters and the mixing of any wool with beaver in making beaver hats, *Tudor and Stuart Proc.* i. 1810.

reign of Henry VIII; that previous to that time the English had worn 'winter and sommer knit caps, cloth hoods and . . . silk thromd hats'.[1] It is difficult to reconcile this statement with Lydgate's mention of 'fyne felt hats'.[2] Whatever the date of English manufacture, felts were so extensively worn by 1566 that protective legislation for the cap-makers had to be passed.[3]

Sixteenth-century felt hats were faced or lined with velvet or silk.[4] Felt was the usual material for the 'sugar-loaf', also for the hat described in *Honest Whore*; and the Spanish felt 'or the like counterfeyte' was, according to Stowe's *Survey*, 'the most commonly of all men temporal and spiritual taken to use'.[5]

Straw Hats

Sharp's account of expenses for the Coventry Mysteries of 1453 records 'iiij stre hatts', which seems to be the earliest known reference in English drama to straw hats.[6] An inventory of the goods of Sir John Fastolfe, made six years later, includes 'ij strawen hattes',[7] showing that they were worn by private persons, but whether they were imported or English made is impossible to determine; it is reasonable to suppose that plaiting straw for hats was a countryside occupation long before such hats were manufactured commercially.

Tradition connects the manufacture with Mary Queen of Scots, who, observing their success in Lorraine, 1552, brought back some of the hat-makers to Scotland to teach her own people. After her death, her son, James I of England, took the Lorrainers to England, finding shelter for them under protection of the Napier family.[8] These were evidently not the first foreigners of the 'mystery',

[1] *Annales* (Howes), 870.
[2] *Minor Poems*, 105.
[3] *Statutes at Large*, 8 Elizabeth, c. 11.
[4] 1571, Ellis, *Letters*, 11. iii. 74; 1580, *Durham Wills*, xxxiii. 66; *Surrey Rec. Soc. Pub.* xiv. 237; also contemporary portraits.
[5] 2 *Honest Whore*, 1. i. 368; *Survey*, ii. 195.
[6] 190. In the British Museum is a small figure dated *c*. 700 B.C., wearing a Stephanos which appears to be of plaited straw.
[7] *Archaeologia*, xxi. 255.
[8] Austin, Thomas G., *The Straw Trade* (1870), 15.

however, for among the naturalizations in England, 1530, was that of Martin Johnson, Gueldres, 'strawen hat-maker'.[1]

The straw hat does not seem to have been worn by any except country folk during Shakespeare's age. The 'sun-burned sicklemen' of *The Tempest* wear 'rye straw hats' (IV. i. 136), and 'straw hats shall be no more bongraces' is part of the song of country lasses in *The Rape of Lucrece*.[2]

TAFFETA HAT

Taffeta was a favoured material for hats because it was lighter than velvet, soft, and yet had sufficient 'body' to hold its place; consequently, from the thirties, when Henry VIII set the fashion, to the end of the century, every wardrobe that could afford them contained taffeta hats.[3] Taffeta hats were usually embroidered, pinked, or jewelled. One presented to Queen Elizabeth was of tawny taffeta embroidered in scorpions of Venice gold, with a border of seed pearls;[4] and a white one given her by Sir Julius Caesar, 1590, was trimmed with rubies and diamonds.

'Taffeta pipkins',[5] scorned by Gertrude as unfit for a lady, or for a lady's sister, were small French hats with a large crown pleated into a narrow brim. After 1600 ladies such as Gertrude expected to be, wore large-brimmed, high crowned felts, so that taffeta hats were worn only by persons of incomes too small to support fashion.

[1] Page, *Denization and Naturaliza-tion*, 136.

[2] III. iv. (vol. v. 213), Jonson, *Epi-gram to Lady Wroth*: 'He that but saw you wear the wheaten hat,' &c. Greene, *Works*, ix. 265: 'having on his head a strawne hat steeplewise'; *Lover's Complaint*, 8: 'Upon her a head a platted hive of straw Which fortified her visage from the sun.'

[3] 1533-4: 'hat of taffety . . . vj s viij d,' *Archaeologia*, xxv. 555; 1539, *Letters and Papers Henry VIII*, xiv. 2, 342: 'for 7 hats of taffeta for my lord'; 1553, E. 154/2/39, inventory goods,

Duke of Northumberland; 1558, *Lan-cashire and Cheshire Wills*, liv. 12, 139, valued at 3s. 4d. each; 1563, L.C. 9/57; 1565, A.O. 1/1106, hat of velvet lined with 'taphata pinked'; 1577, *Court Leet Rec. Southampton*, i. 161; 1578, *Richmond Wills*, 276, valued at 6s. 8d.; 1582, *Durham Wills*, xxxviii. 66, 15s. each; ibid. 103: 'ij fyne taffyte hates' £1; 1596, L.C. 2/82; 1601, *Sur-rey Rec. Soc.* xiv. 181.

[4] *Prog. Elizabeth*, ii. 261.

[5] *Eastward Hoe*, I. ii. 23; *Amends for Ladies*, II. i. 80: 'finicall taffatea pipkin.'

Thrummed Hats

Thrums were the unwoven threads[1] at the ends of cloth
or silk. A felt hat so made as to leave projecting ends of
the threads upon the surface to form a pile or nap was
called a thrummed hat.[2] Such hats had been worn in
England since before 1525,[3] but during Elizabeth's reign
when velvet, silk, and beaver were desired, thrummed hats
seem to have been the wear of the lower class, represented in *Merry Wives of Windsor*.[4]

Since the nap or thrum on a hat was raised by rubbing,
any turning of a hat around in the hands was called thrumming. 'Thrumming of hats', therefore, became proverbial
for indecision or time wasting;[5] hence: 'I'de nere stand
thrumming of caps for the matter,' of *Tu Quoque*.[6]

Hood

The hood, which was the oldest style of head covering,
dates to Anglo-Saxon days, and was revived periodically
thereafter.[7] Hoods were exclusively woman's wear in the
sixteenth century. Those worn previous to the *coquille*,
or French hood, were ugly and heavy, with broad back
curtain or lappet, and narrow side lappets which hung
from a peaked or gable front. They were worn over a caul,
and often with a bongrace; and since the jewelled or embroidered frontlet fitted rather closely about the face, the
effect was stiff, severe, and unbecoming even to lovely
faces.

The French hood was softly pleated, of velvet, tissue,

---

[1] *Rot. Parl.*, 8 Henry VI, xxiii.

[2] Florio, 1611, '*Gottonare*, to cotton, to frize, to thrum, or set a nap
upon'; 'Felts are of two kinds: bare
and thrummed', *Statutes at Large*,
I Edward VI, c. 6.

[3] 1525, Harl. MS. 4217, 11: 'Hattes
thrommed with silke of diverse col-
lours'; 1535, *Bury Wills*, xlv. 26; 1552,
Statutes at Large, 5 & 6 Edward VI,
c. 24; 1566, *Durham Wills*, ii. 262;
1582, ibid. xxxviii. 66: 'two silke

thromed hattes'; 1587, *Lancashire and
Cheshire Wills*, li. 120.

[4] IV. ii. 82.

[5] Florio, 1611, '*Nicchiare*, to stand
thrumming of hats or to speak doubt-
ful words or hang off and on as if
more would make all well.'

[6] Sig. H. ij verso; *Women Beware
Women*, III. iii. 17.

[7] See examples *O.E.D.*; *The Paston
Letters*, 121, 476, 487, give excellent
descriptions of fifteenth-century hoods.

or other silk, with a round front. Since it was worn over
the back of the head as far as the ears, the face had a
becoming frame of hair. Of course, such hoods were easily
disarranged.[1] Though these hoods were used in a Greenwich masque,[2] 1514, mentioned in *The Pardoner and the
Friar*, 1520 (p. 7), and purchased for 'Katyne and Anne'
Lestrange in 1530,[3] they are not spoken of as an English
fashion until 1540, when chroniclers, describing the costume of Anne of Cleves, note that she wore a 'French
whode whiche set furth her beautie and good visage', and
'thene begane all the gentylwomen of Yngland to weare
French whoddes with bellements'.[4] For thirty years thereafter Royal wardrobe accounts and bequests of gentlewomen[5] alike contain references to this 'far fetched, dear
bought' style which called forth the famous condemnation
of Latimer in his Lenten sermon[6] before Edward VI,
1550. Even as late as 1587, Philip Gawdy, writing to his
sister Anne, concerning court styles, stated: 'For cappes
and french hoodes I fynde no change in the world whatsoever.'[7] By the nineties, however, Court ladies had begun
to wear hats, and found French hoods less desirable.

The lower class, represented by Tibet Talkapace of
Roister Doister (II. iii. 41), were wearing French hoods by
the fifties, and the *London Prodigal*,[8] 1605, shows them at
that date to be peculiar to citizens' wives. 'Paris hoads'
were purchased for lady attendants at the funeral of Queen

[1] *Devil is an Ass*, I. i. 110.

[2] 1548, Hall, *Union Families Lancaster and York*, xxij: 'Out came sixe
ladies . . . with French hoddes on their
heddes.'

[3] *Archaeologia*, xxv. 509: 'French
hoods w^t byllym^{ts}.' 1527, de Guez,
Grammaire, 906: 'Le chaperon à plis,
the french hode.'

[4] *Chronicle of Grey friars*, 43. Hall,
836–7; but Holinshed, iii. 814, wrote:
'This daie she was apparelled after the
English manner, with a French hood,
which became her exceeding well.'
The hoods of Anne of Cleves were
thereafter ordered in France, 1541,
State Papers Henry VIII, i. 695.

[5] 1545, E. 351/3025, 4½ yds. velvet
are needed for six 'ffrenchhoods and
billements'; 1558, *Test. Leod.* xxvii.
191; 1561–8, *Durham Wills*, ii. 273,
288, valued at 10 to 16s.; 1553, *Middlesex Sessions Rolls*, i. 14, stolen: 'unum
ornamentum de serico vocat. French
Whoodd', value 26s. 8d. In 1532 a
French hood cost 14s., *Archaeologia*,
xxv. 556; 1553, 18s. 9d. *Antiq. Rep.*
i. 66, 1547, *Malone Soc. Coll.* II. i. 198:
'a French hode of tyeshew.'

[6] *Sermons*, i. 253.

[7] Egerton MS. 2804, fol. 41.

[8] Sig. B 4. They are priced at 16s.
in the inventory, 1589, of J. Johnson,
merchant, *Durham Wills*, xxxviii. 211.

Elizabeth, but no further mention of them is made in
Royal wardrobe accounts, and Moryson wrote that the
style was definitely out, even for 'the graver sort of married women'.[1] *The City Madam* (IV. iv. 32) pictures the
distress of proud Lady Frugal, forced to wear this fashion
which was so antiquated as to appear ridiculous.

ACCESSORIES OF HEAD ATTIRE

BILLIMENTS

What means this gorgeous glittering head attir?
How ill beseeme these billaments of gold.
(1591, *Tancred & Gismund*, v. ii. 65–6.)

To wear her 'biliments of gold' every day was the
highest ambition of Tibet Talkapace in *Roister Doister*.[2]
These billiments were borders or circlets worn on the
fronts of hoods or around the head, like a fillet.[3] They
were made of goldsmith's work, precious stones, pearls,
velvet or silks embroidered or edged with pleated cypress
or lace.[4]

[1] *Itinerary*, iv. 235. See *Alchemist*,
II. vi.

[2] II. iii. 43. Cf. *Robin Conscience*,
Hazlitt, *Early Pop. Poetry*, iii. 238,
'and goeth in their billaments of fine
pearle and gold'; *Rape of Lucrece*, vol.
v. 213, 'and Billements with golden
studs'.

[3] Florio, 1598, '*Cercéglio* . . . billiment or border that women weare
upon their heads'.

[4] 1541, *Letters and Papers Henry
VIII*, xvi. 618: 'upper and nether habil-
ments of goldsmiths work for the
French hood'; 1541–2, *Statutes of
Realm*, 33 Henry VIII, c. 5, 'whos
wiff shall were any Frenche hood or
bonnet of Velvett wth any habilment
past or egge of gold perle or stone';
1546, 'foure upper billyments of
goldesmithyes worke, and foure nether
billyments', L.R. 2/115; 1553, *Richmond Wills*, xxvi. 76, 'my perell bely-
ment both the upper and the ondre';

1555, *Fardle of Facions*, II. vii. 161:
'The abillements of their heades are
much like the frontlettes that the magi
doe weare'; 1570, Egerton MSS. 2806,
'One yarde of crymsen Satten to make
habilliaments: and one yarde quarter
of blak ssarcnet to lyne the same. For
making of the whodde three billiments
of vellat with gathered sipers to them';
1584, 'an upper and nether abillement
of gold; the upper abillement contayn-
ing eleven peces, syx of them lyke
harts, the other fyve crownes imperiall
garnished with sparcks of rubyes, dyamondes and perles; the nether contayn-
ing 17 peces, eight of them lynks of
perles, and two sparkes of dyamondes,
the other nine peces sett with roses of
sparkes of dyamondes, smale rubyes in
the midest of either of them'. These
handsome billiments were a New
Year's gift to Queen Elizabeth, *Prog.
Elizabeth*, ii. 426.

BONGRACE

Bongrace was a projecting front brim or shade worn
with bonnets, caps, or coifs to protect the wearer from the
sun and so preserve her good grace or beauty. As its name
implies, it was a French fashion, but was called after 1575
a 'shadow'. From the time of the introduction of French
hoods to England, i.e. about 1514, the bongrace became
necessary, for these hoods offered no protection for the
face. A piece of velvet shaped like an eye-shade was one
form of bongrace, though many women used the long
flap of the French hood, which ordinarily hung behind,
folding it to shade the forehead 'like a pent house', as
described in *Mary Magdalene*.[1] The Pardoner of *The
Pardoner and the Friar* used this new fashion to offer the
crowd a choice relic—the bongrace of Our Lady,

> which she ware with her French hood
> When she went out always for sunburning. (P. 7.)

These velvet bongraces, which were also detachable, were
sometimes sold as separate articles, and were to be found, in
the late sixteenth century when they had become *démodées*
at Court, in the packs of pedlars[2] on and off the stage.

The bongrace, or shadow, of the latter part of the century was of linen, cypress, network, or lace, and the 'set'
of this shadow became the object of special care on the
part of ladies.[3] Moryson tells of the passing of the old
bongrace. Writing of the women of Denmark, he says:
'The married Gentlewomen goe with their heads covered
with a fine linnen coyfe, and weare upon their foreheads a
French shadow of velvet to defend them from the Sunne,
which our Gentlewomen of old borrowed of the French, and
called the Bonegraces, now altogether out of use with us.'[4]

---

[1] 1566, sig. C iiij verso. Plate VIII.

[2] 1595, *Pedler's Prophecy*, sig. D 1.
For other references to velvet bongraces, see 1566, *Richmond Wills*, 183;
1569, *Durham Wills*, ii. 303; 1583,
ibid. xxxviii. 74.

[3] Harrison, 1591, *Orlando Furioso*,
410, describes their fastidious care in
arranging these shadows. 1580–1,

L.C. 9/71, shadow of network edged
with needlework; 1591, *Durham Wills*,
xxxviii. 211, network shadows. 1586–
7, L.C. 9/77, shadow of cypress with
a border of gold and silver embroidery.
They are called shadows in *Mydas*, I.
ii. 80.

[4] 1605–17, *Itinerary*, iv. 215.

Shadows, of course, went out of fashion with hoods. The Jacobean lady wore a large hat to protect her complexion from sunburning.

FILLET

A fillet was a 'little long band or narowe ribben where-with women doe wreath or bind their haire'.[1] In the six-teenth century, fillets were worn over the top and sides of the head and fastened in the back, to keep the hair smooth. This smoothness was especially desirable when the French hood was worn. When women began to dress their hair on 'rolls' and 'palisadoes', fillets were no longer necessary. *The Four PP, Pedler's Prophecy, Mydas*, and *Lingua*[2] men-tion fillets.

FRONTLET

'Your frontlets lay by' sings Valerius in *The Rape of Lucrece* (III. iv). Though frontlets changed their shape with the fashion of head-dress, hood, or hat, they remained essentially bands which served to enrich the coiffure or hood of ladies.[3] They were made of gold, of velvet, or of satin embroidered with gold, or of needlework,[4] and were worn with cauls, hoods,[5] &c.

Since frontlets usually cast a shadow on the forehead, a frown or a sullen expression was called a frontlet, as in *Lear* (I. iv. 208). They are named in many plays from *The Four PP* to *Lingua*.[6]

[1] Baret, *Alvearie*.

[2] *The Four PP*, p. 7; *Pedler's Prophecy*, sig. D 1; *Mydas*, I. ii. 78; *Lingua*, IV. vi. 25. 'Rolls' were stuffed pads worn under the hair to raise it *pompadour* fashion; 'palisadoes' were wire rolls which served the same purpose.

[3] Known in France, 1338, and in England about a century later, *Rot. Parl.* vi. 287. A sumptuary law of 17 Edward IV permits wives and daughters of persons having posses-sions of yearly value of £10 to use and wear frontlets of black velvet, Addit. MS. 7099.

[4] 1502, *P. P. Ex. Elizabeth York*, 68; 1504, *Paston Letters*, iii. 470;

1506, *Test. Ebor.* liii. 258; 1523, *Archaeologia*, xxxviii. 369; 1536, L.C. 9/57—all of these accounts listing gold frontlets. 1530, *Shuttleworth Accts.* xli. 362, 'frontlet of blewe velvet' cost 7s. 6d.; 1546, L.R. 2/119, frontlet of purple satin with 'purles and pipes of gold'; 1611, L.R. 2/121, of purple satin garnished with 'damask purle'. 1565, A.O. 3/1106, 'iiij virg de laqueo de nedlework pro v frontlets'.

[5] 1523, *Letters and Papers Henry VIII*, iii. 2, 1254; 1526, ibid. iv. 2, 1225; 1524, *Churchwardens' Accounts St. Mary Hill*, 125.

[6] *Four PP*, p. 36; *Lingua*, IV. vi. 25; *Mydas*, I. ii. 77, &c.

PASTE

'Cony skins for old pastes' is the burden of the Pedlar's cry in *The Pedler's Prophecy*,[1] as he seeks to barter his wares with the country folk. Paste, from *passe*, border, was a border of rich material as velvet, lawn, &c., decorated with embroidery or gold, or a jewelled circlet worn on the fronts of French hoods, or on the heads of brides. Pastes were used in the revels at Greenwich, 1527, the earliest reference noted,[2] and the wedding apparel of Mary Neville, 1530, included 'pasts'.[3] A statute of 1541 forbade wives of persons below a certain rank or income to wear 'any French hood or bonett of Velvet wth any habiliment past or egge (i.e. edge) of gold perle or stone'.[4]

The Great Wardrobe Accounts between 1537 and 1565 contain numerous references to 'frows pastes' in lawn, lace, and jewels, as do also other wardrobes and historical accounts.[5] They evidently went out of fashion with the French hoods to which they were a necessary accessory.

[1] Sig. D 3. For a more complete discussion of pastes, see 'Cony Skins for Old Pastes', *Phil. Quart.* x. 84.

[2] *Letters and Papers Henry VIII*, iv. 2, 1606: 'Hire of a serklet and a rich paste.'

[3] *Chetham Soc. Pub.* xli. 367. Also Machyn, *Diary*, 246.

[4] *Statutes at Large*, 33 Henry VIII, c. 5.

[5] 1537, E. 315/455; 1545, E. 351/3025; 1565, A.O. 1/1106; 1561, L.C. 9/56; 1554, *Camden Soc. Pub.* (1850), 50; 1550, *Mid. MSS.* 402; 1603 (funeral Queen Elizabeth), L.C. 2/44, &c., *Repentance Mary Magdalene*, sig. (C iiij, verso).

XIV

LEATHER AND FOOTWEAR

THE early Anglo-Saxons used undressed skins for their footwear, but tanning must have been practised before Norman occupation, for the Cordwainers' Guild—including tanners, curriers, shoemakers—was reconstituted in 1131.[1] There were many tanners, curriers, and shoemakers in Oxon., Essex, and Surrey towns during the thirteenth century,[2] and by 1321 the Guild had grown enough to secure an act preventing non-members from exercising the 'mistery'.[3] Thirty years later the Cordwainers were one of the thirteen companies who elected members to the Common Council in London.[4] By this date the policy of specialization had produced the Statute of Labourers which forbade shoemakers to tan leather and tanners to make shoes.[5] Statutes in 1485 and 1503–4 further divided the operations of leather preparation and shoe-making.[6]

With the growth of these industries in the sixteenth century, legislation was needed to check deceitful practices in tanning,[7] and finally to regulate the whole process of shoe-manufacture.[8] Until the seventeenth century

---

[1] Cunningham, *Growth of English Industry and Commerce*, i. 652. Leather is mentioned attributively in 1000, and by name in 1225, *O.E.D.* Rogers says the tanning of leather was probably a by-product in most villages in England. *Six Centuries of Work and Wages*, 46.

[2] *Oxford Hist. Soc. Pub.* xxxvii. 3, 7, 10. In 1380, poll tax returns showed four saddlers, twelve tanners, twelve skinners, in Oxfordshire alone, ibid. xviii. *passim*.

[3] Ibid. xxxii. 121.

[4] *Let. Bk. F.*, 237–8.

[5] 25 Edward III, c. 4; also 13 Richard II, c. 12; 21 Richard II, c 16; repealed 1 Henry IV, c. 3; revived 2

Henry VI, c. 7.

[6] 1 Henry VII, c. 5; 19 Henry VII, c. 19.

[7] 2 & 3 Edward VI, c. 11.

[8] 5 Elizabeth, c. 8. Some interesting observations on this Statute for Tanners are in the Lansdowne MS. 5, art. 58. Only six of the fifteen clauses could be kept because the framers of the statute seemed ignorant of tanning processes. Lansdowne MS. 20, art. 4, contains a letter from the Recorder of London to Lord Burghley stating that the manner of tanning varied in every shire; even the waters varied greatly, the chalk waters of Chiltern Hills being the best. Oak bark seemed preferable to ash for the 'owes'; and the quality

XVI. James, Duke of Hamilton. Costume of 1623. Black velvet
doublet, hose and cloak; embroidered hanger; French 'fall', matching
cuffs; scarlet stockings; silk lace-edged garters; silver-coloured shoes,
lace shoe-roses ornamented with spangles

National Gallery

Surrey towns—notably Chiddingfold, Bermondsey, and Southwark—led in the production of leather goods, but Oxfordshire had reached first place by the reign of James I.

Leather for footwear—classified by a statute of 1603 as shoes, boots, buskins, startups, slippers or pantoffles[1] —was made from the hides of deer, goats, sheep, and domestic cattle, neat; the hide of the ox producing the most enduring leather. Horse hide was forbidden by this statute. Spanish leather, of which the best was made in Cordova, must have been used very early in England for it gave the term *cordwain*, originally leather made in Cordova, to the language; this fine-grained, coloured leather was tanned and dry-curried by a process at first known only in that city.[2] The best cordovan leather was, according to Florio, 1611, made from the skin of the *musmone*, a cross between a sheep and a goat, which was bred in Corsica and Sardinia. This leather was a favourite with Elizabethans, and quantities were imported.[3] It naturally is named in Tudor and Jacobean drama.[4] In order to encourage the home industry, Englishmen were urged to wear neat's leather, and scorn the Spanish product.[5] The figure of speech: 'as proper a man as ever trod

of the leather depended for the most part upon the skill in making the 'owes' and changing the hides at the proper time from 'owes' to 'owes'. This Statute was revised by 1 James I, c. 22. Ash or oak bark, tapwort, malt, meal, lime, sheep and hen dung were allowed in the 'woozes'. Twelve months' immersion in the vats was required for sole-leather; and nine months' for upper-leather.

[1] *Statutes at Large*, 1 James I, c. 22. 'The steere, the hayefer and the calfe Are all called neat.' *Wint. Tale*, I. ii. 125. Florio, *Second Frvtes*, 7: 'Two paire bootes, one Spanishe, the other neates lether.'

[2] Sir Thopas wears 'shoon of corde-vane', 2, line 1922. For numerous items of coloured Spanish leather see the wardrobe accounts of Edward IV,

1480. The wardrobe account of Richard III for his coronation inclu-ded '2 paire slops, 2 paire shoon, 8 paire botes of Spanish leder', *Archaeo-logia*, i. 397. Henry VIII, 1536, bought six pair Spanish leather bus-kins, ibid. ix. 252. In spite of the popularity of Spanish leather, the hides tanned in England and Turkey were considered the best that were im-ported into Venice, 1545, *C.S.P.V.* v, entry 358.

[3] These skins were a usual part of the cargo of English ships returning from Spain: (? 1595), *C.S.P.D.* cclv. 56.

[4] *Loyal Subject*, IV. vi. 39; *Faithful Shepherdess*, I. i. 21; *The Magnetic Lady*, III. iii. 106.

[5] *The History of Sir Thomas Wyatt*, sig. E 2 verso.

upon neat's leather' came to mean as good a man as ever
walked. This expression, found as early as *Misogonus* (IV.
i. 158), c. 1550, occurs also in *Old Wives Tale*, *The
Tempest*, *Julius Caesar*,[1] and other plays.

The wearing of pantofles and galoshes over shoes and
boots—a French mode—and the 'huge, slovenly, unman-
nerly and immoderate tops' of boots especially fashionable
during the reign of Charles I, were the subject of much
criticism, a writer of 1629 estimating that one pair of such
boots used the leather of 'six pair of reasonable men's
shoes'.[2] Because of this 'prodigality of legs and feet', leather
cost more in England during this reign than ever before.[3]

Leather is mentioned in the drama not only for footwear, but for aprons,[4] jerkins,[5] gloves, &c. Because of its
softness, Spanish leather was the usual material for jerkins
of leather,[6] which were often slashed, laid with gold lace,
and trimmed with buttons.[7]

Buff, a leather made from ox hide—originally from the
hide of the wild ox or buffalo—was dressed with oil and
finished with a velvety surface. It was wear-resisting, so
that it was said to be 'everlasting' or of 'durance', as in
Comedy of Errors, *1 Henry IV*, and *Westward Hoe*.[8] Buff
leather was probably ancient, but it seems never before to
have been as much in use as it was in the sixteenth and
seventeenth centuries. The gentlemen attendants of Lord
Cromwell, 1539, wore buff jerkins; and buff was the usual
material for military men and those in charge of law en-
forcement, as many allusions in the drama indicate: *Honest
Whore*, *Henry IV*, *Elder Brother*, *Malcontent*, *Ram Alley*,
Unnatural Combat,[9] &c.

---

[1] In order of mention: Peele, *Works*,
vol. i. 324; II. ii. 75; I. i. 28.

[2] 'Leather', *Social England Illustrated*, 326.

[3] Ibid. 327.

[4] *Jul. Caes.* I. i. 7.

[5] *All Fools*, II. i. 303; *Troilus*, III. iii.
268. A leather jerkin lined in the collar with satin was made for the Master
of Hunstanton, 1520, *Archaeologia*,
xxv. 461.

[6] *Dutch Courtezan*, I. i. 3.

[7] 1546, 'jerkin de corrio hispani
sciss et ligat cum laquos passaymayn
de auro', E. 351/3025; 1553, 'a jerkin
of white spanishe lether garnished with
p'cment lace of gold with lj dozen bot-
tons of gold', E. 154/2/39.

[8] In order of mention: IV. iii. 26;
I. ii. 49; II. ii.

[9] *1 Honest Whore*, I. ii. 52: 'The
warrior marches in buff'; *1 Henry IV*,

The most popular leather for gloves was cheverel, made
from the skin of the kid of wild goat, which was so pliable
that it could be stretched from 'an ynch to an ell broad',[1]
a quality which afforded dramatists many opportunities
for comparisons of cheverel with wit and conscience.[2]

FASHIONS IN FOOTWEAR

Four kinds of footwear worn during Elizabethan and
Jacobean times are suggested by a conversation in *The
Devil's Law Case*:

Win. 'He wore no shoes.'
Cris. 'No! What then, pumps?'
Win. 'Neither.'
Cris. 'Boots were unfit for his journey.'
Win. 'He wore tennis-court woollen slippers for fear of the creak-
ing, Sir.'[3]

The lowest cut footwear covering only a part of the
foot was known by the generic term of slipper. Overshoes
such as pantofles, chopines, pattens, and chamber slippers
were of this type; those covering all of the foot, but having
only a single sole[4] were called pumps; those covering the
foot to the ankle or a little above, such as 'corks', brogues,
startups, were shoes; and those extending to the calf or
to the knee were designated boots.

As regards fashion in cut or shape of footwear, the
general tendency of the period was from low pumps to
high boots; from width to narrowness in toes, passing
from squareness through various degrees of roundness to
points,[5] and returning to squareness by 1625; from flat-
ness to height in soles, developing in the last years of the

---

1. ii. 52; *Elder Brother*, v. i. 15; *Malcontent*, v. ii. 82; *Ram Alley*, Dodsley,
x. 330; *Unnatural Combat*, III. i. 31;
Silent Woman, III. i. 53, mentions buff
doublets.
   [1] *Rom. & Jul.* II. iv. 90. The first
noted occurrence of cheverel is in
Coventry Mysteries (1841), 241, *O.E.D.*
   [2] *Hen. VIII*, II. iii. 32; *Tw. N.* III.
i. 13.

[3] IV. ii. 401–5. Compare the footwear made by the Court shoemaker
for Prince Charles in 1618: white,
grey, and waxed boots; polonian and
tennis shoes; pumps, pantofles, and
chamber slippers, E. 101/434/9.
   [4] A single-soled shoe indicated one
without an inner sole.
   [5] Sharp toes are mentioned in *King
and No King*, v. i. 325.

sixteenth century into double or high corked soles for
both men and women; from lack of attached heel to high
'Polonian' heels.[1] Throughout the sixteenth century,
vamps of the slipper type were made in one piece seamed
at the back, or in two pieces—back and front—seamed at
the arch. The sole was separate. Silk materials, of which
velvet was the favourite, and leather—sometimes perfumed—were used.[2]

Between 1533 and 1540, footwear was cut low at the
back and instep. Square toes began to go out of fashion
by 1540, broad toes by 1570.[3] About 1550 the front of
the low footwear began to be cut longer, reaching towards
the ankle; by 1580 it had reached the ankle, and by the
end of the century the 'corks' were made with an extended
front, forming a 'tongue' over which the back vamp
fastened at the ankle by latchets or tie; or, in the case of
pumps, by an extended front ending in a curve or peak
slightly above the ankle. By this date, soles had thickened,
cork being the most popular material. The following account from the cost of footwear for 'Mrs. Dorothy Bacon',
between February and April, 1594, shows a preference
for cork soles: 'one payer of pantables rased'; 'one payre
tawney spanish leather shooes corked'; 'one payer straw
colour spanishe leather shoes corked'; 'one payer high
corked shoes'; 'one payer velvett shoes'.[4] Slashing of the
fronts of footwear was practised to about 1560, when
pinking, i.e. puncturing, or cutting merely the surface of
the leather, largely superseded it.[5]

[1] Cotgrave, 'Souliers cambrez, shooes
which have hollow, raised or Polonian
heeles'. 1611, Rowlands, 'More Knaves
Yet?' Works, II. 5: 'Bootes and stockins to our legs doth finde Garters,
polonia heels and rose shooe strings.'
Fitzgeffrey, Notes from Blackfryers,
1617, F. 1: 'mounted Pelonianly until
he reels.'
[2] 1535, Philobiblon Soc. Misc. VII.
ii. 12, materials for footwear made for
Anne Boleyn, 1545, E. 101/423/14,
shoemaker's bill; 1551, Ellis, Letters,
II. ii. 215; 1558, Lancashire and

Cheshire Wills, xxxii. 177; also sections
in this study: pump, pantoffle, &c.;
City Madam, I. i. 113:
'Where are my shoes?'
'Those your ladyship gave order,
should be made of Spanish perfum'd
skins?'
[3] 'His shoes of the old cut, broad at
the toes and crosse-buckled with
brasse.' 1596, Lodge, Wits Miserie . . .
Incarnate Devils, IV. 27.
[4] Bacon MSS., Univ. Chicago.
[5] 1560, A.O. 1/1106: 'calcear, pro
fĉur xxlj par. de calceis de velvett

XVII. King Charles I. 1629. Red satin suit embroidered in gold and silver; white gloves, gauntlets embroidered in gold and silver; buff-coloured boots; French 'fall'. Paned doublet, white lining; ornamental points at waistline and knee. Scarf

Metropolitan Museum of Art, New York

Boots, which had been worn always by travellers and horsemen, became fashionable wear in the last few years of the sixteenth century—a fashion which grew in popularity until the years 1620–35, when all gallants were booted and spurred as if ready to ride.[1]

A variety of fastening was practised in footwear. Cloth and silk 'gave' a little, and could be pulled on the foot. Buckles, ties, and laces were used on leather shoes. Most of the boots were made to fit the leg and had to be pulled on or off by force; hence the comic scenes employed in drama, of getting off the master's boots. Ties, which were at first small bows, grew in width and length, and in intricacy of knotting.[2] A yard to a yard and a quarter of ribbon was allowed for each shoe-tie.[3] These ties became the symbols of courtship, their colours varying according to the progress of the lover's suit for his mistress's affections. The lady bestowed her own ties as favours, the fortunate recipients of which wore them in conspicuous places about their persons.[4]

These ties gradually developed into roses; or rather, the dress-shoes were fastened by small ties, and the fastening concealed by rosettes. The date of the introduction of these rosettes into England has been much disputed, though it is generally agreed that the fashion came from France. The date of the first French usage is equally uncertain. Merimée, whose historical accuracy in detail is well known, mentions 'souliers avec des rosettes couleur de feu' in a description of a costume representative of the year 1572,[5] but the writer has found no sixteenth-century

stitchd pinkd sciss et ravelled corked cum velvett ranes stitchd cum serico lin cum satten et skarlet.'

[1] *Cupid's Whirligig*, line 36: 'But he is a Gentleman I can assure you, Sir, for he walks always in boots.'

[2] *Northward Hoe*, I.i. 228: 'Drawer, tye my shoe; tye the new knot as thou seest this.' Also *Lingua*, sig. G 2.

[3] 1599, *Every Man Out of His Humour* ('after the second sounding'), 'A yard of shooetye.' Account of William Freke at Oxford, *Eng. Hist.*

Rev. VII. 92: '2 yards Ribband to make shooestrings'.

[4] 'A bashful suitor that is ravish'd with
A feather of your fan, or if he gain
A riband from your shoe, cries out, *Nil Ultra.*'
    Parliament of Love, II. iii. 89.
' . . . Shooe-string . . . that he putteth through his eare.' Rowlands, *Dr. Merrie-man*, ii. 22.

[5] *Chronique du règne de Charles IX*, pp. 23, 229. His description of M. de

allusions to shoe-roses in France. In England a few portraits—such as the anonymous one of Sir Jerome Bowes
circa 1583—show small rosettes on shoes, but since even
dated portraits are not conclusive evidence a student should
be careful in accepting Planché's statement that 'shoes
and roses are seen in the earliest paintings or prints' of the
Elizabethan period.[1] Ribbon ties are abundant; but they
do not resemble the rosettes known as roses which are represented in seventeenth-century portraits. Such roses were
formed of ribbon or lengths of lace gathered into circles
of graduated sizes, so that, placed in order, they resembled a
rose. Metal lace was fashionable, and frequently spangles
and oes were added to shoe-roses to increase the glitter.

Roses of cypress were in Royal favour as trimming for
gowns and doublets, as indicated by Elizabeth's wardrobe
accounts of 1578–90,[2] but no mention of their use on
shoes is made. As the accounts are detailed, one may be
justified in assuming that roses on footwear did not become
the mode until the nineties. One reference suggestive of
roses on garters or shoes occurs in the mock articles 'to
be observed by the Knights of the noble Order of the
Crescent', *Gesta Grayorum*, 1594. The seventeenth article
states: 'You shall weare bootes and spurs, more to shew
your knighthood, than to save silk stockings, garters and
roses.'[3] A definite reference to roses on shoes is made in
Hamlet, 1602.[4] The fashion soon became popular and
was satirized in drama[5] and poetry. In 1606 the author
of *Friar Bacon's Prophecy* praises the former times,

Turgis, who wears roses of flame-
colour ribbon on the guard of his
sword, his doublet, and his shoes, suggests Faeneste's reply to Enay (D'Aubigné, *Baron de Faeneste*, 1617, ch. ii),
when the latter asks, 'Vous avez des
roses en Hyver?' Faeneste responds,
'. . . sur les dux pieds, trainantes à
terre, aux dux jarrets, pendents à mi-
jamves, au vusc du perpunt, une au
pendant de l'espeio, une sur l'estomach,
au droit des vrasarts et aux coudes.'

[1] *History of British Costume* (London, 1913), 287.

[2] Egerton MS. 2806, fol. 137.

[3] *Prog. Elizabeth*, iii. 322.

[4] III. ii. 291: 'Two Provincial roses
on my razed shoes.' John Tradescant,
who in 1556 made a catalogue of the
varieties of roses in his garden, lists
white Province Rose: red Province
Rose. Cotgrave, 1611, mentions both
Provence and Provins roses.

[5] *Cynthia's Revels*, I. iv. 118 (quarto); *Devil is an Ass*, I. i. 130; 1614,
Hutton Accts. 210: garters and roses,
£1 10s.

> When roses in the garden grew,
> And not in ribbons on a shoe.
> Now ribbon roses take such place,
> That garden roses want their grace.[1]

As is the tendency of all fashions to go to extremes, shoe-roses grew 'great',[2] 'overblown' enough to hide 'gouty ankles'[3] and 'splay feet',[4] and correspondingly expensive. Howes's continuation of Stowe's *Annales* noted that men of rank were wearing shoe-roses costing five pounds apiece, and Peacham stated in his *Truth of Our Times*, published 1638, that such roses cost from thirty shillings to thirty pounds[5]—a price equal to that named in Luke's lecture to his sister on such extravagances in footwear as 'roses worth a family'.[6] For Court women the shoe-roses went out of fashion with the farthingale; for the courtiers by 1635. After that date, the extravagant ribbon-tie, which was even larger than the shoe-rose, replaced the latter. Since the reign of Charles was the reign of boots the interest in shoe-roses was superseded by an interest in decorative boot-tops.

[1] Hazlitt, *Early Popular Poetry*, iv. 283.

[2] *Silent Woman*, II. i. 122.

[3] *White Devil*, v. iii. 104.

[4] *Roaring Girl*, iv. ii. 9.

[5] *Annales*, 1039. *Truth of our Times*, 61–2.

[6] *City Madam*, iv. iv. 115. Cf. *If This Be Not a Good Play*, vol. iii. 357: 'Some who eate subjects up, and ware Whole Families in their shoo-strings.' Since the dresses of women were very long, their footwear seldom is represented in portraits. Very clear illustrations are shown in the Geerarts portrait of Queen Anne of Denmark, 1610; and in the no less familiar portrait of Mary Darcy, Countess Rivers, 1617.

FOOTWEAR IN THE DRAMA

BOOTS

BOOTS, a term of uncertain origin, represent an ancient[1] kind of footwear which covered the foot and leg, reaching above the calf.[2] Allusions to boots are so numerous in the drama that only a few characteristic ones need be considered.

Until the last twenty years of the sixteenth century boots were fashionable only for riding, but by 1585 gallants were wearing them to the exclusion of almost all other footwear; and from 1625 until the Puritan age boots were the mode for every one. The King, his courtiers, the clergy, university students, attorneys, lawyers, clerks, merchants, mechanics, servingmen, went every day booted. Boots were made of soft leather, usually Spanish, which would ruche; and their wide tops—called 'ruffles'—turned down, displaying the embroidered or lace tops of the boot-hose, or the silk stockings of the wearer as Fastidious Brisk describes.[3] The ruched or 'quail-pipe'[4] boots were affected by gallants with 'small-timbered' legs who wished them to appear masculine size.

Boots cost one to two shillings a pair during the second half of the fifteenth century; but were higher in the sixteenth, costing from two shillings and eight pence in the thirties, and six to fifteen shillings by the nineties.[5]

BROGUE

Brogues, the Irish name for shoes, were ankle-high footwear of untanned hide, without lining.[6] The early

---

[1] Worn by Anglo-Saxons but were not common. First noted occurence of the word in English was 1323. *O.E.D.*

[2] *Albumazar*, II. iii. 35: 'Such a speech turns my high shoes strait boots.'

[3] *Every Man Out of His Humour*, IV. vi. 111–12: 'One of the rowels catch'd hold of the ruffle of my boot, and being Spanish leather, and subject to tear, overthrows me, rends me two

pair of silk stockings. . . .'

[4] *Blurt, Master Constable*, II. i. 17. Cf. *Romance of the Rose*, 7261–2: 'And high shoos knopped with dagges, That frouncen like a quaile-pipe.'

[5] Rogers, *Agriculture and Prices*, iii. 522, 563, 564, 568; vi. 574, 575, 581. *Durham Wills*, xxxviii. 328.

[6] 1586 is the earliest noted use of the term: *O.E.D.* 1610, *Camden's*

brogues were of undressed leather with the hair inside, made in one piece and fastened to the foot by thongs. The sixteenth-century brogues seem to have had soles which were sewed to the uppers by thongs and the shoe then turned inside out. Brogues usually prevented the wearer from walking quietly.[1] They were worn by soldiers and by poor persons who could afford no better.[2]

BUSKIN

In the Tradescant Collection of the Ashmolean Museum, Oxford, is a pair of buttoned leather boots with thick soles and heels known as 'Queen Elizabeth's buskins', which answer in height, at least, Vernon's description of *cothurnus* as a fashion of 'buskin which commeth over the calfe of the legge'. Buskins were made of leather,[3] velvet,[4] cloth of gold,[5] and were furred,[6] trimmed with lace, or clinquant, and fastened by buttons, laces, or buckles.[7]

The buskin was probably a survival of the high, thick-soled boot worn by Greek tragedians, to which there are numerous references in the drama.[8]

CORKED SHOES

In 1462 the importation of 'botes shoen or corkes' was forbidden.[9] 'Corkes' was then a name for overshoes with cork soles; but during the next century were of two kinds: 1, a low dress-shoe with a thick cork sole; 2, overshoes such as the chopines and pantofles. Since many writers,

---

Britain (Holland), i. 123: 'They buckle upon their feet a pair of Broges made of raw and untanned leather up to their ankles.'

[1] *Cymb.* IV. ii. 214.

[2] The furnishing of soldiers in Derbyshire, 1600, included two pair of brogues to each man, *Rutland MSS.* i. 375.

[3] *Archaeologia*, ix. 252: 'sixe paire Spanishe lether buskynnes.' The earliest reference to buskins noted in English is in 1503, when they were bought for the queen's use, *P. P. Ex. Elizabeth York*, 85, 86. They were worn by women as well as by men.

[4] 1547, L.C. 2/3; 1572, Egerton MS. 2806; Hall, 1533, *Chronicle*, 635.

[5] Ibid. 609, 619, used by maskers.

[6] 1543-4, *P. P. Ex. Prin. Mary*, 151; 1559-60, L.C. 9/53.

[7] *Magnificence*, i. 754; Florio, 1611, '*Manubrette*, buckles for buskins'.

[8] As examples, *The Roman Actor*, I. i. 8; *Returne from Pernassus*, I. ii: 'Marlowe was happy in his buskine muse.'

[9] *Rot. Pal.* v. 507.

unlike Puttenham,[1] called them all corked shoes, without distinguishing between dress-shoes and overshoes, the reader is forced to judge, by the description, which is intended. Allusions to the squeaking of corked shoes in *Antonio and Mellida*, and *Westward Hoe*,[2] are evidently made to the 'corks' which were fashionable from the sixties; but allusions to ungraceful or mincing steps in cork shoes are to the pantofles or chopines.[3]

Although no chopines are mentioned in the Royal wardrobe accounts there are many corked shoes 'de velvet stitched pinked sciss corked, cum velvet vanes, lin cum satten'.[4]

CHOPINES

Dost not wear high cork shoes—Chopines?

(*Dutch Courtezan*, III. i. 112.)

Jonson spelled chopines as if the word were an Italian derivative, *cioppini*,[5] but there is no proof that such a name for shoes ever existed in that language. Wright pointed out in his edition of 'Hamlet' that the word was probably the Spanish *chapin*, and Dr. Skeat[6] explained the English spelling with 'o' as a confusion with the common French *chopine*, a pint-measure. Skinner, 1671,[7] suggested a connexion with *chapa*. Blount,[8] 1681, used the spelling *chapin*. Massinger[9] has employed the Spanish plural *chapines*. Seventeenth-century lexicographers define *chapin* as 'patin soulier de femme fort haut, butini, scarpe da donna sine alla polpa della gamba alte';[10] and *chapines de atauxia* as

---

[1] 1589, *English Poesie*, I. xv. 49: 'Those high corked shoes or pantofles which now they call in Spain and Italy shoppini.'

[2] *Antonio & Mellida*, V. i. 110; *Westward Hoe*, II. ii.

[3] Gosson, *Quippes*, stanza 21; *Wily Beguiled*, Dodsley, ix. 303: '. . . to foot it in a pair of new corked shoes' may refer to any of the three.

[4] 1561-4, A.O. 3/1106; April, 1595, for Dorothy Bacon: '2 payre high cork shoes, 1 payre pantables, 1 payre tawney Spanish leather corked

shoes; 1 payre straw colour Spanish leather corks, 1 payre whitè leather shoes.' Bacon MSS., Univ. Chicago.

[5] *Cynthia's Revels*, II. ii. 60.

[6] *Transactions Philological Soc.* 1885, 79.

[7] *Etymologicon Linguae Anglicanae*.

[8] *Glossographia*.

[9] *Renegado*, I. ii. 51; *Love's Sacrifice*, II. iii. 111.

[10] Oudin, *Tesoro de las tres lenguas española françesa y italiana*. Compare also Cotgrave: 'Chappins, high slippers for low women.'

'sorte de patins fillolez, & peins delicatement d'or, d'argent & autres couleurs'.[1] Since these definitions seem to describe the footwear known in England as chopine, the word is probably a corruption of the Spanish original.

How early chopines were known in Spain and Italy, or from which country they were introduced into England seems impossible to ascertain. A description of the footwear of English women in 1554, written by one of King Philip's retinue, notes that 'acá en esta tierra las mugeres gastan pocos chapines y mantos como allá en esa tierra',[2] but nothing in the description indicates whether the *chapines* were the chopines of later times or only pattens.

Puttenham[3] and Jonson[4] refer to them as being worn in Spain and Italy. Bertelli,[5] 1563, shows Spanish women wearing them, but they were worn in Italy at least in 1494. Canon Casola[6] in that year wrote that the women of Venice were wearing 'shoes called *pianelle* so high that only slaves supporting them keep them from falling'. In 1611 Coryat stated that all Venetian women were wearing 'chapineys', some half a yard high, and that the women of wealth were 'supported eyther by men or women when they walke abroad, to the end they may not fall'.[7] 'The Italian in her high chopeene'[8] is referred to in Heywood's song of England's adoption of fashions from all countries, but 'her fine high shoes like the Spanish lady', mentioned in *Bartholomew Fair*, suggests Spanish origin. They seem,

---

[1] Oudin, *Le thresor des trois langues espagnole, françoise et italienne.*

[2] *Viaje de Felipe*, 119.

[3] *Art of Poesie*, 1589, i. 15, 19. O.E.D. records the first instance of the use of the word in English as 1577. Weidtz who travelled in north-west Europe in 1529 gives a drawing of an Irish woman wearing low chopines.

[4] *Devil is an Ass*, iv. i. 69.

[5] F. Bertelli, *Omnium fere gentium nostrae aetatis habitus nunquam antehac editi.* Bertelli copied this figure from the anonymous *Recueil de la diversite des habits qui sont de présent en usiage tant es pays d'Europe, Asie, Affrique et*

illes sauuages, Paris, 1562.

[6] Canon Pietro Casola, *Pilgrimage to Jerusalem* (1907), 144.

[7] *Crudities*, i. 400. Fynes Moryson also mentioned the height and consequent tendency to cause the fall of the wearer, *Itinerary*, iv. 172.

[8] *Challenge for Beauty*, vol. v. 66. Tradescant recorded among the varieties of his Museum: 'choppenes 20 sorts', and 'Choppenes for Ladyes from Venice.' Only three pairs are in the present Tradescant Collection in the Ashmolean Museum. Through the courtesy of the Keeper, the author was allowed to examine these.

however, to have been associated in Elizabethan minds with Italy rather than with Spain, and were probably an Italian importation into England.

Coryat described the chopine as 'a thing made of wood and covered with leather of sundry colours. . . . Many of them are curiously painted; some also I have seen fairly gilt.'[1] All extant specimens which the author has examined, however, are constructed of a base of leather fitted to a column of cork four to eighteen inches high, on the top of which is a sole of leather. The cork is placed in layers, part of the centre of each layer being cut out, probably to lessen the weight. The column of cork is covered by fine leather, or silk, and decorated by paint or embroidery. Jonson refers to them as being of goldsmith's work set with diamonds. The chopine was held to the foot by a piece of pinked or decorated leather over the toe, or two pieces of leather or silk fastened by ties over the ankle, as illustrated in Plate XVIII.

Chopines were evidently worn on the stage, for Hamlet speaks of them as the footwear of one of the players (II. ii. 455), and Donusa, in the *Renegado*, orders her chopines to be taken off (I. ii. 51). Were they only stage property? Wilson's *Ram Alley*,[2] 1611, seems to satirize a fashion which is not merely a stage convention:

> To see a bride trip it to church so lightly,
> As if her new chopines would scorn to bruise
> A silly flower.

And Bulwer, 1658, definitely vouches for their usage in England: 'What a prodigious affectation is that of chopines where our ladies imitated the Venetian and Persian ladies.'[3]

PANTOFLES

The term, pantofle, spelled in a variety of ways during the Elizabethan period,[4] is derived, according to Min-

---

[1] *Crudities*, i. 400.
[2] Dodsley, x. 367.
[3] *Artificial Changeling*, p. 550.
[4] 'Pantophle', Greene, Grosart ed. *Works*, vol. x. 119, xi. 238; 'pantoffles',

Stubbes, *Anatomy of Abuses*; 'pantocles', *Richmond Wills*, 1573, 241; 'pantyples', *Durham Wills*, xxxviii. 264; 'pantable', *Cobler's Prophecy*, sig. B 2 verso.

a

b

XVIII. *a.* Lady's pantofle, embroidered in coloured silks. *Circa* 1610
Metropolitan Museum of Art, New York

b. Lady's chopines, Venetian, early 17th century. Kid 'pinked'.
Fine leather. The tallest is 15 inches high

Photograph by Archives Photographiques, Paris

sheu, from the Greek πᾶν φελλός, all cork.[1] This kind
of shoe is very ancient,[2] and was probably of Oriental origin. There is no means of determining the date of its
introduction into England; it is mentioned in 1494, and
Weidtz, who travelled in Europe 1529, shows an Englishman wearing a pair.

The pantofle, as suggested by *Endymion*[3] and *Friar
Bacon*,[4] was constructed of a cork sole thickening towards
the heel, with a piece of leather, velvet, &c., over the front
of the foot up to the instep. The shoe had no upper at
the heel, but was like the modern 'mule'. The inside sole
and toe-piece were, of course, richly lined. During the
second half of the sixteenth century, when pantofles were
in universal favour at Court and among gallants, rich
materials were used in their making: satin, scarlet, Spanish
leather, velvet, cloth of silver, taffeta, &c., and they were
pinked and trimmed with metal lace and spangles and
worked with silk.[5] (Plate XVIII.)

Since the pantofles had no uppers at the heel they were
hard to walk in and, in the words of Stubbes, 'the wearer
had to knock and spurn at every wall stone or poste, to

---

[1] *Guide Into Tongues.*

[2] Quicherat, *Histoire du costume en
France*, 79, tells of a pair of leather
with thick sole found on the skeleton
of an aristocratic woman of the fourth
century. 'Elles sont en cuir, pointues
et relevées du bout, sans quartier, et
montées sur une épaise semelle de
liége.'

[3] 'Because your pantables be higher
    with corke,
  therefore your feete must needs
    be higher in the instep.'
          (II. ii. 33).

[4] 'If it please your lordship, I will
gather up all your old pantophiles and
with the corke make you a Pinnis of
five hundred tunne.' *Works*, iii. 47.
See also Alunno, Francesco, *La Fabri-
co del mondo*, 210: 'Pianelle pantofole
sono spetie di calzari col souero.' i.e.
sughero—cork.

[5] 1552, *Archaeologia*, xviii. 320, 'a
pair of pantacles of brydges sattin for
the lord of misrule'; 1576, A.O.
3/1109: 'pro fcur xv par. crepid et
pantobles de velvet stitched cum serico
sciss. et ravelled, lin. cum sattin et soles
scarlet'; 1578, Egerton MS. 2806:
'Spanish lether Showes and Pantables:
one peire embr̄., another peire layed
with silver lase, three peire lyned
with taphata and the other stitched
with silke of sundrye coloures.' 1580,
Stubbes, *Anatomy of Abuses*, 57: 'some
be of white leather, some of black, and
some of red; some of blacke velvet,
some of red, some of greene, razed,
carved, stitched all over with silke,
and layd on with gold, silver, and
such like.' 1588, L.C. 9/79, 'pro fcur
11 par pantobles de panno argento
liniat cum sattin alb.' 1617, E. 101/
434, delivered to the shoemaker to
garnish pantofles: gold and silver lace,
spangles.

keepe them on his feete'. And 'with their flipping and
flopping up and down in the dirt, they exaggerate a
mountayne of mire, and gather a heape of clay and bag-
gage together, loding the wearer with the importable
burthen'. Pantofles were made shorter than the shoes
over which they were worn, and since their soles were
sometimes two inches thick, the heel of the wearer's foot
hung over the sole, suspended several inches above the
ground. This shortness probably explains Fleire's statement which has puzzled commentators: 'I am one of their
leaders, for their shooes are so hie, and their heeles so
short.'[1]

The wearing of cork shoes possibly originated with
courtesans, so that the expressions 'short heeled', as in
Widow's Tears and *May Day*, or 'much cork under their
heels', 'corke heeld sex', as in *Rape of Lucrece*,[2] indicated
wantonness. Porter, cognizant of the difficulty of walking
on high cork soles and of the association of such footwear
with wanton characters, played upon the word awry, when
he wrote: 'For maides that wear corke shooes may step
awrie.'[3] Two other expressions arose from the use of
pantofles: 'to swear to, or on, a pantofle'; and 'to stand
upon one's pantofles'. The former indicated servitude; the
latter pride. 'To swear by' or 'on a pantofle' probably
came from the custom of a page's carrying the master's
pantofles: 'As your page, I can. . . . Carry your pantofles.'[4]
Phao's statement: 'There I did weare pantophles on my
leggs, here doe I beare them in my hands,'[5] indicated
that he had become a servant. Similarly, the page's reference to being 'sworn to the pantofle', *Unnatural Combat*,[6]
means only that he has been raised to the position of personal servant to Theocrine, or may indicate that the page

---

[1] *The Fleire*, II. i. 76. It explains
Judith's advice: 'Use him as thou
doest thy pantable, scorn to let him
kiss thy heel', *Westward Hoe*, II. i.
487.

[2] *Widow's Tears*, III. i. 152; *May
Day*, IV. iv. 6; *Rape of Lucrece*, vol. v.
211.

[3] *Two Angry Women of Abington*,
line 676.

[4] *The Spanish Curate*, IV. i. 45.

[5] *Sappho & Phao*, I. ii.

[6] III. ii. 107–9. Dr. McKerrow has
discussed this question in his edition of
Nashe's *Works*, IV. 256. See also *New
Way to Pay Old Debts*, I. i. 101.

actually went through an initiation ceremony, part of which was the taking of an oath upon a pantofle.

Since the pantofle had a very high sole of cork, the wearer was elevated, and therefore proud; hence the expression 'to stand upon pantofles' indicated pride. Examples of this expression are common in sixteenth-century literature: ' . . . and walked on his stately pantacles: setting all at naught that I could say to him';[1] 'stand upon thy pantofles like a new-elected scavenger';[2] or from *The Taming of a Shrew*:

> Sander speake a good word for me, and thene I am so
> Stout and takes it upon me, and stands upon my pantofles
> To them out of all crie.'[3]

The traditional dishabille or lack of pride in dress of the rejected lover is suggested in a slightly new way in Breton's 'In Praise of Virtuous Ladies', in which the spurned lover not only tears open buttons, and throws off his hat, but flings away his pantofles.[4]

PUMP

A pump was a single-soled, low shoe, which fitted the foot closely without ties;[5] but in the latter part of the sixteenth century, latchets appear on low shoes which resembled pumps. These latchets, which were tied together in front, must account for Bottom's injunction to his troupe: 'Get . . . new ribbons for your pumps,'[6] for shoe-roses, seemingly, were not worn until the seventeenth century.[7] Romeo's 'Then is my pump well flowered', which is usually explained as an allusion to shoe-roses, merely means that his pump is 'pinked'.[8]

Pumps were used by ladies and gentlemen as well as

[1] Harvey, *Letter Book*, 14.
[2] *Northward Hoe*, III. i.
[3] II. v. Also 'He standeth upon his pantables and regardeth greatly his reputation', Saker, *2 Narbonus*, 99. 'Thus far I stand on my pantuffles', *Carde of Fancy*, Grosart ed., iv. 104.
[4] *Works*, ii. 63.
[5] 1555, Watreman, *Fardle of Facions*, II. iii. 124: 'Their shoes are not

fastened on with lachettes, but lyke a pompe close about the foot.'
[6] *Mid. N. D.* IV. ii. 38.
[7] See chapter on roses and shoes. Pumps with roses were ordered for the pages at the marriage of Princess Elizabeth, 1612, *Archaeologia*, xxvi. 392.
[8] *Rom. & Jul.* II. iv. 66.

by servants. 'To-day in pumps and cheverill gloues' is a description of part of a lady's costume in 1594.[1] Jonson refers to ladies' use of pumps in *Cynthia's Revels* and *Every Man Out of His Humour*.[2] Cost of mending or buying pumps for ladies is noted in Lord Howard's *Household Book*.[3] They are part of the knight's attire in Beaumont's *Masque of the Inner Temple*, 1612; and part of the skipper's costume in Campion's masque at the Earl of Summerfield's marriage, 1613.[4]

Pumps were the footwear of servants. Gabriel's pumps were 'unpinked in the heel'; Sir Bounteous addresses a footman as 'Pumps'; and to Simon's question, 'What's he approaching here in dirty pumps?' Aminadab answers, 'A footman, sir.'[5]

Pumps were made of velvet, satin, tuft-taffeta, or other silks or cloth; also of light leather,[6] and, since they did not add to the height of the wearer, they were associated with comedy, as pantofles were associated with tragedy. They were therefore used in the masques of Beaumont, and Campion, mentioned above, but their presence in Bottom's 'Pyramus and Thisbe' is unexplainable, unless they were used as part of the parody, or, as the usual footwear of Bottom's fellows, were not changed.

The Wearing of Pumps and Pantofles

As has been said, pumps were single-soled shoes, and when they were made of fine materials for ladies or courtiers they were naturally unfit to wear on the street. The thick-soled pantofle was therefore slipped over the pump when the wearer went out; but so rich did the pantofles soon become, that the fashion of wearing both pumps and pantofles indoors and out superseded all other modes of footwear. Dekker notes this fashion in *1 Honest Whore*,

[1] *Cobler's Prophecy*, sig. D 3.

[2] In order of mention: III. iv. 67; IV. ii. 34.

[3] 122; for children, 67, 123.

[4] Beaumont's masque, *Prog. James*, ii. 599; Campion's, ibid. 713.

[5] In order of mention: *Tam. Sh.* IV. i. 136; *A Mad World, My Masters*, III. i. 25; *Mayor of Quinborough*, v. i. 17. Pumps purchased for servants of the Shuttleworths, *Accts.* 1612, cost from 12 to 22 pence a pair, xxxv. 200; 1574, *Mid. MSS.* 446.

[6] Great Wardrobe Accounts 1560–73, L.C. 9/53; L.C. 9/72; A.O. 3/1106; A.O. 3/1109, &c.

when Mateo speaking figuratively to Gaffer Shoomaker says: 'You pul'd on my wife's pumps, and then crept into her pantofles.' (i. xiii. 472.) Pumps and pantofles were worn especially by courtiers and those who wished to be taken for courtiers. When Round Robin and his fellows made ready to go to court, 'on their legs thay had fine yellow stockings; pumps and pantofles on their feet'.[1] Also, in *The Woman Hater*, Lazarillo will bid to his feast:

> All short-cloak'd knights, and all cross-gartered gentlemen
> All pump and pantofle footcloth riders.[2]

The custom of wearing the two kinds of footwear together, and the difficulty of keeping pantofles on the feet —mentioned by Stubbes—are satirized by Harington:

> Now Sextus twice hath supt at Sarazens head
> And both times homeward coming drunk to bed;
> He by the way his Pantofles hath lost;
> And grieved both by the mock, and by the cost,
> To save such charges, and to shun such frumps,
> He goeth now to the tavern in his pumps.[3]

GALOSH

Galoshes present a complicated problem, inasmuch as footwear of that name either changed its character through the ages, or the term was a generic one for any kind of overshoe. Sixteenth- and seventeenth-century dictionaries do not agree, defining the galosh as: 'a sole', 'a sole with latchets to tie it on', 'a wooden shoe of one piece without fastening', 'a shoe worn over other footwear', 'a sock of cloth'.[4]

[1] *Gentle Graft*, 167.
[2] *Woman Hater*, I. ii. 22–3.
[3] *Epigrams*, ii. 52. See also D'Aubigné, *Aventures du baron de Faeneste* (ed. 1617), ch. ii.
[4] 1440, 'Galegge or galoch, under soling of mannis ffette,' *Promptorum Parvulorum*. 1539, 'Galloches, L. Gallicae', Estienne, *Dictionaire François-latin*. 1570, 'Galga, solea, sandalium', Levins, *Manipulus Vocabulorum*. 1572, 'Shoe called Galloge or Patten which hath nothing on the feete but only Latchettes'. Bossewell, *Armorie*,

1599, 'Gallochas, a kind of sock of wool to wear in shoes. Shoes with wooden soles.' Percyval, *Bibliotheca Hispanica*. 1611, 'A wooden shoe or patten made all of a piece, without any latchet or tye of leather and worne by the poore clowne in winter'. Minsheu, *A Guide into Tongues*. Rider, Hierosme, Phillips, Blount, and other lexicographers—English and foreign—define the term, which seems to have existed in all the Romance languages, in about the same way as the above.

Antiquarians add little. According to Strutt,[1] the *gallica* from which the galosh is supposed to have been derived 'were a species of sandals fastened with fillets or thongs about the feet and ankles'. Racinet defines them as 'chaussures à semelle de bois que les Gaulois portaient en temps de pluie'.[2] Quicherat states they were specifically 'chaussure rustique à double ou simple semelle'.[3]

Historical records do not support these inferences. On October 16, 1400, the London Pouchmakers petitioned 'that the making of galoches of wood ... which was formerly by the Pouchmakers invented and established shall be under their governance and rule ... inasmuch as there is great default in this respect, as well as to false and not durable leather as to false workmanship. . . .'[4] Some leather entered into their construction or the Pouchmakers would not have been their inventors or supervisors. French inventories of the fourteenth and fifteenth centuries indicate that leather, cloth, and cork were used in the making of galoshes, and in the specifications for the French galosh of 1452, wood is not mentioned.[5]

The conflicting statements cannot be reconciled except by the conclusion that galosh was a generic term for an outer shoe of several kinds, of which the patten was one —a conclusion warranted by Cotgrave's definition of *porte-semelle* as 'the upper leather of a Patten which we now call a Galoche, though improperly; for the true Galoche (sayes Nicot) hath no leather belonging to it'. Buckles

---

[1] *Dress and Habits of the People of England*, London, 1842, I. xc.

[2] *Le Costume historique*, i. 203.

[3] *Histoire du costume en France*, 59.

[4] Riley, *Memorials London*, 1276–1419, 554–5. 1463, Edward IV forbade importation of galoches.

[5] 'Que toutes galoches tant sciées comme entières, tant à cuirs pleins, croisées comme annelez et les brides derrière soient: c'est assavoir ceux de cuir de noir, de cuir de vache et cloue, et les autres de tel cuir comme il appartiendra bons et souffisans, et que les galoches qui seront siées du long, d'un espan et au dessus, soient assemblées de cuir de vache, et clouez chacune charnière et assemblée de 8 clous et les autres mendres comme il appartiendra, les brides et croisées cousues bien et souffisamment, et clouez les treppointes d'icelles galoches de 4 clous de chascun costé, et les boucles qui y seront qu'elles soient de bon potin, du moins bien attachées at cousues et corroyez comme il appartient'. Gay, *Glossaire archéologique*, i. 756. *Galoche* was used in France by the Queen, 1392, ibid.

were associated with galoshes from Chaucer's time,[1] and were used as fasteners even in the seventeenth century, for in 1607, 'sixteen gold buckles with pendants and toungs to buckle a pair of golosses with gold' were purchased for Prince Henry.[2]

The galosh was worn by all classes of society, women as well as men. Though Gay's[3] investigations led him to think that the early French galosh was a dress-shoe, the English one was an overshoe used as a protection from mud or wet. 'I would his Portugall skinne were tann'd into Spanish Leather,' says the clown of King Sebastian, 'and either cut into some slovenly boote to be dabled in the durt without a galoach, or sniped into Saint Martin's jerkin.'[4]

PATTENS

Etymologists agree that the origin of the term *patten* is obscure, but suggest *patte*, paw, i.e. sole of the foot, as the most probable origin.[5] The word has been incorrectly used by writers on costume to designate patten, galosh, cork-shoe, pantofle, and chopine. Though all five added to the height of the wearer, the galosh and patten were chiefly foul-weather overshoes. The chopine and pantofle, which represented a later development of the overshoe, had soles of cork. Each of the five had a different method of attachment to the foot.

The patten, known in England as early as 1390, was first a man's overshoe. Its construction changed little through the ages. It was a simple sole, more or less thick, sometimes carved into heel and toe instead of being a single, heavy, solid piece. A light wood was necessary, and pattens of 'aspe' were therefore considered 'the most easy for the wearing of all estates, gentiles, and other

[1] 'Ne were worthy to unbokle his galoche', *Squire's Tale*, line 1386.

[2] *Archaeologia*, xi. 93.

[3] Sir Timothy Hutton's accounts for 1614 lists galoshes, 16. A pair for a woman is mentioned in the *Household Bk. Howard* (1625), 225.

[4] Thomas Heywood, *A Challenge for Beauty*, vol. v, 10. 'Let this suffice from a private country knight that lives among clouted shoes, in his frize jacket and galloshes.' *Nugae Antiquae*, i. 311.

[5] Meyer-Lübke, *Romanische Etymologisches Wörterbuch*.

people, of any timber that groweth'.[1] The thickness, length, and width of the sole varied according to the desires of the wearer. The patten was attached to the foot by one or two straps over the ankle.

Because of their wooden soles and because they did not fit closely and therefore moved as the wearer walked, pattens made a clacking noise, especially on flagstones. French ladies of the fifteenth century recognized their loved ones by the sound of their pattens. In Martial d'Auvergne's *Les arrêts d'amours*, a lover asks judgement against his rival to prevent him from attracting the lady's attention in any way, especially from clacking his patten when he entered the church porch.[2]

Since making noise with pattens was considered bad taste, a vulgarly talkative tongue was said to 'run on pattens'. Tibet Talkapace revenges herself on Mumble-crust's sarcastic, 'Your tong is not lame!' by the counter-accusation, 'Yet your tongue can renne on patins as well as mine',[3] and Diccon, speaking of the vulgar Dame Chat, declared: 'The tongue it went on patins by him that Judas solde.'[4]

Pattens, as has been indicated, were used to elevate the feet of the wearer above dirt or wet,[5] and were a permanent fixture on some boots made for out-of-door wear. They were used throughout the sixteenth century, though the wealthy persons preferred the more decorative pantofle.

STARTUPS

Startups were shoes of rough or raw leather, reaching above the ankle,[6] but the term was sometimes applied to the buskin or brodequin made of fine cloth or silk, espe-

[1] *Statutes at Large*, 4 Edward IV. c. 9. Because this wood was used also in making shafts, patten-makers were forbidden by statute (4 Henry V, c. 3) to use any aspen except that which was unfit for shafts. Hundreds of pairs of pattens were imported into England during the early fifteenth century, *Port Bk. Southampton*, 138, &c. Nobility sometimes wore leather pattens.

[2] 'Le V arrêt'.

[3] *Roister Doister*, I. iii. 24.

[4] *Gammer Gurton's Needle*, II. iv. 35.

[5] 'He was fayned to come on pattins because of the great wett.' Harvey, *Letter-Book*, 153.

[6] Vernon, 1575, '*Pero*, startups, a shoe of raw leather'; *Pride and Lowliness*, 33: 'A payre of startuppes had he on his feete.

That lased were up to the small of the legge.'

cially those used in Court Revels.[1] The leather startups were worn during the early seventeenth century by rustics, porters, as indicated by *The Family of Love* (IV. iii. 60), clowns, as in *The Picture* (v. i. 134), but the earliest noted reference to them occurs in the will of J. Mauleverer, gentleman,[2] 1517.

GAMASH

Gamash was probably derived from the French *gamache*, which is defined by Monet, 1635,[3] as 'triquouse, botine de drap, brodequin de drap à semèles de cuir ou sans semèles, servant à cheval et à pied'. Percyval, 1591,[4] described the Spanish *poloyma*—equivalent of *gamache*—as hose without feet, a description which agrees with Florio's '*scaffoni*, gamaches or upper stockings'. It may have changed its character, acquiring a sole, in the seventeenth century; in which case Holme's definition: 'Gamashes, buskins, or startups',[5] would confirm that of Monet. The Lord Chamberlain's accounts for 1601–3 list gamashes as 'caligae'.[6]

Literary references are not informative. One can easily infer that gamashes were leggings or loose hose extending to the knee, or above, but soles are not mentioned. Some gamashes made the leg look larger. Importuno informs Piers Penniless that 'no French gowtie leg, with a gamash upon it is so gotche and boystrous' as the word 'tropologicall'.[7] That they were loose is suggested by Middleton's description of Oliver Hubburd: 'he wisheth the decrease of his lands and the increase of his legs, that his calves may hang down like gamashoes.'[8]

The earliest French allusion to *gamache*, noted by Gay, is 1591, so that it probably did not become an English fashion until after that date. Gamashes were made of cloth

[1] Feuillerat, *Revels*, 1572, 159; 1573, A.O. 3/907, 'a pair of Russet taffeta startoppes'.

[2] *Test. Ebor.* lxxix. 83: 'j par sotularium quae dicuntur stertuppes.'

[3] Gay, op. cit., i. 757.

[4] *Bibliotheca Hispanica*.

[5] Bk. iii, ch. 1, p. 13: '. . . are either

Laced or Buckeled downe the outsides of the legs, and reach only to the instep of the foot.'

[6] L.C. 9/92: 'pro iij par. caligarum vocat gamasshos.'

[7] Nashe, 'Have With You', *Works*, iii. 41.

[8] *Works*, viii. 51.

or silk, according to the taste of the wearer. A pair noted in Lord Howard's accounts, 1622, were of frieze;[1] Laverdure's were of cloth of gold.[2]

They were sometimes fastened by buttons. The Gardener of Campion's entertainment for the Queen, 1613, wore 'buttoned gamachios',[3] and wardrobe accounts frequently mention buttons in connexion with them. As Monet notes, they were worn both 'à cheval et à pied'.

STOCKING

A stocking was a covering for the foot and leg to, or slightly above, the knee. 'Long stocking' or 'tall stocking' was used of the long hose extending from foot to thigh, which was worn with trunk hose.[4]

Stockings were called also 'netherstocks', as in *Henry IV*, and *Lear*,[5] in contrast to the breeches, trunks, or other hose which were 'upperstocks'. Thus, Henry VIII had 'hoosyan of skarlette upper-stocked with yalowe damaske', 'nether stocks de panno alb' with 'upperstocks de satin alb embraudered'.[6] Stowe's record that the stockings of Henry VIII were of cloth or cut out of ell-broad taffeta is borne out by his wardrobe accounts, but the further statement that silk stockings were practically unknown in England until Mistress Montague presented a pair to Queen Elizabeth in 1560 seems questionable. The first silk stockings made in England were presented to Edward VI;[7] and knit silk netherstocks and knit woollen netherstocks are listed among the effects of the Earl of Northumberland,[8] 1553. In 1566 payment was made to one of Queen Elizabeth's silkwomen for six pairs of 'blacke silkeknytt hoose'.[9]

[1] *Household Bk.* 187: 'Fryse to make my Lord a pair of gamasses.'
[2] *What You Will*, II. i. 16.
[3] *Prog. James*, II. 634.
[4] *Malcontent*, I. i. 116; *Devil's Law Case*, III. i. 180. The 'long stocking' was *démodé* by the end of the first decade of the seventeenth century, *Ram Alley*, Dodsley, x. 278.
[5] *1 Hen. IV.* II. iv. 132; *Lear*, II. iv. 10 (pun).
[6] 1537, *T. R. Misc. Bks. Exch.*, 455;

1548, E. 351/3026, 'netherstocks de kersey de divers colours'. 1557, *Richmond Wills*, 107, 'a pair of hoose and a pair of stokks of hoose'. The Latin of these records is a strange hybrid!
[7] *Anciens Vêtements*, iii. 162; *Annales* (Howes), 867.
[8] E. 154/2/39.
[9] Add. MS. 35328. An interesting letter concerning the purchase of foreign silk stockings for the Earl of Leicester, 1578, is reprinted in Wright,

The seekers for the North-west Strait, 1580, were advised to take 'for a show of English commodities' certain cloths and 'knit stocks of silke of orient colours, knit stockes of Jersee yerne of Orient colours, and stockes of kersey of divers colours',[1] for both men and women. The finest worsted stockings then came from Jersey, so that the name stood for worsted both in accounts and in the drama.[2] English stockings, silk or wool, must have been hand-knit, for a knitting machine was not invented until 1589 and not put into use for a decade.

Stubbes[3] describes stockings of Jersey, worsted, silk, 'thred', crewel, 'knitte with open seame downe the legge, with quirks and clocks about the anckles, and sometimes interlaced with golde and siluer threds', not an exaggerated description to a reader of the Queen's wardrobe accounts.[4] These embroidered stockings afforded dramatists many a satirical line and pun,[5] especially on the clocks. Silk stockings soon became the 'only weare' among gallants, for they showed off the comeliness of the wearer's leg much better than did the woollen ones, said characters in *The Hog Hath Lost his Pearl*, *Every Man In His Humour*, and *The Roaring Girl*,[6] but the prices of seven to forty shillings a pair forced some of the gallants to have their stockings of old-fashioned colours 'new dyed' in order to have the *dernier cri* in costume colours.[7]

Times of Elizabeth, 84. The writer promised to go to Granada and get better ones than those he was sending.

[1] *Hakluyt Soc.* vii. 123.

[2] 1580, E. 154/3/13: 'carnation Jearsie stockins,' *Scornful Lady*, I. i. 170. Knit stockings had the disadvantage of fallen or broken stitches, which, if not caught in time, unravelled the entire stocking; *Spanish Gipsy*, II. i. 161; *Bartholomew Fair*, Ind.

[3] *Anatomy of Abuses*, 46.

[4] Egerton MS. 2806 contains numerous items of silk stockings 'wrought at the toppes and clocks with venice golde and silver'; *Devil's Law Case*, I. i. 180: 'daintie embroydered stockings.'

[5] *Devil is an Ass*, I. i. 130; *Northward Hoe*, II. i.

[6] In order of mention: Dodsley, xi. 432; I. iii. 43; IV. ii. 8.

[7] 1577, Ellis, *Letters*, II. iii. 74, worsted stockings for the Earl of Essex 6s. 10d.; 1578, Lord North, *Archaeologia*, xix. 299, silk 40s., yarn 30s.; 1589, *Chetham Soc. Pub.* xli. 382; 1605, *Hutton Accts.* 204: '1 pair carnation silke stockings' £1 18s.; 1614, ibid.: 'dying of my silke stockinges 1 s.'; 1618, *Household Bk. Howard*, 73, worsted, 30s., silk 40s.; 1624, Sir John Francklyn, *Archaeologia*, xv. 160, silk, 28s. to 40s. A pair of silk stockings for Lady Darcy, in 1583, cost £5—the highest price noted, *Hist. Hengrave*,

BOOT-HOSE

'A paire of boote hoose of blacke clothe' was purchased for Henry VIII in 1536.[1] At that date boot-hose were unadorned, footless leggings worn under the boot to protect stockings and long hose from stain. The poor class of persons continued to wear woollen boot-hose such as Grumio assumed at Petruchio's wedding,[2] but the wealthy used fine linen, scarlet lined with velvet, and similar materials.[3]

Boot-hose soon became more ornamental than useful. They were 'wrought' in needlework, as in *Love's Cure*,[4] embroidered in silks, or in purls of gold thread, 'flourished with oes', slashed, fringed, and lace trimmed.[5] Stubbes' description of these hose is not exaggerated:

'They have also bootehose whiche . . . be of finest clothe that may be got, yea, fine enough to make any band, ruffe, or shirte . . . and they must be wrought all over from the gartering place upward, with needleworke, clogged with silke of all colours, with byrdes, foules, beastes, and antiques purtraied all ouer in sumptuous sorte . . . the very needelworke of some one payre of the boote hoose to stand some in foure pounde, sixe pounde, and some in ten pounde. Besides this, they are made so wide to draw ouer all, and so long to reach up to the waste.'[6]

When boots with wide tops became fashionable, the tops were carefully 'ruffled' below the knees, and the boot-hose arranged within these wide tops so that the embroidery or lace showed to best advantage. When the gallant rode on horse, the long tops were drawn up over the riding hose. The ordinary price of plain or slightly ornamented boot-

---

214. Edward Allen evidently used sober colours in winter. He gave orders that his 'orynge tawny stokings of wolen be dyed a very good black . . . to wear in the winter', Greg, *Henslowe Papers*, London, 1907.

[1] *P. P. Ex.* 251.

[2] *Tam. Sh.* III. ii. 69. 1564, *Durham Wills*, ii. 217.

[3] 1577, *Durham Wills*, ii. 422, linen; 1588, *Lancashire and Cheshire Wills*,

liv. 139; 1614, L.C. 9/97, linen; 1607, L.C. 9/94, three-fourth yd. scarlet, 1 yd. velvet required.

[4] I. ii. 106.

[5] 1564, L.C. 2/58: 'un par. Bootehose.vird.orn.cum serico rubeo.' 1605–6, L.C. 9/94, 'pro embrod. toppes unius pār botehose opat.cum. purles et owes argent'; *Gull's Horn Book*, 76, fringed boot-hose.

[6] *Anatomy of Abuses*, 61.

hose was two to twelve shillings,[1] but needlework increased their cost enormously.

References in the drama, of which those in *Knight of the Burning Pestle* and *Knight of Malta*[2] are representative, are uninformative allusions.

GARTERS

Sixteenth-century garters, which were bands tied usually just below the knee, were much ornamented. Henry VIII wore garters of goldsmith's work, and of ribbon garnished with diamonds;[3] Queen Elizabeth had garters of rich taffeta and sarcenet edged and fringed with gold, and of cypress edged with bone lace, or ornamented by 'laid work'.[4] Cypress garters were worn by the middle class as well as the nobility.[5] Though the ladies' garters were, to their regret, invisible,[6] men's were ostentatiously displayed. They wore 'more taffaty for a garter than would serve the Gally dung-boat for streamers',[7] gemmed, spangled, adorned by 'roses all befringed with gold' (Plate XVI), or made entirely of gold lace. Garters cost from a pound upward,[8] though Jonson's price of fourscore pounds a pair[9] was apparently exaggerated. Those who could not afford silk used worsted such as crewel, a practice which afforded dramatists innumerable puns.[10]

When a lover became melancholy, he went without garters as a sign that he was no longer interested in appearances—a custom satirized in *As You Like It*, *Woman*

---

[1] 1523, *Eng. Hist. Rev.* vii. 98; 1579, *Archaeologia*, xix. 299; 1588, *Lancashire and Cheshire Wills*, liv. 139, 1624, *Archaeologia*, xv. 161.

[2] In order of mention: III. iv. 16; IV. i. 120.

[3] 1517, E. 101/418/13; 1528, *Letters and Papers Henry VIII*, IV. ii. 2243; 1536, *Archaeologia*, ix. 250.

[4] 1565, A.O. 3/1106; 1578, Egerton MS. 2806; 1593, L.C. 9/85; 1601, 9/92.

[5] *Durham Wills*, xxxviii. 227.

[6] *Devil is an Ass*, II. i. 429; *City*

Madam, I. i. 134. Ladies wore their garters just below the knee, with the stockings rolled above the garters.

[7] *Devil's Law Case*, II. i. 183; Rowlands, *Melancholy Knight*, ii. 6.

[8] 1615, *Hutton Accts.* xvii. 212, £1 10s. For references to rich garters, *Patient Grissel*, line 1157; 1638, Peacham, *Truth of Our Times*, 78.

[9] *Devil is an Ass*, I. i. 127; 1624, *Archaeologia*, xv. 161, garters and roses, 11s. 6d.—a low price.

[10] *Alchemist*, I. i. 202; *Lear*, II. iv. 8, &c.

*is a Weathercock, Fair Maid of the Exchange, How a Man may
Choose a Good Wife from a Bad,*[1] and many other plays.

Cross-garters, which were placed around the leg below
the knee, twisted crosswise in the back, brought forward
above the knee, and tied in a bow on the side, were fashionable from the sixties, and though still used by gentlemen
after 1600, according to *The Woman Hater,*[2] their decline
began with the introduction of knee-length breeches, and
by 1600 they were worn chiefly by old men, Puritans,
pedants, footmen, and rustic bridegrooms.[3]

SLIPPERS

In 1527 when the King had hurt his foot at tennis and
had to wear one slipper, his noblemen assumed black
velvet slippers in sympathy.[4] Slippers were low, easily
slipped-on footwear chiefly for indoors. They were made
of woollen or silk cloth, leather, and in the case of pantofles
—also called slippers—with cork soles.[5] They were
usually embroidered, as in *Patient Grissel.*[6] The cloth
variety was noiseless,[7] but allusions to creaking slippers
—probably leather soled—betraying the night walker
are common in drama.[8] There was little difference, except
in size, between the slippers worn by men and those worn
by women. A Spanish visitor to London in 1553, and an
Italian visitor in 1618, both wrote that women wore men's
slippers.[9]

[1] In order of their mention: III. ii. 403; I. ii.; I. i. 268; sig. B 3 verso.

[2] The woodcut of John Heywood in the 1562 edition of his *Epigrams*, shows cross garters, and they are fairly common in portraits painted before 1600. *Woman Hater*, I. ii. 26: 'All short-cloaked Knights, and all cross-gartered Gentlemen.'

[3] Jonson, *Masque of Christmas* (Gifford ed.), vol. vii. 259; *Lover's Melancholy*, III. i; *Tw. N.* III. ii. 82; *Two Angry Women of Abington*, line 490.

[4] *C.S.P.V.* iv, entry 105.

[5] Slippers of velvet, *What You Will*, II. i. 14; of cloth of silver, *Women Beware Women*, IV. i. 55; see also 1522,

Camden Soc. Pub., O.S., xlv. 128; *Philobiblon Soc. Pub.* vii. 13; 1551, Ellis, *Letters*, II. ii. 215; Royal MSS. 7 F, xvi. 136: 'Itm seevyn paire slippars of the Spanishe fassion corked and garnyshed with gold.' Slippers are mentioned in the wardrobe of Edward IV, but were worn at the beginning of the century.

[6] Line 2425; also, 1578, Egerton MS. 2806, 1322, 'three peire taphata slippers embr̃ wth lace of silver lyned wth Satten & scarlet'.

[7] *Silent Woman*, I. i. 200.

[8] *Northward Hoe*, III. i, &c.

[9] Muñoz, *Viaje de Felipe Segundo á Inglaterra*, 120; *C.S.P.V.* xv. 112.

XV

COSTUME ACCESSORIES

GIRDLE

A GIRDLE was a fitted belt, fastened in front, used by women to confine their garments at the waist, and by men to support the hanger for the sword. Women's girdles were made of goldsmith's work, silk, or ribbon,[1] and usually had pendant ends. Attached to the lady's girdle were ribbons or chains, on which hung her fan, pomander, mirror, or muff.

Men's girdles were made of gold, silver, embroidered silks and velvets,[2] for their dress costume; and leather, usually embossed, as in *Every Man Out of His Humour*, for wear with armour or for sports. The embroidery was in silk, spangles, precious stones, or pearls.

HANGERS

Attached to a man's girdle was the hanger, which consisted of one or two straps and a plate or pad to which was buckled the scabbard of the sword. (Plate XX.) A gentleman wore a rapier and a dagger, or was attended by an armed servant. A person of the middle class often wore a broadsword and carried a parrying shield or buckler. Hangers, especially wrought or embroidered, were gifts of ladies to their favourites, as Greene's *Tu Quoque* suggests. Bridegrooms gave them to the masculine wedding guests, as in *Scornful Lady*, and young men offered them in payment of wagers, as in *Hamlet*.[3]

[1] 1543, *P. P. Ex. Prin. Mary*, 116, goldsmith's work; 1557, *Lancashire and Cheshire Wills*, lxi. 257; *Bury Wills*, 136, silk; 1547, *Archaeologia*, xxi. 472, ribbon; 1620, *Household Bk. Howard*, 122: 'three yards of broad ribben to make my lady a girdle.'

[2] *Every Man Out of His Humour*, IV. vi. 102; *Tragedy of Dido*, II. i. 601.

[3] *Tu Quoque*, sig. (H 4 verso). *Scornful Lady*, II. ii. 286; *Hamlet*, V. ii. 157; *What You Will*, V. i. 40; *Love's Cure*, I. iii. 1; *Your Five Gallants*, I. i. 323. In 1605 Sir Timothy Hutton paid £3 for pr. hangers of 'neadlework', *Hutton Accts.* 204.

GLOVES

A glove was a covering for the whole of the hand—one with a separate sheath for each finger. Although gloves were worn three thousand years ago—one of tapestry-woven linen with a brilliant scale pattern was found in the tomb of Tutankhamen—the date of their introduction to Europe and to England is unknown. In the reign of Aethelred II, 974–1016, a society of German princes gave him five pairs of gloves as part payment for the protection of their trade.[1] The earliest reference to glove in English literature is that in *Beowulf* (line 2085), though that indicates a sack, rather than a covering for hands.

Since glovers were originally a part of the leathersellers' organization in England, little is known of the early manufacture. The Glovers of Perth, Scotland, are said to have received a charter in 1165.[2] Individual glove-makers are named in records in Colchester, 1295, Benning-worth, 1327, St. Martin (Worcester), 1375, and the Glovers of London were recognized as a separate organization *circa* 1349.[3] The manufacture must have been adequate for home needs by 1463; in that year, King Edward forbade the importation of gloves into England.[4]

No article of costume is so rich in associations as is the glove. Possibly because of their use in ecclesiastical ceremonies, and in law, gloves were symbolic of trust and honour. When Alcibiades appears before Athens, the senators ask for his glove as a pledge of protection:

> Throw thy glove,
> Or any token of thine honour else,
> That thou wilt use the wars as thy redress.[5]

Slender's and Biron's oaths can hardly be regarded as sacred, but rather as following the custom of sixteenth-century gallants who swore by the nearest visible object

[1] Strutt, op. cit. i. 44.

[2] Beck, *Gloves*, London, 1883, 136.

[3] Colchester, see Cunningham, *Growth English Industry*, i. 229; Ben-ningworth, *Worcester Lay Subsidy Rolls*, 20; St. Martin, *Worcester Origi-nal Charters*, 103; London, *Let. Bk. F*, fol. clxix.

[4] *Statutes at Large*, 3 Edward IV, c. 4.

[5] *Timon of Athens*, v. iv. 50 seq.

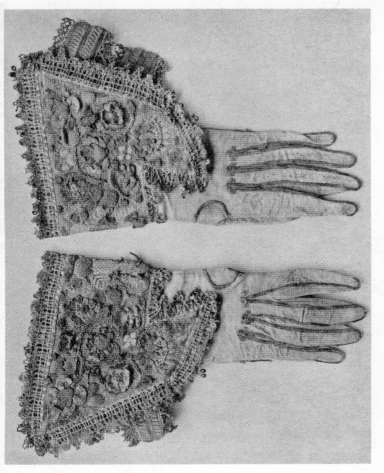

XIX. Early 17th-century gloves, embroidered in coloured silks and metal
thread; gauntlets edged with gold lace, spangled

Metropolitan Museum of Art, New York

XX. Gentleman's girdle and hanger, embroidered in gold and coloured silk

Victoria and Albert Museum

whether it be a beard, mask, fan, or the tip of a lady's ear.[1]

A glove was often sent as a gage, and worn in the helmet or hat as a symbol by which one's enemy could be recognized and challenged on the day of combat—a custom excellently illustrated in sixteenth-century drama by King Henry's exchange of gloves with Williams, and the latter's subsequent meeting with Fluellen, to whom the king had given the glove.[2] To pluck the glove from the hat of a fallen enemy signified victory over him. As a wager of battle, a glove was cast down by the defendant in a quarrel and taken up by the accuser, who thus signified his acceptance of the challenge. To show that his heart was true to Cressida, Troilus declared: 'I will throw my glove to Death himself.'[3]

Gloves were used as memorials, favours, betrothal or wedding gifts. Portia begs Antonio for his gloves as a keepsake; Cressida, parting from Troilus, gives him her gloves as a favour; Prince Hal declares he will go into the stews 'and from the commonest creature, pluck a glove', and wear it as a favour; but Welford of *The Scornful Lady* refuses Abigail's glove as a favour. Drayton describing the departure of the Spanish troops for France tells how, of 'the nobler youth', 'One ware his mistress' garters, one her glove'. Middleton opens *Blurt, Master Constable* with the entrance of five gallants 'with gloves in their hats as if returning from war'. 'Thy men are turned to women', complains Parmenio, 'thy soldiers to lovers, gloves worn in velvet caps instead of plumes on graven helmets.' Edgar refers to the custom when he tells Lear of his former life, that he had been a serving man of love: 'curled my hair, wore gloves in my cap'.[4]

Betrothal gloves and those given as favours to wedding guests were obligatory. Mopsa reproaches the clown for

---

[1] *Wint. Tale*, IV. iii. 417; *Two Gent.* IV. i. 10; *Cynthia's Revels*, II. ii. 18.

[2] *Hen. V*, IV. i. 229; IV. vii. 164; IV. viii. 26.

[3] *Troilus*, IV. iv. 63.

[4] *Merch. of V.* IV. i. 427; *Troilus*, IV. iv. 71; *Rich.* II. v, iii. 17–18; *Battle of Agincourt*, line 483; *Scornful Lady*, III. i. 16; *Blurt, Master Constable*, I. i; *Alexander and Campaspe*, IV. iii. 23; *Lear*, III. iv. 85.

failure to give her the promised 'sweet gloves'; Claudio sends Hero gloves of 'excellent perfume'. Rowlands, in his *Whole Crew of Gossips*, satirically indicates the popularity of a girl by her 'chalking up' forty-five suitors behind the door, and receiving more gift gloves than she could wear in a lifetime. A fascinating collection of laws pertaining to woman's rights, published 1632, shows that betrothal gloves and other gifts of the fiancé to his fiancée could be 'demanded back and recovered if matrimony doe not insue', but there was an exception: 'si sponsus dedit aliquid & aliquo casu impediuntur nuptiae, donatio penitus rescinditur nisi osculum intervenerit'; then the fiancé could recover only one half.[1] But law favoured the woman. She could recover all gifts that she may have made to her betrothed. The groom paid for the wedding gloves, as the Clown in *Winter's Tale* laments. When Lady Haughty arrives at the wedding of Epicoene and Morose, she indignantly exclaims, 'We see no ensigns of a wedding here. Where be our scarves and gloves?' Such gloves were, indeed, an expensive item. Machyn records in his *Diary* that 'Wylliam Belleffe wyntoner' who was 'mared in saint Pancras parryche the XXVII day of January ... gayff a C payre' to wedding guests.[2]

Due to the misinterpretation of an ambiguous passage in Stowe's *Annales*,[3] editors of English literature and costume books have credited Edward de Vere with the introduction of perfumed gloves into England; but such gloves were known there, though probably of foreign manufacture, fifty years previous to the return of de Vere from Italy with his souvenirs of 'gloves, sweete bagges, a perfumed leather jerkin and other pleasant things'. Among the expenses of apparel provided for the marriage of Elizabeth Nevile, January, 1526, is the item:

[1] *The Lavves Resolvtions of Women's Rights or The Lavves Provision for Women*, Lib. ii, sec. 32, p. 72. For references to betrothal gloves, see *Wint. Tale*, IV. iii. 236; *Much Ado*, III. iv. 61; *Amends For Ladies*, II. iii. 40; Rowlands, *Whole Crew of Gos-sips*, ii. 7.

[2] *Diary*, 247; *Wint. Tale*, IV. iv. 236; *Silent Women*, III. ii. 251; see also *Miseries of Enforced Marriage*, I. i; *Scornful Lady*, I. i. 170; Greene, *Works*, xi. 227.

[3] (Howes), 868.

'for a pair of Perfumed Gloves 3 s 4 d.'[1] Henry VIII received a pair from his gunner in 1540,[2] and Princess Mary was presented with a pair four years later.[3] Spain may have originated perfumed gloves; they were known there as early as 1523. Gasparo Contarini mentions forty pairs, worth upward of 200 ducats, offered as prizes for a joust between the Emperor and nine other lords opposing the Duke of Najara and followers of Seville.[4] Spanish perfumed gloves are constantly alluded to as the best: 'He will perfume your gloves most delicately, and give them the right Spanish titillation.' 'Your Spanish titillation in a glove, the best perfume.'[5] Perfuming gloves 'after the Spanish manner' was a long process, requiring five successive immersions in preparations of wine, waters of white lilies, roses, orange flowers, oil of benjamin, powdered cinnamon, nutmeg, cloves, citron, storax, civet, and ambergris.[6] So lasting was the resulting scent, that no after-treatment could remove it.[7] By 1580 England was making 'gloves of all sortes, knit and leather', and 'gloves perfumed',[8] but, if one believes satirists, 'there is no man can be contented with any other glove than is made in France or in Spain.'

The favourite materials for gloves were the skins of the stag, 'scheppys', 'doos', and kids, the latter called cheverel; and silk materials such as satin and velvet.[9] A pair reputed to have belonged to Henry VI, made of brown leather lined with deer-skin, is among the collection in the Public Museum, Liverpool; one worn by Mary, Queen of Scots, which is of buff-coloured leather with a gauntlet embroidered in silver wire gimp and coloured silks, and lined with crimson satin, is at the Saffron Walden Museum;

[1] *Chetham Soc. Pub.* xli. 365.
[2] *P. P. Ex. Henry VIII*, 370.
[3] *P. P. Ex. Prin. Mary*, 156.
[4] *C.S.P.V.* iii, entry 711.
[5] *Sir Giles Goosecap*, ii. i. 307; *Alchemist*, iv. ii. 14.
[6] Garzoni, *La Piazza Universale*, 281; Markham, *English Housewife*, 150, 154.
[7] *Cynthia's Revels*, v. iv. 390–4.

Perfumed gloves were also called 'washed'.
[8] Hakluyt, *Voyages*, iii. 270.
[9] L.C. 2/3, coronation of Edward VI: 'For embroidering 11 paire of gloves of white sattin laid with venice & damaske silver'; 1618, E. 351/3088: 'stag lether gloves well sented and wt deepe ffrindges.' Plate XIX shows a handsome pair kid gloves.

a pair presented to Queen Elizabeth at Oxford—and now in the Ashmolean Museum—is of white kid with gauntlets fringed in gold and embroidered with gold gimp; and an unusual pair given by James I to Sir Edward Denny, and presented by his descendant, Sir Edward Denny, to the Victoria and Albert Museum, is made of leather with gauntlets of red satin bands and gold lace. Whether Sir Epicure Mammon's desire for gloves 'of fishes' and birds' skins' was imaginary or founded upon reality is difficult to determine, but wardrobe accounts do not mention them and there are no extant examples in museums.

An Italian in England, 1618, who gave a lively account of the customs and dress of the English, wrote that 'all wear very costly gloves. This fashion of gloves is so universal that even the porters wear them very ostentatiously.'[1]

HANDKERCHIEF

'Handcoverchieffes' are found in the wardrobe of King Edward IV.[2] Presumably they were a French fashion since they were known in France 1313. By the sixteenth century the name had been shortened to handkercher,[3] and handkerchief. They were one of the costly accessories necessary to every fashionable man and woman of this period, and were usually carried in the hand to show their richness. Some were of cutwork as in *Bartholomew Fair*, some edged with gold and tassels as in *Chaste Maid in Cheapside*, some 'spotted' with embroidery as was Othello's.[4]

[1] *C.S.P.V.* xv. 270.

[2] *Wardrobe Accts. Edward IV*, 122, the earliest reference noted in England, but they were common in France a century earlier. Gay, op. cit. i. 148, gives references 1313.

[3] 1531, *P. P. Ex. Henry VIII*, 104.

[4] *Bartholomew Fair*, IV. i. 215; *Chaste Maid in Cheapside*, III. ii. 51; *Oth.* III. iii. 435. Stowe (Howes), *Annales*, 1039, states that in 1558 'maydes and gentlewomen' gave their favourites, as 'tokens of their love', little hand-kerchiefs three or four inches square, 'wrought round about, and with a button or tassel' on each corner and in the middle, 'the best edged with gold lace'. See also 1601, E. 154/3/24; 1623, *Household Bk. Lord Howard*, 206, handkerchiefs 'wrought' and with 'layd work' (couch-work) of gold cost 9s. 6d. each. See also chapter on embroidery. Handkerchiefs of lower class persons were, of course, less expensive. 1564, *Durham Wills*, ii. 216; *Lancashire and Cheshire Wills*, li. 260.

MUCKINDER

Be of good cheer; take my muckinder and dry thine eyes.
(Tale of a Tub, III. i. 53.)

Muckinder[1] is a vulgar term designating a handkerchief, or a square of linen used as a table napkin. It is
associated with children, infirm persons, and the low class.
Armin uses the word in connexion with fools and children.
John[2] and Jack Oates[3] put on 'cleane muckinders' in
preparation for a London trip and for visitors. 'Babycake',
of Jonson's *Masque of Christmas,* who was dressed like a
boy, wore a muckender (iii. 106). Holofernes[4] is com-
manded: 'Wipe your nose. Fie, on your sleeve! Where's
your muckinder your grandmother gave you?' The woodcut to *Two Maides of Moreclacke,* 1609, illustrates the method
of fastening the fringed muckinder to the girdle of the
wearer, for children and old folk had difficulty in keeping
handkerchiefs about their persons. This woodcut might
well serve as an illustration to the Captain's remark in
Beaumont's *The Captain.* Picturing his friend as a rheu-
matic invalid, he teasingly says:

> We'll have a Bib for spoiling of thy Doublet,
> And a fringed Muckender at thy Girdle.
>
> (III. v. 64.)

MASKS

No lace-woman, nor baud, that brings French masks.
(Devil is an Ass, II. i. 212.)

Stowe tells us that 'Woman's maskes, Buskes, Muffes,
Fanns, Perwigs, and bodkins were first devised and used
in Italy by Courtezans, and from thence brought into
France, and there received of the best sort for gallant
ornaments, and from thence they came into England

[1] The word first occurs in the English language in fifteenth-century glos-
saries and literature (*O.E.D.*), and had
various spellings: muckiter, mucketter,
muckinger, muckinja, mockadore,
mockedar, &c. Machyn, *Diary,* 32,
wrote 'moketor'. Lydgate's 'Advice
To An Old Gentleman Who Wished
For a Young Wife' tells him: 'For

eyen and nose, the nedeth a mokadow.'
Dr. Skeat, *Mod. Lang. Rev.,* 11, 60,
offers the now generally accepted Pro-
vençal origin, *mucadour.*

[2] *Two Maides of Moreclacke,* xiii.
88.

[3] *Foole Upon Foole,* xiii. 6; *Widow's
Tears,* IV. i. 125.

[4] *What You Will,* III. ii. 53.

about the time of the Massacre of Paris'.[1] But English women were wearing masks in 1554, when Philip of Spain came to England,[2] and they are alluded to in *Mary Magdalene*,[3] 1566.

These masks were oblong pieces of velvet or other silk, lined with soft skin or silk,[4] having holes for eyes, and were used to protect a lady's complexion from the sun, or to shield her from public gaze. When disconsolate, a lady no longer cared for her complexion and threw her 'sun-expelling mask away',[5] though masks were as often used to conceal ill-favoured countenances[6] as to protect beautiful ones. The smaller mask which covered only the nose and part of the cheeks was used for concealing identity of the wearer; the larger ones were protective; hence Autolycus' 'Masks for faces and for noses'.[7]

The 'great ladies', wrote Sir John Harington, 1606, 'do go well masked, and indeed it be the only show of their modesty to conceal the countenance',[8] and an Italian account of English ladies at a Court entertainment, 1618, says that they considered the mask as indispensable for their face as bread at a table.[9] Characters on the stage forbid the women of their families to go on the street unmasked,[10] or express disgust that women should sit 'bare fac't' at an execution 'for feare little holes of their masks should not give their eyes roome enough for such a prospect'.[11] Their bare faces, rather than their presence at the execution, caused the disapproval! The attendant—whether it be servant or husband—carried the accessory which the lady was not wearing, whether it be her fan, mask, or gloves.[12]

[1] *Annales*, 1038 (Howes).

[2] *Viaje de Felipe Segundo á Inglaterra*, 119: 'y algunas andan por Lóndres con sus velos ó antifaces ante el rostro, que parescen á las monjas cuando se quieren tapar por no ser vistas.'

[3] Sig. (C 4 verso).

[4] Velvet, *More Dissemblers Besides Women*, I. iv. 91; taffeta, Middleton, *Works*, iii. 97; satin, *Household Bk.*

Howard, 9; 1603, *Eglinton MSS.*, 'two skins to lyn my masks', 32.

[5] *Two Gent.* IV, iv. 160.

[6] *Lingua*, sig. D 2 verso; *Northward Hoe*, V. i. 121.

[7] *Wint. Tale*, IV. iii. 223.

[8] *Prog. James*, ii. 74.

[9] *C.S.P.V.* xv. 112, 67.

[10] *Women Beware Women*, III. i. 216.

[11] *The Fleire*, II. i. 369-70.

[12] *Edward I*, sc. vi, i: 'Hold, take

MIRROR

Looking-glasses were a passing inuention: I protest the fittest books for Ladies to study upon. (*Lingua*, sig. G 2.)

'And he [Moses] made the laver of brass, and the foot of it of brass, of the looking-glasses of the women.'[1] The rendition 'looking-glasses' in this passage is questionable, but, since the antiquity of the optical instrument for producing reflection has not been established, this rendition may be accepted tentatively, at least, as the first notice of mirrors. Pliny[2] says that glass mirrors were made at Sidon. Extant specimens of Etruscan, Greek, and Roman mirrors, however, are thin disks of metal, polished on one side, and plain, incised, or ornamented on the other.

The Celtic population evidently adopted the use of mirrors from their conquerors. One found in Cornwall— now in the British Museum—has a pattern and handle which indicate native origin. Also in this museum are bronze mirrors found in various parts of England.

Mirrors are not mentioned in English literature until the thirteenth century,[3] but by the fourteenth had become rather common. Those of French manufacture were the most desired, and there are beautiful extant examples made of precious metal and decorated with enamel. In these early centuries, mirrors were designed by artists for persons of culture. Until the Renaissance, they were usually circular; and the majority were mounted in cases of ivory, gold, silver, or bronze.

Steel glasses were in use throughout the sixteenth century, but the Lord Chamberlain's accounts of 1561, lists a 'looking glass of crystall'.[4] Ladies wore their mirrors attached to their girdles by a ribbon or precious chain, and women are so presented in *The City Madam*.[5] Men wore them in their hats, as Jonson shows in *Cynthia's Revels* (II. iii. 67), and Fitzgeffrey accuses the 'changeable

my mask, but see you rumple it not.' 1604, Rowlands, *I'le Stabbe Ye*, i. 34.

[1] Exodus, xxxviii. 8.
[2] *Nat. Hist.* xxxvi. 193.
[3] *O.E.D.*

[4] L.C. 9/55. *Prog. Elizabeth*, ii. 257, New Year's gift for 1578: a pair of mirrors in a case of taffeta, embroidered in pearls.
[5] I. i (stage direction).

silk' gallants of reading 'no books but a looking-glass'.[1] A mirror plays an important part in tragic scenes of *Richard II*, and *Lear*,[2] in the first of which the shattering of the glass is a pathetic exhibition of the King's weakness.

One evidence of sixteenth-century interest in mirrors is shown by the great number of books whose titles include the word 'mirror' or 'glass'. Some of the most familiar of these are Princess Elizabeth's *Miroir or Glass of the Synneful Soul*, 1544; *Mirror of Policie*, 1559; *Mirror of Good Manners*, 1570; *Steele Glas*, 1576; *Mirror For Magistrates*, 1578; *Looking Glass for London*, 1594.

Research has not revealed England's initial efforts in the manufacture of looking-glasses. Goldsmiths and metal workers probably made them to order long before they were produced by quantity. There is no positive evidence of glass-mirror making until the Duke of Buckingham established the glass works at Vauxhall,[3] but when Hakluyt, in 1580, listed the products 'to be taken for a shew of our commodities' by the seekers for the North-east Strait, he included 'Glasses of English making, looking glasses for women, great and faire'. Presumably the last were of English manufacture.

MUFF

Diuel: 'and these two thumbes thrust,
(In open Churches) into braue dames eares.
Damning up attention; whilst the loose eye peeres
For fashions of gowne-wings, laces, purles, ruffes,
Fals, cals, tires, caps, hats, mufs, and pufs.'
(*If This Be Not a Good Play, the Diuell Is in It*, vol. iii, 329.)

The muff was a thick cover, usually in shape of a roll, into which the hands could be placed to protect them from

---

[1] *Notes From Blackfryers*, F. 5. In *Silent Woman*, IV. i, Truewit says that a wooer's powder, comb, and mirror must be his 'dearest acquaintance'. See also Breton, *Works*, i. 62; *The Courtier*, bk. i. In 1614 Matthew Hutton paid 2s. 6d. for a 'looking-glasse', *Hutton Accts.*, 211.

[2] *Rich. II*, IV. i. 289; *Lear*, V. iii.

263. Glass mirror also mentioned in *Rich. III*, II. ii. 51.

[3] A Dutch looking-glass maker was among the foreign residents in Southwark, 1618, *Foreign Residents in England*, 97. Mansell, who secured patents for various kinds of glass in 1615, experimented with mirrors.

the cold. Sixteenth-century ladies and gentlemen carried them chiefly for show. Ladies used them from about 1570,[1] but gentlemen seem not to have adopted the fashion until the beginning of the seventeenth century.

Muffs were of fur or silk materials, the latter embroidered,[2] and were expensive accessories. Young Hutton paid two pounds for 'a riche embrodered muffe in coullers' in 1605, and two muffs for Prince Henry in 1607 cost seven pounds six shillings. One was of cloth of silver embroidered with purls, plate, and Venice twist of silver and gold, and the other of black satin embroidered in silk and bugles.[3] To 'maintain' a person in muffs, as is said in *Lover's Melancholy*, in addition to other luxuries, required a considerable income (i. ii. 69).

PATCH

Patches were small pieces of velvet or silk, cut into various shapes and attached by mastic to the face or forehead to cover a blemish or to attract attention to a beautiful feature,[4] a custom satirized by the Clown in *All's Well That Ends Well*: 'O madam, younder's my lord your son with a patch of velvet on 's face: whether there be a scar under it or no, the velvet knows; but 'tis a goodly piece of velvet.'[5]

Lyly, the first dramatist to mention the mode, refers to velvet patches worn at the temples.[6] Beaumont and Fletcher list various shapes, as stars, half-moons, lozenges;[7] and D'Avenant[8] tells how taffeta chipped into stars and 'fixed in several regions of the face' act as a foil to beauty. Such patches, which had been worn by the courtly during the last decade of the sixteenth century,

---

[1] 1581, Rutz, *Habitus variarum orbis gentium*, illustrates the style for ladies. 'She always weares a muff,' *Cynthia's Revels*, II. ii. 46; *Philaster*, v. i. 400.

[2] *Blurt, Master Constable*, III. iii. 112.

[3] *Hutton Accts.* 204; Prince Henry's wardrobe, A.O. 1/2345/35; *Pasquils Fooles Cappe*, 24: 'He that puts fifteene elles into a Ruffe . . . and twenty thousands crownes into a muffe.'

[4] 1598, Hall, *Satyres*, VI. i. 115: 'Or Gellia wore a velvet mastic patch.' 1611, Cotgrave, '*Moucheron* . . . little black patch thats glued by masticke on the faces of many'.

[5] IV. v. 100–2. *Westward Hoe*, II. i. 142.

[6] *Mydas*, III. ii. 143.

[7] *Elder Brother*, III. v. 67.

[8] *Albovine*, v. i. 157.

became an almost universal custom by 1625. The custom declined during the Puritan reign, but was enthusiastically revived on the restoration of the Stuarts and lasted through the eighteenth century.

POMANDER

Pomander, which originated in the Middle Ages as a preventive of the plague, was a moulded, dried mixture of aromatic substances carried usually in a hollow metal ball, so that the name came to be applied to both the substance and the ball. The recipe given in *Lingua* for the substance requires 'purest garden mold clensed and steeped seven days in change of motherless' rosewater 'incorporated' with laudanum, benzoin, storax, ambergris, civet, and musk.[1] *The Malcontent* recommends 'six grains of muske ground with rosewater and tempered with civet' for renewing pomanders whose scent had 'decayed' (v. i. 17), so that they evidently lost their fragrance (?) unless they were, as the chain of pomander mentioned in *Cynthia's Revels*,[2] 'kept in onyx' after they were balled.

Instead of the dried substance, Italian pomanders sometimes contained a perfume. Some very handsome specimens survive. Some were of gold and jewels and hung on golden chains about the neck or at the girdle of the wearer.[3] Made of the baser metals, they were to be found in every pedlar's pack, of which that in *The Winter's Tale* is a good example (IV. iii. 611).

PURSE

This purse which I would be loth to sweare by unless 'twere
embroidered. (*Cynthia's Revels*, IV. iv. 31.)

'Put money into thy purse'[4] is Iago's advice to Roderigo. When man invented money he probably invented a pouch

---

[1] IV. iii. 1–7. 1561, *Prog. Elizabeth*, I. xxxvi, mentions a little round 'mount of gold to contain pomander in it'. For a discussion of its use in the plague, see 1603, Lodge, *Causes and Cures of the Plague*, IV. 23.

[2] V. iv. 411; *Every Man Out of His Humour*, II. i. 98.

[3] 1554, *Bury Wills*, 45; 1545, *Test. Ebor.* cvi. 228; 1541, *Rutland MSS.* iv. 307; 1578–1600, *Prog. Elizabeth*, passim.

[4] *Othello*, I. iii. 345.

in which to carry it. Representations of Byzantine and Frankish noblemen show them wearing at their girdles such pouches of tooled leather and woven materials, but the term purse is not named in accounts until the twelfth century.[1]

Sixteenth-century purses were made of leather and silks, usually embroidered, and were drawn at the top by strings.[2] Such strings were often, as in *What You Will*,[3] adorned by tassels. They were carried in the sleeve, in hose, or hung at the girdle.[4]

[1] *O.E.D.*

[2] *Othello*, I. i. 3: 'thou, Iago, who hast had my purse

As if the strings were thine . . .' Materials for a ladies' purse, 1524, included 'a quarter and a nail of tawney velvet', 3s. 9d.; a skein of silk, 2d.; an oz. of tawny silk for strings, 1s. 2d.;

'a quarter of bucram' for lining, 2d., *Letters and Papers Henry VIII*, IV. i. 340. 1581, *Durham Wills*, ii. 361, 1½ oz. 'cording' for purses. 1581, L.C. 9/78, a satin purse ornamented with venice silver, silk strings.

[3] IV. i. 120: *Troilus*, V. i. 36–37.

[4] Greene, *Works*, ix. 162, x. 207.

XVI

COSTUME FASTENINGS

BUTTONS AND BUTTONHOLES

BUTTONS were in use in England by the twelfth century, though only for ornament; but Gower's effigy at Southwark shows that shanked buttons had developed by that time. Buttons of silk and gold are listed in the wardrobe accounts of Edward IV; they were used with loops (p. 117) of braid and silk to fasten garments. Judging from his wardrobe accounts, Edward VI established the button and buttonhole mode in England; he had buttons of jewels, gold, thread and silks, embroidered, and adorned in every possible way, with silk buttonholes often in colour contrasting with that of his garments.[1]

Stowe wrote that buttons of silk and thread were unknown to the 'generality' until after 1568;[2] that about that year many young citizens began to wear crystal buttons upon their doublets, coats, and jerkins and 'within a few years after, began the general wearing of buttons of threed, silke, haire, gold and silver threed'. A foreigner who had witnessed Queen Elizabeth's first public entry into London was so much impressed by the number of gold buttons worn by the nobility that he described them.[3]

Dozens of buttons were given to the Queen as New Year gifts, some of gold in her favourite acorn shape, some set with precious stones, some of pearl;[4] and items of buttons in silk 'wrought' in 'purle', spangles, and oes are frequent in the Lord Chamberlain's accounts.[5]

'The generality', as Howes terms them, used buttons of the same material as their costume, as did the 'little

---

[1] L.C. 2/3; L.R. 2/115, &c.

[2] *Annales*, Howes, 1039. Such buttons are inventoried in a small shop in that year, so that they must have been more common than Howes indicated; see *Durham Wills*, xxxviii. 283.

[3] Perlin, 'Description England and Scotland', *Antiq. Rep.* iv. 508.

[4] *Prog. Elizabeth*, i. 294; ii. 52, 300; iii. 448.

[5] 1578, L.C. 9/79; 1586, L.C. 9/77, &c.

well-favoured fellow' of *Mucedorus*,[1] but 'diamond buttoned hose', mentioned in *Lady's Trial* (ii. i. 50), were not unusual for the wealthy. Buttons of gold, enamel, silk, and hair were bequeathed in wills throughout this period, and lace buttons made over moulds were favourites during the reign of King James.[2]

The number of buttons to a garment increased: five dozen to a jerkin;[3] four and a half dozen to a doublet,[4] two dozen to a cloak; seventeen to thirty-six dozen to a cassock,[5] often with a corresponding number of buttonholes; many of which were, of course, merely ornamental. When a doublet that was 'three hours a buttoning'[6] indicated wealth, naturally one with three buttons, as in *Eastward Hoe* (i. i. 139), indicated a beggar. Interest in buttons originated many proverbial expressions of which three from Shakespeare survive: ''Tis in his buttons, he will carry it', a Lincolnshire dialectal way of saying 'he will succeed'; 'take down a buttonhole lower', that is to allow a person to have fewer buttons and so humiliate him; 'on fortune's cap, the very button',[7] meaning the utmost in happiness.

HOOKS AND EYES

An examination of portraits painted during the reign of Henry VIII reveals two kinds of visible fasteners: buttons with buttonholes, and points with eyelets; and, from the thirties, one kind of invisible fasteners, especially on ladies' kirtles and men's jerkins, and doublets. These invisible fasteners were evidently hooks and eyes, for the edges of the garments met smoothly instead of overlapping. Twenty-four pairs of silver hooks and eyes were ordered for a 'frock' fastened only to the waist, which was used at

[1] Dodsley, vii. 240.
[2] Cf. 1578, *Richmond Wills*, 279–80; 1579, *Lancashire and Cheshire Wills*, li. 65; 1593, *Durham Wills*, xxxviii. 212; 1612, *Archaeologia*, xxvi. 386; 1616–17, *Shuttleworth Accts*. xxxv. 224, &c.
[3] 1574, *Hist. Hengrave*, 203.
[4] 1623, *Eng. Hist. Rev.* vii. 99.

[5] Kempe, *Loseley MS.* 426, 'making the cassock wth 23 dozen of button holes'.
[6] *The Old Law*, ii. i. 58.
[7] *M. Wives*. iii. ii. 74; *Love's L. L.* v. ii. 705; *Haml.* ii. ii. 237: 'Happy in that we are not over happy; On Fortune's cap, we are not the very button.'

King Edward's coronation, 1546,[1] and eight for a 'tunica' in 1548.[2] Hooks and eyes were purchased for the Great Wardrobe of Elizabeth by the hundreds, thousands, and the pound.[3] At the end of the century this type of fastener was used on garments of the lower class of persons as well as on those of the wealthy.[4]

By the reign of Charles I, hooks and eyes were placed on hose to join them to the doublets, and the visible points tied in bows were merely ornamental. 'In the old time', remarks Buzzano of *Dick of Devonshire*, 1626, 'gentlemen would call to their men and cry, "Come, trusse me"; now the word is "Come, hooke me"; for everybody now lookes so narrowly to Taylors bills that the needle lance knights, in revenge of those prying eyes, put so many hooks and eyes to every hose and dubblet'.[5]

PINS

London pinners had organized during the reign of Edward III,[6] and the manufacture of pins was so well established in the next century that importation of foreign pins was prohibited in 1483.[7] These wire pins were rather clumsily made, but not until fifty-nine years later was a statute passed requiring that heads be well soldered to the shanks of pins, the shanks smoothed and the points 'well filed . . . and sharpened'.[8] Even then the requirement almost annihilated this manufacture, and within three years had to be repealed. English pins sold for about a penny a hundred;[9] and the French, though

[1] 1546, L.C. 2/3 (2): 'Richard Newporte for 24 paire hookes and eyes of silver for said frock.' Hooks and eyes are in the pedlar's pack of *The Four PP* (printed 1540).

[2] E. 351/3026, 'pro viij par hookes et eyes de Argento et deaurañt pro una tunica de satten crimsen'.

[3] L.C. 2/4 (3); 1581, L.C. 9/73, '800 de hamis et oculis pro dict. tog. diploid, cŏpor, et mani.'; 1579, Egerton MSS. 2806; 1583, A.O. 1/1110. By the end of the century the price of ordinary hooks and eyes had been reduced to a shilling a thousand.

[4] 1573, *Mid. MSS.* 439; 1592, *Durham Wills*, xxxviii. 211.

[5] Bullen, *Old Plays*, II. 63.

[6] *Let. Bk. G*, fol. xlviii; they are mentioned 1356.

[7] *Statutes at Large*, I Richard III, c. 12.

[8] Ibid. 34 Henry VIII, c. 6.

[9] See wardrobe accounts below, also inventories of merchants and pedlars, 1570, *Durham Wills*, ii. 362; 1592, ibid. xxxviii. 211. It is interesting to

better made, averaged a little less. The desire for cheaper or better pins must have induced the statute of 1585 allowing the importation of pins from any country whatsoever.[1]

'There is such doing with their looking glasses, pinning and unpinning', is Tactus' disgusted comment on the time needed to dress a 'nice gentlewoman'.[2] His disgust was only partly justified. In the present age of 'snap' and 'zipper' fasteners, it is difficult to realize how dependent upon pins the sixteenth-century woman must have been. Her ruff or band was pinned to her rebato or pickadil; her rebato pinned to the neck of her bodice; her partlet pinned into the upper part of her kirtle; her kirtle bodice and skirt pinned together; her detachable sleeves pinned into the armseyes, her farthingale pinned to her petticoat; her billiament pinned to her hood; her coif pinned to her hair; therefore, wardrobe accounts are full of items of 'great varthingale pynnes', 'myddel varthingale pynnes', 'smale velvett pynnes'; 'hed pynnes', &c., purchased by gross, thousand, or paper.[3] The time which ladies spent in pinning together parts of their costume was the object of stage ridicule, but detachable bodices and skirts, neckwear, sleeves, foreparts, stomachers, and partlets made up costumes which could not be sewed together, for the infinite variety of colour-combinations and materials was part of the charm of the costume; thus a peach colour satin forepart embroidered with gold, and peach cloth-of-gold sleeves might be worn one day with a black velvet kirtle, and the next, with one of pearl taffeta, and a blackwork stomacher and band be equally beautiful with a kirtle of murrey chamlet or Isabelle saye.

By 1600, however, women's costumes were less varied; detachable partlets and sleeves were out of fashion at Court; hooks and eyes, and buttons, had largely displaced

note that pedlars of Chaucer's age included in their packs pins for women, Leaven of Pharisees, 1380, E.E.T.S. (1880), 12. Autolycus also sold them, Winter's Tale, IV. iii. 228.

[1] Statutes at Large, 27 Elizabeth c. 11.

[2] Lingua, IV. vi. 19.

[3] 1561, L.C. 9/35; 1563–4, L.C. 9/57; Egerton MS. 2806; 1616, Shuttleworth Accts. xxxv. 216.

pins; but the proper 'set' of bands still required their use, and dramatists continued to note that fact.[1]

POINTS

Two doseyn poynts of cheverell, the aglottes of sylver feyn.
(1450, *Coventry Mysteries*, 241.)

The inventory of a London haberdasher, 1378,[2] listed a gross of 'poynts' of red leather—the earliest noted reference. Points were originally the metal tags on thongs of leather, but by the fifteenth century the latter had been given the French name *aiguillette*, and the thongs were then called 'points'. When points bore no *aiguillettes* they were said to be 'untagged'.

A row of points were fastened to the waistline of the hose, and a corresponding row of eyelets made at the waistline of the doublet. After the gentleman had donned these garments, his 'boy' drew the points of the hose through the eyelets on the doublet,[3] and tied the two ends of each point in a bow-knot. This process was called trussing. The breaking of points with consequent parting of the garments was frequently alluded to in comic scenes.[4] Points were used also to tie on the cod-piece, and to tie the doublet sleeve along the front opening, though in this position they were largely ornamental. Points which joined the doublet and hose were replaced by hooks and eyes, but the row of points were sewed on the outside of the doublet by way of ornament, a fashion lasting through the reign of King Charles I.

Previous to the sixteenth century points were made chiefly of leather; thereafter, they were of thread—linen or silk—with *aiguillettes* of various metals, and were priced from three pence to three shillings a dozen—exclusive of the *aiguillettes*.[5]

[1] *Cor.* II. i. 227–8.
[2] *Let. Bk. F*, fol. ccxxii.
[3] *Every Man Out of His Humour*, IV. vii. 21; *Ant. & Cleop.* III. xi. 157; *New Inn*, v. i. 199.
[4] *Tw. N.* I. v. 26; *1 Hen. IV*, II. iv. 242–3.

[5] 1551, *Accts. Lord High Treas. Scotland*, x. 18, 72, 87, 194, &c.; 1562, *Durham Wills*, xxxviii. 211–12; 1593, *Archaeologia*, xix. 299; 1578, *Richmond Wills*, 280, 1597, *Durham Wills*, xxxviii. 283: 11 doz. 'wrought silke' points, 27 doz. 'threed' points; 5 doz.

Ribbon

Pedlars on and off the stage carried 'ribbons of all colours i' the rainbow',[1] for ribbons were very useful in the Tudor and Stuart periods. For the revels of February 19, 1520, ribbon was purchased for lacing bonnets; in 1536 eighty-two yards of 'three nayles' ribbon was used in the wardrobe of Henry the Eighth for 'our frokis'; Princess Mary wore ribbon on her foresleeve in 1543; it served for girdles, hatbands, garters, shoeties, hair and bride laces throughout the Elizabethan and Jacobean ages.[2]

Width of ribbon was measured by the 'nail'—about two and one fourth inches, or by the 'penny'—width of an English penny. Ribbon was sold according to its width, by the piece, yard, ounce, or pound. The 'pennybredth' was usually sold by weight, though it was sold also by the 'pece' of a dozen yards. Therefore one finds in accounts such items as: 'syxe pecis Venysse reabande, pennye bredth of div'se colours'; 'iiij pounds peny bred. riben'; 'ij gross vii dosen verge ribin'; 'V duoden ac vi ac xi virge de Towrs riben diversorum colorum'; 'ij ydes. iij d. ribin'.[3]

The twelve penny ribbon, mentioned in *Staple of News*, was the widest of penny ribbons;[4] and the half penny, named in *What You Will*, the narrowest.[5] It was the latter width which was used for the 'riband in the ear'.

'lether' points. 1620, *Household Bk. Howard*, 123: 2 doz. points for 1 pair breeches.

[1] *Wint. Tale.* IV. iv. 206.

[2] In order of mention: Revels, 1520, *Letters and Papers Henry VIII*, iii. 2, 1550; *Archaeologia*, ix. 249; *P. P. Ex. Prin. Mary*, 138; for other uses, see these accessories; *Rom. & Jul.* III. i. 32: 'Didst thou not fall out with a tailor for wearing his new doublet before Easter? with another for tying his new shoes with old riband?'

[3] In order of mention: 1536,

Archaeologia, ix. 250; 1560, L.C. 9/54; 1562, *Durham Wills*, xxxviii. 211 (valued at 10d. an oz.); 1591-2, L.C. 9/82; 1600, L.C. 9/91; 1610. *Shuttleworth Accts.*, xxxv. 190.

[4] I. ii. 224: 'And have a pair of twelve-penny broad ribands, Laid out like labels.'

[5] IV. i. 81: '. . . he that bought the half penny riband, wearing it in his ear, swearing it was the Duchess of Milan's favour.' *Every Man Out of His Humour*, II. iii. 201: '. . . here be some slight favours of hers . . . this ribband in my ear.'

SHORT TITLE LIST OF PRINCIPAL WORKS CITED

Works cited only once are fully described in footnotes.

MANUSCRIPTS

British Museum

ADDITIONAL MSS., especially 12504, petition from Mayor, &c., of Norwich respecting worsted weavers, Jan. 31, 1618; 25097, customs rates for 1558; 35328, warrant from Queen Elizabeth for payments to tailor, 'verthingale maker', hosier, &c., Feb. 10, 1567. (See footnotes for detailed references.)

COTTONIAN MSS., especially Galba C. i, 42, 43, 45, 78; Titus B. iv, 68; Vit. xiv. 33—all concerning customs and cloth manufacture. (See footnotes for detailed references.)

EGERTON MSS., especially 2804, letters from Philip Gawdy, 1579–1616; 2806, *A Booke of Warrantes . . . towchyng her Maiesties Roobes and Appareill*, 1568–1569.

HARLEIAN MSS., especially 1419, inventory of goods Henry VIII, 1547.

LANSDOWNE MSS., especially vii. 81, letters patent for encouragement of foreign weavers in Norwich, Nov. 6, 1564; xxvii. 65, concerning 'new draperies', 1578; 66, 'Interrogatories' concerning certain 'Bays and Friseaddows'; xxviii. 25, complaint of London against Norwich dealers, 1579; lxxxi. 48, 50, 51, &c., wares brought into London; cx. 37, 73, &c., concerning customs, ccxli, &c. (See footnotes.)

LAUD MSS., Bodleian Library, Oxford.

ROYAL MSS., especially 7 F. xiv. 22, the King's apparel in the hands of Alford, 1535; 23, inventory of wardrobe of the Princess Dowager in Baynard Castle, 1535.

STOWE MSS., especially 774, account-book of Roger North, Jan. 1575–Feb. 1581 and Apr. 1582–Dec. 1582. (See footnotes.)

Public Record Office

AUDIT OFFICE, declared accounts, 1/2339 to 2362, Jan. 1558–1630 (62 rolls), Great Wardrobe accounts.

AUDIT OFFICE, various accounts, 3/1106 to 1121, 1559–1632; 907 to 910, 1571–1632 (26 MSS.), accounts of revels, of keeper of Great Wardrobe, robes of Prince of Wales, &c.

EXCHEQUER ACCOUNTS, E. 101/417/4 to 436/9 (60 MSS.), 1511–1625, various accounts, inventories, &c., New Year's gifts, bills of tailors, mercers, shoemakers, &c. Also E. 3. 1–6. 53, Enrolled Accts. Great Wardrobe, Edward III, IV, Richard II, Henry VI, &c.

EXCHEQUER DEPOSITIONS BY COMMISSIONS. (For detailed references, see footnotes.)

EXCHEQUER BILLS AND ANSWERS, 44 Elizabeth, Mich. Norfolk, 30, &c. (For detailed references, see footnotes.)

EXCHEQUER MSS. Ulnage Accounts. Exch. K.R. Accounts. (See footnotes.)

LORD CHAMBERLAIN, Accounts, L.C. 9/51 to 101, 1517–1632 (50 MSS.) expenses of apparel; L.R. 2/3, 4, 113, 114–19, 121, &c. 1547–1605. inventories, expenses of funerals, coronations, progresses, &c.

PIPE OFFICE, declared accounts, E. 351/3024 to 3099, Sept. 1570–1632 (76 MSS.); accounts of keepers of Great Wardrobe, 3141/3145 (15 MSS.); miscellaneous accounts; expenses coronations, progresses, funerals; E. 154/2/17, 20, 22, 36, 39, 41 (6 MSS.), miscellaneous indentures of goods, inventories of apparel, &c., 1509–53; E. 154/3/ 1, 13, 19, 24, 40, inventories apparel, 1556–1612; E. 154/4/4, 6, 14, inventories apparel, 1613–18.

University of Chicago

BACON MSS., wardrobe accounts.

PRINTED SOURCES

1. *Acts*. *Acts of the Privy Council of England*, 1547–1625 (Rolls Series).
2. *Ancaster*, &c. *MSS*. See *Royal Commission Historical Manuscripts*.
3. *Anciens*. See LINAS.
4. *Antiquarian*. *Antiquarian Repertory*. London, 1780–4.
5. *Antiquary*. *The Antiquary*. London, 1880–1915. 51 vols.
6. *Archives*. *Archives curieuses de l'histoire de France*. Ed. by M. L. Cimber, &c. Paris, Beauvais, 1834–40.
7. ARNOLD, R. *Chronicle*, see *Rates*.
8. AUBIGNÉ, T. A. D'. *Les Aventures du Baron de Faeneste*. Paris, Jannet, 1855.
9. AUVERGNE, MARTIAL D'. *Les Arrêts d'amours*. Amsterdam, 1731.
10. BANSLEY, CHARLES. *A treatyse shewing and declaring the pryde and abuse of women now a dayes*. (Written 1550?) Early Popular Poetry, vol. iv.
11. BARET, JOHN. *An Alvearie or Quadruple Dictionarie*. London, 1580.
12. BEVERLEY. *Beverley Town Documents*, 1900. Selden Soc., vol. xiv.
13. BINET, ÉTIENNE. *Essay des merveilles de nature*. Rouen, 1624.
14. BIRCH, THOMAS. *The Court and Times of James the First*. London, 1849. 2 vols.
15. —— *Memoirs of the Reign of Queen Elizabeth*. London, 1754. 2 vols.
16. BLOMEFIELD, F. *Essay towards Topographical History County Norfolk*, Norwich, 1739–75. 5 vols.
17. BLOUNT, T. *Glossographia or a Dictionary interpreting the Hard Words . . . in our . . . English Tongue*. London, 1681.
18. BRETON. *Works in Verse and Prose*. Ed. by A. B. Grosart, 1879. 2 vols.
19. *Bristol*. *The Little Red Book of Bristol*. Ed. by F. B. Bickley. Bristol, 1900. 2 vols.
19 a. —— *Wills*. See WADLEY.

20. BRUYN, A. DE. *Omnium pene Europae, Asiae, Aphricae . . . gentium habitus*, 1581.
21. *Bury. Wills and Inventories from Registers of Commissary of Bury St. Edmunds.* Camden Soc. Pub. 1850.
22. *Calendar. Calendar of Close Rolls*, 1227–1422 (Rolls Series). (Original MSS. consulted for details.)
23. *Calendar of Patent Rolls*, 1338–1553 (Rolls Series). (Original MSS. consulted for details.)
24. *Calendar of Plea and Memoranda Rolls* (preserved among archives of Corporation of City of London at Guildhall), 1323–81. 22 vols. Ed. by A. W. Thomas. Cambridge, Univ. Press.
25. *Calendar of Letter Books* (preserved among archives . . . at Guildhall), 1296–1497. Ed. R. Sharpe, 1896–1912. Published for the Corporation. (Rolls Series.)
26. *Calendar State Papers, Domestic*, Edward VI, Mary, Elizabeth, James I, Charles I (Rolls Series). (Original MSS. consulted for details.)
27. *Calendar State Papers, Ireland*, 1509–1632 (Rolls Series).
28. *Calendar State Papers relating to English affairs, existing in archives, Venice and other libraries, northern Italy.* Ed. by Rawdon Brown. (Rolls Series.)
29. CALEPINO, A. *Dictionarivm vndecim lingvarvm.* Basileae, 1598.
30. *Calverley. Calverley Charters.* Thoresby Soc. Pub., vol. vi.
31. CAMDEN. *Camden Miscellany.* Camden Soc. vols. ii, iii, iv, 1851, 1855, 1859.
32. *Chronicle Grey Friars.* See NICHOLS.
33. *Churchwardens. Churchwardens' Accounts of St. Mary the Great, Cambridge*, 1504–1635. Cambridge Antiquarian Soc. London, Bell, 1905.
34. —— *Churchwardens' Accounts of St. Mary Hill.* J. Nichols, *Illustrations of the Manners . . . Antient Times in England.* London, Nichols, 1797.
35. —— *Churchwardens' Accounts of . . . Yatton*, 1549–1560. Somerset Record Soc., vol. iv.
36. CLIFFORD. *Diary of Lady Anne Clifford.* London, 1923.
37. COKE, EDWARD. *The Second Part of the Institutes of the Laws of England.* London, 1797. 2 vols.
38. COLLIER, J. P. *Annals of the Stage.* London, 1831. 3 vols.
39. *Compota.* See *Scotland.*
40. COOPER. *Annals of Cambridge.* Cambridge, Warwick, 1842–53. 5 vols.
41. CORYATE, GEORGE. *Crudities hastily gobbled up in five months travells in France, Savoy, Italy, &c.* (Written before 1607.) Glasgow, 1905.
42. COTGRAVE, R. *A Dictionarie of the French and English Tongues.* London, 1611.
43. COX, R. *Les Soieries d'art.* Paris: Hachette, 1914.

44. CROWLEY. *Select Works.* Early English Text Soc., 1872.
45. CUNNINGHAM, W. *The Growth of English Industry and Commerce.* Cambridge, 1922–9. 3 vols.
46. *Curia Regis. Rotuli Curiae Regis* (Reigns of Richard I and John). London, 1922–32. 6 vols. (Record Commission.)
47. DART. *History of Cathedral Church of Canterbury.* London, 1726.
48. DAVIES, R. *Extracts from the Municipal Records, City of York.* Edward IV, Richard III. London, 1843.
49. D'EWES, SIR SIMONDS. *The Journal of all the Parliaments during Reign of Elizabeth.* London, Bowes, 1682.
50. —— *Autobiography and Correspondence.* London, 1845. 2 vols.
51. DOLCE, M. L. *Dialogo nel quale si ragiona delle qualità, diversità, e proprietà dei colori.* Venetia, 1565.
52. DRAYTON, M. *Works.* Ed. by J. W. Hebel. Oxford, 1931–3. 4 vols.
53. DUGDALE, W. *The History of St. Paul's Cathedral in London.* London, 1818.
54. DURHAM. *Wills and Inventories Illustrative of the History, Manners, Language of the Northern Counties of England, from the Registry at Durham.* Surtees Soc. Pub., vols. ii, xxxviii, cxii, cxiv, cxlviii.
55. —— *Account Rolls.* Surtees Soc. vols. cxviii, cxxi, cxxiv.
56. —— *Household Book.* Surtees Soc., vol. xviii.
57. *Early Popular Poetry.* See HAZLITT.
58. EICHSTADIUS, L. *De Confectione Alchermes.* 1634.
59. *Elizabeth. Progresses,* see NICHOLS, J. *P. P. Ex. Eliz. York,* see NICOLAS, N. H.
60. ELLIS, H. *Original Letters illustrative of English History,* 1074–1799. London, 1825–46. 3 Series, 11 vols.
61. ELYOT, H. *Bibliotheca,* 1548.
62. *English. English Historical Review.* London, 1886. Especially vol. vii, account book William Freke while at Oxford, 1619–34; vol. xxix, 'English Foreign Trade Under Elizabeth.'
63. ESTIENNE, F. A. 'A Charitable Remonstrance to the Ladies of France, touching Their Dissolute Adornments', 1570–85. Trans. by Wm. Rooke. *Collectanea Adamantaea,* xxi.
64. ESTIENNE, H. *Deux dialogues du nouveau langage françois italianizé.* Paris, 1883. A reprint of 1578.
65. FAIRHOLT, F. W. *History of the Lord Mayors' Pageants.* Percy Soc. Pub., vol. x.
66. FASTOLFE. 'Inventory of Effects of Sir John Fastolfe.' *Archaeologia,* vol. xxi.
67. FEUILLERAT, A. *Documents relating to the revels at court in the time of King Edward VI and Queen Mary.*
68. —— *Office of the revels in the time of Queen Elizabeth.* Both published in *Materialen zu Kunde des älteren englischen Dramas,* 1908, 1914.
69. *Fifty . . . wills. The Fifty earliest English Wills in Court of Probate, London.* Early English Text Soc., 1882.

70. FITZGEFFREY, H. *Certaine Elegies done by Sundrie Excellent Wits with Satyres and Epigrams.* London, 1620.

71. FLORIO, J. *World of Wordes*, 1598. *Queen Anna's New World of Words*, 1611.

72. —— *His Firste Fruites which yeelde familiar speech* . . . London, 1578.

73. FORTESCUE, J. *Works.* London, 1869.

74. FOSTER, W. *The English Factories in India*, 1618–21. Oxford, Clarendon Press, 1906.

75. —— *Early Travels in India*, 1583–1619. Oxford, University Press, 1921.

76. *Fugger. The Fugger News-Letters*, 1568–1605. Ed. by von Klarwill. G. P. Putnam's Sons, New York, 1926.

77. FULLER, THOMAS. *The History of Worthies of England.* London, 1662.

78. GAGE, JOHN. *The History and Antiquities of Hengrave in Suffolk.* London, 1822.

79. GARZONI, T. *La Piazza Universale di Tutte le Professioni del Mondo.* Venice, 1616.

80. GAY, VICTOR. *Glossaire archéologique du moyen âge et de la renaissance.* Paris, 1887–1928. 2 vols.

81. GERARD, JOHN. *The Herball, or general historie of plantes.* London, 1597.

82. GIBBS, H. E. *The Corporation Records of St. Albans.* St. Albans, 1890.

83. GLEN, JEAN DE. *Des Habits, moevrs, cérémonies, facons de faire anciennes et modernes du Monde.* Liége, 1601.

84. GODEFROY, F. *Dictionnaire de l'ancienne langue Française du IXe au XVe siècle.* Paris, 1881–1902. 10 vols.

85. GOSSON, S. *Pleasant Quippes for Upstart Gentlewomen.* London, 1596.

86. GRANGE, JOHN. *The Golden Aphroditis.* London, 1577.

87. GREG, WALTER W. *Henslowe's Diary.* London, 1908.

88. GUICCIARDINI, L. *Descrittione di tvtti i Paesi bassi, altrimenti detti Germania Inferiore.* Antwerp, 1567, 1581.

89. HAKLUYT, R. *The Principal Navigations, Voyages, Traffiques and Discoveries of the English Nation.* Glasgow, 1903. 12 vols.

90. HALES, JOHN. *A Discourse of the Common Weal of England.* Ed. from MSS. by Elizabeth Lamond. Cambridge Univ. Press, 1893.

91. HALL, EDWARD. *Chronicle* (Henry IV–Henry VIII). London, 1809.

92. HALYBURTON. *Ledger of Andrew Halyburton together with the book of customs and valuation of merchandise in Scotland*, 1612. Ed. by Cosmo Innes, Edinburgh, 1867.

93. HARINGTON, JOHN. *Nugae Antiquae* . . . *Original Papers written during Reigns of Henry VIII, Edward VI, Mary, Elizabeth, James I.* London, 1804.

94. HARRIS, JOHN. *Navigantium atque Itinerantium Bibliotheca.* London, 1705.

95. HAZLITT, W. C. *Inedited Tracts.* London, 1868.
96. —— *Remains of the Early Popular Poetry of England.* London, 1864–6. 4 vols.
97. HEATH, J. B. *Some Account of the Worshipful Company of Grocers of the City of London.* London, 1869.
98. HEATON, H. *Yorkshire Woollen and Worsted Industries.* Oxford, Clarendon Press, 1920.
99. *Henry VIII. Letters and Papers.* See *Letters; State Papers.*
100. —— 'Wardrobe Account of Henry VIII', 1536. *Archaeologia,* vol. ix.
101. HERESBACH, M. *Foure Bookes of Husbandry . . . conteyning the whole arte and trade of Husbandry.* London, 1577.
102. *Hic. Hic Mulier.* London, Purslowe, 1620.
103. HOLINSHED, R. *Chronicles* (1586). London, 1807. 6 vols.
104. HOLME, R. *The Academie of Armorie or a Storehouse of Armorie and Blazon.* Chester, 1688.
105. *Horae. Horae Subsecivae. Observations and Discourses.* London, 1620.
106. (HOLLYBAND.) DESAINLEINS, C. *A Dictionarie French and English.* London, 1593.
107. HOWARD, W. *The Household Books of Lord William Howard of Naworth Castle.* Surtees Soc. Pub., vol. lxviii.
108. —— 'Inventory of the Effects of Henry Howard, Earl Northampton.' *Archaeologia,* vol. xlii.
109. HULME, F. E. *Principles and Practice of Symbolism in Christian Art.* London, 1892.
110. HUNGERFORD. See NICHOLS, J. G.
111. HUTTON, M. *The Hutton Correspondence.* Surtees Soc. Pub., vol. xvii (includes *Accounts*).
112. *James I. Court,* see Birch; *Progresses,* see Nichols, J.
113. JOHNSON, A. H. *The History of the Worshipful Company of the Drapers of London.* Oxford, Clarendon Press, 1914–22. 5 vols.
114. JOURDAIN, M. *The History of English Secular Embroidery.* London, 1910.
115. KEMPE, A. J. *Manuscripts preserved in the Muniment Room at Loseley House.* London, 1836.
116. KENDRICK, A. F. *English Embroidery.* London, Newnes, 1904.
117. —— (and others) *A Book of Old Embroidery.* London, 1921.
118. —— *English Needlework.* London, Black, 1933.
119. KIRK, R. E. G. *Returns of Aliens Dwelling in the City and Suburbs of London from the Reign of Henry VIII to that of James I.* London, Huguenot Soc., 1900–7, vol. iii.
120. *Knaresborough. Wills from Knaresborough Court Rolls.* Surtees Soc., vol. civ.
121. LA MOTHE LE VAYER. *Opuscules ou petits traittez.* Paris, 1647.
122. *Lancashire. Lancashire and Cheshire Wills and Inventories from the Ecclesiastical Court of Chester.* Chetham Soc. Pub., o.s., vols. xxxiii, li, liv; N.S. iii, xxviii, xxxvii.

123. LANG, A. *Social England Illustrated.* Westminster, Constable, 1903.
124. LEAN, V. S. *Collectanea.* Bristol, 1902–4. 4 vols.
125. LEBRIJA, A. *Dictionarium latino-hispanicum et hispanico-latinum,* 1553, 1570.
126. LEGH, G. *The Accedens of Armory.* London, 1562. Also 1568, 1591.
127. LELAND, JOHN. *Itinerary,* 1535–43. Ed. by Lucy T. Smith, London, 1910.
128. L'ESTOILE, P. DE. *Registre Journal . . . de Henry III, IV, Louis XIII.* Petitot, Coll. *Mém. Hist. France,* Ser. I, vols. 45–9.
129. LESTRANGE. 'Extracts from Household and Privy Purse Accounts of the Lestranges of Hunstanton from 1519–1579.' *Archaeologia,* vol. xxv.
130. *Letters. Letters and Papers Foreign and Domestic of the Reign of Henry VIII,* 1519–46. (Record Commission.)
131. *Libelle. Libelle of Englyshe Polycye.* Ed. by George Warner. Oxford, Clarendon Press, 1926.
132. *Liber. Monumenta Gildhallae Londoniensis: Liber Albus, Liber Custumarum.* Ed. by T. H. Riley, London, 1859–62. 2 vols. (Rolls Series.)
133. —— *Liber Custumarum villae Northamptoniae.* Ed. by C. Markham, Northampton, 1898.
134. LINAS, C. *Anciens vêtements sacerdotaux.* Paris, 1860. 3 vols.
135. *Lincoln. Lincoln Diocese Documents,* 1450–1544. Ed. by A. Clark. Early English Text Society, 1914, o.s., vol. cxlix.
136. —— *Lincoln Wills,* 1271–1532, *registered in District Probate Registry at Lincoln.* Ed. by C. W. Foster. Lincoln Record Society Pub., vols. v, x, xxiv.
137. *Lincolnshire. Lincolnshire Wills,* 1500–1617. Lincoln, 1888–9. 2 vols.
138. LYTE, SIR HENRY MAXWELL-. *A History of Dunster.* London, 1909.
139. MACHYN, H. *Diary,* 1550–63. Camden Soc. Pub., 1848.
140. MACPHERSON, D. *Annals of Commerce, manufactures, fisheries and navigation.* London, 1805. 4 vols.
141. MADDEN, F. *Privy Purse Expenses of Princess Mary,* 1536–44. London, 1831.
142. MADOX, T. *The History . . . of Exchequer of Kings of England.* London, 1711.
143. —— *Firma Burgi.* London, 1726.
144. *Malone. Malone Soc. Collections.* General Editor, W. W. Greg. 1907–32.
145. MANNINGHAM, R. *Diary.* Camden Soc. Pub., 1868.
146. MARKHAM, G. *English Housewife.* London, 1631.
147. *Mary. Privy Purse.* See MADDEN, F.
148. MAY, JOHN. *A Declaration of the Estate of Clothing now used within this Realme of England.* London, 1613.
149. MICHEL, F. X. *Recherches sur le commerce, la fabrication et l'usage*

des étoffes de soie, d'or et d'argent pendant le moyen âge. Paris, 1853–4. 2 vols.

150. *Middlesex. Middlesex Sessions Rolls.* Middlesex County Records Soc. Ed. by J. C. Jeaffreson. 1886–92. 4 vols.

151. *Milton. Household Book, Milton Abbey.* Chetham Soc., vol. xli.

152. MINSHEU, J. *The Guide Into Tongues.* London, 1617.

153. —— *Vocabvlarivm hispanico-latinvm et anglicum copiosissimum.* London, 1617.

154. MISSELDEN, E. *Free Trade, or the Means to Make Trade Flourish.* London, 1622.

155. MOENS, W. J. C. *The Walloons and their Church at Norwich,* 1565–1832. Huguenot Soc., 1888.

156. MORATO, F. P. *Del significato de' colori.* Venice, 1559, 1593.

157. MORYSON, FYNES. *Itinerary* (1606–17). Glasgow, 1907. 4 vols.

158. MURATORI, L. A. *Rerum Italicarum scriptores.* Milan, 1723–51. 25 vols.

159. —— *Annali d'Italia.* Rome, 1752–4. 12 vols.

160. MUÑOZ, A. *Viaje de Felipe Segundo á Inglaterra (1554).* La Sociedad de Bibliófilos Españoles, 1877, vol. xv.

161. NICOLAS, N. H. *Privy Purse Expenses of Elizabeth of York. The Wardrobe Accounts of Edward IV.* London, Pickering, 1830.

162. —— *Testamenta Vetusta.* London, 1826.

163. NICHOLS, J. *Illustrations of the Manners and Expences of Antient Times in England in 15th, 16th, 17th Centuries.* London, 1797.

164. —— *The Progresses and Public Processions of Queen Elizabeth.* London, 1823. 3 vols.

165. —— *The Progresses, Processions, and Magnificent Festivities of King James the First.* London, 1828. 4 vols.

166. NICHOLS, J. G. *Inventory of Goods of Dame Agnes Hungerford.* London, 1861. (Reprinted from *Archaeologia,* vol. xxxviii.)

167. —— *Chronicle of the Grey Friars of London.* Camden Soc., 1852.

168. NICOLAY, N. *Les navigations, peregrinations et voyages, faicts en la turquie . . . soixante figures . . . tant d'hommes que de femmes . . . leur port, habits . . .* Antwerp, 1576.

169. NICOT, J. *Trésor de la langve françoise tant ancienne qve moderne.* Paris, 1606.

170. *North. The Booke of the Household Charges and Other Paiments Laid Out by Lord North,* 1575–80. *Archaeologia,* vol. xix.

171. *North Country.* See *Durham Wills.*

172. *Norwich. The Records of City of Norwich.* Ed. by J. C. Tingey and W. Hudson. Norwich, 1906. 2 vols.

173. *Nottingham. Records of Borough Nottingham.* London, 1882. 6 vols.

174. OCCOLTI, CORONATO. *Trattato di Colori,* 1568.

175. OTT, ANDRÉ. *Étude sur les couleurs en vieux français.* Paris, 1899.

176. OUDIN, C. *Le Thresor des trois langues espagnole, françoise, et italienne.* Cologne, 1617. 3 vols. in 1.

177. OVERBURY, T. *Works.* Ed. by Rimbault. London, 1856.

178. PAGE, W. *Letters of Denization and acts of Naturalization for Aliens in England*, 1509–1603. Huguenot Soc., 1893, vol. 8.

179. PALET, JEAN. *Diccionario muy copioso de la lengua española y francesa.* Bruxelles, 1606.

180. *Paston. The Paston Letters*, 1422–1509. Ed. by J. Gairdner. London, 1900. 4 vols.

181. PEACHAM, H. *The Truth of Our Times.* London, 1638.

182. —— *Compleat Gentleman.* London, 1622 (re-edited by T. Blount, 1661).

183. PEGGE, S. *The Forme of Cury.* London, 1780.

184. PERCYVAL, R. *Bibliotheca Hispanica.* London, 1591.

185. *Philobiblon. Miscellanies of the Philobiblon Society.* London, 1854–84. 15 vols. (Vol. vii, account materials furnished by Anne Boleyn, 1535–6.)

186. *Pipe Rolls. The Great Roll of the Pipe*, 31 Henry I, 2–4 Henry II (Record Commission, 1929–30); 5 Henry II–14 Henry III (Pipe Roll Society, 1884–1933. In progress.)

187. PLINY, C. *The Historie of the World.* Tr. into English by Philemon Holland. London, 1601.

188. PORTAL, F. *Des couleurs symboliques dans l'antiquité, le moyen-âge et les temps modernes.* Paris, 1837.

189. PURCHAS, S. *Purchas His Pilgrimes.* Glasgow, 1905. Hakluyt Soc. E.S., 20 vols.

190. RABELAIS, F. *Les œuvres.* Paris, 1868–93. 6 vols.

191. *Rates. Customs of London*, otherwise Arnold's *Chronicle*, 1507.

192. —— *The rates of the custome house bothe inwarde and outward*, &c. London, 1545.

193. —— *The Booke of Rates as well for the valuation of merchandizes as for collection of His Maiesties Customs.* London, 1631.

194. RAWLINSON, H. G. *British Beginnings in Western India.* Oxford, Clarendon Press, 1920.

195. *Richmond. Wills and Inventories from the Registry of the Archdeaconry of Richmond.* Surtees Soc. Pub., vol. xxvi.

196. RIDER, J. *Bibliotheca Scholastica.* London, 1589.

197. RILEY, H. T. *Memorials of London and London Life in the XIIIth, XIVth, XVth Centuries.* London, 1868.

198. RINALDI, G. *Il vago et dilettevole giardino... diuiso in due trattati Nel primo de' qvali si ragiona del significato de' colori.* Pauia, 1593.

199. —— *Mostrovissimo Mostro* . . . Ferrara, 1584.

200. ROBERTS, L. *The Merchants Mappe of Commerce.* London, 1638.

201. ROGERS, J. E. T. *A History of Agriculture and Prices in England, 1259–1793.* Oxford, Clarendon Press, 1866–1902. 7 vols.

202. —— *Six Centuries of Work & Wages.* N.Y., Putnam's Sons, 1884.

203. *Rotuli. Rotuli Parliamentorum*, 1278–1503. London, 1767–1832. 7 vols.

204. —— *Rotuli Hundredorum* (Henry III, Edward I). London, 1812–18. 2 vols. (Record Commission.)

205. ROWLANDS, S. *Complete Works.* Hunterian Club, 1880. 3 vols.
206. *Royal Com.* Royal Commission on Historical MSS. (Documents Illustrative of Hist. . . . belonging to private persons): *Ancaster,* pub. 1907; *Cowper,* 1888–9, 3 vols.; *De l'Isle and Dudley,* 1925; *Egmont,* 1905, 1909, 2 vols.; *Eglinton,* 1885; *Fortescue,* 1892–1915, 9 vols.; *Hatfield House,* 1883–1923, 14 vols.; *Kenyon,* 1894; *Middleton,* 1911; *Portland,* 1891–1931, 10 vols.; *Rutland,* 1888, 1889, 1894, 1905, 4 vols.; *Windsor Castle,* 1902–4, 2 vols.
207. RUTZ, C. *Habitus variarum orbis gentium,* 1581.
208. RYE, W. *England as Seen by Foreigners in Days of Elizabeth and James I.* London, 1865.
209. RYMER, T. *Foedera.* London, 1726–35. 20 vols.
210. SANDYS, G. *Travels . . .* 1610. London, 1673.
211. *Scotland. Accounts of Lord High Treasurer of Scotland,* 1413–1564. Ed. J. B. Paul. Edinburgh, 1877–1914. 11 vols.
212. SHAW, W. E. *Denization and Naturalization of Aliens in England,* 1603–1700. Huguenot Soc., vol. xviii.
213. SHUTTLEWORTH. *The House and Farm Accounts of the Shuttleworths of Gawthorpe Hall in the County of Lancaster* from Sept. 1582–Oct. 1621. Chetham Soc. Pub., vols. 35, 41, 43, 46.
214. SICILE. *Le Blason des couleurs en armes Liuries & deuises.* Lyon, 1528.
215. *Social England.* See LANG.
216. *Somerset. Somerset Medieval Wills,* 1383–1558. Somerset Record Soc., 1901–5. Vols. 16, 19, 21.
217. *Southampton. Court Leet Records,* 1528–1624. Ed. F. C. Hearnshaw, 1905–7. 3 vols.
218. —— *The Oak Book of Southampton. Port Book of Southampton.* Ed. P. Studer. Southampton, 1910–11, 1913.
219. STALEY, J. E. *Guilds of Florence.* London, 1906.
220. STARKEY, T. *England in Reigne Henry VIII.* Early English Text Soc., 1878.
221. *State Papers. State Papers King Henry VIII.* 8 vols. (Record Commission.)
222. *Statutes. Statutes at Large* (Magna Carta to 1761). London, Pickering, 1762–1807. 46 vols.
223. —— *Statutes of the Realm* (Magna Carta to end reign of Queen Anne). London, 1816–24. 9 vols. and index.
224. STEPHENS, J. *Satyrical Essays, Characters.* London, 1615.
225. STOWE, J. *The Annales of England.* London, 1592, 1605.
226. —— *Annales or a generall chronicle of England . . .* continued by Edmvnd Howes. London, 1631.
227. —— *The Survey of London.* Ed. C. L. Kingsford. Oxford, Clarendon Press, 1908. 2 vols.
228 STUBBES, W. *Anatomy of Abuses in England in 1583.* Ed. F. J. Furnivall for New Shakespeare Soc., 1882.

229. STRUTT. *Dress and Habits of People of England*, London, 1842. 2 vols.
230. *Suffolk. Suffolk in the XVIIth Century. The Breviary of Suffolk*, by Robert Reyce. London, 1902.
231. *Surrey. Surrey Archaeological Collections.* Surrey Arch. Soc. 1854– .
232. —— *Surrey Wills.* Surrey Record Soc. London, 1920. Vols. iv, v.
233. TAYLOR, J. *Works.* Spenser Soc., 1870–8. 5 vols.
234. *Testamenta. Testamenta Eboracensia. A Selection of Wills from the Registry at York.* Surtees Soc. Pub., vols. iv, xxx, xlv, liii, lxxix, cvi.
235. —— *Testamenta Karleolensia*, 1353–86. Cumberland and West- morland Antiquarian and Archaeological Soc., Kendal, 1893, E.S. vol. ix.
236. —— *Testamenta Leodiensia*, 1539–61. Thoresby Soc. Pub., Leeds, 1913, vols. xix, xxvii.
237. —— *Testamenta Vetusta.* See NICOLAS.
238. TOFTE, R. *Alba.* Manchester, 1880. (Grosart.)
239. *Tudor. Bibliotheca Lindesiana. A Bibliography of Royal Proclama- tions of the Tudor and Stuart Sovereigns*, 1485–1714. Com- piled by J. L. Lindsay, 26th Earl of Crawford. Oxford, Claren- don Press, 1910. 2 vols.
240. VERNON, J. *A Dictionary in Latine and English.* London, 1575.
241. *Victoria History of the Counties of England.* London, 1903– .
242. *Vocabolario degli Accademici della Crusca.* Venezia, 1612, &c.
243. WADLEY, T. P. *Notes . . . of Wills . . . in . . . Book Wills . . . Council House at Bristol.* Bristol, Gloucestershire Society, 1886.
244. *Wakefield. Wakefield Court Rolls.* Yorkshire Archaeological Rec. Ser., vols. xxix, xxxvi.
245. WATREMAN. *The fardle of facions.* London, 1555.
246. WEEVER, J. *Epigrams in the Oldest Cut and Newest Fashion*, 1599. Reprinted from original with notes by R. B. McKerrow, Stratford, 1922.
247. *Wells. Medieval Wills from Wells*, 1543–6, 1554–6. Somerset Rec. Soc., xl.
248. *Welsh. The Welsh Port Book*, 1550–1603. Compiled by E. A. Lewis, London, 1927. Cymmrodorion Rec. Ser., vol. xii.
249. WHEELER, J. *A Treatise of Commerce wherin are shewed the com- modities arising by a wel ordered Trade.* Middelburgh, 1601.
250. WITHER, G. *Juvenilia*, 1626. London, Spenser Soc. Pub., vol. ix.
251. *Worcester. Lay Subsidy Rolls*, Worcestershire Historical Soc., 1899; *Original Charters*, 1907.
252. WRAY, W. 'The Account-book of William Wray', 1589–95. *Antiquary*, vol. xxxii.
253. WRIOTHESLEY, C. *A Chronicle of England*, 1485–1559. Camden Soc., 1875, 1877.
254. *York. York Memorandum Book*, Surtees Soc., vol. cxxi.
255. —— *Municipal Records.* See DAVIES.
256. YULE, A. *The Book of Sir Marco Polo.* London, 1903, 2 vols.

DRAMA

Editions cited are those used. As an aid to persons to whom these editions are not accessible, act, scene, and line, rather than volume and page are given. In plays which are not divided into acts and scenes, volume and page are cited. In editions in which lines are not numbered, lines have been computed. This computation will only *approximate* the location in the scene, but the author and Press felt that such approximation would be of more use than would reference to volume and page. In case of originals or facsimile editions of plays not divided into acts and scenes, the page signature only is given.

1. ARMIN. *Works.* Grosart, *Occasional Issues* (1880), vol. xxviii.
2. BARIONNA, L. *Misogonus. Early Plays from the Italian.* Ed. W. Bond. Oxford, Clarendon Press, 1911.
3. BARRY, D. *Ram Alley.* Dodsley, *Old English Plays*, vol. x.
4. BEAUMONT, F., FLETCHER, J. *Works.* Cambridge English Classics. London, Cambridge University Press, 1905–10. 10 vols.
5. BROME. *Works.* London, Pearson, 1873. 3 vols.
6. CHAPMAN, G. *The Plays and Poems.* Ed. T. M. Parrott. London, Routledge & Sons, 1914. 3 vols.
7. CHETTLE, H. Tudor Facsimile Texts, 1911–13, used for all plays.
8. COOK, J. *Greene's Tu Quoque or the Citie Gallant.* Tudor Facsimile, 1913.
9. D'AVENANT, W. *Dramatic Works.* Edinburgh, Paterson, 1872. 5 vols.
10. DAY, J. *Works.* Ed. by A. H. Bullen. London, Nimmo, 1881.
11. DEKKER, T. *The Dramatic Works.* London, Pearson, 1873. 4 vols.
12. —— *Non-Dramatic Works.* Ed. A. B. Grosart (Huth Library).
13. DELONEY. *Works.* Ed. F. O. Mann. Oxford, Clarendon Press, 1912.
14. EDWARDS, R. *Damon and Pythias.* Tudor Facsimile, 1908.
15. FIELD, N. *Amends for Ladies.* London, 1582. *Woman is a Weather-cock.* London, 1612.
16. FORD, J. *Works.* Ed. Gifford. London, 1895. 3 vols.
17. FULWELL, U. *Like Will To Like.* Tudor Facsimile, 1909.
18. GLAPTHORNE, H. *Works.* Pearson, 1874. 2 vols.
19. GREENE, R. *Complete Works in Prose and Verse.* Ed. A. B. Grosart (Huth Library). 1881–6. 15 vols.
20. HAUGHTON, W. *Englishmen for My Money.* Tudor Facsimile, 1911.
21. HEYWOOD, J. *The Dramatic Writings.* Ed. Farmer. London, Early English Drama Society, 1905.
22. HEYWOOD, T. *Dramatic Works.* London, Pearson, 1874. 6 vols.
23. JONSON, B. *Ben Jonson.* Ed. by C. H. Herford and P. Simpson. Vols. iii, iv. Oxford, Clarendon Press, 1925. (In progress.) For plays and masques not yet printed in this edition, see Gifford ed., London, 1875, 9 vols.

24. KYD, T. *Works.* Ed. F. Boas. Oxford, Clarendon Press, 1901.
25. LYLY, J. *The Complete Works.* Ed. W. Bond. Oxford, Clarendon Press, 1902. 3 vols.
26. MARKHAM, G. *The Dumb Knight.* Dodsley, *Old English Plays,* vol. x.
27. MARLOWE, C. *Works.* T. F. Brooke. Oxford, Clarendon Press. 1910.
28. MARMION, S. *The Antiquary,* Dodsley, *Old English Plays,* 1875, vol. xiii.
29. MASSINGER, P. *Plays.* Ed. W. Gifford. London, Nicol, 1813. 4 vols.
30. MIDDLETON, T. *Works.* Ed. A. H. Bullen. London, Nimmo, 1885–6. 8 vols.
31. MARSTON, J. *Works.* Ed. A. H. Bullen. London, Nimmo, 1887. 3 vols.
32. MAYNE, J. *City Match.* Dodsley *Old Plays,* vol. xiii.
33. NABBES, T. *Works.* Ed. A. H. Bullen, 1887. 2 vols.
34. NASHE, T. *Works.* Ed. R. B. McKerrow. London, 1908. 5 vols.
35. PEELE. *Works.* Ed. A. H. Bullen. London, Nimmo, 1888.
36. PORTER, HENRY. *Two Angry Women of Abington.* Malone Society Reprints, 1912.
37. PRESTON, T. *Cambises.* London, 1585.
38. ROWLEY, W. *Match at Midnight.* London, 1633. *Woman Never Vext.* London, 1632.
39. SHAKESPEARE, W. *Complete Works* (Standard Edition). New York: Oxford University Press.
40. SHARPHAM, E. *The Fleire.* London, 1615. *Cupid's Whirligig.* Ed. A. Nicoll. Berkshire Series, 1926.
41. TAYLOR, R. *The Hog Hath Lost His Pearl.* Dodsley, *Old English Plays* (1874–6), vol. xi.
42. TOMKIS, T. *Lingua.* Tudor Facsimile, 1913. *Albumazar,* London, 1634.
43. UDALL, N. *Roister Doister.* Ed. J. Q. Adams, *Chief Pre-Shakespearian Dramas.* Boston, Houghton Mifflin, 1924.
44. WAGER, L. *Mary Magdalene.* Tudor Facsimile. 1908.
45. WEBSTER, J. *Complete Works.* Ed. F. L. Lucas. London, Chatto & Windus, 1927. 4 vols.
46. WEVER, E. *Lusty Juventus, Dramatic Writings,* edited J. S. Farmer. Early English Drama Society, 1905.
47. WHETSTONE, G. *Promos and Cassandra.* Tudor Facsimile, 1910.
48. WILKINS, G. *Miseries of Enforced Marriage.* Tudor Facsimile, 1913.
49. WILMOT, R. *Tancred and Gismund.* Tudor Facsimile, 1912.
50. WILSON, R. *Three Ladies of London, Cobler's Prophecy, Pedler's Prophecy.* Tudor Facsimile, 1911. *Three Lords and Three Ladies of London.* Tudor Facsimile, 1912.
51. ANONYMOUS PLAYS. *Calisto and Melibaea.* Tudor Facsimile, 1909.
52. —— *Captain Underwit.* Ed. A. H. Bullen, *A Collection of Old Plays,* 1883, vol. ii.
53. —— *How a Man may Choose a Good Wife from a Bad.* Tudor Facsimile, 1912.

54. ANONYMOUS PLAYS. *Jack Juggler*. Tudor Facsimile, 1912.

55. —— *Knack to Know a Knave*. Tudor Facsimile, 1911.

56. —— *Look About You*. Tudor Facsimile, 1912.

57. —— *Mucedorus*. Dodsley, *Old English Plays*, vol. vii.

58. —— *New Custom*. Dodsley, *Old English Plays*, 1874, vol. iii.

59. —— *Return from Parnassus*. Tudor Facsimile, 1912.

60. —— *Sir Clyomon and Sir Clamydes*. Malone Soc., 1913.

61. —— *Thersites*. Tudor Facsimile, 1912.

62. —— *Trial of Treasure*. Tudor Facsimile, 1908.

63. —— *Wily Beguiled*. Tudor Facsimile, 1912.

INDEXES

Since the purpose of the book is to explain allusions to costume in the drama, references to all other literature have been omitted. The costume index is selective, that of the plays, as far as possible, complete. Figures in italic indicate the pages on which the definition or main discussion is found. The date following each item is that of its first known use in England.

COSTUME

PLAYS